DIARIES

AND

CORRESPONDENCE

OF

THE EARL OF MALMESBURY,

———

VOL. II.

DIARIES AND CORRESPONDENCE

OF

JAMES HARRIS,

FIRST EARL OF MALMESBURY,

CONTAINING AN ACCOUNT OF

HIS MISSIONS AT THE COURT OF MADRID, TO
FREDERICK THE GREAT, CATHERINE THE SECOND,
AND AT THE HAGUE;

AND OF HIS SPECIAL MISSIONS TO

BERLIN, BRUNSWICK, AND THE FRENCH REPUBLIC.

EDITED BY HIS GRANDSON,

THE THIRD EARL.

SECOND EDITION.

VOL. II.

AMS PRESS, INC.
NEW YORK

Reprinted from the edition of 1845, London
First AMS EDITION published 1970
Manufactured in the United States of America

International Standard Book Number:
    Complete Set . . . 0-404-04170-1
    Volume 2 0-404-04172-8

Library of Congress Catalog Card Number: 73-121023

AMS PRESS, INC.
NEW YORK, N.Y. 10003

DIARIES AND CORRESPONDENCE.

ENGLAND.

[THE Coalition Ministry was dismissed by the King on the 7th of December, 1783, and Sir J. Harris, on his return to England, supported the Duke of Portland and Mr. Fox by his vote in the House of Commons. The following letters from Sir Gilbert Elliot were written immediately subsequent to that event.]

LETTER FROM SIR GILBERT ELLIOT TO SIR JAMES HARRIS, SALISBURY.

Beckenham, 1st January, 1784.

MY DEAR HARRIS,—In addition to what I told you last night from Park Street, I have picked up this morning an anecdote or two, which I send you to Salisbury, where I suppose you will be at the arrival of this letter.

Lord Clarendon is Chancellor of the Duchy. The first negotiation with Fox was attempted through Lord Spencer, on whom Pitt or his friends in a manner forced themselves. Lord Spencer went to Fox, however, with a direct proposition from Pitt, the substance of which was to betray Lord North, and make room for Pitt by breaking the Coalition, and turning Lord North out. This honourable proposal was received with the respect it deserved. I believe Fox's only answer was, " Why don't they advise us to pick pockets at once?" They have used various other channels for the same end, and with equal success. Jack Lee* shewed me a letter from John Villiers to himself, written in better language, but the same spirit with his father's compositions, a world of cant about moderation of well-meaning men, apprehensions for his country, fears of a *civil war* (for that is now the burthen of their song, as if a Republic and a civil war were intended by Fox); in short, inviting Jack Lee to share with him in a negotiation similar to the above. Jack does not bite, and will have nothing to do in so dishonourable a business; he thinks it would be disgraceful and unprincipled to take Pitt in on any terms after he has evinced his own profligacy by the means he has used to obtain power. Tom Johnnes, member for a Welsh county, is gone over to them; he always belonged to Thurlow, but held a place under the Coalition, and now rejoins his proper master.

I do not intend to go to town again till Monday. I should be in utter despair about my seat if a dissolution did not seem more and more unlikely.

Your affectionate G. Elliot.

The Duke of Richmond has beset the Prince of Wales, but without the least effect.

LETTER FROM SIR GILBERT ELLIOT TO SIR JAMES HARRIS, SALISBURY.

Park Street, Thursday, 26th February, 1784.

My dear Harris,—I am just come from a general meeting at Fox's, such as you have attended once or twice before. The numbers were very good. The measure to-morrow is to put off the consideration of the King's answer† till Monday. As the House will

* Attorney-General under Lord North's Administration.

† February 20th, Mr. Powis moved an address to the Crown, requesting that the King would take measures for giving effect to the declared wishes of the Commons; *i. e.* to dismiss Ministers. The King's answer, 25th, was

not hear the answer authentically till it is read from the Chair, and as no copy of it is in fact furnished even privately to the members, it was thought more proper, as well as more solemn, and more respectful even to the King, to appoint a future day to take it into consideration, than to come on the spot to any measure founded on words which we shall hear to-morrow for the first time. It is supposed that this will not be much opposed, even by the Ministers. The next question will probably be opposed, and bring on a division. It is intended to postpone the Navy supply till we shall have had time to take some step in consequence of the King's answer. You will observe this is still only *postponing*, not *refusing*, supplies, and the question will be argued on that ground; which it will be the more difficult to resist, as the House has already proved that to postpone is not to refuse, by first postponing the Ordnance estimate till we had taken the measure of addressing, and then voting the estimate on a subsequent day, which, you know, is the history of our proceeding relative to that particular supply. The Mutiny Bill also stands for Monday, and it is intended to postpone also the consideration of that bill till the 8th March.

What the measure on Monday will be, I believe, is not finally determined; it is not known at least. Fox, in speaking to his company to-night, reminded us that it would be necessary for us to make our minds fairly up on the question of how far we would go in the contest; for, if the cause of the House of Commons was to be given up by a want of unanimity amongst ourselves, it would be proper to think of some means to surrender our claims in the manner the least disgraceful, and the least fatal to the House; but, if we thought it right, at all events, to resist the attack, we must determine on the necessary measures. The question of ultimately refusing supplies, and passing the Mutiny Bill for a

That, as no specific charge was brought against Ministers, he could not dismiss them.

short time, were those which we must most seriously consider.   Some gentlemen spoke after him, and I was sorry to observe a sort of boggle about the extreme, but the only decisive measure, of refusing supplies.   I do not doubt, however, of our going through even with this.*   I was glad to hear several members say that they thought they observed a turn beginning in the opinions of the people, and that for that reason dilatory measures were advisable.   I shall be too late.   Good night!   There is bad news from Madras, but I have not time for it.   Distraction in our own Government there, and something like a revolt of the army against Lord Macartney.   General Stewart is sent home by him a prisoner, and I hear the Directors have also superseded him.   Your affectionate   G. ELLIOT.

LETTER FROM SIR GILBERT ELLIOT TO SIR JAMES HARRIS, SALISBURY.

Park Street, Saturday, 28th February, 1784.

MY DEAR HARRIS,—Nothing passed yesterday in the House worth telling you.   The proceeding was exactly what I told you it would be, and the debate was unusually cold and barren.   A number of our friends were shut out at the division, and reduced our majority to *seven*.†   We found seven or eight of them in Mrs. Bennet's room, looking like the foolish virgins somewhere in the Bible.   I mention this that you may know from good authority, and *de bonne foi*, that the reduction of our numbers was really accidental.   The division took place at eight o'clock, which you know is earlier than could be well expected.   The negotiators are still trotting, and I met Mr. Powis this morning at Sir G. Cornewall's door. I understand the present state of the Treaty to be, an

---

* In this expectation Sir Gilbert Elliot was disappointed.
† February 27th, Mr. Powis moved that the King's Message be taken into consideration on Monday, and that the House adjourn to that day. This delay being considered by Ministers as an attempt to obstruct the grant of supplies, was opposed by them, but the motion was carried by *seven*.

understanding between the parties as to all the preliminaries I mentioned in a former letter, and that the
honour of the House of Commons no longer forms the
obstacle to treating; that being actually provided for by
consent of all concerned. I have not heard what the
satisfaction is to be, but I doubt, when I do hear it, that
I shall think it a salvo rather than a substantial satisfaction; as I think nothing short of the disgrace of Mr. Pitt
and his associates can amount to such a reparation for
the past as can give us any security for the future.

These preliminaries, however, being adjusted, Mr. Pitt
has started a new difficulty, by requiring the Duke of
Portland to say in writing that he understood and consented that the negotiation should proceed on a *fair and
equal footing.* You may remember Pitt's using these
words more than once in debate, and you will observe
them put into the King's mouth in his gracious answer
to our address. You will easily see their drift, but will
not, I fancy, quite assent to the pretensions on the part
of Pitt which they imply. The Duke answered, that he
could not subscribe to these words without some explanation of them, for that he did not understand them. The
word *fair* he understood perfectly, and was ready to
promise all it could ever mean, in every transaction in
which he should be concerned. The word *equal,* as applied to the present case, required more explanation. If
Mr. Pitt meant that they should so far be considered as
equal that they should draw lots who should be at the
head of the new Administration, and then name to the
different offices alternately, he would not agree to such a
proposal, because such an Administration, formed on
such a principle, could neither be cordial nor lasting.
Powis carried back this answer, or an answer to that
effect, and desired Pitt to reply. Pitt said he saw nothing in the Duke's reasons which induced him to change
his opinion, or depart from this article. Powis desired
that he would only explain more clearly and precisely
the sense in which his words were to be adopted, adding,
that as for himself he really did not understand them;

and he only begged that he would speak fairly out what his meaning and object was. Pitt at last consented to give a fuller explanation, and is to give it in writing to-morrow morning.

On the whole, I think some forced patched accommodation becomes probable; much as I dislike this issue of our contest, I see that the number of those who think as I do about it is too small, and that there is too much water-gruel in the times to render any more manly conclusion to the public distractions practicable. As you can speculate, however, better for yourself than I can do, I shall content myself to-night with sending you the text, leaving the comment to your own judgment and leisure. I hope my letters will satisfy your desire for *facts*, facts; and that I shall not be accused of wit, as heretofore.

Your affectionate

G. ELLIOT.

LETTER FROM SIR GILBERT ELLIOT TO SIR JAMES HARRIS, CHRISTCHURCH.

Park Street, Wednesday, 10th March, 1784.

MY DEAR HARRIS,—I beg your pardon for not writing to you last night to tell you that Carew decided the vote of the House by going with us. His "coup d'essai" was a "coup de Maître." I shall not like the vote the worse for supposing your conversation with him may have had some share in it. Our numbers were much reduced by the Circuit, and other absences. Nobody went over, not one; but Devonshire Parker voted against us, much to the surprise of those who knew him.

There was a general meeting at Devonshire House yesterday before we went down to the House, where the question of the short Mutiny Bill was proposed, and several persons objected to it; and, that being the case, it was the unanimous opinion that it should not be moved in the House, on the ground that it could not be carried. The consequence will probably be a very speedy dissolu-

tion,—some say, in a week, but I should hardly think so
soon, nor can I indeed positively say it will be at all
before the end of the session; but every friend of the
Ministers treat it as certain, and our friends expect it.
I saw the Duke of Portland, Mr. Fox, and Geo. Byng
to-day, who all consider it as the probable event. I
mention this to shew that you ought to act on that supposition, although it will not be certainly known till it
happens. *

Our battle is converted into a campaign, but it is our
business not to despair of the Commonwealth. In the
mean while there will not be much more contest in Parliament till we meet in a new one; when I say we, I
mean my friends, for I now think it most probable that
I shall be out. The leisure in Parliament may perhaps
be employed profitably without doors; and there all our
activity should be directed.

Your affectionate　　　G. E.

LETTER FROM SIR GILBERT ELLIOT TO SIR JAMES HARRIS,
CHRISTCHURCH.

Park Street, Friday evening.

MY DEAR HARRIS,—There was a short poll of an hour
before Church to-day, in which Fox gained six on yesterday's poll.† All the world, male and female, young
and old, is employed in canvassing on either side. The
numbers unpolled are said to be so considerable, and the
Court has made such a push, that it is thought not impracticable to recover the election. I am not sanguine
enough to give way to this hope, but it is clearly ne-

---

* Pitt dissolved Parliament and obtained a great majority. Sir J. Harris
was again returned for Christchurch, and continued to vote for Opposition.

† The contest for Westminster lasted forty days, the whole time allowed
by law. The candidates were Lord Hood, who polled 6694; Fox, 6234;
and Sir M. Wray, 5998. The last demanded a scrutiny, which delay
caused violent debates in Parliament. Fox was not returned for Westminster until March in the following year, but in the mean time he sat for
the Borough of Kirkwall.

cessary to make what exertions we can; and, indeed, there is so general and so natural a zeal on the subject, that I should be sorry you did not come to town, as I mentioned yesterday. I find your ball at Christchurch is on Tuesday; but, if you set off from Bath soon after the receipt of this letter, you will be in town on Monday soon enough to vote, and may be at Salisbury at night. The poll opens at nine o'clock, and closes at three. If there are any Westminster friends at Bath, you will do a good work in whipping them in. It is Fox's wish to have as many gentlemen as he can on his poll. I reserve myself on the subject which I hinted at yesterday till I see you on Monday. I will stay at home till three o'clock in expectation of your arrival.* Mr. Mundy is thought sure of success in Derbyshire against Curzon.

Your affectionate   G. E.

P.S. Folliot Cornewall is made Canon of Windsor, about 500l. a-year. This is given him as Chaplain of the House of Commons, and he of course retires from that office. The story of Hatsell's being to be Speaker, seems without foundation. The Ministry bring in the late Speaker for Rye; and of course, I suppose, intend to continue him in the chair.

* Sir J. Harris came up, and voted for Mr. Fox.

THE HAGUE.

SIR JAMES HARRIS, when he left Petersburg, was appointed by Mr. Fox to the Hague, in the hope that he would banish the harsh feelings retained by the Republic towards England after the severe lessons we had taught her during the last war; and that the English party, which were identified with the Stadtholder, might recover from the Patriots and French faction the ascendancy they had lost. The Bourbons had been and were still playing the blind and desperate game against us in Holland, which they had successfully used in America; and encouraged the Dutch Democrats with money, and promises to establish a pure Republic independent of the Stadtholder. THEY hoped thus to render the States a French province. OUR object was to fortify the national independence of Holland under its ancient constitution, and recover her friendship and alliance. In this trial of skill we were completely victorious, mainly owing to the boldness and ability of Sir J. Harris, who may be said to have created, fostered, and matured a counter-revolution in the States, which restored to the Stadtholder his power, to England her ally, and left nothing for the King of France but the deeper infection of those dangerous doctrines, which his Ministers, in their eagerness to spread them amongst his enemies, received into the vitals of his kingdom, to burst forth for its destruction in 1789. History affords no instance of a political retribution so rapid and so crushing.

When the Coalition Ministry was dismissed on the 7th of December, 1783, Sir James Harris remained in England. The changes in Administration appeared to occupy the Cabinet, and Holland for a time remained unnoticed. Mr. Pitt (although Sir James voted with the Opposition) eventually confirmed his nomination, and he reached the Hague in December, 1784.

The Emperor of Austria, in 1781, taking advantage of the war between England and Holland, had declar'd the treaty of 1715 (called the Barrier Treaty) null, seized the frontier fortresses, and expelled the Dutch garrisons. Continuing to increase his demands, he afterwards revived an obsolete claim on Maestricht, and insisted on a free navigation of the Scheldt. The Republic of Holland, governed by the three Democrat Pensionaries, Van Berkel, Gyzlaer, and Zeebergen, threw herself for protection into the arms of France, who made bold promises; whilst Frederick the Great was ready to sacrifice his niece, the Princess of Orange, to his French alliance.

England, whose Government and policy naturally appeared unstable and eccentric, had lost all Continental confidence at this second dismission of Mr. Fox.

From the best written account of the Dutch Revolution, by the accomplished Mr. George Ellis, (who was with Sir James Harris at the Hague, and a spectator of the events he describes,) and which was published anonymously in 1789, by Edwards in Pall Mall, I make the following extract:—

" Such was the unpromising and apparently desperate posture of affairs when Sir James Harris began his mission at the Hague. It was necessary he should separate the *man* from the *Minister*, and that by his address and conciliating manners he should rescue himself from that general proscription in which all who bore the name of Englishman had been long involved; that, with an appearance of perfect inactivity, he should connect and unite a scattered and despondent party, and inspire them with unanimity and courage; that he should discover or create channels of sure and secret intelligence; and that, under all those impressions of jealousy which his mission necessarily inspired, he should disappoint the vigilance, and detect and defeat the intrigues, of a wary and powerful faction whose emissaries pervaded every society in the Republic. In all these points ' this subtle and audacious Minister,'* as the French writers emphatically style him, became at last completely successful."

This placed Sir James Harris at once in the first rank

* " Ce rusé et audacieux Harris."—*Mirabeau's Cour de Berlin*, vol. ii. p. 13·

of the diplomatists of his day, and raised his reputation perhaps even to a higher pitch on the Continent than at home, where the victory was appreciated; but the circumstances and difficulties of the struggle were not so well known as by those whose ablest Ministers he had foiled.

Monsieur, afterwards Louis the Eighteenth, in a letter to Lady Malmesbury accompanying a copy of his Translation of Mr. Ellis's work, writes thus:—

"St. Cloud, Aug. 31, 1790.

" MY LADY,—To whom could this weak copy of an egregious picture be more properly inscribed than to your Ladyship? The praise of your noble husband, who perhaps contributed more to that memorable Revolution than the Duke of Brunswick himself, (for he has been the *head*, and the Duke only the *arm*, of it,) will possibly appear displaced in the work of a man who, born on the banks of the Seine, is naturally inclined towards the *Patriotic* side of the question: but, as says Corneille, (whom I should not dare to quote were I not informed how perfectly your Ladyship is mistress of the French language,)

' L'estime et le respect sont de justes tribus
Qu' aux plus fiers ennemis arrachent les vertus ;'

and certainly nobody can help admiring the abilities of a great statesman, which Lord Malmesbury has displayed in the whole transaction."

[The liberal manner in which Mr. Pitt appointed a political opponent to the Hague with a perfect freedom of future Parliamentary opposition, and the conduct and views of Sir J. Harris, and of his leaders, the Duke of Portland and Mr. Fox, in this matter, reflect great credit on all these persons. Sir James served Pitt with all his characteristic energy and zeal, and at the end of his Mission returned, as a matter of course, into the ranks of the Whig Party.]

SIR J. HARRIS'S ACCOUNT OF HIS NOMINATION TO
HOLLAND, 1784.

On Mr. Fox coming into office for a second time, in
1783, he immediately complied with a request I had
frequently repeated, of being recalled on account of my
health from the Court of Petersburg. He gave me a
discretionary power to return home when I pleased, but
expressed his wish that I would remain in Russia as
long as possible. I left Petersburg in September. In
April he wrote me a private letter, to ask me whether
I should object to be employed in Holland. I replied,
that I was willing to be employed in Holland, provided
sufficient time was to be allowed to me to re-establish
my health before I went there; and that the mission,
when I did go there, should, both as to the appoint-
ments and as to the rank, be such an one as I might
accept without the appearance of going backward in my
career. To this he assented. On my coming to England in November, 1783, I asked him most particularly
the terms on which the King meant that I should go to
the Hague. He said, it ought to be an Embassy, both
on my account and on account of the public; but the
King thinks it below his dignity to send a Minister of a
higher rank to the States than they shall appoint here,
and the States intend to name only a Minister of the
second rank. " But," added Mr. Fox, " you shall be
equally an ambassador. Lord Mountstuart declines
Spain, and that embassy is open to you if you like it."
I replied, that such an offer was highly flattering to me,
but there were, on the score of Lady Harris and of my
children, such insuperable objections to my living at
Madrid, that I felt myself obliged to refuse it; that the
Hague raised to an Embassy was the only object which
could induce me to return to the Continent, and that I
had rather have my pension at home than anything
short of that abroad.

Fox approved my determination; said he had much
rather have me in Holland than Spain, as being a place

of such important business, and that he would endeavour to prevail on the King not to attend so scrupu-
lously to a mere matter of etiquette.

Early in December, Fox and the Portland Administration were dismissed; I followed them into Opposition,
and voted constantly with them on every question till
the middle of February, when I paired off with Sir
Whally Gardiner, my health obliging me to go to Bath.
I had renounced all thoughts, both of going abroad on a
public employment, or of receiving any reward for my
services under the new Administration, with none of
whom I had any connexion, and whose manner of coming into office I had so explicitly and avowedly disapproved.

In March (towards the middle of the month), Mr.
Fraser, Under Secretary of State, wrote me word that,
as it was probable the Definitive Treaty with the Dutch
would be shortly signed, an exchange of Ministers
would soon take place between this country and Holland; and he could assure me that it would give the
King's Ministers great satisfaction if they thought I
would not refuse this post, if it was proposed to me
on proper terms.   I returned a general answer, neither
absolutely declining nor accepting the proposal; declaring, at the same time, my sentiments would always
lead me to serve where I could do it with credit and
ability, without committing myself, or appearing to desert my friends and principles.   I wrote by the same
post to Sir G. Elliot, whom I desired to acquaint the
Duke of Portland and Mr. Fox with the overture which
had been made me, to ask their opinion upon the subject, and to assure them that I should strictly abide by
it, be it what it would.   They both, without hesitation,
agreed that I ought to accept; that foreign employ was
perfectly distinct from home politics; and that the first
consideration ought to be, not how best to serve *a party*,
but how to make oneself the most useful to the whole
community.   This the Duke of Portland confirmed to
me from my own conduct in April, when I was in Westminster to poll for Fox; and, from my own sentiments

being so strongly supported by theirs, I was induced to call on Fraser to ask him on what grounds he had written to me, whether with the participation of Lord Carmarthen,* or simply from motives of private regard.

Fraser not being explicit on this point, left me no doubt that his letter was in consequence of orders from the Secretary of State; in which opinion I was confirmed on his asking me, after I had expressed my readiness to serve abroad, whether I should object saying to Lord Carmarthen what I had said to him. I replied, certainly not, but that I would say nothing more, nor even wear the appearance of relinquishing my party, or seeking employment as a favour. Fraser said, I by no means ought; he only wished Lord Carmarthen knew my disposition to continue in the foreign line from my own mouth: he was sure it would give him great satisfaction, and enable him to carry a very agreeable piece of information to St. James's. I accordingly, at two, saw Lord Carmarthen, to whom I expressed my willingness to serve on the Continent, providing no conditions whatsoever were made with me relative to my Parliamentary conduct, and providing the employment offered to me was such as I could with propriety accept. Lord Carmarthen assured me that he had great pleasure from what he had heard; that he could be responsible it would be particularly grateful to the King, who had expressed his concern on being told that I had given up the Foreign line. Our conference was confined solely to these words; it was very short, of course. I returned the same day to Bath: during my stay there I had frequent letters from Fraser, informing me of the approaching conclusion of the Dutch Treaty, and that the Cabinet were unanimous in their wishes that I should go to the Hague. Their only doubt was how to make the Mission worthy my acceptance.

Things were thus circumstanced when I returned to London in May, on the meeting of the new Parliament (Pitt having dissolved the old one). I called imme-

---

* Secretary of State for Foreign Affairs under Mr. Pitt.

diately on the Duke of Portland, stated precisely the situation in which I stood, and begged of him to give me his opinion whether, thus situated, I ought or ought not to vote in Parliament. I begged him to set aside all personal considerations, and to determine solely on the grounds of public propriety; that it was not permission to vote one way or the other that I came to ask, nor by an artful apology to conceal an intended desertion of my party, but merely to obtain his advice, which, let it be what it would, I was determined, at all events, to follow. The Duke replied that he was clearly of opinion that I ought not to vote at all. That he so much wished to have me at the Hague, that he should be extremely sorry if I furnished any handle for Ministers to send another person, which my voting against them would certainly do; and that, even supposing them liberal enough not to attend to the way in which I voted, my publicly appearing in Opposition, immediately previous to my accepting so consequential a post, would give bad impressions abroad; it would impede my negotiations by affording to my adversaries a motive to say that I had not the confidence of the Ministry, and that I was appointed simply in order to be got rid of.

I replied to the Duke that his opinion was that of a most candid and honest man, and, as I before said, my conduct should be regulated by it; but that the world at large, less candid a great deal than himself, and unacquainted with the manner in which this transaction had been carried on, would, on seeing me immediately absent myself from Parliament, and soon after accept a high and lucrative employment, conclude that I had acted on interested grounds, and deserted my party on that account. The Duke answered me, that, to obviate this, he authorized me to declare to any one who should misconstrue my behaviour, that it was not only in consequence of his advice, but in consequence of his express desire, that I had acted as I did; that he himself would say the same to every one who should make any observations on the subject; and that this would very sufficiently justify with all those towards whom it was of any importance to be justified. Fox was of the same opinion, although he was too busy in his Westminster election to be so explicit as the Duke. I therefore did not attend Parliament at its meeting.

The 28th of May, I received a note from Fraser, saying that Lord Carmarthen wished to see me as soon as possible. I went directly to the office. Lord Carmarthen told me that the Definitive Treaty between Great Britain and the States was signed; that an exchange of Ministers was in contemplation, and that all his Majesty's confidential servants were unanimous in their opinion that I was the properest man to be sent to Holland; that they equally agreed that it could not be expected of me to accept that post on the same terms on which I held Russia, at the same time that it was not becoming to send a Minister of a higher rank to the Dutch than they should send here; that, to conciliate this point of etiquette with the personal considerations which were due to me, they (the Cabinet) had come to a resolution to offer me the Hague mission, with the salary and all the emoluments of an Ambassador, but that I should produce in Holland credentials only as Minister Plenipotentiary, till such time as either the States General sent an Ambassador, or till some favourable circumstance should make it proper for me to appear in that character. Lord Carmarthen ended by saying, that he hoped this proposal would be agreeable to me, and that he made it to me in the King's name. I replied, that it was so flattering to me personally, and so advantageous in itself, that it did not require any hesitation as far as relative to myself; that I was only embarrassed how to express my gratitude for a mark of favour so much above my merits and expectations; that it had been my opinion that business would be carried on at the Hague better by having an ostensible Ambassador there, as we should then have carried on our negotiations with the same force as the French, but that I submitted this to the judgment of his Lordship.

Lord Carmarthen said *he* thought as I did, but his sentiments were overruled. The King did not choose to give up a point of etiquette. He hinted the probability and the propriety of my being called up to the Privy Council, in order to give me *a relief* at home and abroad. The same evening, at Carlton House, I saw both Fox and the Duke of Portland, and they both were extremely pleased with what had passed; both approved of what I had done, and both praised the candour of the Ministry. On Sunday I saw the Prince of Wales, to whom I communicated the whole transaction; he, too, expressed his entire approbation, and said some pleasing things on the subject.

LETTER FROM SIR JAMES HARRIS TO MR. FRASER.

Bath, 27th March, 1784.

IN answer to the last paragraph of your letter, I can assure you, that, whatever my political opinions or political leanings may be, they are founded on this invariable principle, a desire to promote, as far as in me lies, the general good of this country. Whenever I can do this without an appearance of abandoning my friends, and in a situation which may look like a promotion, not like degradation in my line, I certainly shall not be backward to listen to any overture which might be made. I confess, however, at the same time, that I foresee so many *humiliating* circumstances which must attend, in these unhappy times, an English Minister abroad, that I scarce can venture to pronounce myself fit to accept such a service. After having got the better of the Spanish pride, and fought at least an equal fight in Russia, it would gall me to the quick to be oppressed and trampled on by the Dutch. But all this is *hors de propos;* you can collect enough of my general sentiments as are necessary to be assured, that, though I may not at this moment be an agreeable subject, yet it is, and ever will be, my intention to be a good and loyal one.

FROM THE MARQUIS OF CARMARTHEN* TO SIR JAMES HARRIS.

St. James's, 22nd October, 1784.

MY DEAR SIR,—I think I begin to smell our official correspondence. In the mean time, however, let me beg of you to come up as soon as your own convenience may permit. I mean to go out of town to-morrow, (to Mims only,) and return on Tuesday at furthest, and shall probably find *le beau Lynden*† déjà arrivé. *Pitt wishes to see you soon;* the Duke of Richmond to hear you are already listening to the soft strains of Belgic croaking. What I most want to hear is a good account of Lady Harris, and to see (vide Pitt supra).

Ever yours faithfully,   CARMARTHEN.

FROM THE MARQUIS OF CARMARTHEN TO SIR JAMES HARRIS.

November 22, 1784.

Extract of a Note from a Gentleman‡ in Berkshire to his Clerk§ in town.

" I DO not suppose it can be right to take any step except hurrying the departure of Sir James Harris, whose presence at the Hague becomes very essential."

A word to the wise is sufficient; I therefore depend upon seeing you on Wednesday night, or, at furthest, Thursday morning. Pray remember me kindly to Lady Harris, and believe me ever, my dear Sir,

Faithfully yours,   CARMARTHEN.

EXTRACT OF A DESPATCH FROM SIR JAMES HARRIS TO THE MARQUIS OF CARMARTHEN.

Hague, 7th Dec., 1784.

YOUR Lordship will, I am sure, make allowances for a despatch written so few hours after my arrival, and

* Secretary of State for Foreign Affairs, and afterwards Duke of Leeds.
† Dutch Minister in London, and a Patriot in politics.
‡ The King.   § Lord Carmarthen.

before I have had time to attend to anything but the ceremonial of my introduction.

There seems now but little doubt that France is determined to support this country against the claims of the Emperor. She has offered the Republic the choice of one out of four of her best generals, Maillebois, Luckerer, May, and Marcange, to command the Dutch army under the Prince of Orange. She has also given them leave to raise a corps of four thousand light troops in France, and has hinted to them her intention of having an army of observation in the Low Countries.

A courier from Berlin, who arrived a few days ago, has brought them assurances equally favourable. The King of Prussia has offered them his assistance to obtain troops from the German Princes, and declared also that he will have an army of observation to wait on that of Austria. These events have raised the spirits of the Anti-Stadtholderian party, and they now look forward to an honourable peace or to a successful war. Much, it is supposed, will depend on the determination of the Empress of Russia: if she supports the Emperor in his claims, the issue of the present contest, it is thought, will be war; if she holds a neutral language, peace.

In regard to the Republic itself, it is now entirely in the hands of Messrs. Zeeberg, Gyslaer, and Van Berkel, Pensionaries of Haarlem, Dort, and Amsterdam. These three direct the Grand Pensionary Blyswick, who now only acts a second part. It must be, therefore, my business to discover, if possible, not what passes in the Assembly of the States General, or even in that of the States of Holland, but *what passes between these persons.* To know this, (if it be ever attainable,) will be a work of time and difficulty; but, till it is attained, my information will be very deficient. In the meanwhile, I may venture to assure your Lordship that the primary object of this Triumvirate is to overset the Stadtholder; and to this every other consideration, even the preventing the opening of the Scheldt, gives way.

The Court of Versailles and the King of Prussia readily concur with them; but the latter, from his connexion with the Princess of Orange,* is not for a *total* annihilation of the office. He proposes, as I am told, that the Prince of Orange should be pronounced incapable of filling it, and his niece appointed Gouvernante, in conjunction with a Council chosen from the Patriotic party. This measure, however, violent as it is, does not still come up to their wishes. They are bent upon introducing a new form of Government.

Things thus circumstanced, there is not, I fear, the most distant prospect of reclaiming this country, or that my Mission will be attended with any other advantage to his Majesty's service than to stand upon record as a proof of his not having abandoned the Republic in the hour of distress.

I, however, will leave nothing unattempted, as far as may be consistent with the rules of caution and prudence, to *animate* our disheartened party, and to induce them to *die hard.*

I arrived here yesterday at three in the afternoon; which I immediately announced by M. Gomm, my secretary, to the Greffier.† He appointed me to go to him this morning at ten. Nothing could be more cordial or more friendly than the Greffier, and I am convinced I shall receive from him the best of advice. He recommended me to attempt nothing more, in the first moments of my mission, than the doing away the impressions which our enemies had given universally here, that we entertain the most inimical sentiments for this country.‡

The President of the week scarcely uttered a word, nor could I draw from him anything more than a bow in

---

* The Princess of Orange was the niece of Frederick the Great.

† Baron Fagel. The place was for life ; and the present Greffier was of the Stadtholder's party.

‡ The Seven Provinces considered as a Republic were governed by the Assembly of the States General, in which each province had one vote. The Greffier was their Secretary and attended at their meetings. The States of Holland were composed of the nobles and the deputies of the towns, and the Grand Pensionary was their Speaker.

answer to the assurances I made him of the King's good-will, on delivering my credentials. On my visit to the Great Pensionary Blyswick, I was determined to set him as much at his ease as possible. I, therefore, began by telling him that, in the present embarrassed circum-stances, I did not expect he could have much to say to me; and that, in fact, I had nothing more to say to him than that although untoward events had placed the two countries in a very different position from that in which they had been accustomed to stand for near a century, yet that the King's sentiments are unalterable, and that he can never be indifferent to the welfare and prosperity of the States General ; that, on all occasions which I might have of doing business with him, he would find me sincere, frank, and true, and that I was persuaded he also would deal in the same manner by me. He was very civil in his reply, lamented past events, and kept pace with me in general assurances of friendship and regard.

The Prince of Orange received me with every appear-ance of satisfaction, and replied with strong expressions of gratitude to the affectionate assurances I had in com-mand to make him from his Majesty. He spoke with great feeling of his own situation; said, that if, when we met last, anybody had told him that the two first wars he should be engaged in were to be one with England and the other with the Emperor, he should have supposed that person to have been insane, but that his happy days were over, and that he looked forward to nothing for himself and his children but *misery* and *disgrace.* I told him that courage and patience might still effect a great deal; that he might be convinced the professions I had just made him were perfectly sincere; and that whenever he could adopt a wise and vigorous system, and would persevere in it with energy and resolution, he might de-pend on such support from my royal Master as could be granted, consistently with the welfare and interest of his own subjects. He appeared somewhat animated by this language, which I was induced to make more pointed than I otherwise should have done, from a report which

reached me just before I went into his closet that he was
actually meditating *a voluntary abdication.*

———

[THE following despatch shows how soon Sir James
Harris formed his plan of effecting a counter revolution in
Holland, and suggested it to the English Government.]

EXTRACT OF A DESPATCH FROM SIR JAMES HARRIS TO THE
MARQUIS OF CARMARTHEN.

(Confidential.)

Hague, 10th December, 1784.

THE only difference which seems to exist between the
interests of Prussia and France is, that the King of
Prussia wishes to preserve at least the form of an Aristocratical Government in this country, (say, in this Republic,) while the object of France is to make it a perfect
Democracy. The King of Prussia feels he can do a great
deal through the Princess of Orange, and France looks
forward to every object she can gain by throwing this
country into a state of anarchy.

The Patriots* are the tools of France. The Princess
of Orange, from her predilection to her own family, and
the Prince, from his excessive weakness, are the tools of
Prussia. The result will probably be the ruin of both.
The House of Orange cannot subsist as Stadtholder, deprived of all its prerogatives; and the Patriots have neither power nor ability to induce the people to submit
quietly to the danger and expense into which they are
going to plunge them.

England has certainly still a party here, but it is
composed of a set of men dejected, oppressed, and divided amongst themselves. Something might be effected
if a chief could be found to head it. The chief ought
to be a Prince of Orange, but not a Prince of Orange

———

* The name assumed by the Dutch Democrats.

like the *present* one. In default of him, it perhaps ought to be *his Majesty's Minister;* but, under the present circumstances, 1 submit it to your Lordship whether it is a post to be filled by one invested with a public character. Nothing can be effected without violence, and the success of violent measures (however well concerted) is too uncertain ever to be attempted by one who must be attentive not to commit the honour and dignity of his Court.

If it were possible by any means whatsoever to gain over the Princess of Orange, to open her eyes to the interests of her children, and to induce her to prevail on the Prince's party to consent to the Emperor's views on the Scheldt, (provided the Emperor would contribute on his side to reinstate the Prince in the full privileges of his high office,) this country might still be restored to its ancient system. But this, I fear, is beyond the reach of negotiation, unless both the King and Prince of Prussia should soon drop. It remains, therefore, to be seen, whether the *people themselves* of this country will not (ultimately) be *roused* to a sense of their situation, and produce, by an *insurrection*, what nothing short of an insurrection can produce. If this should not happen, we might then look forward to the reduction of this country to a state of perfect insignificancy as the best event which can befall England, it being evident that the Republic had better be annihilated than remain as it is.

I feel some apology necessary for presuming to write in so positive a manner so early after my arrival. In common times I should have deferred it to a more distant day, but moments like these admit, I hope, of exceptions; and though, from length of time, I have lost many of my best connexions in this country, yet it is not entirely new to me, and I can, perhaps, more readily catch the temper and feelings of its inhabitants than a perfect stranger.*

* Sir J. Harris had passed eighteen months at Leyden when he left Oxford, and had (as his Journal shows) taken much pains to become acquainted with the leading people at the Hague, and the character of the country. It stood him now in good stead.

[THE following reply shows how little disposed our Government was to interfere in the Stadtholder's behalf by any active or avowed measures.]

EXTRACT OF A DESPATCH FROM THE MARQUIS OF CARMARTHEN TO SIR JAMES HARRIS.

St. James's, 14th December, 1784.

SIR,—Your several despatches have been all received, and laid before the King.   The high opinion of your zeal and activity in his Majesty's service, which your former correspondence must have impressed on the minds of my predecessors in office, is already more than confirmed in my mind by the very ample and accurate report of the present situation of things in Holland, which, a few hours after your arrival at the Hague, you have been able to transmit for his Majesty's information.

Whatever turn the actual differences may take, there appears little occasion for any precise instructions to you, Sir, at this time, in addition to those you received previous to your departure.   The general line of your conduct must ever be regulated by this one invariable maxim, that, desirable as it must ever be to crush, as far as possible, the assumed and despotic influence of France in that country, yet even the attainment of this object must not be purchased at the expense of having to support, at all events, the enfeebled and impoverished remains of a distressed and divided country.

LETTER FROM THE MARQUIS OF CARMARTHEN TO SIR JAMES HARRIS.

St. James's, 14th December, 1784.

MY DEAR SIR,—A thousand thanks to you for your private letters (as well as the *confidential* one, which I have not now time to answer).   Nothing can be more pleasant to me, both as a Minister and (what is to me a much more valuable feather in my cap) your friend, than your two packets. I am sure they will please in other more important quarters. I most highly approve of your projected excursion to Amsterdam;† everything that can be, ought to be known; and, I am sure, you will collect more in a week than   *   *   *   did in seven years. He could neither *stoop to conquer*, nor conciliate.

Supper is waiting; so, I can only tell you Goertz is ordered by the King his Master to make a formal complaint against Simolin on account of the conversation with Lusi at St. James's, which you remember hearing of one day we dined at Kagenech's. I could not help concluding my letter to Fitzherbert to-day with rejoicing at Simolin's being fallen into such good hands. Pray remember me kindly to the good Greffier, and believe me ever, &c.

EXTRACT OF A DESPATCH FROM SIR JAMES HARRIS TO THE
MARQUIS OF CARMARTHEN.

Hague, 17th Dec., 1784.

I HAVE it now in my power to give your Lordship an account of the gradual progress and actual extent of the Prussian influence in this country.

It naturally may be supposed to date its commencement from the marriage of the present Princess of Orange, who came hither strongly prejudiced in favour of her family, and who was attended by Mad[lle] Danckelman, a lady who had brought her up, and who is entirely devoted to his Prussian Majesty. This connexion, however, for many years did not affect either the conduct of the Prince of Orange, or the measures of the Republic, on any material points. It was not till France began to raise a party in opposition to that of the Stadtholder, that its influence began to appear, and from that

---

† Amsterdam was the focus of the French Intrigues with the Patriots, who had a great majority in that town, and had been the first cause of our late war with Holland, by acknowledging our revolted Colonies.

period the interests of the Courts of Versailles and Berlin have increased by mutually supporting each other. During the course of our war with the Republic, the constant language the Prince of Orange heard from Potzdam was, that the only means for maintaining his power and dignity was through the medium of France, and by uniting himself with the town of Amsterdam. The Prince was at that time too well advised not to see the dangerous tendency of such counsels; and, as long as he felt that he had a remnant of party which he could call his own, he was averse to seeking a protection which would compel him to adopt an entire new plan. The Princess of Orange herself also, notwithstanding her predilections, was far from considering it as one which would contribute to the welfare of her family; but, as their old partisans fell off, and as the unpopularity of the House of Orange increased, fear and irresolution wrought a change in their sentiments, and a trifling incident which took place two years ago threw them entirely into the hands of the King of Prussia.

On the 6th December, 1782, some friends of the Prince, more zealous than wise, attempted to raise riots in his favour. Their measures were concerted and executed so ill, that they produced an effect directly contrary to that which was intended, and animated the body of the people so much against the Stadtholder that he thought himself in personal danger. In these circumstances he was weak enough to apply to the King of Prussia, who promised him his support, provided he would no longer oppose the views of France in the Republic. To this I have every reason to fear the Prince has consented, and endeavours to palliate his want of firmness by the hackneyed plea of necessity.

From that time to this day he is effectually under the management of Prussia, as what is styled the Patriotic party is under the direction of France. They however kept their interests and operations distinct, till such time as the Emperor's pretensions on the Scheldt were made known.

The King of Prussia, whose primary object for many years has been to form an alliance with France, considered this as a favourable moment for effecting his purpose. He did not think he paid too dear for it by the total sacrifice of the Stadtholder, who, partly from his own inconsistency, and partly from the apprehensions of the Princess, is become the instrument of his own destruction. He was induced to send, a few weeks ago, an artful and unprincipled man (the Rhingrave of Salm) on a special commission to Berlin, to solicit advice and assistance of every kind. He has obtained a great deal more of the first than of the latter. The King of Prussia declined lending any of his Generals to act under the Prince in his military capacity.

The Princess of Orange is accomplished to a degree, with a strong mind and quick penetration; but she is depressed by misfortunes of every kind. Her domestic life is deprived of happiness, and her public one a perpetual scene of anxiety. Naturally high-minded, she can ill brook the inattention she daily experiences from the bad breeding of the wives of the factious Patriots; and she feels most sensibly the defection of those about her person, who in better days used to pay her servile court.

LETTER FROM SIR J. HARRIS TO THE MARQUIS OF CARMARTHEN.

Hague, Tuesday, 21st Dec., 1784.

MY LORD,—The mail of the 14th instant, which came yesterday, brought me your Lordship's despatch of that date. It gives me very great satisfaction to learn that the letters I have written from hence on the opening my mission meet your Lordship's approbation: I have every possible motive for wishing to continue to deserve it; and you may rely, my Lord, on my sparing neither zeal nor assiduity.

I must entreat your Lordship's patience till I get

more acquainted with the constitution and interior government of this country, before I can venture to give
you information on the practicability of the designs of
the present men in power.   That they extend to an
entire subversion of the Stadtholderate is certain: it is
even to be presumed that they wish to dissolve the ties
of the Act of Union, to destroy what is called here the
Government of the States, by taking the supreme power
(where it has been lodged ever since the time of Prince
Maurice) out of the hands of the Council of State and
Assembly of the States General, who are representatives
of the *Generality*, and by placing it in those of the different *Provincial* Assemblies; in other words, to render
each Province a *distinct* Government by itself.   This independence of the Province will ultimately tend to give
Holland an absolute dominion over the other six, from
its being rather more populous, and that which furnishes
a larger quota of men and money to the Republic than
all the rest together do; it follows that the Pensionaries
of the towns in Holland, and particularly the Great Pensionary of the Province, will then become as much, from
legal authority, the rulers of this country, as they now
are, under the support of faction and popularity.   To
diminish the power of the *Generality*, and to increase
that of each *particular* Province, was the system set on
foot by Barnwelt, pursued afterwards by John De Witt
and the Louverstein party, and which nothing but the
vigilance and abilities of the Princes of Orange of those
days could have prevented being established.

The same means which overset it *then* would possibly
overset it *now*.   It is however but just to point out to
your Lordship one very material difference.   The Princes
of the House of Orange in the times I refer to were, if I
may use the expression, *out of place;* they had the address to make people believe that the distresses and misfortunes of the State arose from a defect in its form of
Government, and that the existence of a chief or Stadtholder was essential to save them from destruction; the
case is now far otherwise.   Every evil which has come

upon the Republic has happened during the actual existence of a Stadtholder invested with more power than
any of his predecessors, and the Patriots have had art
enough to throw the whole blame of everything which
has passed on him. The people, therefore, at this moment are in the belief that the existence of a Stadtholder
will *produce*, not *prevent*, their ruin. To open their eyes
on the subject requires a degree of systematic patience
and courage we are not likely to find, or a series of
fortunate events not likely to happen.

On reading over this sketch of the present situation of
parties here, it will appear evident why France supports
the present leading men and their system, and why these
prefer a French connexion to all others. It is indeed so
evidently their reciprocal interest, that I think it is not
necessary to suppose that either Van Berkel, Zeebergen,
or Gyslaer have been ever corrupted by France. They
find their reward in becoming Regents of the Republic,
and in having their share in the acquisition and distri-
bution of emoluments of every kind.

There is no doubt that these three men have real
weight and influence, and that they derive it principally
from the state of confusion which they themselves have
had the skill to raise. They have certainly much intrinsic merit. They have amongst them judgment,
knowledge, and spirit, and, I fear, many other essential
qualities the opposite party is without. I am satisfied
nothing but a convulsion, which would shake the State to
its foundation, could at this moment wrest the power out
of their hands; but there is no one to direct the storm
(if it could be raised), and, even if it were raised, God
knows in what situation it would leave the Republic!

I shall in my next letter endeavour to give your
Lordship an account of the character of the three Pensionaries. I shall then have nearly exhausted all the
general topics which may be considered as necessary to
form the groundwork of a new correspondence from this
country, and you will not be afterwards troubled with
such diffusive despatches.   I have, &c.

EXTRACT OF A LETTER FROM SIR JAMES HARRIS TO THE
MARQUIS OF CARMARTHEN.

Hague, 21st Dec., 1784.

A FEW private lines, my dear Lord, on public concerns. Would it not be advisable to say a word to them
here on the Naval Force they intend keeping in India
on their Peace Establishment; or is it better that this
subject should be finally discussed where it began, at
Paris? It is, at all events, material for me now and
then to have *something like a public commission*, as,
without some pretext of this kind, I never can get a
sight of the Greffier, who cautioned me, for his sake,
never to come to him, unless I at the same time *went to
Mr. Blyswick.*

This I have hitherto most religiously observed; and,
as I am well aware that during the first days of my arrival I am closely watched, I have seen neither him nor
any of my confidential friends, but in such a manner as
will defeat the most vigilant spies. I observed a link-
boy, who most assiduously lighted me whenever I went
out in the evening, although I had two flambeaux, and
this without asking fee or reward; but as they have no
idea that a gentleman can get up before it is *eight*, and
walk in the rain with a brown surtout and round hat, I
have done all my mysterious business before their eyes
are open.

LETTER FROM SIR JAMES HARRIS TO THE MARQUIS OF
CARMARTHEN.

Hague, 28th Dec., 1784.

MY LORD,—The obtaining a competent insight into
the characters of the *three leading men* in this Republic
appeared to me so essential an object, that I have made
it one of my earliest inquiries. As they never live in
the society with which I mix, and have scarcely any in-

tercourse with foreigners, I can only transmit to your Lordship such information relative to them as I have had it in my power to obtain from such persons as have opportunities of knowing them, and on whose judgment and veracity I may venture to depend.

Van Berkel, Gyslaer, and Zeebergen were all three brought up to the law; a study which in this country does not tend to enlarge the ideas, nor to inspire sentiments of liberality and integrity. It teaches, on the contrary, cunning, chicanery, and narrowness of mind.

Van Berkel, for the first years of his life, followed this profession with no great degree of success at the Hague; and it was the marrying a woman of some fortune at Amsterdam that first carried him to that city, where her connexions and his own abilities raised him in course of time to the post of Pensionary. His principles were from the beginning adverse to a Stadtholderian Government, and some slight he thought put upon him many years ago gave him a rooted hatred to England. To gratify a private pique by a national quarrel seems to exceed the bounds of common rancour, but I am convinced that this motive alone (without ever examining whether the consequences were salutary or detrimental to the Republic) directed his conduct. It was a premeditated plan of revenge, which he had stored up in his mind, and which he was ready to execute on the very first opening. We have seen that he did not neglect his opportunity, and unfortunately has been able to satisfy his inimical disposition towards us with more success than he ever could allow himself to expect.* He is of a temper nearer violence than warmth, steady in his conduct, and not to be driven from his purpose either by fear or persuasion. His professional habits, joined to the acuteness of his mind, enable him very soon to see into the different characters of men; and he possesses, in an eminent degree, the art of working upon their passions. It was he that poisoned the minds

* Alluding to the communications of Amsterdam with the Americans during the war, which were conducted by Blyswick.

of the honest Dutchmen by spreading the most infamous libels against England, in which he has been so
indefatigable and so clever, that he has undone in four
years the work of a century.   The Capellons, the Lyn-
dens, the Alvas, and various others, who really think
they are implicitly following the impulse of their own
consciences and feelings, are only instruments in his
hands, which he employs to inflame the minds of the
vulgar, and to establish a new order of things in the
State.

Gyslaer and Zeebergen, though they also owe their
celebrity to him, and move under his direction, are,
however, of a higher class.   They well know what they
are about, to what their system tends, and are not, like
the names I have just mentioned, the blind tools of an
ambitious leader.   Gyslaer was originally Pensionary of
Gorcum, in which insignificant post he would probably
have remained for life, if it had not appeared (so long
ago as in 1779, when the question was to be debated
whether limited or unlimited convoys should be granted)
to the Amsterdam party that they were likely to lose
their question by a single vote.

Van Berkel immediately turned his thoughts towards
the Pensionary of Gorcum, whom he knew to be young
and ambitious, clever and popular.   He promised him
the first Great Pensionaryship which should drop, if he
could induce his town to direct their deputies to vote
according to his wishes.   Gyslaer succeeded: unlimited
convoys were granted, and he soon after became Pensionary of Dort.   From that time he has been a most
active and inveterate enemy.   As he joins to very fine
parts great eloquence, courage, and spirit, he stands certainly next in rank to Van Berkel.

Zeebergen was first heard of when France, with great
and unexampled insolence, took upon her (in 1779) to
regulate the commercial privileges of the different towns
of the province, according as their political conduct was
conformable or contrary to her views.   Amsterdam was
particularly favoured, and several towns in North Holland

as particularly disgraced.   Zeebergen, then Pensionary
of Haerlem, stood forth and complained, that, as the
principles and behaviour of his town corresponded perfectly with those of Amsterdam, it certainly was entitled
on the part of France to the same distinctions.*   This,
which was probably a concerted measure, pointed out to
the other towns the path they were to tread, and in a
very short time they all subscribed to the doctrines of
Amsterdam, in order to enjoy the same immunities.
Zeebergen continues to direct the political conduct of
Haerlem and its neighbourhood, where he has made a
great many converts ; amongst others, Mr. L'Estevenon,
son of Mons. De Berkenrode, the Dutch Ambassador at
Paris, formerly a violent Englishman, but now as violent
a Patriot.

Zeebergen is a man of calm even temper, patient but
persevering, and a great master of those concealed intrigues, so necessary to keep up the spirits, and increase
the number of a party.   He professes great moderation,
but he is as much in earnest as either of his colleagues,
who find him a very useful and zealous helpmate.   It
must be observed that neither of the three have carried
their ideas beyond the keeping up the spirit of faction in
their own country, and attaining, by this means, the
end they aim at.   They are entirely ignorant of Foreign
politics, and indifferent to every *exterior* consideration of
State; have no idea of looking forward to the consequences of the present position of the Republic, and preparing for the dangers with which it is threatened, otherwise than by temporary expedients.

---

* During our war with America, Amsterdam had, in 1778, signed a Treaty
of Commerce with our revolted Colonies ; and, to induce the other towns to
do the same, France imposed a freightage duty on all Dutch ships, except
those from Amsterdam.—*Ellis and Harris Papers.*

EXTRACT OF A DESPATCH FROM SIR JAMES HARRIS TO
THE MARQUIS OF CARMARTHEN.

Hague, 28th Dec., 1784.

THE answer to the Memorial delivered in by Mons.
Kallicheff,* was sent to that Minister yesterday evening.
It was drawn up in the Secret Committee, who, as I before mentioned, had powers from the States General for
this purpose. I have the honour of enclosing the substance of it, from which it will appear, that though the
answer itself is conceived in very civil words, yet that
they are determined here to abide by their first resolution; and the Pensionary declared in express terms to
the Russian Minister, that the Republic ought to expend
its last shilling rather than submit to so destructive and
humiliating a measure as the opening of the Scheldt.

EXTRACT OF A DESPATCH FROM SIR JAMES HARRIS TO
THE MARQUIS OF CARMARTHEN.

Hague, Tuesday, 4th Jan., 1785.

THE ostensible Governors of the country are still without any official information whatsoever on what is likely
to be the issue of the present impending contest.

The usurpers of the Government, however, I have
reason to believe, are not quite so much kept in the
dark; and, as far as my intelligence in those quarters
can be depended on, it should appear that matters stand
nearly thus:— That, in answer to the French Declaration of the 20th of November, the Emperor has signified
his consent to accept the Mediation of France, provided
that of Russia be annexed to it; and provided, before
any negotiation is entered upon, the Scheldt be declared
open, and he indemnified for the expenses he has incurred, and the losses he has sustained.

* Russian Minister.—The Empress Catherine intimated her intention of
supporting the Emperor's claims.—*Harris Papers.*

The Russian Memorial has damped their spirits, and ought to stagger their faith in the King of Prussia, who has all along assured them they had nothing to fear from that quarter, and who, even at this moment, tells them it does not contain the Empress's real sentiments; that the Austrian interest at Petersburg is on the decline, and that his will very soon prevail there over that of his rival.

I have just heard that Mons. de Maillebois accepts the command of the Dutch army, with the rank of General, but to be raised to that of Field-Marshal on the first promotion.

There is some prospect of a popular commotion at Rotterdam next week, where a woman is to be hanged for no other crime, as the people say and think, than for having worn orange-coloured ribbons.

In a country where party runs so high as in this, and where everything presents itself through the medium of passion and animosity, it is very difficult to observe accurately any alteration in the minds of the people at large, or to distinguish between what is the effect of conviction, or what may be caused solely by disappointment or resentment. It should seem, however, that there is an appearance of discontent, a murmuring amongst some of the leading men of the principal towns, which indicates a disapprobation of the conduct of the Pensionaries. The abuse they make of the ascendancy they have acquired, in several other instances, begins to be felt by many of their more temperate adherents; and their inattention to the Assembly of the States General, their marked contempt of the body of the nobility in every province, joined to their evident inefficiency to direct the State under its present embarrassed situation, seems to raise doubts and alarms in the minds of men, which may in time produce a very salutary revolution in this Government.

As far as relates to England, however, it must be a work of time, or rather a work which must do itself; any attempt to accelerate, any show of interference on our side, would certainly retard, probably defeat, its success altogether.   The unfavourable sentiments of the people against us still prevail.   The prejudices raised in their minds by the indefatigable pains of the Patriots keep their suspicions awake; and, till some national calamity, either internal or foreign, draws their attention another way, and, by pointing out to them new and more deserving objects of fear and hatred, divests them of their present feelings, we must appear to be perfectly quiet, and our operations here carried on out of sight and with the greatest caution: they indeed must be confined to the sole object of recovering the *confidence* of this nation; and it will require a long series of even and soothing conduct to calm their resentment, and to lull them into that state of security in regard to us, so necessary before we attempt to resume any avowed influence in their affairs.

But this system of caution and circumspection is not applicable to the Prince of Orange and the Stadtholderian party; on the contrary, *they* ought to act with vigour, energy, and unremitting attention.   No faults, no mistakes of the opposite party should escape their notice and animadversions; much less should they suffer to pass by disregarded their acts of violence, innovation, and oppression.   They should not idly consume their time in useless attempts to justify themselves, or the still more disgraceful ones of courting their enemies by humiliating concessions.   They should begin by criminating their adversaries, by retorting on them the similar accusations in this quarrel with which the Prince of Orange was charged in the English war.   They should exasperate the people against them by representing them as the cause of all their actual distresses, as a set of men who are going to load them with taxes, who are sold to France and Prussia, and who ultimately intend to divide the Republic between those two Monarchs.

The Prince's situation and character are such, that I dare not press him upon this subject, and I am not sufficiently acquainted with those about him to trust any of them in a matter of such magnitude. To unbosom myself to a weak and false friend would undo me for ever; and the opening is so palpable, that I had rather leave them to the operation of their own senses, than, by risking to misplace my confidence, mar the whole. It is with the less concern that I adopt this method, as the opportunity will not pass away immediately; it may grow even better in the course of a few months; and if it continues to be neglected, and the Stadtholderian party under all circumstances suffer themselves to be trampled upon and oppressed, it must be considered as composed of a set of devoted men whom nothing can save.

EXTRACT OF A LETTER FROM SIR JAMES HARRIS TO THE MARQUIS OF CARMARTHEN.

Hague, 4th Jan., 1785.

THE picture I have ventured to give of the present state of this country is, I really believe, a very true one. You must make allowances, and consider it as only the *first sitting*. A popular insurrection is certainly on the cards, but, if it was once begun, it would be impossible either to direct or to stop its progress.

There is an idle prophecy gone forth that a massacre is to take place this month. The leading faction have very imprudently put arms into the hands of the peasants on the frontiers. The people at large feel the weight of the present oppression, and the consequences of being delivered over to France and Prussia. The nobles of this and the other provinces have their privileges and emoluments wrested from them; even the magistracy are dissatisfied at seeing their Pensionaries usurp, of their own authority, a right of decision which ought to follow, not precede, their consent; every description of men here, in short, have some cause within themselves

for complaint, and they are kept under merely by the
intrigues of the Patriotic faction, (who have address
enough to make them believe that the ills they suffer
are only to prevent greater evils,) and by the insensibility of the Stadtholder, who by his torpitude affords
them a striking example of submission and resignation
difficult to be paralleled in the annals of history.   Were
he to lift up a finger, two-thirds of the country would
obey his call.   It would even be no very arduous task
to excite them without his instigation; but it is not our
business to produce a revolution here, at the risk of
having a distressed and feeble country to support.   Yet,
though *this is not the moment* for stirring, yet it becomes us to be *ripe to stir* when any opening presents
itself; and the subterranean noise is so loud that an
eruption may be nearer at hand than we expect, and
I would not have it take me unawares.

Allow me then to ask you whether just now I ought
to do anything more than behave in so even a manner
as to avoid consequences, and to put myself, if possible,
in a situation to be able, when the battlements rock, to
claim, in case of success, some portion of the merit.
The character of our party here is caution and timidity.
If I saw *despair* amongst them, I should have some
hope; but I flatter myself I shall not appear infected
with their weaknesses if I do not venture to tread firm
till I am sure the ground will bear me.

I submit to your judgment whether there would be
any impropriety some weeks hence in my going to Amsterdam.   There reigns in that city great discontent
with the present mode of governing, and I have now
before me a list of some ten or twelve people who perhaps want only a little encouragement to be brought
over.   If we could overset Van Berkel, the other two
would fall of themselves.   A little urbanity, I find, goes
a great way here: perhaps it is a commodity they are
not used to see coming out of the shop of an *English*
Minister.   It would go still farther at Amsterdam, and
it would give me pleasure to say,

Via prima salutis,
Quod minimè rêris, Graiâ pandetur ab urbe.

In short, my dear Lord, make the most of me. I have no personal fears, and should have no care about my own head being broken, if the same stroke did not affect that of His Majesty's Minister.

EXTRACT OF A DESPATCH FROM SIR JAMES HARRIS TO
THE MARQUIS OF CARMARTHEN.

Hague, 21st Jan., 1785.

THE Prince of Orange presented on Wednesday a letter to the States General, containing a justification of his conduct from the year 1776, (when he first took the Administration of the affairs of this country into his hands,) to the present day. He recapitulated every remarkable event which has happened during this period, and he is particularly attentive to exculpate himself from the accusations alleged against him of being, first, the cause of the war with England, and afterwards of its ill-success. He ends his paper, which is of many pages and well drawn up, with a plan of defence for the Inland Provinces. When this letter was read to the States of Holland, it was treated with an indifference bordering on contempt, and it is to be apprehended that it will not share a better fate when it is produced before those of the other provinces.

This party seems bent on oversetting the present form of Government, without having prepared any other to substitute in its room. France, who will find her account in the total subversion of order, encourages this attempt by every means in her power. Prussia, who never loses sight of breaking up the connexion between the Courts of Versailles and Vienna, affords no real support to the Stadtholder, and every day this country seems nearer approaching its ruin.

[On the 3rd of January, the Emperor's ambition fol-
lowing a new object, he concluded a treaty with the
Elector Palatine, by which he agreed to transfer the
Austrian Netherlands in exchange for the succession of
Bavaria.   The Elector was to take the title of King,
and succeed to all the Emperor's present claims on the
Dutch.   Catherine, although she could not support the
Emperor without breaking through her obligations form-
ed at Teschen, appeared ready to do so.   Frederick was
indignant, and by the activity with which he raised the
German Confederation thwarted the plan.]

EXTRACT OF A LETTER FROM SIR JAMES HARRIS TO THE
MARQUIS OF CARMARTHEN.

Hague, 25th Jan., 1785.

IF the information relative to an exchange of the
Bavarian succession be true, the murder is out: I say,
if it be true; for as yet we have only the King of
Prussia's word for it, and it is an act of too much consequence to be credited without two reputable witnesses
at the least.   This matter is too recently come upon
me, and has taken me too unprepared, for me to look
forward to all its possible consequences, or to know precisely what we are to wish for.

England and Holland gave the Low Countries, by the
peace of Utrecht, to the House of Austria, to serve as a
barrier against France; and if I recollect right, (for I
have not the Treaty at hand,) they cannot be alienated
without the consent of these Powers.   In this treaty-
breaking age, this perhaps does not signify a great deal
either to one or the other of the parties; but we shall
certainly be called upon on this occasion, and I scarce
see how we can avoid giving something like a positive
answer.   I will trust to your Lordship for wording it in
such manner as will be most suitable to our interest
without wounding our dignity.   But as I shall be cer-

tainly pressed hard upon here to declare some opinion, and as I cannot answer like the shepherd in the *Avocat Patelin*, I shall be anxious and awkward till I know your sentiments.

The Elector Palatine, as King of Brabant, with the districts of Juliers and Berg, Dusseldorf, and Ravenstein, without taking into account what may be pared from the Dutch, would be no contemptible monarch; and, if allied with England and the Emperor (become so much a greater power by his new acquisitions), would contribute to the formation of no contemptible an opposition to France, and be in the new system what this country was in the old;—this is the bright side of the medal.

If His Majesty of Brabant, Burgundy, or by whatever title dignified or distinguished, should choose rather to be governed by France than protected by England, (like these Boors,) why then it is the reverse of the medal; in short, it is heads or tails: and I shall not presume to say a word more before I have consulted *Lord Torrington*, who I have no doubt foresaw all this several months ago, and can foretel as accurately as he foresaw clearly all that will follow.

His Lordship has played me a trick which puts the finishing stroke to his character for prudence and penetration. He recommended to me *as his cousin*, and as a man of worth, a Major Byng, who *two* days after he gets to Amsterdam is accused of having issued a false bill of exchange, and who absconds the *third*. That an honest man who is blind, deaf, lame, and dumb, should mistake a rogue for a man of worth is possible; but how he could mistake him for his *cousin*, I cannot well understand : *il abuse de la permission*, and, if there is a general reform in the Government and Governors of the Austrian Netherlands, I hope he will not be forgotten.

EXTRACT OF A LETTER FROM SIR JAMES HARRIS TO THE
MARQUIS OF CARMARTHEN.

Hague, 28th January, 1785.

I HAVE many thanks to return you for your kind ani-
mating letter of the 17th instant. Be assured that my
spirits will not fail me whenever I am to act on *my own
account;* but it is impossible to see without being hurt,
even to dejection, the want of energy and vigour of mind
in the Prince of Orange. Everything at this moment
provokes him to move,—the temper of the people, the
irresolution of the Patriots, the inefficiency of the
French Ambassador,* the confused state of Europe ;
yet, instead of advancing, he retires. Such a man never
can win at any game; and, unless a sleeping potion is
administered to him, total ruin must follow. I discover
daily many great and good qualities in the Princess:
she has a due sense of her situation, and spirit and
abilities *equal to anything;* but he, from that contemptible jealousy ever attendant on imbecility, had rather
be crushed by his own awkwardness than saved by her
dexterity. But enough on this unpleasant disorder in
the State, which, like the tooth-ache, is incurable unless
by drawing the tooth.

I am sure your friendship for me will forgive my asking you, without any preface, a plain question. Is it
intended that I should remain at the Hague ? And do
you and your respectable colleagues think I am worth
the expense I put you to ? It is not a motive of curiosity which induces me to press you for an answer.
Still less does it arise from my not being most perfectly
satisfied with my situation. I only wish, as the French
say, to know *sur quel pied danser.*

It is neither decent as King's Minister, nor agreeable
to myself, to continue any longer in an *Inn.* If I mean
to do anything of notoriety, I must wield the *spit* as well
as the *pen.* Dutch hearts lie to the leeward of their

* Mons. de Verac.

stomachs; and, if I now at this moment make any impression on them, it is from the beef and pudding they
see in the back-ground.

No house, such as I can inhabit, is to be had here
under a term of three or four years: now, to enter into
such a lease, and perhaps to be recalled the moment I
had signed it, would very ill suit my projects of economy;
besides that, it would carry with it something like a hostile intention to this country, " *a glance at our swords,*"
as Sir Joseph Yorke would say.   It is for these reasons I
have explained myself, as I feel that you will, I am sure,
be good enough to give me at least your opinion, if you
cannot any positive assurance on the possible duration of
my mission.   I repeat, I never wish for any other, and
that it is merely *neu fluitem dubiæ, spe pendulus horæ,*
that I apply thus abruptly to your friendship.

EXTRACT OF A DESPATCH FROM SIR JAMES HARRIS TO
THE MARQUIS OF CARMARTHEN.

Hague, 28th January, 1785.

A STRONG fermentation prevails throughout all the
Provinces amongst the peasants, who seem unanimously
determined not to submit to the resolution of the States
General for arming and disciplining them for the defence
of the Republic.   There is scarce a village from Zutphen
to Dort where they are not assembled in great numbers
with orange cockades in their hats, and declaring their
fixed intention not to comply with this order; alleging,
and with great truth, that they pay very heavy taxes for
the maintenance of an army, and that they have a right
to expect that this army should defend them.   Their
dissatisfaction against the present Government has manifested itself in still stronger terms; and I met yesterday,
in a village within five miles of the Hague, at least a
hundred of them armed with clubs, ripe for a revolt and
ready to go any length to support the Stadtholder.

It is painful beyond expression to be forced to say, that not only the Stadtholder has not spirit enough to encourage such a disposition in the people, but that he is the first to declare that he wishes it to be suppressed. His torpitude is unaccountable. There is every reason to suppose that, in the course of the ensuing summer, the Pensionaries, after having divested him of every privilege belonging to the Stadtholderate, mean to create a new form of Government, by declaring that post no longer *hereditary* in his family; yet nothing can awaken him to a sense of feeling. He is neither animated by the spirit of the people and assurances of his friends, nor alarmed by the manifest designs of his enemies; and he beholds with the same callous insensibility the distress of the Republic, his own approaching disgrace, and the inevitable ruin which threatens his family.

I feel, my Lord, that my description may appear harsh ; but, if I forbore to speak plainly on the character of the Prince of Orange, I never could account for the many strange incidents which have happened, and which are certainly still to happen, in the Administration of this country.

EXTRACT OF A DESPATCH FROM SIR JAMES HARRIS TO
THE MARQUIS OF CARMARTHEN.

Hague, 1st February, 1785.

THE leading Patriots in this country are actuated by no motive of public virtue whatever. They are the very tools of France, and, provided they attain their end of subverting the Stadtholderate, are equally indifferent to the fate of the Republic and to that of the liberties of Europe. There are, however, amongst them more moderate ones, not so unprincipled, not so far gone. These begin to be alarmed, and to give way to suspicions, which, had they not been blinded by the prejudices of party, would long since have opened their eyes.

It is supposed that France is to have the Duchy of Luxembourg, Namur with a large territory round it, and the town of Maestricht; acquisitions which were the great objects of the ambition of Louis the Fourteenth, and which he, with all his power and in the midst of his glory, could never obtain. If this be the case, the Austrian Netherlands and the Seven United Provinces come under the immediate controul of France. She surrounds them both. Luxembourg gives her the key of Germany, and she attains the means of gratifying her ambition to any extent.

I can only add to this despatch, that, since this intelligence has reached the Hague, France and Prussia (who for so long a time have always held a similar language) are now in direct contradiction to each other. France proceeds almost as far as threats, to force the Dutch to comply with the Emperor's last proposal.* Prussia goes almost to promises of actual assistance, to induce them to reject them.

I still observe the same line of conduct which I laid down on my arrival. I, however, see with pleasure that the number of our friends increases, that there are many good men amongst them, and that they are disposed to treat me with confidence. I must not long remain in this state of indifference, *if ever anything is intended to be done;* the moment for action approaches very fast, and, if it is lost, may never be recovered. If only the interests of this Republic were at stake, and there was nothing more in agitation than the recovery of a weak and ungrateful ally, I certainly should not deem it a matter of sufficient importance to call the attention of Government from the more immediate concerns at home; but the honour, the welfare, nay, the very existence of England as a *great Power*, appears to be deeply concerned in the upshot of the present crisis.†

* The cession of the Outre Meuse, both banks of the Scheldt from Antwerp to Saftingen, the destruction of the Dutch forts, and ten millions of florins, as compensation for the cession of Maestricht.—*Harris Papers.*

† England was at this moment quite isolated.

[Convinced that the Stadtholderian and English interests could be recovered, Sir James Harris wrote the following urgent letter to Lord Carmarthen.]

LETTER FROM SIR JAMES HARRIS TO THE MARQUIS OF
CARMARTHEN.

Hague, 2nd February, 1785.

My DEAR LORD,—I never in my life felt so deeply interested in the concerns of Europe as at this present instant. I have, perhaps, expressed this sentiment too strongly in my official letters by this post; but I am so impressed with the idea that this is the last favourable moment England will have to resume its proper place amongst the European Powers, that my zeal and anxiety get the better of every other consideration. A strong, explicit, and friendly declaration, nearly to the effect I have taken the liberty to mention in my inclosure A, would lead us to that certainty we have long wanted, and force the Emperor either to return to his former connexions with us, or to pronounce that he gives them up for ever. Should this be the case (which I begin to suspect it will), we then (forgetting all past transactions) must turn towards *Prussia.* The moment Austria gives up all ideas of ever uniting with England, Prussia must renounce every hope of forming an alliance with France; and the Courts of London and Berlin, though they may be without reciprocal inclination, or reciprocal esteem, will have much more binding cement to unite them—reciprocal interest. England must necessarily adopt one of these two plans: if she trims, or regulates her conduct on half measures, she gives *tête baissée* into the designs of her enemies.

I know, my dear Lord, from frequent conversations with yourself and Mr. Pitt, how inconvenient, even to distress, it would be, to risk a war. I feel this inconvenience, and would submit to any temporary evil rather than expose the country to such a risk. But it is not

the evil of the day we are to attend to; it is to those
many great and inevitable ones with which the completion of the views of the Emperor are pregnant, and
which, if we allow them to go their time, will in the
end crush us entirely. I admit that repose and tranquillity are due to us—that they are both agreeable
and essential; but we are surely not so fatigued, or so
indolent, as to lie down to sleep when there is a probability of our throats being cut before we wake.

I have not a grain of opinion or regard left for Catherine — would she had her Petruchio again! Her
sending Markoff to Denmark to counteract our interests
there, has damned her for ever in my esteem: it is useless to talk reason, sense, or sound policy with her.
As for Joseph,* his ambition is *greater* than his wisdom;
his means, I trust, are *less*. As for this country, I will
be bound to shake its bogs to their foundations (if they
have any) the moment you lift up your finger. I am
in charity with the Prince of Orange since yesterday,
and begin to think some spirit may be injected into his
character by making use of a proper squirt.

Though unnecessary, I cannot but again urge the
expediency of an *immediate* and *determined conduct.*
We had better be maimed than killed; better lose a leg
or an arm now, than have our brains knocked out this
day se'nnight. As for myself, I would subscribe to any
loss. I would not, indeed, sacrifice my children, for
that would be a Heathen and Jewish offering; but I
would sacrifice that which I believe Abraham loved
better than he did Isaac — my fortune, rather than
see England lie dormant under the present circumstances.

Excuse me, my dear Lord, if I write thus warmly.
It is neither the effects of wine nor of love, for I have
just dined alone, and have not seen a white apron since
I have been in Holland. It is the picture of my true
and genuine feelings, which I never shall be ashamed or
afraid to communicate to so good and valuable a friend
as yourself.

* Emperor of Austria.

CONSIDERATIONS UPON THE STATE OF EUROPE in 1785, submitted to His Majesty's Government on the 2nd of February, by Sir James Harris.

THE SITUATION of Europe appears never to have been so critical at any epoch since the breaking out of the Thirty-years' war, as it is at the present moment.

The labours of the ablest politicians to distribute power and influence with an equal hand during the five years which preceded the conclusion of the Peace of Munster have long since lost their efficacy. The system established by that memorable Treaty has been constantly referred to, and as constantly deviated from, in all subsequent negotiations; and although it be still quoted with a kind of reverential awe, yet its principles are no longer to be traced in the operations of any of the Cabinets in Europe.

The revolution in the relative strength of many of the great Powers which took place immediately after that period, and the introducing into the political scale a power unknown till then, and one so singularly constituted as that of Russia, has rendered these principles so obsolete, that they are no longer applicable to the interests of the present times, nor in any degree equal to preserve the balance they were originally intended to poize. A new order of things has arisen, and a new system (long since become necessary) seems at length on the eve of working itself out.

It would be an idle waste of time to enumerate the different interests of the different Courts of Europe. It would be still more so to speculate on what may, or may not, be the future designs of each of them. We are, however, in possession of a sufficient number of *data* to be able to ascertain with a great degree of probability that the moment is not very distant when England will be called upon to take, once more, a share in the concerns of the Continent; and one may venture to pronounce, that the line of conduct she holds at this important conjuncture will decide whether she is again to become a leading power, and regain her former influence, or whether she is to remain exposed to all the dangers of an isolated system.

The Emperor, after having formed various claims upon the United Provinces, seems now to have discovered that his real intentions are bent on a much more solid and important aggrandizement of his dominions, by an exchange of the Austrian Netherlands, under certain restrictions, for the Electorate of Bavaria and the Upper Palatinate. In this plan he is evidently assisted by Russia, and as evidently opposed by Prussia.

It remains to be seen how France will act, and it is of the utmost importance for England to be prepared to take advantage of the state of suspense and dilemma to which she appears to be reduced. France must either wholly oppose, or wholly approve this step; or she must endeavour to steer a middle course, and consent to it on terms. If she opposes it, England will have an easy part to act. She has nothing to do but to hold a neutral language, to give the belligerent powers time to weary and exhaust themselves, while she takes leisure to recover her own vigour, and not appear at all till she can stand forth in a way to give that turn to the contest which may be the most consistent with her interest, and the best suit her dignity. To effect this, nothing more is required than patience and steadiness of behaviour, with a watchful eye to all that passes.

If France adopts either of the other two lines of conduct, the prospect for England will not be so fair. She must then necessarily take a more active part.

The Low Countries, from time immemorial, have been looked upon as a double barrier, on one side as that of the Empire, on the other as that of what are called the Maritime Powers. They were considered as such as well when they were in the possession of the Dukes of Burgundy, as when they made a part of the Spanish Monarchy. They were intended to be held

under this tenure by the young Prince of Bavaria, and
were given, for this purpose, to the House of Austria by
the Treaty of Utrecht.   The experience of more than
three centuries, and the united opinions of the wisest
Ministers, concur in proving the real importance of this
barrier. *Its existence has ever been deemed essential to
the interests of Europe in general, and to those of England in particular, but it is destroyed the moment the
Low Countries either belong to France directly, or are
governed by a Sovereign devoted to her influence :* and this
must be the case, whether France consents *ipso facto*
to the Emperor's proposal, or if she comes into it on
conditions of her own suggesting.*

To defeat the pernicious effects of the full concurrence
of France, must be a trial of force.   To counteract those
which may arise from her conditional acquiescence with
the Emperor's views, must be a trial of skill.   In the
first case, the whole support of Prussia, with that of
much the largest part of the Germanic body, may certainly be relied on; probably that of Denmark also, if
well managed; and even of this Republic, would the
Stadtholder suffer himself to be directed, — for, were
England and Prussia to unite in their operations here,
were proper advantage taken of the dispositions of the
people, were the conduct of France clearly stated to
them, and were the friends of the Prince assured of a
support, I have little doubt that either the Patriotic
body would soon dissolve of itself, or become an easy
victim to a short popular insurrection.

If we estimated the degree of force collected together
from such a confederacy, we should find it not much
inferior to that of the opposite party.   It would be, at
least, sufficient to make a powerful stand against so dangerous an innovation; and the consequences of the most
unsuccessful contest, even, could hardly be more unfa-

* This sentiment is underlined in the original MS., as if the writer attached particular importance to it.   The " experience of three centuries,
and the united opinion of the wisest Ministers," are now set aside, and the
son-in-law of the King of the French is made King of Belgium by the
consent of England.

vourable for Great Britain than those which would inevitably and immediately ensue to her from France having the command of that whole extent of coast which reaches from Ostend to the Texel, and from the Emperor's being driven so far into the Continent as no longer to have any point of reunion with the Maritime Powers.

If France consents to enter into a negotiation with the Emperor on this commutation of territory, and expresses a readiness to agree to it on certain advantages to accrue to her, it will then be the interest of England to set on foot a counter negotiation, and to endeavour to anticipate, by activity and address, the views of the Court of Versailles.

In that case, the plain and natural way seems to be by direct application to the Court of Vienna, stating in clear and explicit terms the nature of the tenure of the Low Countries; reminding the Emperor that by the Treaty of Utrecht they are unalienable, and, this Treaty still existing in its full force, England claims an indisputable right to be consulted, and expects to be attended to, on any projected alteration. That, however, as she is invariable in her wishes to give satisfaction to the Emperor, and to contribute, on every occasion not incompatible with her own safety, to the greatness of the House of Austria, she will not oppose this exchange of the Low Countries, provided it be stipulated that he forego his claims on the United Provinces; that Luxembourg and Namur shall never be ceded to France, or to any other Power whatever; but that he keep them himself, to enable him, in conjunction with the Elector of Bavaria, to form on one side a barrier for the safety of the Empire, on the other for that of England and Holland; and that a treaty to regulate the nature of this barrier, and to insure its duration, be immediately concluded between His Imperial Majesty, the Elector of Bavaria, England, and Holland.

If the Emperor subscribes to this proposal, the old system is preserved under another shape; and it is so manifestly advantageous to him, that, if he declines it, there cannot be the smallest doubt that his principles are inimical to a degree against England, and that, in conjunction with his two powerful allies, he meditates views of ambition, which, if not opposed in time, will overset the liberties of all Europe.

EXTRACT OF A DESPATCH FROM SIR JAMES HARRIS TO THE MARQUIS OF CARMARTHEN.

Hague, 4th February, 1785.

THE first battalion of Dutch, and the first battalion of Swiss Guards, are ordered to return from Breda, to which place they marched about six weeks ago. The disposition which prevails amongst the peasants throughout the whole Province of Holland is the motive of this order.

Several of the most enterprising of these are taken into custody here and confined. They are to be tried by a Special Commission, and it is supposed the Patriotic faction mean to punish them with *death*; a measure which (as I have before observed), from its violence, is more likely to irritate than appease a people of the temper of this nation.

EXTRACT OF A DESPATCH FROM SIR JAMES HARRIS TO THE MARQUIS OF CARMARTHEN.

Hague, 8th February, 1785.

TWO messengers arrived here from Paris on Saturday last; one to the States General, the other to the French Ambassador. They bring the accounts I mentioned in my last as expected. The Emperor has now formally declared that he is ready to give up the Scheldt on the conditions announced by Mons. de Vergennes. He even insinuates that the cession of Maestricht will be the only point on which he shall invariably insist. The answer was despatched from hence on Sunday. Their High

Mightinesses express their willingness to consent to the sending two Ministers Plenipotentiary, to be chosen from amongst the Deputies of the States, to Vienna, in order to carry on the negotiation under the eye of the Emperor himself, with instructions to explain the nature of the pretended insult offered to his flag.   They repeat what they before said relative to Maestricht, that they can neither absolutely promise, nor absolutely refuse, compliance with this demand; and that they are ready to discuss all the other points in the fullest and most satisfactory manner.

The courier received by the French Ambassador brought him instructions to press in the strongest terms an acceptation of the Emperor's offers.   The answer the States General have made will sufficiently prove to your Lordship the attention they are inclined to pay to this new recommendation on the part of France.

There is little doubt that, if a war does take place on the Continent, it will not arise from the disputes between this country and the Emperor; for, besides that both parties have in some measure receded from their original pretensions, I have very good reason to believe that the Patriotic faction here, from a conviction that their meditated projects on the interior Government of the country can only be brought to maturity in time of peace, have consented to pay to the Emperor a very considerable sum of money by way of indemnification, which, however, will not appear in the Act of Pacification, or make part of the instructions to be given to their two Plenipotentiaries.   It will be a *secret* and shameful submission, to which France alone is to be privy.

The King of Prussia continues urging the necessity the Republic is under of putting itself in a state of respectable defence.   He still advises them not to trust to the pacific disposition at Vienna, and even goes so far as to hint that the professions of France are fallacious.

It is evident now that the Patriots sacrifice every *public* consideration to their own *private* views.   The possibility of the Stadtholder's regaining his power and influence when at the head of an army, has brought them to subscribe to terms they themselves were the first to reprobate a few weeks ago. As they can place little or no reliance in the standing army of the Republic, which must be ever more or less inclined to the interests of the Stadtholder, they intend to make use of the different volunteer corps. It was with this view also, and under the supposition that they might be as easily led, that they put arms into the hands of the peasants; which, however, has produced an effect contrary to their expectations.

LETTER FROM SIR JAMES HARRIS TO THE MARQUIS OF CARMARTHEN.

Hague, 15th February, 1785.

My dear Lord,—My official letter to-day is dry and very uninteresting. This is in great measure owing to the real sterility of matter; but it would have been perhaps less so, if I was not vexed and out of humour.

We have had the ball at our foot, and yet shall lose the game. The torpedo swims round us, and flaps us all with his fins; never were mortals composed of such inanimate clay, so void of every spark of Promethean fire, as the Prince's friends. I have not time nor inclination, neither indeed is it necessary to tell you to-day what a golden opportunity has been lost—lost, I fear, never to be recovered; because nothing can succeed where confidence, courage, and cordiality are wanting. This is not an official letter; and I am writing to my *friend*, not to the *Secretary of State*.

After all, however, my dear Lord, do not suppose that I despond; I only rail to prevent a jaundice, and to be able to *turn and turn again* before I give up the cause. The Gordian knot may be untied as well as cut; and, if we have not an Alexander, we may find a Fabius. It is for this reason that I have signed the lease of my house for five years; that I am making up my mind to dulness and gravity; my eyes to black teeth and white lips; my nose to the stench of tobacco and unwashed toes; and my stomach to cheese, butter, and herrings. The experiment will cost me a few moral as well as physical indigestions; but in five or six months I hope to become as square and solid, mentally and corporeally, as the most massive burgomaster in the Republic.

EXTRACT OF A DESPATCH FROM SIR JAMES HARRIS TO THE
MARQUIS OF CARMARTHEN.

Hague, 18th February, 1785.

THE few people in the Republic that are not entirely absorbed by party views consider a revolution in the Government of the Low Countries as an event of the utmost importance, and many of the principal leaders in the ruling faction do not scruple to declare that they will renounce all connexion with France, if, in the result, she is to be put in possession of Luxembourg and Namur.

Unassisted and ill-supported as I am, it is not in my power to derive any very material benefit from this disposition. I can only occasionally descant on the general importance of *a barrier*, and endeavour, by repeating the same hackneyed argument, to keep their *alarms* awake on this subject. I dare not move forward, from the certainty that I should immediately be left alone; and, if I ever mean to effect anything, it must be after I have impressed strongly on the minds of people that I am not only an indifferent but an inattentive and indolent spectator of what is going forward.

In regard to what relates to the disputes between this country and the Emperor, they remain precisely in the same situation; neither can anything new be expected till a week or ten days hence, when the answer from Vienna may be returned.

The situation of the interior Government of this country becomes every day more and more turbulent, and it appears impossible to me that this summer should elapse without some violent convulsion.

EXTRACT OF A DESPATCH FROM SIR JAMES HARRIS TO THE MARQUIS OF CARMARTHEN.

Hague, 25th February, 1785.

THE Patriotic faction press harder on the Stadtholder than ever, and are proceeding to lengths which must soon put the spirit of the people to the test. A placard was published yesterday, prohibiting, under the severest penalty, any demonstration of joy or festivity on the 8th of March, the Prince of Orange's birth-day, particularly the wearing Orange cockades. This placard is drawn up in terms the most injurious to the Prince.

The first effects will naturally inspire fear, for the punishments held out extend to death itself; but it must, in the end, work up a spirit of vengeance in the most tame and passive minds, as it conveys a principle of wanton tyranny and oppression equal to a decree of the Inquisition itself, and which cannot but alarm a people who, though not easily moved, have at all times been very tenacious of their liberty, and very strenuous in their defence of it.

The plausible pretext of this edict is an apprehension, from what has lately happened in the villages, that, on the 8th of March, the people may be disposed to be riotous, and that it is necessary to keep them in order.

The people, in the course of yesterday, tore down the placard mentioned in the beginning of this letter, and express their greatest indignation at its contents. Another is now published, with an offer of 14,000 florins to whoever will discover those who have been guilty of this contempt of Government, and the Patriots seem determined to support oppression by violence.

EXTRACT OF A DESPATCH FROM SIR JAMES HARRIS TO THE
MARQUIS OF CARMARTHEN.

Hague, 11th March, 1785.

THE name and character of the Rhinegrave of Salm
is not unknown to your Lordship. By betraying the
Prince of Orange, and by paying court to the French
party, from a very unnoticed and insignificant officer he
of a sudden became charged with a very important commission, and was sent to Berlin under the specious pretext of raising a corps, but, in fact, with a view to sound
the real intentions of His Prussian Majesty relative to
the Republic. The sphere he moved in was entirely
new to him; and though, from his own reports, his success was complete, yet your Lordship will have heard
much truer accounts from Mr. Ewart.

His want of veracity, or want of prudence, has involved him since his return in a very serious dilemma.
He asserted some days ago, in a mixed company, that
the King of Prussia told him that Duke Lewis of Brunswick held a secret and treacherous correspondence with
the garrison of Maestricht, with an intention to deliver
up the town to the Emperor. An accusation of such a
nature made against a person in the situation of the
Duke could not pass unnoticed. It soon became a State
consideration, and the Prince of Orange was applied to
by Deputies from the province of Utrecht on the subject.

The Rhinegrave was sent for, and he asserted to the
Prince what he had before said at table; adding, "that
the King of Prussia had given it him in charge to make
it known here."

The fact being thus solemnly avowed by him, he was
the next day (Monday last) examined by the Secret
Committee, where, not without hesitation and embarrassment, he again repeated what he had said, with this
not immaterial difference, that the King of Prussia had
permitted him, not *charged* him, to tell it here. On
being asked why he first mentioned it in a mixed com-

pany, rather than to the Stadtholder, or to the Ministers of the Republic, he replied, "It was through *delicacy*."

I have no doubt myself that the whole is an egregious falsehood; that the Rhinegrave of Salm, without looking to the very serious consequences with which so heavy a charge, if not supported by evidence, must be attended to the accuser, made it to gratify the animosity of the Patriots against the Duke, and with a view ultimately to criminate the Prince of Orange.

[Sir James Harris was not to be diverted from his determination of rescuing Holland from the Patriots, either by the supineness of the Prince of Orange, or the natural caution of Mr. Pitt in the matter. He was also ambitious of gaining the whole credit of the affair, if his views succeeded. The following letter is the first of a series of correspondence which he carried on with Mr. Ewart, who was only our Secretary of Legation at Berlin under Lord Dalrymple, but who practically transacted most of the business at that Court. I have not room to publish the whole, but its object was to prepare the minds of the Prince of Prussia and his friends for an intervention in favour of the Stadtholder in the event of Frederick's death. Mr. Ewart entered most warmly and ably into the cause, and gained over Hertzberg, &c.]

EXTRACT OF A DESPATCH FROM SIR JAMES HARRIS TO MR. EWART, BERLIN.

Hague, Tuesday, 15th March, 1785.

I HAVE such convincing proofs of your abilities and zeal, and so just a reliance on your prudence and secrecy, that I have no scruple of opening myself to you confidentially on the present state of affairs. I must premise that *I speak from myself alone.* Our *Principals* at home are too much occupied with the House of Commons to attend to what passes on the Continent; and, if any good is ever done there, it must be effected through the King's Ministers *abroad*, and not by those about his person. Long experience has taught me this; and I never yet received an instruction that was worth reading. This preface is necessary, in order to regulate your mode of conduct, if you should think proper to take any steps in consequence of what I am going to write.

The manner in which France recommends to this Republic to accede to the Emperor's demands, and his preferring that the negotiation should go on at Paris rather than at Vienna, leaves little doubt but that these two Courts perfectly understand each other, and that their alliance is far from being near its conclusion.

The Empress is more or less drawn into this connexion, and the Emperor has been either artful or lucky enough to carry his favourite point, that of keeping his two allies at the same time, and the making them both subservient to his purposes. Holland is already sacrificed to his ambition; and we may, without the gift of prophecy, look forward to much more violent attacks upon the liberties of Europe, if these three great Powers move in concert. The Bavarian exchange stands next in order; but it is certainly not the last, or the least important. If I am not mistaken in my conjectures, (which, after all, can only be founded on presumptive proofs,) another inference is to be drawn: that Prussia is, and has been, egregiously duped by France, and is placed in so isolated a position, that the duration of its power, notwithstanding its intrinsic force and the great abilities of the King, will become precarious, if it is to resist alone so formidable a league. England stands in the same predicament. The effect of this compact will, perhaps, reach us later, but as surely and as fatally as Prussia. Single, we must sink; united, we may resist; probably with success, certainly with vigour.

I know enough of the personal and private feelings of the two Courts to be aware that they will stand in the way of this measure. I have partaken of these feelings myself at times as strongly as any one; but it would be weak (even to criminality) to suffer them to prevail against reason and conviction. I am satisfied the King of Prussia acts up to this doctrine; and that if he once saw that every chance of breaking up the Alliance of 1756 was at an end, that France has been making a fool of him for these ten years, and more especially a few months back, through his brother Henry, he would readily turn his thoughts towards us; and we should be more flimsy and insufficient than, I hope, any Administration can be in England, if we shrunk from any overtures he made us. And this leads me to the motive for troubling you with this letter; which, if I was not persuaded you are as zealous and as warm in the service as myself, you never would have received.

Is it not possible for you, either through Hertzberg himself, through Count Goertz, or through, perhaps, some still better channel in your possession, to sound the dispositions of the King? to state to him the palpable treachery of France? that he has been all along lulled into security by the fallacious language of that Court, who are at the same time aggrandizing his rival, and sacrificing his niece and her family here; that their union with the Emperor is stronger than ever; and that, whatever assurances they may give His Prussian Majesty, they will certainly support the Emperor, both in the exchange of Bavaria and in the election of the King of the Romans, and in all his other attacks on the rights of the Germanic body.

If this idea could be once impressed on the King of Prussia's mind, (and I conscientiously believe it to be a true one,) it is impossible he should not promote a connexion with us; and, I repeat, our Ministers must be mad or blind, if, circumstanced as Europe is at this moment, they did not eagerly listen to any proposals coming from your quarter.

To encourage His Prussian Majesty, it might be suggested to him that Denmark might perhaps be got immediately.

It may also be added, (and I can assert it more positively, as it comes immediately under my department,) that, if England and Prussia were to unite in their operations here, both the Republic and the House of Orange might be still saved. All these considerations, not futile ones, nor founded in imagination, apply, in the event, to the welfare of his crown and permanency of his power. If he admits the first point laid down, all the rest follows.

I submit it entirely to your discretion to make any use of this letter you please; only, recollect it is a *private* one, therefore do not commit me *Ministerially*. As an individual, I have no objection to being quoted to a certain degree, which I leave to your prudence to regulate. I must add, that Mr. Thulemeyer and myself are on nothing more than a footing of civility. He is shy in speaking to me on business, and has shrunk from several openings I gave him on this score. He is an unesteemed man of no character, and I confess to you that I could never trust him if we had any serious matters to transact together. I strongly suspect also that he is devoted to France by closer ties than those of principle.

I shall now put an end to this unmerciful quantity of figures, only entreating you to recollect that all this is a transaction between ourselves; an attempt of two zealous citizens to labour in their vocations, it does *not yet* concern our official capacity as men in office.

EXTRACT OF A DESPATCH FROM SIR JAMES HARRIS TO THE MARQUIS OF CARMARTHEN.

Hague, 18th March, 1785.

I HAVE every reason to be satisfied with my reception at Amsterdam; the appearance of an English Minister in that city was a kind of phenomenon, and I could easily perceive that it gave pleasure, also, my wearing

the appearance of being pleased with their civilities
and attentions, and my living with men of every description without distinction.

As my sole view in this first visit was to accustom
the inhabitants to see me amongst them, I avoided as
much as possible all conversation on the times, or an
affectation of forming any particular connexion. I lived
rather more with the Patriots than the Stadtholderians,
and in my expressions confined myself solely to the
general assurances that England could not be indifferent
to the political existence of Holland, nor see without
concern any incident which might tend to decrease her
weight in the balance of Europe.

In other respects I endeavoured to appear rather
addicted to dissipation than business, and to enter into
all their amusements with a much greater share of glee
than I really felt.

I found much more moderation and good sense than I
expected to meet with, and, by proper management, I
am far from despairing that the first ray of light may
break out in this city; but much patience, temper,
and urbanity are necessary.

[Sir James Harris went to England on leave of absence in March, and returned to the Hague at the end
of July. He pressed upon Mr. Pitt and Lord Carmarthen the importance of our rescuing Holland from
French influence, and its feasibility by the Stadtholder
and people themselves, if England would lend her moral influence: but Mr. Pitt was afraid of a war; the
King was equally adverse to the risk; and Lord Carmarthen and the Duke of Richmond were the only Cabinet Ministers who at this time viewed the matter in
the same light as Sir James.]

EXTRACT OF A DESPATCH FROM MR. EWART TO SIR JAMES
HARRIS.

Berlin, 4th April, 1785.

FROM the actual dispositions of the King of Prussia,
and from the nature of the late transactions between
this Court and the Regency of Hanover, I thought it
right to enter indirectly upon the subject of your confidential letter, in my official correspondence; and I
flatter myself that the general view contained in my
late despatch will have met with your approbation. I
shall now resume the consideration of the different
points more at length, and endeavour to reduce the
substance of two private conversations with Mr. Hertzberg within the bounds of a ciphered letter.

The most essential particulars may be deduced from
the three leading principles which I attempted to establish in my letter to Mr. Fraser.

First, That the King of Prussia seems now to be well
convinced of the permanent existence and vigour of the
Alliance of 1756.

Secondly, That his great object is to regain Russia;
and that he looks forward to the Empress's death, or
to a change of system, more eagerly than ever.

Thirdly, That the new Germanic League constitutes
a principle of re-union between England and Prussia,
which may serve as a basis to a closer connexion.

With regard to the first point, a variety of circumstances have tended of late to increase the suspicions and
distrust which the King has long entertained of the
French Cabinet; and the more favourable impression
made on his mind by the assurances of Prince Henry
has been entirely obliterated by their conduct in the
Bavarian affair, and their treachery towards the Dutch.
His Majesty has no longer any doubt of the Emperor's
having obtained the irrevocable approbation of France to
the projected exchange, and is not ignorant of their conjoint views on Germany. They have been even so impo-

litic as to avow that they consider the scheme as favourable to the interests of France. Further, the King has assurance that the favourite object of France is to extend her dominions to the Rhine, and that the Emperor consents to this important acquisition of territory and influence. These considerations, added to many others, have given rise to the formation of the long ago projected Germanic Confederacy, and would certainly induce His Majesty to take other precautions immediately, could he be made to entertain any hopes of soon regaining Russia.

This leads to the second principle, upon which Mr. Hertzberg* lays very great stress, insisting particularly on the danger to which this country would be exposed in having Russia for an enemy in the present circumstances. Mr. Hertzberg informed me that his Court has most positive assurances that the wished for change will take place at the Empress's death, and considers the establishment of the great Northern Alliance as a necessary consequence. That, in the mean time, the greatest caution and circumspection are necessary on the part of this Court, on account of the King's age and infirmity, which would render a war a very great misfortune for this country during His Majesty's lifetime ; but that, in event of the King's death, he should no longer be under any apprehension, but would recommend openly and engage that immediate overtures should be made to the Court of Great Britain.

This led to the consideration of the political sentiments of the Prince of Prussia, and of his desire to adopt that system. This Court has been negotiating for some time with the Regency of Hanover, and has had several communications with the King our Master, on the subject of the Germanic League. The Duke of York has transmitted to Potzdam the copy of a letter from His Majesty, expressing strongly his approbation of the scheme, and His Majesty's wishes, as Elector of Hanover, in the defence of the liberties of the Empire.

---

* Prussian Minister for Foreign Affairs.

As His Royal Highness the Duke of York takes a
very active part in the negotiations carrying on between
Berlin and Hanover, and is very much attached to this
Court, I submit it to your consideration, if it might not
be advisable to make him better acquainted with the
situation of affairs, and to explain to him the propriety
there would be to have England enter into the confederacy as a leading party with Prussia.

After what I have said, I need scarcely repeat, that
everything conspires at present to favour the accomplishment of your judicious and necessary political system.   Mr. Hertzberg has undertaken to communicate
privately to the King the ideas suggested by your letter;
but he is obliged to proceed with the greatest caution, as
Prince Henry of Prussia is his inveterate enemy, and has
great influence in the Cabinet through Count Finckenstein, who is likewise much attached to the French party.

EXTRACT OF A LETTER FROM SIR JAMES HARRIS TO
MR. EWART, BERLIN.

St. James's, 19th April, 1785.

LORD CARMARTHEN, to whom I have communicated
every part of our private correspondence, cannot sufficiently applaud your zeal and ability.

His Prussian Majesty mistakes in supposing England
averse to Continental measures.   We wish to make part
of some solid, I say, of some wise and solid Continental
system, and do not intend that any should be concluded
without us.

If the King of Prussia has entirely foregone his views
on France, and if he is actually convinced, and firm in
his opinion, that the Treaty of 1756 is indissoluble, our
business will do itself ; if he is disposed to act explicitly
and with good faith, if he has got rid of his idle prejudices concerning the Government of this country, he
may rest assured that we shall readily meet him half-way.
But *this* must be clearly and specifically ascertained

before we can venture to commit ourselves *officially*;
and I need not, I am sure, point out to you how essential it is that this should be the primary object of your
investigation.   I, in my private and individual capacity,
am persuaded that France and Austria are acting in
perfect concert; and, if the reports received at Potzdam
are similar to those which come here well authenticated,
His Prussian Majesty must entertain the same idea.
This is real ground for negotiating an eventual connexion between England and Prussia ; and, this principle admitted, all the secondary considerations will be
very easily arranged.

Mons. de Hertzberg does me too much honour in
asking my opinion on Russia and Holland.   I can have
no objection in speaking freely to him, after the confidential and friendly manner in which he opens himself
towards you.

The Empress's interest must be opposed by the same
means, or, by what is more feasible, by making her
perceive the Emperor is amusing her with false hopes;
that France is his great and only object, and that she
is drawn into the connexion in order to be the instrument and tool of their ambition.   If this could be clearly
stated to her ; and if, at the same time, it was made to
appear that the Emperor, instead of the great man she
thought him, is an irresolute, timid, and shallow character ; anger and shame would go a great way towards
inducing her to break off her connexion with him.   As
for money, it certainly would go far at Petersburg, but
without intrigue and negotiation it will effect nothing ;
as even Prince Potemkin himself cannot, on certain
points, get the better of his Imperial Mistress's firmness
and obstinacy.

As to Holland, the King of Prussia must have so many
better channels of intelligence than myself, that my ideas
on that country can be little worth.   If, however, the
Courts of London and Berlin were to act together there,
and to unite their force, we should undoubtedly make a
powerful resistance against the French party, if we could

not entirely overset it. We must first make the Patriotic party see that the French are deceiving them; and then, that they are deceiving themselves in supposing that the powers and privileges they are wresting from the Stadtholder through the means of the Free Corps will, on the formation of a new Government, devolve on them. It will evidently go to the people at large, and a democracy, not an aristocracy, will ensue. This ought to be the general language; and it contains two such palpable truths, that they cannot fail striking all dispassionate minds. Besides this, some particular language should be held to particular people, to Gyslaer, to Du Moulin, and to Peter Paulus. The first is ambitious, enterprising, and young, and, I have reason to believe, dissatisfied with his party. The other has always professed himself a friend of the Prince's; and, though now a seeming Patriot, would certainly be reclaimed the moment it was his interest to be so. As to the third, he is a new man of weight and consequence, from his extreme popularity and activity, and would undoubtedly join that party where he saw the greatest probability of gaining celebrity and fortune. Such are my ideas on the state of Holland. I have only to add, that I do not think we should move too fast, or, by precipitating matters, occasion an alarm which would defeat our purposes. The French, if once they begin to get unpopular in Holland, will very rapidly, if left to themselves, get detested. Security always makes *them* insolent.

_____

[The following statement is inserted here as in the order of dates, although it has no reference to Sir James's present mission.]

ACCOUNT OF MY FIRST CONFERENCE WITH THE PRINCE OF WALES AT CARLTON HOUSE.

Wednesday, April 27th, 1785.

HE began by saying, that, as he was convinced of my sincere regard for him, he wished to make me acquainted with his situation—to communicate it to me fully, and to consult me upon it.   He said he must, in order to be clear, refer back to that period when his Establishment was settled.   This, he added, was first of all thought of in Lord Rockingham's Administration; then in Lord Shelburne's; but not finally determined on till that of the Duke of Portland.   The original ideas of the then Ministry were, to give him 50,000*l.* to pay his debts, 50,000*l.* to fit him out, and 100,000*l.* a-year exclusive of the Duchy of Cornwall.   The King, after having apparently approved of this arrangement, refused ultimately to agree to it.   The Ministers were on the point of going out;* but the Prince of Wales being told that Lord John Cavendish was against it, and that the King had referred to Lords North and Stormont (as his old friends) to decide on the propriety of his conduct, he (the Prince of Wales†) insisted that they should stay in, and that he would not be the cause of a revolution in Ministry, or have it said he ran counter to the King's pleasure in his first outset.   In consequence of this, he received 30,000*l.* to pay his debts, and 30,000*l.* to equip him, with 50,000*l.* a-year out of the Civil List.   He found his house unfurnished; that, and many other expenses,—some necessary to his rank,—some, as he confessed, incurred by the natural imprudences of a young man,—soon involved him in debts to a very considerable amount.

In the autumn of 1784‡ he wrote to the King, stating his embarrassed situation, and signifying his wish to travel in order to retrench.   The idea of his travelling was reprobated, and, after several letters had passed, the King desired the Prince of Wales to send in an *exact* statement of his debts, giving him to understand he would liquidate them.   This the Prince did *en gros.* It was kept four months, and then returned on the

* Lord Carlisle, Mr. Fox, and Lord Keppel.—Original Note.
† This affair was negotiated between the Prince and Charles Fox by Colonel Leake.—Original Note.
‡ He at the time mentioned this to me.—Original Note.

King's saying it was not exact—the articles were not specified. The Prince sent it back again, with every article minuted by his Treasurer, except one of 25,000*l*., which was lumped, and which he could not account for. (He told me it was borrowed money, and that he was obliged, in honour, not to tell from whom he got it.) The King objected to this reserve—insisted on its being explained. The Prince persisted in his refusal, alleging the motive of secrecy to be one of honour. The King replied, that if it was a debt he was ashamed to explain, it was one he ought not to pay. Here the matter ended. The Prince's debts increased, and with them his embarrassment and distress. He now owes 160,000*l*. He ended this discourse by telling me that, circumstanced as he was, he saw no means of relief left but by going abroad—that he only wanted to ask me whether he should distress me or not if he was to come to the Hague in a private character, and whether I could present him as such. He added, he would rather not come at all (though it was his resolution to travel) than distress me, or oblige me to act improperly. Our subsequent conversation was nearly as follows:

H.—I should be very sorry, Sir, to see you in Holland otherwise than in a character which would allow me to receive you in a manner conformable to the sentiments of respect and affection I bear your Royal Highness; but your coming abroad without having obtained the King's consent implies that you will come after it has been refused you, and, you may rest assured, in that case I shall receive orders how to act towards you before your arrival; and those orders, let them be ever so much in contradiction to my feelings, I must obey.

P.—Certainly. I should be the last person to wish you to do otherwise. But what am I to do? Am I to be refused the right of every individual? Cannot I travel legally, as a private man, without the King's consent?

H.—I think it very immaterial for Your Royal Highness to know whether you can, or cannot, legally travel without His Majesty's consent; since it is evident that you cannot with any propriety to the public, or satisfaction to yourself, cross the seas without it.

P.—Why not? I wish to travel on a plan of economy; to be unknown; to live in retirement.

H.—Without entering into the almost impossibility of Your Royal Highness making so rapid a transition in your ways of life, I confess I see no event would give me so much pain as an Englishman, as to see a Prince of Wales abroad under such a description. He ought never to appear but with all the splendour attached to his rank. Never to lose sight that he always will be a character who comes under the observation of all Europe. That any deviation from his rank, any acting beneath his situation, would remain fixed upon him through life; and that the idea of his travelling on the grounds he proposed would ruin him both here and on the Continent.

P.—I feel what you say: but what can I do? The King proposed to me to lay by 10,000*l.* a-year to pay my debts, at a time when, with the strictest economy, my expenses are twice my income. I am ruined if I stay in England. I disgrace myself as a man.

H.—Your Royal Highness, give me leave to say, will find no relief in travelling the way you propose. You will be either slighted, or, what is worse, become the object of political intrigue at every Court you pass through. You will perpetually hear things which will hurt your feelings, and to which, from the situation you will have put yourself in, you cannot reply. In a political light, you will injure equally both the King and the nation, and in a still stronger degree yourself.

P.—But if I avoid all great Courts? If I keep to the smaller ones of Germany, can this happen? I may there live unnoticed and unknown.

H.—Impossible, Sir. The title of the Earl of Chester will be only a mask which covers the Prince of Wales, and, as such, your actions will ever be judged. A

Grand Duke of Russia or a King of Sweden may emerge from their frozen dens, and, after having shown themselves to half Europe, return, to be thought no more of; and even these shower gold around them, and, so far from saving, exceed their usual expenses: and shall a Prince of Wales travel with less dignity, less liberality than them? A Prince of Wales, born to the highest rank in Europe, who never can be withdrawn from the eyes of all men, who is in a situation to be seen, to be estimated, to be criticised by all!

P.—You think I mean to go to France. I shall keep to the Empire, and perhaps to Italy.

H.—What I say applies to all countries, Sir. As for France, I hope never to see a Prince of Wales there on any other purpose than that which carried the Black Prince; or ever to hear of his being at Calais, but to fix the British standard on its walls.*

P.—But what can I do, my dear Harris? The King hates me. He wants to set me at variance with my brother. I have no hopes from him. He won't let even Parliament assist me till I marry.

H.—But there exists so cordial an affection between Your Royal Highness and the Duke of York, that I should think he might be employed most usefully to reconcile the King to Your Royal Highness. It cannot be a difficult task when undertaken by a brother.

P.—If he thought it possible, he would come over immediately. He has often expressed his concern at our disunion, and declares he never will leave the Continent till he can see a prospect of bringing the King to enter into my situation.

H.—Surely, Sir, the King could not object to any increase of income Parliament thought proper to allow Your Royal Highness?

---

* Sir J. Harris's Anti-French sentiments so strongly expressed here and elsewhere, did not exceed those of his contemporaries. During the first seventy years of his life, viz. from 1746 to 1815, England was constantly in a situation either of open hostility or diplomatic enmity with France, and he was himself employed for thirty years in opposing and thwarting her policy.

P.—I believe he would. He hates me; he always did, from seven years old.

H.—His Majesty may be displeased and dissatisfied with Your Royal Highness, but surely he cannot hate you; and I am convinced nothing would make both him and the Queen so happy as to restore their affections to you. It would be the greatest blessing to the nation, and the greatest comfort to the Royal Family.

P.—It may be so, but it cannot be. We are too wide asunder ever to meet. The King has deceived me, he has made me deceive others; I cannot trust him, and he will never believe me.

H.—I am sorry Your Royal Highness thinks so. The confidence and kindness with which you hear me perhaps make me speak more freely than I ought, but I think Your Royal Highness should try every possible means before you carry into execution your plan of travelling. I am certain it would in no one respect alleviate your situation; on the contrary, that it would add to Your Royal Highness's unpleasant feelings.

P.—I will think it over, but I see no option. We will meet again soon. I have great reliance on your opinion, and am disposed to attend to you, because I am convinced you have no interested motives in advising me.

NOTE FROM HIS MAJESTY GEORGE III. TO THE MARQUIS OF CARMARTHEN.

Queen's House, 10th May, 1785.

THE Despatches arrived by the Dutch mail of yesterday are so material, and, if Britain is to take any part at present, so pressing, that I approve of Lord Carmarthen's, if possible, assembling the Cabinet this morning. On reflecting on what Lord Carmarthen mentioned on Friday, of the Lord Chancellor's suggestion that some concert of Petersburg and the Hague with Prussia might be effected if some person could speak openly to the King of Prussia, I can devise but one means, the sending Sir James Harris for a few days to Potzdam, to state the situation of things personally to the King of Prussia. His having been Minister at his Court, and his now being the one in Holland, makes him the natural person for so delicate a commission, which his own talents render also highly eligible.*

SECOND CONFERENCE WITH THE PRINCE OF WALES.

Monday, 23rd May, 1785.

ON Saturday, May the 21st, the Prince took an opportunity of saying many obliging things to me at an assembly at Mrs. Sturt's, in St. James's Square. I was induced, in consequence of this civility, to ask permission to reclaim his promise of allowing me to wait upon him again at Carlton House. He appointed the Monday following, at two P.M. My motive for requesting this interview was, that I had received vague assurances from Lord Carmarthen (Secretary of State for the Foreign Department, and who spoke after Mr. Pitt, First Lord of the Treasury) that Ministry would not be adverse to increase His Royal Highness's income, providing he would consent to appropriate a share of it to liquidate his debts, renounce going abroad, and be reconciled to the King.

Before I opened this subject to him, I consulted both the Duke of Portland and Mr. Fox; and both of them expressed their approbation of the measure, and their wishes for me to mention it to the Prince.

After waiting some time after the hour appointed on Monday, he sent for me up into his dressing-room. Our conversation was nearly what follows:

P.—If you are come, my dear Harris, to dissuade me again from travelling, let me anticipate your kind intentions, by telling you I have dismissed that idea from

---

* Lord Cornwallis was sent to Berlin for the object mentioned by the King in this letter.

my mind. I see all my other friends, as well as yourself, are against it, and I subscribe to their opinion.

H.—I should not have presumed to have mentioned
that subject again to Your Royal Highness, from an
apprehension that I should have nothing agreeable to
say relative to it; but after what you have told me, Sir,
allow me to express my infinite satisfaction on hearing
you have given up a plan, in the execution of which I
am confident Your Royal Highness would have met disappointment and mortification.

P.—I am glad to have pleased you, at least, if I have
not pleased myself. Yet I am sure you will be concerned
to see the distressed and unbecoming light in which I
must appear by remaining in England.

H.—This had better appear here (admitting it to be
the case) than to strangers. But, Sir, the purport of
my troubling Your Royal Highness was to obviate this
unpleasant circumstance.

P.—How so?

H.—I have thought, Sir, with great anxiety on all you
said to me when I was last admitted to your presence,
and, if you will allow me, I will lay before you the result
of my reflections.

P.—Most willingly.

H.—If Your Royal Highness will give me leave, I will
propose to Mr. Pitt to increase your revenue to 100,000*l.*
a-year, on two conditions. The one, that you will set
aside 50,000*l.* of it to pay your debts; the other, that
you will cease to be a man of party, and reconcile yourself to the King. I should have named a third, Sir; but
Your Royal Highness, by declaring to me that you had
given up all idea of leaving the kingdom, had subscribed
to it before it could be proposed.

P.—Your good-will towards me deceives you. The
attempt would be useless. Pitt would not carry such a
proposal to Parliament: the King would not hear of it.

H.—This, Sir, is exactly what I mean to try. *You*
certainly shall not be committed; and the refusal shall
be given to me alone, who am ready to appear as a vo-

lunteer in your service, which I consider, circumstanced as you are, to be a national one.

P.—I thank you; but it will not do. I tell you the King hates me. He would turn out Pitt for entertaining such an idea; besides, I cannot abandon Charles* and my friends.

H.—Mr. Fox and the Duke of Portland have told me often, Sir, that they by no means wish Your Royal Highness to condescend, on their account, to take any share in party concerns. They have repeatedly declared that a Prince of Wales ought to be of no party. I will be responsible that all the sensible and respectable men of that party think the same. You are to be governed, Sir, in your high station, by considerations very different from those which are to regulate the conduct of a simple individual, let his rank be ever so great.

P.—Well, but admitting this, and supposing that I can get rid of a partiality in politics you seem to condemn, I tell you, Harris, the King never will listen to it. Pitt dares not mention it to him; or, if he did, is he strong enough in the House of Lords to carry it through?

H.—But, Sir, I pre-suppose a reconciliation between you and His Majesty. Surely this would be grateful to the King himself, and most particularly so to the Queen.

P.—Why, my dear Harris, will you force me to repeat to you that the *King hates me?* He will never be reconciled to me.

H.—It cannot be, Sir. If you order me, I will ask an audience of him, and fling myself at his feet.

P.—I love you too well to encourage you to undertake so useless a commission. If you will not credit me, you will, perhaps, credit the King himself. Take and read all our correspondence for these last six months.

The Prince here opened an escritoire, and took out a large bundle of papers, which he read to me. It consisted of various letters which had passed between him and the King, beginning with that in which he asked

* Charles Fox.

his leave to go abroad in autumn, 1784, as mentioned in my first conversation.

It is needless to attempt to relate precisely the contents of this correspondence; it is sufficient to observe that the Prince's letters were full of respect and deference, written with great plainness of style and simplicity. Those of the King were also well written, but harsh and severe; constantly refusing every request the Prince made, and reprobating in each of them his extravagance and dissipated manner of living. They were void of every expression of parental kindness or affection; and, after both hearing them read, and perusing them myself, I was compelled to subscribe to the Prince's opinion, and to confess there was very little appearance of making any impression on His Majesty in favour of His Royal Highness. I resumed, however, the conversation as follows:

H.—I am hurt to a degree, Sir, at what I have read. But still, Sir, the Queen must have a reconciliation so much at heart, that through her and your sisters it surely might be effected.

P.—Look ye, Harris; I cannot bring myself to say I am in the wrong when I am in the right. The King has used me ill; and I wish the public knew what you now know, and was to pronounce between us.

H.—I should be very sorry, indeed, Sir, if this was known beyond these walls; for I am much mistaken if the public would not pronounce a judgment widely different from that you think. It is not sufficient, Sir, for the King to be wrong in *one* point, Sir, unless you are in the right in *all;* and, as long as any part of your conduct is open to censure, the voice of the public (considering your relative situations) will always go with the King.

P.—That is a cruel truth, if it be true what you say; but it is of no use to investigate it; my case never will go to that tribunal. You are, however, convinced of the impracticability of your scheme; as much, I hope, as I am of your kind regard in proposing it to me.

H.—I would not willingly renounce an idea, which, by its accomplishment, is to relieve Your Royal Highness from a state of distress, and, I may say, discredit, and place you in one of affluence and comfort. May I suggest, Sir, the idea of your marrying? It would, I should think, be most agreeable to the King, and, I am certain, most grateful to the nation.

P. (*with vehemence*).—I never will marry! My resolution is taken on that subject. I have settled it with Frederick. No, I never will marry!

H.—Give me leave to say, Sir, most respectfully, that you cannot have really come to such a resolution; and you *must* marry, Sir: you owe it to the country, to the King, to yourself.

P.—I owe nothing to the King. Frederick will marry, and the Crown will descend to his children; and as for myself, I do not see how it affects me.

H.—Till you are married, Sir, and have children, you have no solid hold on the affections of the people, even while you are Prince of Wales; but if you come to the throne a bachelor, and His Royal Highness the Duke of York is married and has sons to succeed you, your situation, when King, will be more painful than it is at this moment. Our own history furnishes strong examples of the truth of what I say.

The Prince was greatly struck with this observation. He walked about the room, apparently angry. I moved towards the door, saying, " I perceive, Sir, I have said too much: you will allow me to withdraw. I am sure I shall be forgiven an hour hence."

P.—You are forgiven now, my dear Harris. I am angry with myself, not with you. Don't question me any more. I will think of what you said. Adieu! God bless you!

I left England in June, and saw the Prince no more in private. In December following a report took place, of the Prince having formed a serious connexion (it was called marriage) with Mrs. Fitzherbert; and in March,

1786, he declared his resolution of setting aside 30,000*l.*
a-year to pay his debts, and reduced his establishment,
sold his horses, &c.

It is clear to me both these ideas were in his mind
when he spoke with me, and that the great obstacle in
the way of his accepting my proposal was Mrs. Fitzherbert.

The Duke of Portland and Mr. Fox were as much
surprised at his rejecting my proposal as I could be, and
at the time could not account for it.

The connexion with Mrs. Fitzherbert has taken place
since I have seen them.

During my stay in England in May, 1785, an attempt
was made by the Cabinet through me and Mr. Ewart to
sound the ground at Berlin. The event proved the
King of Prussia to be averse to any connexion with
England.*

EXTRACT OF A LETTER FROM SIR JAMES HARRIS TO MR.
EWART, BERLIN.

Hague, Tuesday, 7th August, 1785.

The best effect that the League just now concluded at
Berlin can, in my opinion, produce, will be the determining necessarily, in some shape or other, the King of
Prussia's political sentiments relative to England. I
have a full confidence in Mons. Hertzberg, and I believe
him perfectly sincere in his professions ; but I will confess to you freely, that I have not the same faith in those
of his Royal Master. I clearly perceive a backwardness
in him to extend the effects of his connexions with England beyond the limits of the Empire, and that he still
wishes to have it in his power to say to France, " that
he has entered into no engagements contrary to her in-

* I have not thought it necessary to publish this correspondence.

terests, or which stand in the way of his joining in
alliance with her whenever she wishes to promote it."
While he is thus cautious of committing himself, he has
by no means the same scruples of committing us; and
though he discriminates very specifically, when speaking
of his own conduct between the Hanoverian Regency and
English Ministers, yet he very artfully wishes the English Minister at Petersburg to communicate the confection of the League to the Empress, where he well knows
it is even more reprobated than at Vienna itself.   This,
joined to the manner in which he declined in May
coming into a general system with Great Britain, and his
still invariably advising the Princess of Orange to keep
on terms with France at least, afford me room for entertaining doubts of his not having entirely renounced his
hopes of gratifying himself in his plan of forming a connexion with the Court of Versailles.

I must do the Princess the justice to say, she was
very open and candid: she did not conceal from me the
repeated admonitions which had come from Potzdam,
recommending her to endeavour to conciliate the interests of France here with those of the Stadtholder;
and that it was His Prussian Majesty's opinion, in the
present situation of Holland, that it was through France
alone the Prince of Orange could preserve even a remnant of his authority.

Her Royal Highness, though she avowed her deference
to her uncle's advice, and that she had followed it, yet
was ready to agree with me that no real or permanent
good could result from it; that the interests of France
ever must clash with those of the Prince, and that the
Houses of Bourbon and Orange ever must remain implacable enemies.

From this it was easy to lead her to confess that
England could alone secure her family, and of course
no difficult task to induce her (which was the butt-end
of my conversation) to use her endeavours to persuade
her uncle to alter his measures here; and I have reason
to believe she writes by this post nearly to this effect.

She promised to communicate to me the answer from Potzdam.

As to the situation of this country, it is not materially altered since my absence; for though the people's eyes begin to open, and there reigns a general discontent against the French Legion, yet the faction is still preponderant, and cannot be overset unless the Orange party has a powerful support from without.

England and Prussia acting in concert, and with sincerity and wisdom, would, I have reason to believe, very soon set everything to rights.

EXTRACT OF A LETTER FROM SIR JAMES HARRIS TO THE MARQUIS OF CARMARTHEN.

Hague, 9th August, 1785.

I AM dissatisfied with Woronzow. Why, if so well inclined as he professes himself, such a manifest predilection for Austria? Why cannot a good Russian be English as well as Austrian? I wish the whole of his conduct be not part of a very dangerous plan,—*a League, indeed*, between the two Imperial Courts and France.

Russia is the first dupe in this plan; Austria, the second; and France has the lion's share. At all events, we cannot move with too much precaution.

If the Empress has been idle enough to be tart and crusty with us, and not to take our confidential communication as she ought, we should put down this humour to her sex, and not condescend to reply to it in the same tone. I think the longer we remain at the window the better. The passengers know we *can* walk down stairs if we like it, and that we observe what they are about as they go along, and rather expect they should not forget we are looking at them.

I have expressed very faithfully my sentiments on the state of this country, as well as the means of acting. I consider the country as gone, as I do not see anywhere

that kind of spirit necessary to save or support it.　It
will be a bog the less in Europe, *et voilà tout.*

The people at large are, beyond a doubt, recovering
apace from their errors, and the popular tide will probably soon run in a contrary current from what it has
done for the last six years.　The middle class, and also
the more temperate members of the aristocratical party,
begin to reflect seriously on the situation of their
country.　They see the military power on the eve of
being lodged entirely in the hands of a Frenchman, and
the civil government placed in those of two or three
factious leaders, unequal in point of abilities to its administration, and of whose principles and integrity their
opinions begin to waver.　But this conviction comes too
late; and, whatever their alarms may be, it is now no
longer within their reach to wrest the power from those,
where their own want of foresight and hasty conduct have
thought proper to vest it.　The French system is too far
advanced, and has taken too great a degree of consistency,
to be overthrown by deliberations, resolutions, and various other means of delay, which we find have been so
often practised with success in the annals of the Republic.

The Pensionaries remain in full possession of their
authority, and, riveted in this, they have little to fear
from the ill-will of the people, and the existence of both
the French party and that of the Pensionaries are now
so intimately connected, and depend so entirely on each
other, that no intrigue, however well managed, can separate them.　The knot must be cut, not untied, and the
King of Prussia's half-measures rejected, whenever any
real good is meant to be effected here.

In the meanwhile, my Lord, and till we can see a little
more clearly on what we are to depend, there remains
only for me to endeavour to suspend the signature of the
Alliance with France; to get, if possible, the powers now
in the hands of the Dutch Ambassadors at Paris, revoked,
or, at least, an order sent to them that they should not
proceed to the actual conclusion of the Treaty till they

received fresh instructions from hence. The time which would be gained by this delay would, in all probability, produce some material events, and be well employed in fomenting that spirit of discontent and uneasiness which prevails here.

To effect a suspension of the exercise of the full powers now in the hands of the Dutch Ambassadors at Paris, I see but two ways. The one, to engage one or more of the Provinces to enter a protest against them at an assembly of the States. The other, by putting an end to those idle fears the faction here has so artfully fixed in the minds of the Dutch East India merchants, that England has hostile views on their possessions.

As to the first, though it is difficult, and I believe almost unprecedented, to *resume* a solemn act of the States, yet I do not think it absolutely impracticable. The situation of Europe is not the same as it was a year ago. The Emperor's views of aggrandizement in Bavaria, which, *though stopped, are not laid aside,* and the formation of the German League, furnish very plausible pretexts for holding forth to this country the ineligibility of their entering into engagements with a Power whom they might be immediately called upon to assist in a war, while the Republic itself would be, otherwise, in a state of peace and security.

These and similar arguments, which would naturally present themselves in the course of conversation, would, I should hope, not be totally unattended to in the present temper of several of the Provinces, and I mean not to lose a moment in employing them with some leading people in Zealand and Gelderland.

The setting these *Provinces* at variance with that of Holland will be a great step towards that confusion which alone can produce order; and, if afterwards it can be contrived to divide the *towns* of Holland against Amsterdam, matters would soon go right.

As to the second point, it appears to be a much easier operation, since nothing more is necessary than to declare our readiness to enter into any commercial arrangements with the Dutch East India Company which may be advantageous to both countries, and even a reciprocal guarantee of our respective possessions. This is a kind of bait I think they could not resist, particularly as many of the Dutch Directors are well disposed; and though they may have been inspired with groundless apprehensions of England, yet they certainly would not be averse to listen to any friendly overtures coming from our quarter.

EXTRACT OF A DESPATCH FROM SIR JAMES HARRIS TO THE MARQUIS OF CARMARTHEN.

Hague, 12th August, 1785.

THE manner in which the Emperor seems disposed to persevere in his original demands, and the conduct of the Court of Versailles, are certainly not agreeable to the Pensionaries; but they are now so much in the hands of France, that not only the duration of their power, but in a great measure their personal existence, depends on the French system preserving its preponderance here. They dare not, therefore, oppose anything France recommends, but must subscribe implicitly, though perhaps sometimes reluctantly, to its mandates, let them be what they will.

Things being thus situated, there is little doubt what will be the issue of this business. The negotiation for peace may be protracted, but it certainly will be concluded: it would be idle to attempt to fling any obstacle in its way;· and on this point matters must be left to take their course.

My efforts must be all directed to prevent that the signing of this Treaty and of the Alliance* should go hand in hand; and I have some faint hopes that they may not be entirely fruitless, partly from what I may be able to effect through some of our friends in the Provinces, and partly because I think I perceive some

* Between France and Holland.

sparks of spirit discovering themselves in the nation at
large; and that, as they have begun to think, they
may, by management and caution, be brought to act.

I am not ripe to give your Lordship an account of
several steps I have taken with a design to promote
this purpose, or of various others I have in contemplation. I feel so strongly the necessity of releasing this
country from the French yoke, that the means of effecting it employ my whole thoughts.

I have not seen either the Prince or Princess, or any
member of the Government lately. I wish to appear
an inactive and unconcerned spectator, as I perceive I
am more than commonly watched, and, what is very
flattering, I am told, feared by the French party.

EXTRACT OF A DESPATCH FROM SIR JAMES HARRIS TO
THE MARQUIS OF CARMARTHEN.

Hague, August 16th, 1785.

THE instruments I have to employ to counteract their
measures are so unequal to any great purpose, that it
is almost impossible to employ them effectually. There
are not indeed wanting men of parts and abilities, nor
many who see the situation of their country and its
interests in their true light; but they are so disconnected amongst themselves, so overawed by the clamour
and violence of faction, so intimidated by their enemies, and so jealous of each other, that it is a most
arduous task to bring them to act, and still more so to
prevail on them to submit to anything like a systematic
direction. I have to move, therefore, with the greatest
caution, fearful lest, when I trust one friend, I displease
several others; and still more so, lest, in times like these,
those who till now have appeared staunch in the cause,
should be disposed to purchase their peace with the opposite party by betraying my confidence.

I am also not a little circumscribed in my operations,

from the present perplexed state of Europe, and from the difficulty of pointing out to them what power they ought to rely upon, and look up to for support and defence. I even cannot venture to promise them anything specific from my own Court, and am reduced to the hackneyed and seldom efficacious argument when it stands single—"the necessity of maintaining the honour and dignity of their country, and standing forth in support of its rights and independence."

I, however, flatter myself I have not been quite unsuccessful in operating on the minds of some of the principal people in Zealand, whom I have seen secretly several times on the subject, and who, from their local position, as well as from their rooted jealousy of Holland, are the most liable to receive such impressions as I could wish to give. They have promised me to try to induce the States of their Province to advise a suspension at least of the Signature of the Alliance with France, and I have furnished them with a very sufficient number of good reasons why this advice ought to be followed.

I only apprehend what I have mentioned before, that my friends will not agree amongst themselves, and defeat the end they aim at, by narrow personal jealousies, and want of confidence in each other. I have also been talking to some of the Deputies from Gelderland and Friesland, and endeavoured to work them up to my purpose. In the first of these Provinces (which is the seat of the Dutch nobility) there are many steady friends, but, from their inability and indolence, the whole Province is led by one man, Mons. De Lyndende Hemmen, formerly of the right side, but whose principles have given way to his interest, and who now, though attached to the person of the Prince, is a creature of France. This man has unfortunately obtained the character of worth and great integrity, merely because he is circumspect, taciturn, demure, and precise.

EXTRACT OF A DESPATCH FROM SIR JAMES HARRIS TO
THE MARQUIS OF CARMARTHEN.

Hague, 19th August, 1785.

I HAD another private conference yesterday with the
Princess of Orange.   Her motive for wishing to see me
was simply to justify herself from any blame in not
having as yet an answer from Berlin (which ought in
the common course of post to be received) since our first
conversation, and she attributes this delay to the King
of Prussia's illness.*   Her anxiety on this subject was
certainly not feigned, and I am convinced she feels that
neither she nor her children ever can expect any cordial
or efficacious assistance from Berlin, and that she looks
up to my Royal Master as the only real support the
House of Orange has left.   She spoke with much good
sense and great sensibility on her own position; and,
with much address, though without losing her dignity,
endeavoured to interest me deeply in her situation.   I,
on my side, spared no pains to gain her confidence, and
to persuade her that I mean nothing but good to her
and her House.   She talked of temporizing, and the
necessity of treating her opponents with a degree of
management.   I took the liberty of controverting this
conduct, from a conviction I am under, that the success
of the faction is owing principally to the irresolution and
pusillanimity of the Prince's party.

She promised to see me again on Tuesday, and settled with me how our meeting might take place without
suspicion.

* The Princess had continued to urge Frederick to take her husband's
part against the Patriots.

EXTRACT OF A DESPATCH FROM SIR JAMES HARRIS TO
THE MARQUIS OF CARMARTHEN.

Hague, 23rd August, 1785.

I RETURNED late last night from some visits I thought
it advisable to make to several of my acquaintance at
their country-houses in the neighbourhood of Amsterdam.

I found, amongst the people with whom I have been
living since Friday, and who are all more or less concerned in the regency of the towns (of course enemies),
strong symptoms of discontent, and an evident alarm at
the turn the affairs of the Republic were likely to take.
Several went so far as to profess themselves absolute
converts, and to declare they have gone too far; but
they are all infected with the same spirit of timidity
and cowardice, and no one dares take the lead, or be the
first to stem the torrent. My language to them all, of
whatever description or party, was, that England wishes
nothing but to see the Republic recover its rank in Europe, and resume that influence and weight it had held
under every form of government for so many years.

EXTRACT OF A DESPATCH FROM SIR JAMES HARRIS TO
THE MARQUIS OF CARMARTHEN.

Hague, 26th August, 1785.

A VERY few words on political subjects passed between the Princess of Orange and myself at the ball on
Wednesday, but they were not immaterial ones.

She said, the answer from Potzdam was far from
what she wished; that the King declined positively
taking an active part here; that he advised patience,
moderation, and resignation—a word, she said, *qui lui
serrait le cœur*, as it carried with it the idea of being
totally abandoned by him: that she, however, imputed
this cold insensible conduct of her Uncle's entirely to

infirmity and old age; since, at the same time that he held this desponding language, he recommended to her strongly to be on her guard against the French, to resist the influence of their party, and to treat *me* with confidence, since her only support could come from England.

It was impossible in the crowd and confusion of a ball, and watched on all sides as we were, to enter into anything like a regular conversation, and what I have just written was said at many different parts of the evening.

EXTRACT OF A DESPATCH FROM SIR JAMES HARRIS TO THE MARQUIS OF CARMARTHEN.

Hague, 2nd September, 1785.

I AM just returned from a long and secret interview with the Princess of Orange in the gardens of the House in the Wood. As it was of my seeking, I opened the conversation by telling Her Royal Highness what had passed between me and the Prussian Minister,* and by observing, that I had used towards him a reserve I certainly should never assume when I had the honour of conversing with her.

On her bowing assent, I proceeded by saying that the crisis in the affairs of this country, so often talked of, seemed to me to be now really at hand; that the moment the peace is signed with the Emperor, the Alliance with France would be actually concluded; and that, whatever might be the reports of the day (propagated designedly to deceive), the Patriots would undoubtedly make peace on any terms. That peace concluded, and the Alliance signed, they would as certainly carry into execution what was the consummation of all their

---

* Mr. Thulemeyer, a man who deservedly became as much discredited at his own Court as he had been at others. He had tried, by pretending to side with the Stadtholder, to elicit from Sir J. Harris the intentions of his Court. Sir James knew him to be in the pay of France, and corresponded directly with Berlin through Mr. Ewart.

wishes,—a subversion of the Stadtholderate, and probably a crimination of the Stadtholder, &c.

Under these circumstances, I submitted it to Her
Royal Highness's judgment to pronounce whether a plan
of moderation and caution was, in fact, either more or
less than a tame and unconditional submission to the
yoke.

If His Prussian Majesty would take the lead here,
the English and Stadtholderian party might soon recover, and good order at home, as well as consideration
abroad, be restored to the Republic; that the stake,
in every sense of the word, was worth playing for; and
the most unsuccessful struggle to obtain it could not
be attended with worse consequences than remaining in
a state of torpid inaction; and that the doing nothing,
because the attempting something appeared hazardous
and difficult, would be an apology posterity would never
believe to have come from a Prince of Orange, married
to a Princess of the House of Brandenburg.

I was careful as I spoke to watch very accurately
the changes in the Princess's countenance. I could
clearly perceive she felt as I could wish the oblique
insinuation I aimed at—the want of cordiality and
sincerity in her Uncle, that she was deeply impressed
with the melancholy situation of her family, and that
want of courage and energy made no part of *her* character.

She was so overpowered by the many different ideas
which had occurred to her during my speaking, that it
was some time before she was sufficiently recovered to
answer me; and, when she spoke, she held a very different language from that she used in our first interview.

She admitted everything I said to be strictly true,
agreed with me in the consequences of the alliance with
France, in the desperate designs of the Patriots, and
that she and her House stood on the verge of its ruin.
She lamented even to reproaches the conduct of the
King of Prussia, which she did not impute to any de-

ficiency in his Minister's reports, but to his own political system, which prevailed over every other consideration.

She ended by saying, that, as we were most entirely agreed as to the pressing urgency of the moment, she was also afraid we should be agreed as to the impossibility of devising any means which could be employed with the smallest hope of success. I told her I was ready to hear and obey her orders; that she well knew, if England singly was to attempt anything here, it would only aggravate the evil, and that any overt act of mine would be extremely ill-judged.

She intreated me to prevail on your Lordship to write to Mr. Ewart, or to allow me to do it in your name, in such a manner as to enable him to state the precise situation of the Prince and this country to the King of Prussia; to convince him that delay is fatal, that it will lose both Her and the Republic for ever; and that it is his interest to stand forth immediately in support of its existence, lest he should feel obliged to do it when it will be too late,—that it should be held out to him as a part of a general system equally necessary to his interest as to his reputation. She dwelt particularly on the word *interest*, and, I could easily see, knows her Uncle's character perfectly well.

I must add, before I conclude, that she promised to write precisely in the same style to Potzdam she wishes we should write in, and that she would show me her letter. She likewise has allowed me to see her whenever I please in the same way I saw her this morning; but it is a permission I must use with the greatest caution, as a discovery would give rise to many unpleasant consequences.

Before I dismiss this subject, I must observe that in this, and in all the preceding conversations I have had with the Princess of Orange, I could clearly perceive that she was by no means on a footing of confidence with the Prince; and that although she never mentioned his name but with an appearance of respect, that she neither trusted him herself nor was trusted by him. I fear this disunion extends still farther than public subjects; that they are as little agreed on domestic ones; and this circumstance makes it a very difficult task to obtain the confidence of the one, without losing that of the other.

EXTRACT OF A LETTER FROM SIR JAMES HARRIS TO MR. EWART, BERLIN.

Hague, Monday, 5th September, 1785.

I AM very happy to have a safe opportunity of opening myself truly and confidentially to you ; of communicating to you more fully than the nature of the post would admit the several conversations I have lately had with the Princess of Orange, as well as what has passed between me and Mons. de Thulemeyer.

From these several pieces you will be able to collect, with as much precision as the subject will admit of, the relative situation of the Courts of Berlin and London, as well towards each other as towards what is passing in the Republic.

If His Prussian Majesty means ever to serve his niece, he must do it now; if he does not, his assurances of affection are mere words, and his proffers of assistance at a distant day an idle mockery.

I cannot impute this coldness to age and infirmity. There is no risk in the attempt when undertaken in concert with England; on the contrary, a show of timidity is much more likely to induce a character constituted like that of the Emperor to disturb the general tranquillity, than a show of resistance and opposition. His Prussian Majesty knows his rival too well to be ignorant of this, and I again repeat my fears that there is something *false and hollow within.* If this is not the case, there only remains to suppose that either Mr. Thulemeyer is not faithful in his description of the position of this country, and that through ignorance, prejudice, or partiality he misrepresents the truth; or (which I have some reason to suspect) that there is a secret correspondence going on between some of the Patriots and some one at Potzdam, and that they, to prevent the King of Prussia being uneasy about the fate of his niece, instil into his mind the notions his Ministers here and at London repeat. In either of these cases it is important to undeceive him. I have endeavoured to enable you to do it as far as lay in my power, by withholding from you no one article of intelligence which relates to this country.

The Princess knows I despatch this messenger, and *in general* the tenour of what I write; but it is known to no one else, not even to the Prince.

EXTRACT OF A DESPATCH FROM SIR JAMES HARRIS TO THE MARQUIS OF CARMARTHEN.

Hague, 9th September, 1785.

MESSENGERS are arrived within these three or four days from Paris, Vienna, and Petersburg.

Those from France bring an account of the opening of the conferences, and that the negotiators met on every point, except on that which is to settle the sum to be paid for the redemption of Maestricht, and another relative to the cession of the county of Dalheim. On these two the Imperial Ambassador declared his Master would stand out. The latter must be complied with *in toto;* and, in the former, no diminution will be made lower than ten millions of florins.

The Dutch Ambassadors, on their side, declared their inability of complying with either of these proposals.

The two messengers from Vienna confirm this resolution; and they were despatched one after another at a very short interval, to inform the States that a very considerable body of troops, to the amount of 10,000 men, were actually in march towards the Austrian Netherlands.

The courier from Petersburg brings also orders to the Empress's Minister here, to press the conclusion of the disputes with the Emperor; and M. Kallitcheff, without giving in a Memorial, expressed verbally the wish of his Imperial Mistress yesterday, to the several members of this Government, in very strong terms.

There is little doubt that from all these considerations peace will be concluded. In the mean time, however, they are not idle here; and the Prince of Orange means, I am told, to give orders for the whole garrison of Rotterdam, and for all that of the Hague, to be in readiness to march towards Breda on the shortest notice.

The dread of being attacked on the 15th is very great, and the faction are urging the Court of France in the strongest terms to prevail on the Emperor to give them longer time.

Your Lordship will readily conceive what a state of confusion all these external objects of dismay, joined to its internal dissensions, create in this country, and that it is impossible it can remain long as it is.

I leave nothing unsaid or untried to make them feel that it arises solely from their having abandoned their *ancient system*, and I think every day the number of converts increases: but as long as the power remains invested where it is, nothing can be done; and the present rulers must either be absolutely overset, or be brought to renounce their principles and connexions, on conditions of their own seeking.

Yesterday the States of Holland took a leading measure towards depriving the Prince of Orange of the direction of the army. They called an extraordinary assembly, under the pretence of the danger of a popular insurrection; and determined, in order to be prepared against this event, that the guards should be doubled, and military patrols, both of horse and foot, parade the streets from sun-set till sun-rise, and that orders to this effect should be given by the *Gecommitteerderade*, not as hitherto, by the Prince of Orange.

The distress and confusion of this country is already

at such a height, and increases so fast, that it is impossible, as long as things remain as they are, to expect that any thing salutary or good can be effected anywhere. The minds of every class of individuals partake of the fermentation of the State, and are not to be fixed to any object which requires cool and temperate investigation.

I am equally attentive to a still more material point, the flinging delays and difficulties in the way of the French alliance. My agents are at work, both in Zealand and Gelderland, but it is impossible for me to hear from them without running a risk of being discovered. I gave them at their departure full instructions, which I made them take down in writing; and, if a spirit of error and folly had not gone forth throughout every part of the Republic, I should have some hopes of success.

EXTRACTS OF A LETTER FROM SIR JAMES HARRIS TO THE MARQUIS OF CARMARTHEN.

Hague, 9th Sept., 1785.

I AM the more anxious to obtain the Princess of Orange's confidence, as, if ever Europe recovers its senses sufficiently to admit of the formation of a wise system, the great *Remora* which would stand in the way of this country becoming a part of it, would be the Princess of Orange's predilection for Prussia, and her disposition to attend to no other minister here than the minister from Berlin. Now, if I can once fix on her mind the idea that England is a more *natural* friend to her and her family, and united by stronger ties to the House of Orange than those of simple consanguinity,— which, if His Prussian Majesty acts as I expect him to do on the present occasion, I think I shall be able to effect,—I then may hope to have a considerable share of her confidence, and some direction of her political conduct. This, and not any idea that His Majesty of

Potzdam ever will co-operate here with us, is the motive of my present behaviour. I flatter myself it has your sanction, since, as far as I recollect, it is nearly consonant with the ideas we seemed mutually inclined to adopt in one of our last conversations. My only fear is, that whilst I am getting round the Princess I shall lose the Prince. He is so jealous, not of her virtue, but of her sense and power, that he would not even go to Paradise by her influence; and she has so mean an opinion of his capacity, and, in general, that kind of contempt a high-spirited woman feels for an inferior male being, that I see no hopes of bringing them to that degree of cohesion so highly necessary for the accomplishment of my future plans.

Hitherto I have carried my cup even; and indeed it is not so much myself I fear, as the operations of spies and officious informers, from whose eyes and tongues no one is safe.

EXTRACTS OF A DESPATCH FROM SIR JAMES HARRIS TO THE MARQUIS OF CARMARTHEN.

Hague, 13th Sept., 1785.

A VALET DE CHAMBRE, just arrived from Vienna, despatched by the Deputies, adds to our apprehensions by confirming the account of the march of 10,000 men towards the Low Countries; and by repeating that Prince Kaunitz had again declared to them, that, if the preliminaries were not agreed on by the 15th instant, the Emperor was determined not to afford them an hour's more delay. The Patriots, however, either really have not these fears, or affect not to be impressed with them.

They say, and with some degree of truth, that they are intended to intimidate and to force the Republic to hasten the business, but will disappear the moment His Imperial Majesty is informed of their readiness to meet him half-way, and of the fixed intention of France not to abandon them.

This fixed intention of France not to abandon them, and the confidence with which they speak of it, is founded merely on Monsieur de Vergennes having said, that, as the Republic was ready to treat on such reasonable terms, " il pouvait leur assurer que le Roi de France exigerait de l'Empereur de suspendre toute démarche hostile bien au delà du 15 Septembre."

The spirit of party, however, prevails over every other consideration; and at an hour when the enemy is at their gates, when decision and expedition are of the last importance, they are on every side thwarting the Stadtholder in his orders, and depriving him of his military authority.

EXTRACTS OF A DESPATCH FROM SIR JAMES HARRIS TO THE MARQUIS OF CARMARTHEN.

Hague, 16th Sept., 1785.

THE Princess of Orange, with her children, left the House in the Wood yesterday morning at six, and at three in the evening the Prince Stadtholder set out for Breda, attended by several officers of his suite. I had a conversation of considerable length with the Princess of Orange on Wednesday evening. I was to have accompanied her to dine yesterday at Mynheer Vanderhop's, near the Zuyder Zee, on which she is to embark for Friesland; but the obligation I think myself under to avoid any step which might expose Her Royal Highness or myself in my Public capacity to the scurrilous remarks of the infamous libellers of this country induced me to waive this invitation.

Her Royal Highness's soundness of understanding and rectitude of mind never appeared to me so conspicuous as on this occasion; and I shall be ill able, in my endeavours to transmit it to your Lordship, to do her that justice she deserves.

After informing her of the reasons which induced me to decline the honour of dining with her on Thursday, I told her I was come to receive her commands, and to ask of Her Royal Highness in what, or how, during her absence I could the most contribute to promote her interests and those of her family, &c.

The Princess received these assurances with the strongest appearance of gratitude and respect. " But," said she, " the fate of the House of Orange is determining very fast. No intervention, no assistance, I fear, can save us; an unaccountable series of unforeseen events, a want of concord amongst our friends, and a doubtful, irresolute conduct on our side, (which we now lament when it is too late,) has brought us to a state of distress and difficulty from which we never can recover." On my not appearing to acquiesce in this, she went on by saying, " My despair, Sir, believe me, is not a sentiment of weakness or dejection; it unfortunately is the result of reflection: deceived and betrayed on all sides, we have discovered too late the whole extent of the designs of our enemies, and the inefficacy and lukewarmness of our friends. I leave the Hague possibly never to return to it. A few days will wrest from the Prince every remnant of authority, and I trust he is too high-minded to consent to remain *un Stadthouder en peinture.* The life of political anxiety I have led for so many years, and of which I have seen the Prince so strongly partake, makes me behold with more than indifference my children driven from the succession and honours of their ancestors. They are too young to know ambition, or to regret the rank they now fill. I trust they will be happier in a less splendid situation."

Her Royal Highness here was forced to pause, but without suffering her emotion, which was very strong, to have vent, she presently continued by saying, " I have been often advised, and the advice has been pressed on me almost to importunity this morning, to separate my interests and those of my children from the interests of the Prince; but to *this* I will *never* subscribe; my principles withhold me from it, and, if they did not, I am not so circumscribed in my judgment as to be ignorant that to divide the House of Orange would be to ruin it for ever, and to add disgrace to misfortune.

"I may," said she, "at times wish the Prince possessed many qualities he has not, and that he could be divested of several he has; but these feelings I conceal in my own breast, and they neither have nor ever shall influence my own conduct. I am bound to share his fate, let it be what it may; and I trust in God to be enabled to meet it with firmness and resignation."

It was impossible for me to do anything but hear, admire, and compassionate this unfortunate Princess. To have interrupted her in the thread of her discourse, would have been as unfeeling as disrespectful. As, however, I could perceive she was more than commonly agitated, I was convinced something besides the result of mere reflection gave rise to what she said ; I therefore with the most cautious respect endeavoured, by several questions which naturally followed each other, to search what was the *immediate cause* of this fit of despondency, and which she certainly had not (at least to anything like such a degree) the night before, when I had the honour of sitting next to her at supper, and conversing much with her.

After some hesitation, and a visible increase of uneasiness, she confessed to me that Mons. de Maillebois (deputed, as she supposed, by the Court of Versailles) had been audacious enough to propose to her to *give up the Prince*. That she should contribute to his (Mons. de Maillebois') having the command of the army; that then he would undertake to put into her hands the Stadtholderian power, or, to use his own words, "un pouvoir qui vaudroit bien celui du Stadthouder." *

She rejected these offers, she said, with the disdain they deserved; but they opened the whole of the gloomy prospect to her eyes at once; and the little delicacy with which the proposal was made, proved to her that the

---

* Her uncle Frederick offered to make her Gouvernante of the States, if she would come into his and the French policy ; but she nobly refused the temptation.—*Harris Papers.*

plan of her enemies was brought to perfection, and that
nothing short of a miracle could prevent its execution.

I neither was, nor affected to be, surprised at this conduct of Mons. de Maillebois.   I did not endeavour to
soften her indignation against him, or to take from the
Court of Versailles its share in this project.   I observed,
however, that it was very extraordinary that the King of
Prussia, her uncle and avowed protector, should have
been the first person who advised the Prince to select
Mons. de Maillebois from amongst the three French
General Officers who were proposed; and that I was convinced, when he knew what had passed, he would be
very sorry to have been instrumental to his being placed
at the head of the Dutch army.

I promised faithfully it should be mentioned nowhere
but in a confidential despatch to your Lordship, and that
I would be responsible that it never should transpire.

I confess, my Lord, I am not without my suspicions
that it is the Court of Berlin, not that of Versailles,
which has directed this measure.   My suspicions are
founded, not only on what may be called probable conjecture, but arise from my knowing that there subsists a
great intimacy between this French General and Mad^{lle}.
Dankelman, who is full as much Prussian Minister here
as Mons. Thulemeyer himself.

Her Royal Highness mentioned one thing more to me,
which she said also added to her embarrassment, and
with this too she assured me she had acquainted no one.
Peter Paulus had waited on her, under pretence of taking
leave, and held out to her the possibility of a union with
the Patriots, and that, if some certain points in the regulations of 1747 were altered, he thought a coalition a
very practicable measure.

She asked me what I thought of this proposal.   I
replied without hesitation, that it was *false* and *dangerous;* that the Patriotic party stood on such high
ground just now, that it was idle to think of treating
with them; that the terms they would prescribe would
be humiliating and disgraceful, and would lead to every-

thing that was bad, with the aggravated circumstance (if she listened to them) of her becoming a kind of accomplice in the ruin of her House. That either this was the case, or the Patriots felt they were playing a deep stake, and were seeking insidiously to shelter themselves under the sanction of her authority; that, therefore, no attention should be now paid to what they said; that, indeed, some time back such an accommodation might, perhaps, have been brought about in an advantageous manner, but that, from what Her Royal Highness had just done me the honour to say to me herself, their project was now brought to perfection. Of course, to suppose any good could be derived from a junction with them was either supposing them to be composed of a description of men infinitely weak, or infinitely honourable, which certainly was not their character. I dwelt the more on this, as I was fearful despair might make her catch at this slight twig; and, before I left the subject, I made her reflect that Maillebois's proposal of separating her from the Stadtholder, and that of Paulus of uniting her with the Patriots, coming on the *same day*, and at a moment when she was upon the eve of her departure, and not likely to see the Prince for some weeks, was a remarkable circumstance and well worth attending to.

On my taking leave and again making my offers of service, she said, " Recommend me and my children to the King your Master; I hope I never shall be unworthy of his protection."

She told me she would write to me if she had anything to communicate, and put me in a way of writing to her by a safe conveyance.

Heads of what the King of Prussia said to Lord
Cornwallis,* at Sans Souci, the 17th Sept., 1785,
sent by Mr. Ewart to Sir James Harris.

His Majesty assured me that he was equally desirous
of friendship and connexion with the King of Great
Britain, but said that we must first take a view of the
political state of Europe.—That the balance of Power,
which England had so long and strenuously supported,
was lost. — That France, Spain, Austria, and Russia
were in alliance; and that Holland was in the power of
France, to whom the ruling party were totally devoted.
—That England and Prussia were *isolés*, without any ally
whatever; that these two Powers alone were not a match
for that mass which he had described.—That England
would have to contend with the fleets of France, Spain,
Holland, and perhaps Russia.—He should have upon
his hands the armies of France, Austria, and Russia.—
That although, from some fortunate circumstances, such
a contest had been maintained, it was not a game to play
often. He said France and Austria were closely connected, because France wished to be able to turn her
whole force to her marine, and against England; and
that the Emperor's alliance secured her from a continental war. That this was so favourite a point with
France, that she even consented to the alienation of
Bavaria, although it was guaranteed by her to the Duke
of Deux Ponts.

He stated that Austria had hold of Russia, both by the
Empress and her favourite, Prince Potemkin : that the
Emperor flattered the former with conquests on the
Turks, and even the possession of Constantinople; the
latter with promises of being Hospodar of Wallachia
and Moldavia. That in this situation of affairs he did
not think it would be wise to give alarm to all the great
Powers of Europe by a treaty between England and

* Lord Cornwallis was sent to sound the sentiments of Frederick towards
an English alliance.

Prussia. He considered England as his Ally, and hoped the King of England would look on him in the same light. That he felt the utmost anxiety for the affairs of Holland from his connexion with the House of Orange, and from his desire of preventing Holland from becoming, in fact, a Province of France. He was convinced violent means would not do, unless we had a force to support them. He was apprehensive that the interference and activity of our Minister at the Hague would do mischief if it was discovered.

He then expatiated on the necessity of endeavouring to detach some of the powers from the great league, and pointed out Russia as the principal object. He said, if Russia could be got over, he was ready to sign a triple alliance.

EXTRACT OF A LETTER FROM THE MARQUIS OF CARMARTHEN TO SIR JAMES HARRIS.

St. James's, Sept. 19th, 1785.

THE King of Prussia is outrageous with poor Lusi* for having intimated the expediency of writing to Lord Cornwallis upon the subject of a nearer connexion between the two Courts; he tells him he has been guilty of an *effronterie*, which deserves the most exemplary punishment; in another letter supposes he must have *le diable au corps* to have been guilty of such an indiscretion, and threatens him with his heaviest displeasure if not more discreet in future. His poor penitent Minister sends a copy of a despatch for his justification, and, after wishing rather to sacrifice his life than incur his Master's displeasure, throws himself on the clemency of that mild and merciful Monarch.

Had His Prussian Majesty seen my letter to Lord Cornwallis, he need not have been *alarmed* at the idea of our pressing him to form an alliance; as the chief pur-

---

* Prussian Minister at London, an Italian by birth, and a man of no consideration.—*Original Note.*

port of my despatch was directing his Lordship to get all possible information from His Majesty, and in return to give him as many civil *words* as possible, but not to commit this Court in the smallest degree by the remotest idea of any thing like an alliance.

EXTRACTS OF A DESPATCH FROM SIR JAMES HARRIS TO THE MARQUIS OF CARMARTHEN.

Hague, 20th Sept., 1785.

MY accounts from Friesland are more satisfactory. The Princess arrived there on Friday amid the acclamations of the people, who crowded in shoals on the shore to receive her. The same rejoicings were manifested in the several towns through which she passed on Saturday, and not " one *unpleasant symptom*," says my correspondent, "has yet shown itself." If we could be permitted to hope that it was possible for Her Royal Highness to regain Friesland, and for the Prince to recover Zealand, so as to make these two Provinces act in constant opposition to that of Holland, it would shake the power of the Patriots, and be a strong curb on their dangerous designs.

EXTRACT OF A DESPATCH FROM SIR JAMES HARRIS TO THE MARQUIS OF CARMARTHEN.

Hague, 24th Sept., 1785.

THE messenger who is to bring the important decision of war or peace is not arrived. The only symptom of spirit which has appeared is in Zealand; which Province has entered its protest against the discretionary powers given to France, and supported their opinion by many strong and able reasons. I hear nothing new either from Breda or Friesland. I understand that in a very short time Prince Louis of Brunswick means to publish an account of the attempt made to seize his papers. Mons. d'Aroz, originally an accomplice, has turned informer, on thinking himself ill-used by the Rhingrave of Salm. Both the Rhingrave and Mons. de Maillebois* are undoubtedly concerned in this affair. The latter has offered 2000 louis for a letter of his now in possession of the Duke.

It is now near eleven o'clock, and no messenger is arrived; I cannot venture to detain the packet any longer. The Great Pensionary was up all night, expecting a messenger, and, I am told, is under the greatest anxiety lest the negotiation should break off.

EXTRACTS OF A DESPATCH FROM SIR JAMES HARRIS TO THE MARQUIS OF CARMARTHEN.

Hague, 27th Sept., 1785.

A VERY few hours after I had despatched my messenger to Helvoet on Saturday, a courier arrived from Paris with the preliminaries between the Emperor and this country, signed by the Imperial Ambassador and the Ambassadors of this Republic at the French Court. I have the honour of enclosing a copy of these preliminaries.

It is probable not more than four of the Provinces will concur on this occasion, (which ought to invalidate the whole measure,) but, in all the late transactions, that article of the Act of Union, which states unanimity to be necessary when any great State question is to be determined, has been set aside, and the plurality been deemed sufficient to carry a question. Zealand, Friesland, and Gelderland are the Provinces which most likely will not consent, either to ratify the prelimi-

* Maillebois and the Patriots employed some adventurers to seize Prince Louis's papers, in hopes of finding a correspondence between him and the Stadtholder, which might be used against the latter. Prince Louis had been guardian to the Prince of Orange, and Regent of the States during his minority.— *Ellis, Rev. of Holland.*

naries, or to pay their quota part of the ten millions of florins.

The Patriots know the secret of the King of Prussia's conduct perfectly well, and how to rate his show of anger and displeasure at them, and his expressions of regard and affection for the House of Orange. France keeps them fully informed on this subject; and they will, I am persuaded, treat this feeble demonstration of support in the same inattentive manner they treated the Memorials which were sent from Potzdam a few years ago. His repeated insinuations that England should not appear in any transaction in Holland, and the apprehensions he expresses that *my* supposed *activity* here may do harm, are strong proofs of his not being seriously disposed to bring this country back to its ancient system.

EXTRACT OF A LETTER FROM SIR JAMES HARRIS TO MR. EWART.

Hague, Friday, Sept. 30, 1785.

SIR,—The nature of a cyphered letter will not permit me to enter so fully as I could wish into the many interesting points contained in your despatches. I sent them to England by the first post, accompanied with an account of the *impression* His Prussian Majesty's conduct is likely to produce, as well here as in the rest of Europe.

I have no reason to believe that there exists in the mind of the Stadtholder any serious intention to abdicate his high office, and that this assertion is founded on anything more than a few words he spoke in a burst of passion the day the command of this garrison was taken from him. Mons. de Thulemeyer was misinformed when he advanced this intention as a positive fact; and the imputing it to so base a motive as personal fear, is neither truth nor justice. To separate the Prince and Princess would be, in my opinion, to put the finishing stroke to the House of Nassau, and to add *disgrace* to misfortune. I believe this also to be the sentiment of the Princess.

The Patriots know full well the motives of the King of Prussia's forbearance, and that whatever answer they give, he will be withheld, from considerations more important to him than the restoration of the Stadtholderate, from proceeding to any lengths against them. The letters, for form's sake, are sent to *the Provinces*, whilst the answer is preparing *here*, which will be certainly declinatory, and perhaps not even civil, to His Prussian Majesty's tender of Mediation.

You may be assured their primary object is to overset the Stadtholderate. All their efforts have pointed at this; for this they have disgraced their country, by introducing confusion at home, and exposing it to danger and shame abroad.

You have effected a great deal, for it is *very important* to have got at the Prince of Prussia's sentiments. I rely much on him, or rather on the decisive events his *accession* must produce.

You will, I am sure, forgive me for having written freely. In matters of business sincerity is the strongest proof of confidence.

EXTRACT OF A DESPATCH FROM SIR JAMES HARRIS TO THE MARQUIS OF CARMARTHEN.

Hague, 4th October, 1785.

I FLATTER myself, by next post, to write your Lordship pleasing intelligence from Zealand; a very strong protestation against the preliminaries is arrived this morning from that Province, where my efforts to do good will, I trust, not be entirely ineffectual.

EXTRACTS OF A DESPATCH FROM SIR JAMES HARRIS TO THE
MARQUIS OF CARMARTHEN.

Hague, 11th October, 1785.

A PERFECT concord between the Prince and Princess,
and making it appear manifestly and beyond doubt that
every attempt to separate their interests (whether coming from dangerous enemies or from weak friends), will
be reprobated with indignation, is the primary object at
this moment. Not a day should be lost in impressing
the people with this idea. A contrary one prevails, and
does more harm to the Stadtholderate than can be expressed.

Though it is, perhaps, not equally necessary to make
it public, yet, to the very few on whom he can rely, the
Prince should declare his fixed intention of never submitting to any terms of accommodation with the Patriotic faction; no connexion can subsist between him
and them that would not be both unsafe and dishonourable to him, nor any division of authority be made that
would not be as disgraceful as unwise. There should be
no shadow of doubt left of the Stadtholder wavering on
this point.

LETTER FROM MR. PITT TO SIR JAMES HARRIS.

Oct. 13th, 1785.

MY DEAR SIR,—I ought to make many apologies for
the trouble I am going to give you. The subject of it
is one not uninteresting to our domestic situation, and
if in the busy scene with which you are surrounded you
should have any leisure to give to it, you will I am sure
not think your time misspent in anything that gives a
chance of improving the resources on which so much
depends both at home and abroad. I have been inclined
to think, that, among the few things in Holland which
could be imitated with advantage, one is a considerable

article of Revenue, arising from the *tax on successions.**
I have seen a translation of the two edicts by which it
was imposed, said to have been in 1723 and 1743, but
am not sure whether it is correct.   If it should fall in
your way to obtain any information to be relied upon
relative to the detail of collecting this tax, how far it is
supposed to be fairly paid, what is its average produce,
and whether any inconveniency is complained of—especially by persons in *trade* from the necessity of discovering the amount of any property they succeed to — I
should be very much obliged to you for such particulars;
as they will furnish the means of judging whether any
similar system could be adapted to the situation of this
country.   Having intruded upon you so far on the subject of Finance, I cannot deny myself the pleasure of
adding, that the general state of our revenue is improving daily.   We are, I believe, already in possession of
very near a million surplus beyond all our probable
annual expenses, and shall, if the same course of prosperity continues, find ourselves very different in the eyes
of Europe from what we have been for some time.

I will not suffer myself to say anything on the politics to which you are a witness, or on those of the
Continent, for they seem in truth still too mysterious
to form any conjecture on the turn either of them may
ultimately take.   I have only to add the most sincere
assurances of the esteem and regard with which I have
the honour to be, dear Sir, your most obedient and
faithful humble servant,   W. PITT.

---

* Sir J. Harris gave Mr. Pitt the desired information respecting the
Dutch Legacy Duties, and the latter accordingly imposed them upon this
country.

EXTRACTS OF A DESPATCH FROM SIR JAMES HARRIS TO
THE MARQUIS OF CARMARTHEN.

Hague, 18th Oct., 1785.

THE Preliminaries were ratified in the Assembly of
the States General yesterday morning, with the approbation of the four Provinces of Holland, Utrecht, Overyssel, and Groningen.   The other three formally pro-
tested against them; and the four which have ratified
them, far from sanctifying the measure with their approbation, justify their conduct only from necessity.*

Mons. Thulemeyer has talked more sensibly and more
openly to me within these few days than he ever yet has
done, and I am glad to find from Mr. Ewart, that his
letters to Berlin correspond with the language he holds
to me.   He has gone so far, in conversing with me, as
to confess the injudiciousness of every step his Master
has taken here for these last four or five years past, and
has not scrupled to declare that he has been the dupe of
France.

He exclaims with great acrimony against the Patriots,
against Mons. de Verac, and the Rhingrave, and, in
short, talks a language so unlike that he held a month
ago, that I am puzzled which way to take him.   Mad^{lle}
Dankelman, in her way, expresses the same sentiments;
and, whatever may be the *real* views and opinions of
the King of Prussia, he has certainly instructed his
Ministers and Agents to hold him forth as dissatisfied
and displeased with France.

I am not at all surprised that the contents of the
Princess of Orange's letter to me should not appear to
your Lordship to correspond with what her Royal
Highness said to me before she left the Hague.†   I

---

* This was a breach of the constitution, which required unanimity.
† This letter requested Sir James not to correspond with Her Royal
Highness any more, as being too dangerous, and the cause hopeless.

can only observe, that though it came by a messenger, yet that it passed through the hands of Mons. de Larrey, that Mons. de Larrey is devoted to the King of Prussia, and that her Royal Highness, not without reason, suspected the letter she wrote to me would probably be perused by him, and shown to Mons. de Thulemeyer before it reached me. I would willingly believe that she would have expressed herself differently in a personal interview, when she was not under the fear of having her sentiments betrayed.

The Patriots all agree in the idea that the Stadtholderate must be overset, but they are divided as to the means of oversetting it. Van Berkel and Zeebergen are for forcing the Prince of Orange to return hither (which they pretend they have a right to do), in hopes of making him, by repeated provocations and from the petulance of his character, the instrument of his own downfall. Gyslaer and Paulus are for disuniting him and the Princess, and by a division of, and gradual diminution of the Stadtholderian power, to reduce it imperceptibly to nothing. The first two, in order to prevail on him to return hither, are luring him with an appearance of moderation. The order is *suspended* for striking his arms from the colours, &c.

The two others affect to give in to the King of Prussia's views, and to say that their objections are not to the Stadtholderian government, but to the person of the Stadtholder, and that, if the authority of a Stadtholder was in the hands of a *proper person*, they would readily support it. They point out the Princess as the person they mean, and spare no pains to gain her by flattery and praises. But they are all four equally false and dangerous.

Things thus circumstanced, (and your Lordship may rely on the veracity of what I say,) I have taken the only step from which I could possibly hope to effect any good, by writing to the Stadtholder the following letter.

[Sir James Harris now took upon himself to address the Prince of Orange directly, in the hope of infusing into his Royal Highness some of the spirit and energy which he saw was necessary to the maintenance of his power. During Sir James's last visit to England he had completely gained over Lord Carmarthen to his views, and his friendship with that nobleman encouraged him to undertake a responsibility in all his actions, for which the cautious spirit of our Administration could give him no warrant.]

LETTER FROM SIR JAMES HARRIS TO HIS SERENE
HIGHNESS THE PRINCE OF ORANGE.

Hague, Oct. 16th, 1785.

SIR,—Your Highness will, I hope, impute my venturing to transmit to you the enclosed paper, to the only possible motive which can exist for my so doing,—to a sincere and uniform desire of serving you, and an earnest wish of seeing you, on some future day, in a situation to be called upon to restore tranquillity and consideration to this unfortunate Republic. I shall not affect to enforce what I say by professions. Your Highness knows well of how little value they are; but a Minister from England never can mean to deceive or mislead you, more particularly one who has had the happiness to know you for so many years, and who adds to principles of duty, sentiments of early attachment and regard.

It is not my *private opinion*, which I should never presume to intrude on your Highness, but that of those from whom I hold the right of addressing you, on whose affection and constant support your Highness may most religiously reckon, that if you were to adopt a plan similar to that set forth in the annexed paper, and to act up to it firmly and systematically, that you would immediately and at once check the violence of the ruling faction, embarrass their operations, and ultimately lead the nation at large to apply to you for support and

assistance.   Such a manly and resolute conduct also
would startle your enemies, would encourage your friends,
and give you throughout Europe that reputation which
ever belonged to the House of Nassau.

The ruling faction has no claim to call upon you to
return to the Hague.   Sir, by depriving you of some
of your most essential rights, they have in a manner
rescinded the most sacred resolutions of the State, and
it is insulting you to expect that *you* should be bound
by resolutions which *they* have made no scruple to violate.   You may rest assured, Sir, that it is their fixed
and determined resolution to overset the Stadtholderate;
that their views are not personal, but general; and that
the Court of Versailles concurs entirely in this plan.
The agreement between them was mutual; and, the
Patriots having now done the work of France, France is
to do theirs.   Any attempt to modify their virulence,
to disconnect them, or to obtain from them a share
of the authority they have usurped and still maintain,
would not only be fruitless, but most pernicious.   To
propose terms of accommodation or to sue for a coalition would betray a weakness, and from this apparent
weakness they would derive real strength.   A very
recent event (the issue of which is still depending)
proves beyond a doubt the truth of what I say, that
moderation and lenient measures (from whatever high
authority they come, will avail nothing.

The time may arrive, Sir, when more efficacious
ones may be employed, and when your Highness may
be called upon to vindicate your rights in a manner
more becoming the high blood which flows in your
veins.   Till then nothing remains to be done but to
lie by, to remove yourself and your family from the
scene of action, to protest respectfully but with becoming spirit against every infringement on the pre-
rogative of a constitutional Stadtholder ; and not, by
listening to any insidious plans of accommodation which
may be artfully held out, fix on the minds of posterity
the impression that you were an accomplice in the

destruction of a country your ancestors have thrice saved from ruin.

EXTRACTS OF A DESPATCH FROM SIR JAMES HARRIS TO
THE MARQUIS OF CARMARTHEN.

Hague, 25th Oct., 1785.

THE three ruling Pensionaries are losing ground in their respective towns. A great number of the Regents are against Zeebergen at Haarlem; at Dort, Gyslaer's credit is declining very fast; and the magistrates of Amsterdam are by no means satisfied with Van Berkel. I do not choose to soil myself by meddling in the dirty intrigues of these towns; but, if the Prince had a party he could call his own, some one of its members might be selected for this purpose, and with management and address this formidable Triumvirate be drawn from their posts.

The rise of our funds, and the increase of the wealth and prosperity of Great Britain, seem to have a great effect on the Continent, and to undeceive those nations who were taught to believe we were no longer equal to have a weight in the balance of Europe.

It is now necessary for me to give your Lordship a further account than I have hitherto thought it necessary to do, of what I have been, and still am, doing in Zealand, and of the effects it has produced.

From my general knowledge of the sentiments of this province, and from the character of its inhabitants, I immediately, on my return from England, considered it as the one the most proper to work up to my purpose. Its interests also corresponded with my intentions. The cessions made to the Emperor pressed harder on Zealand than on any other part of the Republic, and its welfare was more intimately and more immediately affected by a French alliance. I made it, therefore, my chief business, partly by myself, and partly through Count

Mirabel,* on whose friendship I cannot too much insist, to convey to the Deputies of that province here, such kind of intelligence and observations as were the best suited to my views.   I kept them informed of what is never thought of here, the close connexion between the general affairs of Europe and the particular one of this country.

It would be idle to enumerate to your Lordship the various arguments I produced to support my doctrines; they are too palpable to be mentioned, and in any other country but this they would have needed no prompter.

Besides this attempt to influence the reports of the Deputies to their constituents, in which I was lucky enough to succeed beyond my wishes, I thought it expedient to send some one into Zealand on whom I could depend, and who, besides conversing with the different Regents at large, would more particularly apply his attention to Mons. Van der Spiegel† (since he became Pensionary of the province), of whose good sense, sound principles, and uncommon acuteness, I had heard so much.   I selected for this purpose Baron Kinckel‡ and Mons. Van Citters (the elder), the first from his zeal and enterprising spirit, the other from his excellent understanding and personal influence, and both from their tried attachment to the good cause.

I had no need to point out to men thinking like these, how notoriously the Union of Utrecht had been violated, and that from the whole of their conduct the three Pensionaries seem to have no other view than to make Holland the absolute Sovereign over the other Six Confederate States.

---

* Sardinian Minister.   The Sardinian Consul, Triquetti, was in our pay, and Sir James's principal agent.   He was a most active and useful fellow, and a true Italian of the sixteenth century.

† A man of first-rate talent, and of unimpeachable character.   He died in exile at Lingen, in Westphalia, in 1800, after the French had conquered his country, and had thrown him into prison for refusing to acknowledge their dominion.

‡ Kinckel was a clever man, and an Admiral in the Dutch service.

The able and zealous conduct of these two gentlemen has exceeded my expectations. It was to their activity that we owe the strong, spirited, and able protestation of the province of Zealand against the peace; and it is through them also that the Pensionary Van der Spiegel has promised me that he will leave nothing untried to induce the province to suspend the instructions given to the Dutch Ambassadors to sign the Alliance.

If Zealand formally and seriously insists on a revision of the instructions given to the Dutch Ambassadors in Oct. 1784, the Patriots cannot, in their present situation, venture so far to violate the most solemn acts of the Constitution, as to set such a resolution at nought, and go on with the negotiation of the alliance.

If to the opposition of Zealand I should be able to add that of Gelderland (at which I am working), it will be a great point.

The Prince and Princess will, I trust, not let Friesland slip through their fingers; and, if we get *three* provinces to join, it will then be time to talk of a separation from the Union, and to threaten to leave Holland to itself if it continues to act with such tyrannical and unconstitutional oppression.

I have till within these few days, by never absenting myself from society, and by affecting to seek for dissipation and amusements of every kind, carried on my operations without suspicion; but Peter Paulus (and, of course, the other Patriots) has now got wind of what I am about, and I must be doubly on my guard.

Paulus dined with me on Thursday last, and from his caressing, insidious manner, raised doubts in my mind that he had views of imposing on me. He since has expressed his alarms to one of my friends, and I must expect to have the whole force of their opposition to encounter. The foundation, however, is laid; and their efforts will, I trust, come too late to prevent the superstructure.

I do not presume to say what conduct England ought to observe on this occasion, but some of our

friends think that some *ministerial* symptom of our not
being totally indifferent to the concerns of the Republic
and its present operations, would come well-timed, and
have a good effect.   If I did not feel it was going
beyond the bounds of my mission, I should venture to
transmit their ideas to your Lordship, but I cannot re-
solve to do it without your permission.

EXTRACTS OF A DESPATCH FROM SIR JAMES HARRIS TO THE MARQUIS OF CARMARTHEN.

Hague, 1st Nov., 1785.

THE fermentation among the Patriots increases
hourly; they seem almost desperate, and determined to
run every risk, and to submit to no terms.   They talk
of the dissolution of the Union as a desirable incident,
and that Holland can stand and act alone better than
with such weak and spiritless confederates.

They mean to reject the King of Prussia's Mediation
without reserve, and to attempt to criminate the Prince
in every instance they can devise.

The three Pensionaries during the recess (which ends
on Friday) have been at their respective towns endeavouring to rally their forces and recover their popularity.

The result of all this will appear very shortly; the
crisis is drawing nearer every day; and it is, at least,
some consolation to me, that, if we are to fall, we shall
fall more like men than I could have expected a few
months ago.

The people at the Hague are ripe for insurrection.
The absence of the Stadtholder is felt throughout every
class of the Burghers; and they meditate a petition,
signed by 5000 of them to the States General, praying
them to desire the Stadtholder to return.

Such a number of discontented men of the description and character of the Dutch got together, will claim

attention, and make the Patriots think very seriously of what they are exposing themselves to. I should be sorry, however, if any use was as yet made of the people.

Besides the impossibility of directing a mob, or stopping its effects in time, I do not think that the moment is come for employing it. The danger must be still nearer; the pain more sensibly and more generally felt than it is yet, to be certain a struggle between the popular body and the aristocratical one would meet proper support, and be attended with that certainty of success which should be made evident before the blow is struck; to attempt it and to fail would be an irreparable evil.

LETTER FROM SIR JAMES HARRIS TO THE PRINCE OF ORANGE.

6th Nov., 1785.

MONSEIGNEUR,—Le zèle qui m'anime pour les vrais intérêts de Votre Altesse Sereine et de toute sa famille m'engage à vous confier dans le plus grand secret, que d'après mes notions le temps approche où la fermeté et la grandeur d'ame de Votre Altesse doivent être mises à toute épreuve.

Le plan qu'on se flatte d'exécuter est d'intimider Votre Altesse par des menaces, et de l'engager par toute sorte de mauvais traitemens à abandonner de gré ou de force la Régence.

C'est le moment où il importe de manifester l'énergie d'une ame supérieure aux évènemens et digne du sang qui coule dans vos veines.

Il seroit, ce me semble, à propos de protester hautement contre toute entreprise contraire à vos prérogatives légitimes, de ne s'arrêter ni à des menaces ni à des insinuations insidieuses, de vous maintenir prêt à répondre avec dignité à tous les griefs qu'on affecte d'alléguer à votre charge, et d'en appeler enfin à la nation comme juge de vos actions, et de la droiture de vos sentimens politiques.

Espérez, Monseigneur, qu'en vous réglant ainsi l'Europe entière applaudira à de si nobles efforts, et que vous ne sauriez pour lors manquer d'appui ni de ressource pour vous et pour votre maison.

Si la franchise avec laquelle je parle vous offense, Monseigneur, je vous offense par un excès de zèle et d'attachement que je ne saurois supprimer.

LETTER FROM SIR JAMES HARRIS TO THE MARQUIS OF CARMARTHEN.

Hague, 8th Nov., 1785.

MY DEAR LORD,—My life is a perpetual canvass, and my house like the Adam and Eve, or George and Vulture Inn, at a Middlesex meeting. Could we rally our voters and form a party, I should go on cheerfully, and with spirit; but to hear three-fourths of the Republic tell me they wish well to the cause, and then proceed with a list of reasons why they dare not publicly espouse it, provokes me beyond the limits of my patience. I am every day more confirmed in my opinion, *that trade narrows the mind*, and that a nation which is *nothing but commercial* must end like this, in becoming despicable, enervated, and woe-begone.

This must be my first and my last trial. We have a great deal to win, and a very little to lose. A man who lies on the ground may get up, but he cannot fall lower. This is nearly the situation of me and my friends.

Woronzow cannot be such a fool as to believe what he says, or think us such fools as not to see that Russia wants to change her system, and fix on England the charge of mutability. He has totally alienated poor Kalitcheff, and, by so doing, has left him like a blind beggar without his dog; the unfortunate man had no

confidence in anybody but me, and, now he is told
to mistrust me, he knows not where to take shelter.

Kalitcheff grows shyer every day; he and Woronzow
justify strongly the phrase of *La Crédulité des Incré-
dules.* They believe everything but truth.

DESPATCH FROM SIR JAMES HARRIS TO THE MARQUIS OF
CARMARTHEN.

Hague, 8th Nov., 1785.

My Lord,—The following intelligence may, I believe,
be considered as perfectly authentic ; the channels
through which I have received it leave me no doubt
of its being a faithful account of the plan the ruling
faction have resolved on.

I must begin by premising to your Lordship that
the whole of what I am going to write has been concerted with France; that it has the sanction, and will
have the support, of France, throughout every part of
it; and that, when I mention the ruling faction here,
I consider the Court of Versailles as making a very
material part of it.

Their plan is, by persecution, and by operating on
the fears of the Prince of Orange, to force him to re-
linquish the administration of the Stadtholderate, and
to retire to his possessions in Germany. They have
some charges against him not totally void of foundation,
and their own art and his weakness will furnish them
with many specious and affected ones. They mean to
bring these forward with all the publicity possible, and
to terrify him with the idea that his conduct has been
so highly criminal against the State, that his head is
liable to be brought to the block. His imagination is
already strongly impressed with this dread, and, in conversing with me, he has often said, the Patriots mean
to treat him as the Republicans did Charles the First.

They do not intend to alter the hereditary succession

of the Stadtholderate, but they propose taking on themselves the education of the Prince of Orange's children, and to send the two young Princes to be brought up in France (as it is said), however incredible, under the tuition of the Rhingrave of Salm.

I need not point out to your Lordship the pernicious tendency of this plan, nor how completely it will answer every purpose of the Patriots, without exposing themselves and their party to the danger which would inevitably attend a direct attempt to subvert the Stadtholderate entirely, and to substitute a new form of government in its place. It will leave strength enough in the hands of the executive power to keep the democratical faction from rising, and not enough to controul the aristocratical authority. It will satisfy France by making the House of Orange dependent on the towns of Holland, which province will be always dependent on France.

I confess, my Lord, my inability of devising any new means of counteracting it, or that anything else can be done than by repeatedly urging to the Prince the necessity of adhering firmly to the advice conveyed to him in my last letter.

I ought, perhaps, according to rule, to have waited for an answer to my first before I had sent a second; but it is not a time to consult etiquette, and it is the cause, not the man, which is to be supported.

As for the Princess, I am at a loss how to act. I dare not write to her, as well because I know of no channel through which I can send my letters to her that would not subject them to be read by the Prussian Minister, as because I am not certain whether they would find her in the same principles with which she left the Hague.

I confess, I cannot easily submit to give up my faith in her good sense, and in the veracity of her character; and I incline to believe that fear, and deference for the King of Prussia, make her act frequently in contradiction to her judgment and feelings. Her chief reliance, I must needs think, is in her brother,* and he seems to bid fair to act on very different principles from his uncle.

EXTRACT OF A DESPATCH FROM SIR JAMES HARRIS TO THE MARQUIS OF CARMARTHEN.

Hague, 11th Nov., 1785.

I HAVE prevailed on Colonel Bentinck to go to Loo, where he will say all I wish to be said, and observe all I wish to know. The great object is to prevail on the Prince to do neither more nor less than what is traced out for him. Every appearance of concert must be most carefully avoided. He must be made to feel that, before he can be restored to his privileges, the Republic must be recovered from its present erroneous system. To begin by supporting him would be commencing at the wrong end; it would mar the cause at once; and he ought to know that, without being named or even thought of, his power will gradually rise as that of France sinks. He must not, therefore, expect avowed and open, but indirect and concealed, support from England; neither must he think himself forsaken or neglected if he is not consulted, or advised of all that is going forward.

It would be of infinite consequence, if it were possible, to prevail on the King of Prussia to make even a show of disapprobation here at the French Alliance. I have ventured to press Mr. Ewart on this subject. I see such an opening for success, that I would pronounce it *certain* if I had but the remnant of a party on whom I could depend. But the pusillanimity and torpitude of this nation are not to be described. I must, however, work with the tools I have, trusting to your Lordship's indulgence for the rest.

* Afterwards King of Prussia.

EXTRACT OF A LETTER FROM SIR J. HARRIS TO
MR. EWART.

Hague, 11th Nov., 1785.

THE answer to the King of Prussia will probably
have been shown or read to you by Mons. de Hertzberg. I am anxious to know how it will be received.
It was drawn up at Versailles, and, unless there is a
secret and concealed plan of intelligence between the
King of Prussia and France, must, I think, give offence
at Potzdam. If the King lets the matter rest here,
he has done more harm than good. The only possible
means of serving the House of Orange, and of saving
this country from falling into the hands of France, is to
oppose the violence of the ruling party by violence.
They may be frightened, but cannot be persuaded; and
nothing short of menaces, well supported, will make any
impression on them.

If you could prevail on the King of Prussia to declare
himself against the conclusion of the French Alliance as
a measure which may lead this Republic into a system
contrary to his interests, it would be of great effect, and
come most remarkably well-timed.

It is of the utmost consequence you should fix in the
minds of the Prussian Ministers, and in that of the
Prince of Prussia *if you cannot get at the King*, that
any separation of interests of the Prince and Princess
of Orange would be equal ruin to them both. It is the
favourite plan of the Patriots.

I trust His Prussian Majesty thinks differently, and is
not to be deceived by so gross an imposition; but I am
not without my misgivings that Baron Thulemeyer recommends it, and that the Princess herself is now and
then tempted to approve it. But I repeat that, if it is
adopted, the House of Orange is gone for ever, and this
country sunk into a French province.

[Mr. Ewart most ably fulfilled these instructions, and it was mainly owing to Sir James Harris's foresight of the importance of gaining over to the Orange party the future King of Prussia, that his decisive intervention in 1787 resulted.]

EXTRACT OF A DESPATCH FROM SIR JAMES HARRIS TO
THE MARQUIS OF CARMARTHEN.

Hague, 15th Nov., 1785.

ON Sunday morning a courier arrived from Versailles with the definitive Treaty of Peace, signed there the 8th instant; and yesterday one of Mons. de Brantzen's secretaries brought that of an alliance concluded the 9th, between the Court of France and the States General.

Both these events have been for so long a time fore-told as certain, that they can only be considered as the completion of the system of the party which has usurped the government of this country. They take no one by surprise, or unprepared; but I must, in justice to every thinking member of the Republic, say that, far from giving them pleasure, they have raised in their minds strong sensations of concern and apprehension. The unjustifiable precipitancy with which the last of these measures has been carried into execution, proves that the ruling faction here felt they had no time to lose, and that, to secure to themselves a duration of power and influence, it was necessary, at any price, to purchase the support of France.

The Province of Zealand exceeds my most sanguine expectations; it has already declared its strong disapprobation of a French Alliance, and may, if properly supported, be led any lengths. I have sent a friend on whom I can depend to Middlebourg; he went away yesterday, and is furnished with proper materials for keeping up the spirit of the province.

Utrecht seems coming round fast, and I am far from thinking it impossible, when it is made evident here that England is not entirely indifferent to the well-being of the Republic, that the *majority* of the provinces will refuse to ratify the Alliance. I have little doubt, however, that in this case Holland would take the ratification on itself, and that France would consider that as sufficient: but such a manifest violation of the Act of Union would be as good a weapon in our hands as any one we could have; and the attempt will, I flatter myself, be thought worth making.

If it is attended with the smallest degree of success, much good may arise from it; if it fails, it will stand on record that England did not see her old friend and ally depart from every principle of political wisdom without holding out her hand to save her.

EXTRACTS OF A DESPATCH FROM THE MARQUIS OF CARMARTHEN TO SIR JAMES HARRIS.

St. James's, 17th Nov., 1785.

SIR,—Your very important despatches by Frome, and by the Dutch mail, together with their several inclosures, have been received and laid before the King.

In obedience to His Majesty's commands, the confidential servants of the Crown have taken their contents into their most serious consideration; and I am now, Sir, to inform you of the result of their deliberations, which, having met with His Majesty's most gracious approbation, will point out to you the line of conduct you are to observe at this very critical and important period.

The great and important object of your attention must be, to prevent, if possible, the ratification of the Treaty of Alliance already signed between France and the United Provinces. Difficult as this attempt may appear, perhaps it is not absolutely desperate. Should this event, however, actually take place, and a measure so alarming to the interests of this country be formally concluded, it must then become our care to endeavour to excite such an opposition to the ruling party who have brought it to perfection, as at least to render the effects of it as little pernicious as possible to our own prosperity and safety.

The expediency of the measure proposed by you, Sir, of presenting a *Memorial* to the States General, and thereby giving a public and convincing proof of the King's friendly attention to the welfare of the Republic, as well as paternal regard to the interests of His Majesty's own dominions, naturally became the subject of our most serious and deliberate consideration; and after having given the utmost attention to the reasons which you have urged with so much ability in support of your proposal, and weighing the consequences likely to result from a different line of conduct, we agreed that a Memorial* ought to be presented, &c.

DESPATCH FROM SIR JAMES HARRIS TO THE MARQUIS OF CARMARTHEN.

Hague, 25th Nov., 1785.

I AM now to give your Lordship a more full account than it was in my power to do on Tuesday, of the effects the Memorial I presented that morning has produced, and of the various steps I have since taken in consequence of it. It absorbs the general attention of both parties, and is the topic of universal conversation.

As I found it met the warmest approbation of our friends, and that it was sought after with great avidity, I had it printed this morning in the Dutch and French Gazette at this place, and I have little doubt of its producing the best effects on the minds of the people at large.

* This Memorial did little more than assure the Dutch of His Majesty's continued interest in their affairs; but Mr. Ellis describes it in his work as producing a great effect in the States, in raising the desponding spirits of the Stadtholderian party.

It is particularly adapted to please that part of the nation (by far the most numerous) who are perfectly neutral, who have no political leanings whatever, are averse to all foreign connexions, and whose ideas are all centred in trade, and who consider the importance of this country to consist not in its political, but in its commercial consequence. It is to these that I particularly address myself, under the entire conviction that, if we can bring their system to prevail, we shall ensure to ourselves in time complete success.

I intend going very shortly to Amsterdam and Rotterdam, and endeavouring to fix on the minds of the trading inhabitants of these two great cities the imminent danger to which the French Alliance exposes their wealth and credit. The protest from Zealand, and my Memorial, have, I know, already claimed their attention; and the recollection of their losses is still too fresh in their memories not to make them dread the idea of another rupture with England.

It was by operating on the fears and interests of the merchants, that Mons. de la Vauguyon broke the first link of the connexion between England and Holland. It is lawful to take advantage of his lessons, and attack our artful and persevering enemies with their own weapons.

I shall continue, my Lord, to cherish and encourage the glimmering prospect of recovery which just appears to us. If, from the nature of the business, I should be sometimes compelled to move before I can receive any specific instructions from your Lordship, I must rely on your candour and indulgence to forgive me if I err.

Colonel Bentinck is returned from Loo. He says nothing can be more judicious than the conduct and sentiments of the Princess, that she sees very clearly the inability of the Stadtholder's party to come forward, and that the Stadtholderate can only be saved indirectly.

He repeated to me, from her, almost word for word, the same expressions she used the day of her departure from hence, and her assurances that no consideration should ever prevail on her to separate herself from the Prince.   That all proposals tending to that point, from *whatever quarter they came,* would be rejected by her; and that, if the Prince was forced or frightened away, she was determined with her children to accompany him.   She expressed her obligations to His Majesty in the most respectful and grateful terms, and entreated me to convey her high sense of them on every proper opportunity.

As for Him, I wish I could say the accounts were equally advantageous. Irresolution, anger, despair, and timidity rule him by turn, and the whole of his conduct is so light and inconsistent, that the further he is off the better.

EXTRACT OF A DESPATCH FROM SIR JAMES HARRIS TO THE MARQUIS OF CARMARTHEN.

Hague, 2nd Dec., 1785.

THE French Ambassador was not so well received at Amsterdam as the partisans of that Court affected to give out he had been.   There was no deputation of the Magistrates, no complimentary speech, and, except a great dinner Van Berkel gave him, his reception was not different from that of other persons of distinction who come there.   He, however, succeeded in the point on which he was the most alarmed; and news was brought here yesterday by Mons. Abbéma, one of the most violent of the Amsterdam Patriots, that the council of that town had, with only *one* dissentient voice, agreed to the ratification of the Treaty with France.

This does not afford me a very promising prospect of success, but I am, however, still determined to go there to-morrow.   Attention and cordial assurances never can do harm; and, if they cannot raise a spirit of opposition in the minds of our friends, they will, at least, take from our enemies the faculty of describing me as inimical in my views to the Republic, and striving to raise a fermentation in the State. Patience, temper, and forbearance are the principal ingredients I must employ, and with these I do not despair in time to make the French party feel that England still exists in Holland.

[The following is the first intimation of Mr. Pitt's conversion to the *active policy* recommended by Lord Carmarthen and Sir J. Harris.]

LETTER FROM THE MARQUIS OF CARMARTHEN TO SIR J. HARRIS.

St. James's, Dec. 6th, 1785.

MY DEAR SIR,—I have this moment received a letter from Mr. Pitt, in which he expresses himself inclined to think that " you ought to be instructed (without delay) to *redouble every possible effort* within the next fortnight, if the Stadtholder's timidity has not rendered all opposition to the French Alliance desperate."

EXTRACT OF A DESPATCH FROM SIR JAMES HARRIS TO THE MARQUIS OF CARMARTHEN.

Amsterdam, 8th Dec., 1785.

I CAME here on Saturday last, and have been employing the intermediate days in attending to the main object of my journey hither. As I was well aware that I should be most minutely watched, it was expedient for me to avoid any marked application to business, and I have endeavoured to give my visit, as much as possible, an air of curiosity, by accompanying Lady Harris to see the many objects worthy notice which this city affords.

Previous to my arrival, I was informed that there were insurmountable difficulties attending the presentation of a petition similar to that I had proposed; not because there were not grounds sufficient, nor because there were wanting a number of persons in trade who admitted the truth of every part of it, but because the power of the ruling faction was at so high a pitch just now, and their proceedings so arbitrary, that no one could be found bold enough to be the first to set it on foot.

I have since verified, from my own observation, this account of my friends, and am reluctantly forced to abandon (at least in this town) a measure from which I flattered myself much good might be derived. If, however, I have been compelled to renounce all hopes of obtaining this public mark of alarm, I do not despair of having impressed on the minds of several individuals of weight the dangerous consequences with which the French Alliance may be attended.

EXTRACTS OF A DESPATCH FROM SIR JAMES HARRIS TO THE MARQUIS OF CARMARTHEN.

Hague, 13th Dec., 1785.

THE Peace is only ratified by the four Provinces which originally agreed to it. Friesland, Gelderland, and Zealand have *refused their consent*, and declared their intention of not contributing their quota to the sum of money to be paid to the Emperor. The States of Holland flatter themselves, I understand, to raise these ten millions by a loan in this country, at three per cent.; but I should much doubt its being filled at a moment when capital can be placed out at so much higher interest, and in full as good security, both in France and England. They will, however, strain every nerve rather than lay on new taxes, as well because there does not remain a single article of luxury or necessity that is not already overcharged, but because on this occasion they must studiously avoid displeasing the people, to whom in general the Peace is already very obnoxious.

As to the Treaty of Alliance, it would have been ratified by only three Provinces, if the Prince of Orange would have afforded me the most trifling assistance, or, indeed, if he would have only seemed to approve what I was doing. In Gelderland everything went in perfect conformity to the plan I had proposed. The majority of the Diet were prepared to reject the Treaty of Alliance; and it would have been actually rejected if the Prince of Orange, through Mons. de Lynden de Hemmett, had not declared his wish that it should be otherwise, giving for reason, that, as he was resident in this Province, such a conduct would expose him to the accusation of using an undue influence in the deliberation of its States!

In Friesland, matters were taking the same turn, and marred precisely in the same manner. Too inconsiderable to oppose the will of the Province of Holland without a certainty of support, both Gelderland and Friesland were in a manner compelled to give up their opinion, and vote with the majority. The ratification passed without a debate, and will be sent to-day by a messenger to Fontainbleau.

Your Lordship may judge, from the violent proceedings of the French party here, how strong they feel themselves; how much they set all opposition at defiance; and how impossible it is, deserted as I am by the Stadtholder, unsupported by any of my colleagues, and surrounded by spies and emissaries, and with no one assistant who unites judgment with courage, or good-will with influence, to make any favourable impression here, or to shake in this, their first hour of triumph and glory, the power of the usurping Faction. I think I may venture to say I have left nothing untried. I have been moving in all the Provinces where I thought I could produce any effect. I have attended to the great towns of Holland, and endeavoured to spread a just alarm among the commercial part of their inhabitants. I have been striving to create a party by working on those passions most likely to predominate, on the fear, on the vanity, and on the avarice of those with whom I have been dealing; I have spared no pains to efface the idea of England's entertaining any resentment against the Republic, and held everywhere, and to all descriptions of men, the language of friendship, temper, and moderation. To those only who were absurd or vain enough to suppose that the cordial style in which my Memorial of the 22nd Nov. was conceived was the effect of fear, I have taken the liberty to express myself differently, and to point out to them (in case they should be so inconsiderate as to join their new ally in a war) the dangerous enemy they would have in England, and the weak and inefficient friend they necessarily must have in France, from the topographical position of the two kingdoms.

Every attempt to prevent the final ratification of the Alliance having proved abortive, it now becomes my duty to turn my thoughts towards such measures as may more or less conduce to hinder its effects from producing all those evils with which it seems to be fraught. Although every hour I pass in this country ought to correct me of that sanguine disposition towards which I naturally incline, yet I still am very backward to despair, and, while I see anything which is likely to be attended with the remotest prospect of success, I shall not willingly quit the field.

What I have been doing for these last six weeks has let me more into the character and temper of these people than as many years would under different circumstances. I am satisfied, in my observation both on those who govern and on those who are governed, that things cannot remain long as they are, that they never will take a degree of consistency under the present form, and that the prevailing system of the day being founded on French intrigue from without, and on passion and

personal pique from within, will fall to pieces with the
first political convulsion in Europe, which must in some
shape or other, since the work of yesterday, reach this
Republic. It seems to me, therefore, to be our business
to keep awake, as much as we can, the attention of those
on whose minds I have already fixed a degree of alarm
relative to the consequences of this Alliance.

The only means which occur to me for keeping this
disposition from dying away is, to remind them from
time to time that the Treaty they have so inconsiderately
subscribed to is not of a *defensive* alliance, but of an
offensive one, and that it must inevitably, sooner or
later, involve them in the quarrels of their great neigh-
bours.

We may begin by asking, whether the Treaty is
purely defensive, as expressed in the preamble? And
if it is, how we are to understand what is meant by the
Fourth Article, which stipulates that succours are to be
granted by the Republic to France *en tout cas où Sa
Majesté Très Chrétienne éprouverait des hostilités par
mer*, without any exception of aggression, or any pro-
vision being made for the refusal of succours, supposing
the attack to be wantonly provoked by France for the
purpose of raising a war?

Besides these questions, which may all be couched in
terms of the most friendly inquiry, we have to observe
to the Republic, that these engagements are contrary to
the Triple Alliance of 1717, which Mons. de Vergennes,
very artfully, and from no friendly motives to this country, took care should be inserted in the last treaty of
peace between England and France, though he suffered
it to be omitted in that between England and Holland. Your Lordship will forgive me for throwing
these various suggestions on paper; my wish to strain
every nerve to save a sinking cause must serve as my
apology.

EXTRACT OF A DESPATCH FROM SIR JAMES HARRIS TO THE MARQUIS OF CARMARTHEN.

Hague, 16th Dec., 1785.

I HAVE received this morning the strongest assurances that the Province of Zealand is determined to persist invariably in its present principles, that it will go any lengths to which I choose to push it, and is ready to separate from the Union, and put itself under the immediate protection of England. I replied with expressions of great applause to the laudable spirit they manifest, and encouraged it by every vague assurance I could make. I avoided, however, touching on their offer of throwing themselves into the hands of England, till I know in what manner your Lordship orders me to receive it.

DESPATCH FROM THE MARQUIS OF CARMARTHEN TO SIR JAMES HARRIS.

St. James's, Dec. 23rd, 1785.

SIR,—The idea of the Province of Zealand separating itself from the Union, and recurring to the protection of England, can by no means be encouraged in the extent the very proposal implies. That so respectable a part of the Republic should endeavour to resist the despotic system of the present ruling faction, is most desirable: but when the bare supposition of the serious consequences which might result to this country, even from the Seven Provinces engaging us in a war, though for the maintenance of our common interests, demands no trifling degree of consideration; the defection of one single Province cannot, by any means, justify a risk on our part of such a nature.

DESPATCH FROM SIR JAMES HARRIS TO THE MARQUIS OF
CARMARTHEN.

Hague, 6th Jan., 1786.

My Lord,—The States of Holland met yesterday,
but, contrary to the general expectation, they came to
no important resolution on any one subject whatever.

The delay in their decision is only a putting off of
the evil hour: when it does take place, it will come
with all that violence and inveteracy which generally
characterize a triumphant faction; and the Stadtholder
may expect that, after his privileges are gradually
wrested from him, they will proceed to more serious
extremities, and bring various accusations against him
for neglect of duty and misconduct in the high trust the
States have reposed in him.   At the head of these
stands the charge of preventing the Dutch fleet from
being sent to Brest in 1782;* and, besides this, which
in the present temper of their Government, is likely to
be treated in a very grave manner, they have, I understand, four or five others, taxing him with remissness
and inattention, both in his direction of the army and
in his preparations for the defence of the Republic, as
well in the English war as in that with the Emperor.

It is needless to inquire on what these charges are
founded; they are brought, not for the sake of justice,
but make part of a plan which, your Lordship will have
seen from my despatches, has been long in agitation.

There is no doubt what will be the event; the accusations will all be deemed just.   The Stadtholder will
be under the heavy imputation of having, in several
instances, betrayed his trust.   Grounds will be laid for
a criminal process against him, and, with this object
of terror in their hands, the Faction will have attained

* M. de Vauguyon had demanded for his Court ten ships from the Dutch
to join the French fleet; but Admiral Hartsink and the Captains asserted
that they could not comply with the order, as their ships were unfit for sea.
They were accused by the French of being bought by us, and betrayed by
the Stadtholder.—*Harris Papers.*

to what I pointed out to be their ultimate aim, so long
ago as last year; and the Stadtholder be reduced, either
to leave the country and abdicate his office, or else to
fling himself at the feet of the Patriots, and to hold it
under their controul and good pleasure.

I prevailed on a person on whom I can rely to go to
Loo yesterday, and I desired him to regulate his language according to what he found to be the temper of
the Court. If he perceived the Princess convinced in
her own mind that there is no safety for herself and
children but through France, I requested him to give
me the quickest information possible of it, but not to
make any attempt to alter her opinion; but if he perceived Her Royal Highness to be wavering, and not
unmindful of those elevated sentiments she expressed to
me at her departure, I then instructed him to use every
argument in his power to induce her not to give in to
the insidious views of France and the Patriots. That
it was more honourable for the moment, and would in
the event be certainly more advantageous, for the
Prince and her to continue at Loo, than to return to
the Hague circumscribed in their power, and submitting to regulations prescribed to them by a set of
men, their avowed enemies; to make her feel that every
privilege which they consented to give up would never
be restored them, while they would ever have a right
to reclaim those which were taken from them by force.
That, in the course of a few years, events must occur
from without which would call the attention of France
from this country, and from within which would divide
the Patriots amongst themselves. That this would be
the hour for the Prince to assert his rights and privileges, and that then there would not be wanting
Foreign Powers who could give him efficacious assistance; that it was better to wait for these events with
patience, firmness, and resignation, than by one precipitate and despondent act diminish for ever the power and
greatness of her family.

EXTRACT OF A DESPATCH FROM SIR JAMES HARRIS TO
THE MARQUIS OF CARMARTHEN.

Hague, 13th Jan., 1786.

THE person who was so good as to go to Loo at my
request, returned from thence yesterday. His report
may, I believe, be depended upon. He found the
Prince just as I described him, strongly agitated by
various passions; not sufficiently collected within himself to have any opinion of his own; too suspicious and
mistrustful to adopt that of others; and withal so neglectful in fulfilling the common duties of his office, as
to furnish every day, by his remissness and inattention,
fresh grounds of complaint against his administration of
the Stadtholderate.

As for the Princess, he describes her as thoroughly
feeling her situation; acknowledging freely that the
support held out to her by her uncle, the King of
Prussia, is an inefficacious, if not a fallacious one; yet at
the same time confessing she has followed his advice,
and concurred with his Minister here in soliciting the
good offices of France.

From what he observed from her behaviour, as well
as from what he heard during his short stay with the
Court, he seems convinced that the King of Prussia has
the sole and entire direction of the Princess; that she
ultimately subscribes to everything he advises, even
when it is in contradiction to her own judgment.

He assured me that all the letters from Potzdam recommended her, in the strongest manner, to avoid every
appearance of acting in concert with me, and that she
had been repeatedly blamed in them for having treated
me with so much confidence during her last residence at
the Hague.

While the heads of the House of Orange at Loo are
thus instrumental in hastening their own downfall, nothing passes here which gives the smallest room to hope
that the intervention of His Prussian Majesty will be
productive of any good consequence whatever.

EXTRACT OF A DESPATCH FROM SIR JAMES HARRIS TO
THE MARQUIS OF CARMARTHEN.

Hague, 17th Jan., 1786.

THE plan of the French and Patriotic party for
annulling the Stadtholderian influence, or rather for
getting it into their own hands, seems hastening to its
maturity.

Van Berkel's reply to the Prince's memorial is ready,
and will shortly be published. It is more eloquent than
argumentative, and calculated solely to depreciate the
Prince personally, and to inflame the minds of the people against him.

The French Ambassador now does not conceal what I
was satisfied he had been about these last six weeks,
and avows that his Court has given him orders to
communicate with the Prussian Minister on whatever
may concern the regulations to be made relative to the
Stadtholder. I must, however, add, in justice to Mon.
de Thulemeyer, that he is by no means satisfied with
the effect of these instructions; and that he sees clearly
France means nothing more than to gratify the King of
Prussia with a semblance of acting with him, while,
in fact, its real and cordial co-operation is with the
Patriots.

As soon as Van Berkel's reply has had time to be
dispersed, and to have produced the effect it is expected will be produced by it, I understand that conditions will be then drawn up, and proposed to the
Prince to sign.

I cannot precisely specify them; but I know that
they in general amount to the depriving him absolutely
of all his power, and vesting it in the hands of a council, which council is to be composed of the leading Patriots themselves.

It therefore remains to be seen whether there still
exists enough of the ancient partiality for the House of
Orange in the people to resent this opprobrious behaviour towards it.

It also remains to be seen, when the Patriots have usurped the Executive as well as the Legislative power, whether the people will submit patiently to so new and irregular a form of Government; for it will neither be an aristocracy nor democracy, but an oligarchical administration, acting under the impression of foreign influence.

To these events we must look forward with patience; we cannot accelerate them, much less can we produce them.

EXTRACT OF A DESPATCH FROM SIR JAMES HARRIS TO THE MARQUIS OF CARMARTHEN.

Hague, 20th Jan., 1786.

THE donation of the two line-of-battle ships to France passed the States of Holland yesterday. In order to induce those of Friesland to subscribe to it, it was agreed to purchase two 74-gun men-of-war the Frieslanders began building some years back, but which the distressed state of their finances prevented their finishing.

EXTRACT OF A DESPATCH FROM SIR JAMES HARRIS TO THE MARQUIS OF CARMARTHEN.

Hague, 3rd Feb., 1786.

As more favourable accounts of the King of Prussia's health are come from Potzdam, and his immediate dissolution no longer appears a probable event, the Faction (from everything I can learn) are determined to carry into execution, without loss of time, their views against the Stadtholderate.

The town of Amsterdam has declared the answer Van Berkel has made to the Prince's memorial, and which, as I have already mentioned, is a performance full of acrimony and personal invective, to be perfectly conformable to their sentiments and opinions, and as such it will be read to the States of Holland when they assemble.

The great point, " to whom the command of the garrison here belongs," will be then discussed; and I am afraid that it will be given against the Prince.   This once determined, the Faction proceed in the execution of their plan; and in a very few weeks we shall probably see the whole of the executive power wrested from the Stadtholder.

It is needless, I trust, for me to say that I can do nothing in favour of the Stadtholder.   Besides the no-weight of an English Minister here at this moment, the Prince himself has put it out of my power to assist him, by the infinite pains he takes to declare he has no relation or connexion whatsoever with me.

EXTRACT OF A DESPATCH FROM SIR JAMES HARRIS TO
THE MARQUIS OF CARMARTHEN.

Hague, 21st Feb., 1786.

I HAVE reason to believe that the States of Holland will again break up, without having come to any final resolution relative to the command of the garrison at the Hague.

The Prince declares he will not subscribe to any terms which may tend to diminish essentially the dignity and influence of the Stadtholderate; and Mons. de Lynden de Blytterswyk, who, as I mentioned in my last, was sent to sound the way, found him too irritable to undertake the commission, and is returned without having ventured to show to his Highness the conditions he had in his pocket.

There is undoubtedly a strong fermentation amongst the people here, and a growing animosity against the French and the Patriots.   But it will avail nothing, unless it were to be directed by an able chief; and, should it break out now, it would, like all unsuccessful insurrections, only tend to give weight and strength to the party it was meant to suppress.

Your Lordship will probably have heard, that, to a very long, elaborate speech, full of compliment and flattery, which the Dutch Deputies made to the Emperor on taking leave, His Majesty confined his answer to these words: " Messieurs, je suis bien aise d'avoir fait votre connoissance."

EXTRACT OF A DESPATCH FROM SIR JAMES HARRIS TO THE MARQUIS OF CARMARTHEN.

Hague, 24th Feb., 1786.

THE French influence here is at its highest pitch, and it bears down everything before it. I have lately discovered, to a certainty, what I had always the strongest reason to suspect, that they support their party here not only by intrigue and cabal, but by the expending immense sums of money in bribery and corruption; and that to maintain their interest in the different towns of this Province alone it costs them yearly upwards of 50,000*l.*

The sudden turn in the conduct of the Provinces on the East India business was, I have little doubt, produced by the same means.

The very Deputies who, two days before the proposal for the East India Reform came before the States General, promised me to vote against it, were the first to give their vote for it; and their countenances, when I taxed them with breach of promise, betrayed evidently to what I was to attribute it.

I am unalterable in my opinion of what will happen relative to the Stadtholder. The Faction wait in hopes to force him to consent to their terms, and to make the subversion of the Stadtholderate his own act and deed.

LETTER FROM SIR JAMES HARRIS TO THE MARQUIS OF
CARMARTHEN.

Hague, 28th Feb., 1786.

MY DEAR LORD,—What I mentioned to you some
posts ago, of the Court of Versailles having set the King
of Prussia at ease relative to the Bavarian Exchange,
has been since confirmed to me from two channels,
neither of them contemptible ones.   It has been even
hinted to me, that this *quieting draught* was sent and
delivered by Mirabeau,* who gave out that he went to
Berlin to be received at the Royal Academy there.

In addition to the information I have received, I
must needs confess, as well from what is passing under
my eyes as from the incoherent language and sham confidence of the Prussian Cabinet towards Lord Dalrymple,
that I strongly admit in my own mind the belief of a
secret understanding and fellow-feeling between Prussia
and France, and that they say to each other, as Molière's
doctors, "*Passez moi la rhubarbe, et je vous passerai le
séné.*"   "Let me alone in Holland," says France, "and
you, Prussia, shall have nothing to fear in Bavaria."

My Danish colleague here is a person from whom
neither use nor instruction can be extracted.   He has a
mouth, which, if it went on in a straight line, would
undoubtedly extend from ear to ear; but, as it makes
an angle of forty-five degrees with his chin, it begins
when he laughs, or rather grins, at his left eye, and
ends at his right ear.

---

* Mirabeau was an unaccredited agent of France at Berlin.   His letters
from thence were published in a book entitled "La Cour de Berlin, par un
Voyageur;" and much has been said as to whether they were genuine.   In
the first leaf of a copy at Heron Court, the following note by the second Lord
Malmesbury decides the question :—"On the 27th April, 1834, I met Prince
Talleyrand at dinner at Lord Tankerville's.   The Prince was at that time
Ambassador at our Court from that of the Tuileries.   In alluding to this
work, I remarked that it was generally attributed to Mirabeau.   Prince
Talleyrand observed, "Mais oui, c'étoit bien lui qui l'a écrit."   I added,
that it appeared to me to be the correspondence of an *agent* at that time of
the French Government.   Prince Talleyrand immediately replied, "C'étoit
avec moi qu'il correspondait."

EXTRACT OF A DESPATCH FROM SIR JAMES HARRIS TO THE
MARQUIS OF CARMARTHEN.

Hague, 3rd March, 1786.

In consequence of the resolution I mentioned in my
last, it is now ordered, that, while the States of Holland
are sitting, military honours should be paid to no one;
that they are to receive them on their meeting and on
their breaking up; and that each member has a right
to pass during the assembly in his carriage through a
gate, which till now was only open to the Stadtholder.
His arms were also effaced from the colours of the Dutch
Guards a few days ago, and those of this Province substituted in their place. The Prince may judge from
these proceedings of the little reliance to be placed on
the moderation and forbearance of the Faction.

The Chamber of Zealand protests violently against the
conduct of the other Chambers of the East India Company, and threaten to separate their stock and interests
from the general mass.

EXTRACTS OF A DESPATCH FROM SIR JAMES HARRIS TO THE
MARQUIS OF CARMARTHEN.

Hague, 7th March, 1786.

As I have some information I think it important for
your Lordship to know without loss of time, I send over
a *valet-de-chambre*, on whom I can depend, with these
letters, in a Scheveling fishing-boat.

The Rhingrave of Salm, whose departure I mentioned
in my last, carries, for the approbation of the French
Ministry, the plan the Faction have adopted relative to
the future existence of the Stadtholderate. It is, that
the Prince of Orange should be set aside, and that the
Princess should be declared Gouvernante during the

minority of her children, with a council appointed to assist her in the direction of all affairs, as well military as civil.

This council, in whom the whole authority of the Stadtholder will reside, is to be composed of the leading Patriots; and Salm has modestly proposed and obtained their consent, that he should preside in it himself, at the head of the Military Department.

This plan, which is nearly the same I mentioned to your Lordship long ago, has been finally resolved on, upon the Prince having positively refused to subscribe to any conditions which obliged him to renounce the constitutional privileges of the Stadtholderate. The Princess, *I am assured*, thinks like the Prince, and has declared she is determined to abide by his fate, let it be what it will.

The King of Prussia, from the beginning, has been acquainted with every step the French and Patriotic faction have been taking here relative to the Prince.

However important the intelligence contained in my other letter of this date may appear, I should not have thought it *by itself* of a nature sufficiently pressing to have authorized the sending away a special messenger. France has intimated to those of the Faction in whom she places the greatest confidence here, that *a rupture with England in Asia* is not at a very distant period. That it is, therefore, of the utmost consequence that no time should be lost in increasing the naval and land force of the Republic in that quarter of the world.

In consequence of this insinuation, the leading Patriots have come to a resolution, *amongst themselves*, to send, as soon as they can be got ready, four ships of the line, and four frigates, with as many troops as the ships will hold over and above their complement, to the Cape, where they are to remain for further orders. Mons. de Cotleuri, whose name I have more than once mentioned, is the person the French employ here to carry through this part of the negotiation. His language is, that our power in India is exorbitant, and our intentions hostile to a degree; that we must be kept down there, at any rate, &c.*

EXTRACTS OF A DESPATCH FROM SIR JAMES HARRIS TO THE
MARQUIS OF CARMARTHEN.

Hague, 10th March, 1786.

THE *Vroedschap*, or Council-Chamber, of Amsterdam decided yesterday, that the command of the troops in garrison at the Hague belonged to the Stadtholder as Captain-General of the Union, and not to the Committee of the States of Holland. The question was carried by a majority of six votes (twenty against fourteen).

I confess I am not so sanguine as many of the Prince's friends, who think it will be attended with great advantages to him, and give a decisive turn to his affairs in this Province.

I sincerely wish I may be mistaken, but, after the information I sent your Lordship in mine of the 7th March (the authenticity of which I cannot doubt), I scarce can see a possibility of the Stadtholder's recovering his influence by anything short of a revolution effectuated by force.

---

* At the end of the last year, France, with the intention of attacking our territories in India, prevailed on the Patriot leaders to transfer the direction of military affairs there from the Dutch East India Company to themselves. They asked that four ships of the line should be fitted out, and that the Directors should take French troops into their pay. Sir James Harris exerted himself to the utmost to exasperate the East India Company against the Patriots and their Allies, and eventually succeeded in thwarting their object.—*Harris Papers.*

DESPATCH FROM SIR JAMES HARRIS TO THE MARQUIS OF
CARMARTHEN.

Hague, 17th March, 1786.

MY LORD,—The following incident has happened since
I made up my other letters of this date, and I have learnt
the particulars barely in time to catch the post. Your
Lordship may recollect, that according to the new regulation of the honours to be paid to the States of Holland
during the time of their sitting, one was, that a gate,
known by the name of the Stadtholder's Gate, should be
opened to the members to and from their way to the
assembly.

The mob was so great yesterday, the first day of these
honours taking place, that, although the guards had been
doubled, none of them thought it prudent to pass through
this gate, particularly as it led to a drawbridge on which
the populace was assembled. To-day about four P. M.,
on the breaking up of the assembly, Mons. Gyslaer ordered his coachman to drive through it. The mob, who
had taken post on the bridge, refused to let him pass,
and endeavoured not only to stop the horses, but to push
his carriage over the chains into the canal.

As this resistance was expected, a considerable body of
soldiers were at hand, who immediately came to the relief
of the Pensionary of Dordt, and dispersed the people.
The ringleader, a hairdresser, established from his infancy
at the Hague, is the only person taken into custody as
yet ; but, as the civil magistrates are very active in their
researches, it is probable several others will be discovered
before to-morrow. Never was a plan so ill-combined, or
so ill-executed.

The people will be too closely watched ever to be able
to make a second attempt, and this first having failed,
only tends to give strength and energy to the Faction.

There is no doubt but this unfortunate hairdresser
will be condemned to die; and I hear that Gyslaer is preparing all his eloquence to excite the States of Holland

to-morrow to revenge this daring attack on their rights as Sovereigns of the Province.

EXTRACT OF A DESPATCH FROM SIR JAMES HARRIS TO THE MARQUIS OF CARMARTHEN.

Hague, 21st March, 1786.

THE States of Holland have ordered that the hair-dresser, who attempted to stop Mons. Gyslaer's carriage on Friday, should be considered as accused of High Treason, and be tried, not by the Court of Holland according to the common course of justice, but by the Committee of the States. The trial began yesterday. He rests his defence on his having seized the reins because he was in danger of being run over. It, however, has been clearly proved on the other side, that he had used several threatening expressions before the assembly broke up; and that, when he was seized by the civil power, he turned round to the mob, and reproached them bitterly for having abandoned him.

There is little doubt indeed, from the temper of the times, and from the spirit of the Faction, that, even supposing this unfortunate man to be innocent, he would be found guilty and condemned to die; but I fear it will come out in evidence that it was a premeditated attack.

The obtaining intelligence becomes every day more and more difficult. The friends to the old cause, disheartened by ill-success, gradually leave the Hague, and retire to the distant Provinces. The more timid ones dare not see or speak to *me*, and many whom I found well disposed on my arrival have gone over to the opposite party.

The Hague itself is more like a besieged town than an open village, the guards are doubled during the day, and the streets at night are covered with patroles. The police has, I am told, twelve hundred spies in its pay, and no one of the smallest consequence can stir without being attended by one or more of these emissaries.

EXTRACT OF A DESPATCH FROM SIR JAMES HARRIS TO THE
MARQUIS OF CARMARTHEN.

Hague, 24th March, 1786.

SENTENCE of death was pronounced yesterday on the
hairdresser, who stood accused of High Treason for disobedience to the Placards of the States of Holland. He
was brought to the scaffold this morning between ten
and eleven, but was reprieved on the moment the exe-
cutioner was putting the rope round his neck.

It would be perhaps uncandid not to attribute this act
of mercy solely to principles of humanity, yet some are
not wanting who assert that it was the effect of fear ;
and, indeed, to judge from the number of troops employed to surround the gallows, the States were under
strong apprehension of a popular insurrection. Everything, however, passed off in perfect tranquillity ; and I
think there is every reason to be assured that this ill-
concerted attempt will be the only struggle the inhabitants of the Hague will venture to make against the
oppression of the ruling Faction, who, after this event,
will govern them with more severity than ever.

My accounts from Amsterdam are rather favourable.
The division among the Regents increases daily, and the
majority are on the right side. The violence and abuse
of the opposite party seem to have animated them, and
personal invective has given them that degree of union
and spirit no public consideration could ever produce.

I think it prudent to take no share whatever at so
early a period in this altercation, but to let matters
ferment, and the breach widen.

I therefore confine myself in my language to terms of
general applause and encouragement, and to my endeavours to keep up my personal connexions at Amsterdam, and to obtain regular and authentic information.

EXTRACT OF A DESPATCH FROM SIR JAMES HARRIS TO THE
MARQUIS OF CARMARTHEN.

Hague, 28th March, 1786.

THE whole of the proceedings on the hairdresser's trial have been arbitrary to a degree, and in direct contradiction to the mode of trial prescribed by law.

The prisoner was convicted without sufficient evidence ; after he was condemned, a confession was extorted from him under the hopes of being pardoned ; and after this confession they cruelly kept him in suspense till the very moment his sentence was to have been executed.

The power of pardoning for capital crimes has ever been considered as belonging to the Stadtholder ; on this occasion the States of Holland assume it themselves.

EXTRACT OF A DESPATCH FROM SIR JAMES HARRIS TO THE
MARQUIS OF CARMARTHEN.

Hague, 31st March, 1786.

IT is not on the cards at this moment to reclaim this country. Everything both foreign and domestic concurs to throw it into the arms of France, where it must remain till some convulsion in Europe forces it into its natural position, or till there exists here a party wise and powerful enough to wrest the government from the hands of the present usurpers.

The Stadtholder *had* such a party ; but, as he did not know how to avail himself of it while it existed, it cannot be supposed that he can restore it from its ashes.

It will require a length of time, and a degree of management and conduct scarcely to be expected, before the division which prevails in the Regency at Amsterdam can be formed into a steady and real opposition. The discontented Regents are of such motley characters, so little versed in public business, and so disconnected with each other, that although they may be brought to act in concert and vigorously on some point where they consider the municipal privileges of their great city as invaded, yet I much doubt that the same energy and union would extend to a more general principle, or that they would hold together in a regular and systematic attack on the present ruling Faction.

I have had a long and serious conversation on this subject with Mons. De Rendorp, one of the reigning Burgomasters, who is at the head of this set, and who directs all its operations. He is a man of excellent parts and great activity, and who carries his views as far as I could wish them to go. But neither he nor I are so sanguine as to be blind to the many difficulties to be got over before this *third party* can be shaped into a form ; and it is to be feared, even supposing it should not perish in its infancy, the space of time which must elapse before it can attain to any degree of consistency, will be sufficient for the French and Patriots to have accomplished all their designs and completed the ruin of the Republic.

___

EXTRACT OF A DESPATCH FROM SIR JAMES HARRIS TO THE
MARQUIS OF CARMARTHEN.

Hague, 7th April, 1786.

THE Court of Versailles declares that she will not suffer any Foreign Power whatever to interfere in the internal arrangement of the Government of this country ; and that, if any one should attempt it, *she will oppose such interference by force.*

Mon. de Verac has orders to signify immediately this determination of his Court verbally to the Pensionary of Holland, and to the Leaders of the Faction ; and it is expected, I am told, he will soon be instructed to express it in a regular Memorial to the States General.

The Faction are greatly elated with this intelligence ; and, confident in their strength, seem to set all opposition at nought. They will proceed, without loss of time, in the execution of their plan ; which, I have little doubt, will end in a total subversion of the Stadtholderate. The Prince of Orange will not hear of the terms they propose to him ; and I am almost equally sure that they will be rejected by the Princess.

EXTRACT OF A DESPATCH FROM SIR JAMES HARRIS TO THE MARQUIS OF CARMARTHEN.

Hague, 5th May, 1786.

I AM happy to inform your Lordship, that the Dutch East India Company have rejected both the ideas suggested by Mon. De Cotleuri, and will neither hear of any additional fortifications in their settlements nor admit a body of 6000 French troops into their service.

I got just in time to hear their determination on the last of these points, and to furnish them with additional arguments for putting a strong negative on it.

EXTRACT OF A DESPATCH FROM SIR JAMES HARRIS TO THE MARQUIS OF CARMARTHEN.

Hague, 16th May, 1786.

I AM sorry to say that I have every reason to believe that my opinion relative to the inefficacy of the friendly party at Amsterdam was but too well founded. My letters from thence describe it as indolent and timid, and giving way every day to the threats and violence of their antagonists.

I expect to-day or to-morrow the Pensionary of Zealand, Mon. Vander Spiegel, who comes to the Hague almost purposely to see me. If he answers the description I have heard of him, he is greatly superior to all those with whom I have had hitherto to deal. A very few conferences with him will probably clear up what ought or ought not to be done with the Province of Zealand.

DESPATCH FROM SIR JAMES HARRIS TO THE MARQUIS OF
CARMARTHEN.

Hague, 26th May, 1786.

I AM now to transmit to your Lordship, as accurately
as my memory will permit me to do, an account of two
very interesting conversations I have had in the course
of last week with Mon. Vander Spiegel, Pensionary of
Zealand.

After a few general observations on the melancholy
situation of this country, and animadverting on the
various causes to which it was to be attributed, he came
to that of his own Province, and entered fully into the
state of persecution and oppression to which Zealand was
exposed under the direction of the present Rulers of the
Republic.

He said he had long since seen the storm gathering,
and had done everything in his power to prevent its
breaking ; but, not succeeding in that, he had spared no
pains to prepare his Province to meet it with becoming
spirit and resolution.

That, in conformity to these sentiments, Zealand had
uniformly, and from the beginning, opposed and pro-
tested against every measure brought forward by the Faction ; and its political doctrines were become so evident,
that it was no longer in its power to retract ; and, now
that matters were hastening to a crisis, Zealand had no
choice left, but either submitting to a dishonourable and
oppressive capitulation with the Patriots, or else to throw
themselves on the protection of some Foreign Power ; that
the choice, in his opinion, did not admit of a doubt ; and
that it was on this important point he wished to speak to
me, flattering himself that in the course of what he had to
say he should be able to do away the scruples which he
understood existed on our part, and make it appear that
it was as greatly for the advantage of England to take
Zealand under its protection, as it was for that of Zealand
to court and solicit the protection of England.

Being thus induced to speak, he went on by saying,
"that it was the firm intention of the State of Zealand
to persist in instructing that portion of the East India
Company which belongs to their Province to refuse positively to consent to the reform adopted by the other
three-fourths in the administration of Indian affairs.

"Zealand is ready to consent that their share of the
East India Company shall be annexed (*incorporée* was
the word) to that of England, to whom they will make
over a participation of *all the rights* they hold by
charter, both in Europe and in Asia, provided the whole
trade be carried on under the English flag, and that
England will consent to afford the same protection ('la
même sauvegarde') to the Zealand ships in India as to
its own."

Mon. Vander Spiegel stopped here, to see the effect
this proposal had upon me ; and I made no difficulty of
expressing to him my feelings.

I declared that it was the strongest mark of attachment and confidence which could be given, and would, I
was persuaded, be considered as such by my Royal
Master and his confidential servants ; that it was in
itself so vast a matter, and comprised so many incalcu-
lable consequences, that it was impossible for the mind
to embrace them all at once, or to pronounce (without
taking in consideration how it might terminate for England) whether, by our closing with their proposal, it
might not lead to events which would leave even the
Province of Zealand in a worse situation than that in
which it now stands.

"You imagine," said the Pensionary of Zealand, "that
it would immediately produce a war ?" I answered, I
confessed I did. "And you think, perhaps," added he,
"that the risks to which a war would expose you are
greater than the advantages either you or we can obtain
by it ?" I replied, I was strongly inclined to apprehend
they would be so. "I was prepared," said Mons. Vander
Spiegel, "to meet your objection, and, with your permission, will combat your opinion with openness and
freedom." I begged he would.

"In the first place," said he, "we do not require that
the arrangement we propose should take place immediately. We are sure of receiving our next returns from
India, and can consequently go on upon our own bottom
for a twelvemonth longer. It is at the expiration of that
term we shall call upon Great Britain for protection, and
content ourselves till then with a promise made immediately and ministerially, that it will not be refused us.
Under that sanction we shall proceed with security, and
prepare everything for the event which is to happen.

"*You* suppose," said he, "a war will be the consequence. *I* think otherwise ; and am disposed to believe
that Great Britain, standing forth the declared friend of
Zealand, and Zealand's not hesitating to say she will
separate herself from the Confederacy of the Union if her
rights are contested, is likely to spread a terror amongst
the Patriots, to give encouragement to those who are well-
disposed, and to contribute to restore the ancient system.
If this should be the effect," added he, "you will admit
it to be a most salutary one, and I shall have obtained
the completion of my wishes.

"France is by no means ready for war ; and, if she
were, it is doubtful whether she would think the object
of sufficient magnitude to draw the sword. Besides,
England will only be following her example, and doing
in Zealand what *she* has been about in Holland. If
France has a right to be partial to her friends in the
Republic, England surely is allowed, and even is called
upon, to protect us. If Sweden has a right to lend the
Port of Gothenburg to France, Zealand has equally one
to lend Flushing to England.

"But," said he, "admitting *war* to be the consequence,
let us duly weigh the risks with which it would be
attended against the advantages which might be obtained
from it, and see which will sink the scale.

"Zealand, though, from its population, and the quota
part it pays, is only reckoned a tenth part of the Belgic
Confederation, is, nevertheless, from her local situation,
by far the most important Province of the Union. It has
the only port in the Republic (Flushing) capable of

admitting large ships-of-war, at the same time that it is the key of all the trade between Holland and Flanders.

"On the east and south it is surrounded by the Scheldt; on the north by the Maese; and six frigates would protect it against any possible invasion by land. Its position gives it the command of the German Ocean; secures the Baltic trade; and an English fleet stationed at Flushing would effectually prevent any vessel from coming out of the Texel undiscovered. It is filled with sailors, has arsenals well stored, and docks for repairing and building the largest ships; the very privation of which would throw insurmountable impediments in the naval armament of the Dutch.

"No junction between the French and Dutch fleets could take place; the French would never venture amongst the shoals and currents of the North Sea, without having one port where they could take shelter; and the Dutch must either go North about, or through the Channel.

"Essequibo and Demerary also," added he, "are under the sole direction of Zealand; and these, as well as our share of the East Indian Trade, will also be at the disposal of England.

"Such are the advantages," continued he, "which would arise to England from having a free exclusive use of the Ports of Zealand;" and he concluded by saying, that "all these advantages would belong to France, if we left Zealand to its fate; for notwithstanding all his efforts, and the spirited temper of the Province in general, it must, if abandoned, inevitably bend under the yoke of the Patriots." He hoped, therefore, I would take into consideration what he had said, and, if I was impressed myself with the importance, endeavour to give the same impression at home.

I told him it was my duty to make faithful Reports of whatever I heard of a public nature, but that I never presume to annex to my Reports any opinion of my own; that I took care to relate as accurately as I was able; but that it remained in the breast of my Royal Master to direct what measures were, or were not, the most eligible to be pursued.

LETTER FROM SIR JAMES HARRIS TO THE MARQUIS OF
CARMARTHEN.

Hague, 26th May, 1786.

AFTER knowing nearly what are your Lordship's sentiments relative to the defection of Zealand, I could almost
have wished not to have been forced to have heard Mr.
Vander Spiegel on the subject; but besides the utility
which might result from a knowledge of the sentiments
of the man, who has certainly the best understanding in
the Republic, I hope neither the manner in which I encouraged him to speak out, nor that in which I terminated
our conversation, will in any means have pledged my
Court, or distress your Lordship in the smallest degree
for the reply you may think proper to make.

It is evident, beyond a doubt, that Zealand is the *last
hold* we have here, and that, if we lose it, we shall not
have the remnant of a party left in the Republic ; but I
am very far from pronouncing that it is equally evident,
that, if we give in to the Pensionary of Zealand's proposal,
we shall increase our influence and reinstate the ancient
system.   On the contrary, if I may speak freely, I think
this much more likely to be done by a total secession on
the part of England from the affairs of this country; by
leaving it to struggle under the pressure of anarchy,
ignorance, and oppression; and, by letting it feel the madness and iniquity of its present leaders, compel it to have
recourse to new measures.

In regard to the various advantages which would result
from England's being able to dispose of Zealand in any
way she pleases, it is a *military*, rather than a *political*
calculation; and, even admitting all Mr. Vander Spiegel
says to be true, these advantages may still be purchased
at too dear a rate.   It depends on various considerations
of infinitely more magnitude than those which come immediately under my care, to determine on their solidity.

EXTRACT OF A DESPATCH FROM SIR JAMES HARRIS TO THE
MARQUIS OF CARMARTHEN.

Hague, 6th June, 1786.

NOTWITHSTANDING what I advanced in my separate
letter of the 26th May,* I submit to your Lordship's
judgment the outlines of a measure, which, if it meets His
Majesty's approbation and is properly supported here, it
is thought may still prevent the French influence from
rooting itself in this country, and contribute to reinstate
the principles of the ancient system.   It is at all events
certainly the last trial that can be made under the
present circumstances, and, if it is either rejected or
should fail, no hopes of effecting anything good remain.

The Provinces from the beginning, hurt at the dicta-
torial conduct of Holland, seem at this moment disposed
to manifest their dissatisfaction in a decided manner;
and, if they were to be well advised, and saw an appearance of support held out to them, might be soon led to
unite in a body, and form a mass of regular and systematic opposition.

The Prince of Orange's visit to Zealand, together with
a general discontent which pervades the whole body of
the people, fills the Patriots with anxiety and uneasiness.

In consequence of this situation of doubt and dilemma, which exists on one side, and of the favourable
symptoms which appear on the other, Mons. Vander
Spiegel is of opinion that something might be attempted,
and the plan he has formed in his own mind is this:

"That the Prince of Orange should forsake that wavering conduct he has hitherto observed; that he should
assume a decided character; and, having obtained no one
good by affecting to be of no party, put himself at the
head of that which can alone maintain him in the possession of the prerogatives of his high office.   That he
should treat the Patriots as enemies to his House, and to
the established constitution of the State; and, acting up

* Recommending non-interference for the present.

to these principles, oppose the operations of France, and look up to England as the only Power who can afford him or the Republic sincere and real support. That if the Prince can be prevailed on to listen to this salutary advice, and to declare resolutely and openly that he means to pursue a line of conduct consonant to it, then Great Britain might, without exposing herself, and with infinite utility to the States, step forward and give some ostensible mark of her readiness to support every measure which may be adopted to preserve the Stadtholderian form of Government, and to restore a political union between the two countries."

The Pensionary of Zealand undertakes himself the most arduous part of this task, and is ready by every argument in his power to endeavour to impress the Prince of Orange during his readiness at Middleburg with a sense of the necessity of doing something for himself, if he expects his friends ever to do anything for him.

We have agreed on a means of his letting me know how he succeeds ; and he expresses his earnest wish, that, if he should be fortunate enough to make a proper impression on the Prince, England should then take up her part in the business, and give in such a Memorial as would serve to evince to the friends of the good cause that she had not forsaken them, and make it appear to the Republic at large how different the true and genuine political sentiments of Great Britain were from those the Faction thought proper to ascribe to her.

A manly declaration coming so unexpectedly from the Prince during his residence in a Province which brought about the Revolution in 1747, backed by all the support which, though not expressed, would be inferable from such a Memorial,—coming, moreover, at a moment when the Patriots are embarrassed,—it is thought would give them a severe shock ; and, if the measure was followed up with vigour and method, might possibly put an end to their political existence.

The co-operation between Mr. Vander Spiegel and myself is to be carefully concealed from the Prince (at least for a time), as he is of so suspicious a turn, and so jealous of being governed, that it is probable the umbrage he would take at this circumstance would make him blind to all the advantages he might derive from the measure.

I have only to add, that my hopes on this occasion are buoyed up by those of Mr. Vander Spiegel. My deference to his opinion is not slightly founded. He is the only man the Patriots dread, the only one the other side *universally* acknowledge as *superior to them all.*

EXTRACT OF A DESPATCH FROM SIR JAMES HARRIS TO THE MARQUIS OF CARMARTHEN.

Hague, 13th June, 1786.

It is matter of real satisfaction for me to perceive that your Lordship's sentiments, relative to the expediency of making a stand if possible against the progress of the French influence here, concur so entirely with those expressed in mine.

The plan was so fully explained in my last, that, as far as relates to its texture, I have nothing more to add. Its success depends on its being executed *in time;* and your Lordship is already acquainted with the dates, both of the meeting of the States of Holland, and of the Prince's arrival in Zealand. The mainspring of the whole transaction is the Stadtholder.

From the state of the Provinces there is every reason to expect that three of them will warmly concur with the Prince and Zealand.

Amsterdam, if properly managed, will certainly also go with us. That city must be treated with delicacy, and be well assured that no idea is entertained of diminishing the high rank and influence its opulence and consideration entitle it to in the direction of the Government of the Republic. Other towns in this province are also to be got at, and I only wait for a determination to set my emissaries at work at Dordt and Haarlem ; Rotterdam will come round the moment it has a prospect of support held out to it, and I do not despair of dividing even this whole Province throughout, so as greatly to fetter its operations on the present occasion.

The whole of this favourable change, which seems to have come about so unexpectedly, is owing solely to the glaring attempt made by the Faction to take the supreme direction of the East India Company into their own hands, and to render it subservient to the purposes of France.

EXTRACT OF A DESPATCH FROM SIR JAMES HARRIS TO THE MARQUIS OF CARMARTHEN.

Hague, 23rd June, 1786.

As far as my own expectations go, I am already arrived much beyond what I could ever presume to have hoped. Four Provinces, and I trust the town of Amsterdam, are ready to co-operate with the Prince under the influence of England, to restore the constitutional Government of this Republic ; and it scarce admits a doubt, if the Stadtholder will join us, that we shall drive the Pensionaries from their strongholds, and wrest the reins of Administration from their hands.

The reception of the Stadtholder in Zealand has exceeded all expectation. Mynheer Vander Spiegel made him an excellent speech at the head of the States the day after his arrival, and the next day all the towns (except Zuriczee) sent him a deputation of their magistrates.

LETTER FROM SIR JAMES HARRIS TO THE MARQUIS OF CARMARTHEN.

Hague, 27th June, 1786.

As the hour of action draws nearer, I am sorry to say I find the alacrity and courage of my friends flag ; they return to their favourite system of procrastination as a dog to his vomit, and it is next to impossible to keep them to the collar. I have carefully concealed from

them all, except Vander Spiegel's confidant, the attempt
I am making in conjunction with him on the Prince. I
have by this means brought them all to promise, to a
man, that if he moves they will move also, from the conviction they are under that nothing can put him in
motion. This is all I can wish for, as my coming forward is only *conditional:* it is, however, painful and
tedious beyond description to work with such tools; it
is like mending a pen with a scythe, or mowing grass
with a penknife.

The people are too ready to second us; and I do not
know which I most fear, their over-eagerness, or the
backwardness of those of a higher class. You would not,
I am sure, my dear Lord, desire to be here, if you felt
the unpleasant anxiety of all these contradictory circumstances; and particularly if, as I do, you saw the greatest
possibility of success likely to be lost from the flaccid
and sluggish character of those with whom you were
acting.

EXTRACT OF A DESPATCH FROM SIR JAMES HARRIS TO THE
MARQUIS OF CARMARTHEN.

Hague, 27th June, 1786.

THE French party here seem totally occupied in the
support of the Free Corps; * and I should not be surprised if the attempt to suppress them in the Assembly
of the States of Holland should produce a serious
tumult.

The people of the Hague, in defiance of repeated
orders to the contrary, cover themselves with orange-
coloured ornaments, and are so ripe for insurrection that
it is no easy matter to keep them quiet.

It is one of my most anxious solicitudes that they
should not be put in motion too soon; and I recommend
it most earnestly to my friends to dissuade them from
committing any overt act which may expose them to the

* Democratic Militia.

rigour of the new laws, before our party is strong enough
to bear them through. I know, beyond a doubt, that the
Faction wish for nothing so much as an event of this
kind ; and I am in my own mind persuaded that among
those who wear the orange-coloured ribbons there are
many of their own adherents, who are instructed to provoke the people to be riotous, purposely to furnish the
Patriots with an argument for the necessity of keeping
up the Free Corps.

EXTRACT OF A DESPATCH FROM SIR JAMES HARRIS TO THE
MARQUIS OF CARMARTHEN.

Hague, 4th July, 1786.

I RETURNED from my excursion in the neighbourhood of
Amsterdam late yesterday afternoon. The chief object
of my visit was to keep up the friendly disposition which
begins to show itself in the conduct of that city, and
which can only be maintained by a constant and unremitting attention. Mons. Vander Spiegel gives me to
understand that everything goes on as well as can be
expected, and pledges himself, for his Province, to receive
the friendly Declaration of His Majesty with all the sentiments of gratitude and respect it so justly calls for. He
assures me, that he has the best hopes of the Stadtholder's perseverance, and that he finds him eager in his
endeavours to re-establish his interest in the Provinces.

Things being thus circumstanced, I have determined to
give in my Memorial to-morrow. I shall to-day see some
of the friendly Deputies of Gelderland, Friesland, Zealand,
and Utrecht, and desire of them to be careful that it be
taken *ad referendum*. This will give an opportunity to
each Province to give its opinion separately on its contents. It is an excellent sign, that nothing relative to
the measure proposed has transpired. I have been obliged,
in order to obtain it a proper reception in the Assembly
of the States General, to trust various persons; and nothing serves more to prove their zeal and sincerity than

their having kept the secret so religiously. The French suspect I am about something, and their friends are hard at work ; but I believe none of them guess we are so ripe for execution.

EXTRACT OF A DESPATCH FROM SIR JAMES HARRIS TO THE MARQUIS OF CARMARTHEN.

Hague, 7th July, 1786.

ON Wednesday morning I delivered in to the President of the week, the Memorial* I had it in command to present to their High Mightinesses. According to the established custom, I waited first on the Pensionary of Holland and the Greffier, and gave to each of them a copy.

The President of the week, Mons. Voerst Vander-Bergel, of the Province of Overyssel, whom I had worked up through my friends to give a proper reception to the communication I was about to make to him, exceeded everything I could have wished, and, forgetting the responsible character in which he stood, pledged himself to go any lengths to serve me.

At eleven o'clock the Memorial was presented to the States General, and immediately taken *ad referendum* by six of the Provinces, Holland alone voting it as merely a simple communication. This was more than I expected. I reckoned upon four of the Provinces, but I could not flatter myself that the whole Generality† would have given the same vote.

The States of Holland are adjourned for three weeks, and this intermediate time will be employed by both

---

* This Memorial stated, that His Britannic Majesty disavowed all intention of interfering in the domestic concerns of the Republic, but expresses his earnest wish, " that the Government should be preserved in those hands to which it has been intrusted by the Constitution, and founded on principles established by the unanimous consent of the whole nation."

† The geographical term for the Six Provinces annexed, by the Act of Union, to Holland.

sides in canvassing the Provinces. I trust, as we stand on high ground, we shall not lose our advantage ; and that, in spite of the virulent opposition of Holland, I shall obtain a becoming and satisfactory answer to my Memorial. If this can be effected, the corner-stone of the party may be considered as laid ; and if there is no relaxation on the part of the Stadtholder, or negligence on my side, it may gradually gain strength and consistency.

To-morrow, all those friends who have so well assisted me dine here ; and I shall make a point of assembling them frequently at my house, fully persuaded, that besides the consideration I myself shall acquire from treating them hospitably, the bringing them together often will contribute more than anything else to give them courage and confidence.

I have had the Memorial translated into Dutch, in a way to lose none of its force and energy, and it will appear to-day in several of the Dutch newspapers.

EXTRACT OF A DESPATCH FROM SIR JAMES HARRIS TO THE
MARQUIS OF CARMARTHEN.

Hague, 11th July, 1786.

MY Memorial seems, from the impression it makes, to have perfectly answered the purpose for which it was intended. The conduct, as well of our friends as of our adversaries, proves that it has come remarkably well timed. The first express great satisfaction at receiving this public mark of countenance and support from England, and begin to acquire a degree of vigour and union which may produce the most happy consequences ; the latter, whom it had taken quite by surprise, are alarmed and embarrassed, and, ignorant of what has given rise to this step, do not foresee how far it may extend.

They are more particularly uneasy at the vote given unanimously by the six Provinces against that of Holland, for taking my Memorial *ad referendum*.

EXTRACT OF A LETTER FROM SIR JAMES HARRIS TO THE
MARQUIS OF CARMARTHEN.

Hague, 14th July, 1786.

I HAD very great pleasure from your kind private
letter of the 11th, which came to hand this morning ;
I am truly happy you approve my conduct. As long as
I have this approbation, I shall not regret or repine at
any fatigue or labour with which my mission may be
attended. You will, I hope, not forget that I cannot
command success, neither can I alone promote it ; I
trust, therefore, I shall not be judged after the event of
the present contest—which, after all, is as likely to be a
defeat as a victory. My endeavours have been to bring
matters to a struggle, and to prevent this nation bending
under the yoke of France, without lifting up a finger in
its defence.

The assurances of support I held out to the Prince in
my letter to him, and which you think rather too strong,
are perfectly conformable to the verbal instructions I was
honoured with in the Cabinet previous to my coming to
the Hague. We risk nothing. If the Stadtholder as-
sumes that degree of spirit and vigour I require of him,
our *countenance* alone, without any *real support,* will
bear him through with success ; if he does not assume it,
the bargain is void. I still, too, return to my old theme—
*France never will fight for this country, not even if Eng-
land was to attempt to reduce it by force.*

EXTRACT OF A DESPATCH FROM SIR JAMES HARRIS TO THE
MARQUIS OF CARMARTHEN.

Hague, 18th July, 1786.

THE Faction are straining every nerve to subdue in its
infancy the party which is forming against them; and as
the Patriots are well aware, if it gains head, that their fall
is certain, they seem determined to proceed to extremities
in order to prevent its progress.

Their agents are employed on every side in encouraging the Free Corps, and in endeavouring to work them up to their purpose. Van Berkel went in the night disguised, on Saturday, to Utrecht, and was in conference for some hours with the chiefs of the seditious Burghers of that town ; Gyslaer, as I before said, is in Gelderland, and will probably visit both Groningen and Friesland before his return. Inferior agents are dispersed about in the smaller towns in this Province; and their rendezvous for communicating reciprocally their intelligence is at Leissendam, a village upon the canal between the Hague and Leyden, and where probably the first sparks of insurrection in this neighbourhood will appear.

The Rhingrave of Salm returned from Paris on Sunday night, and the whole tribe of French Emissaries have been since constantly shut up with him.

My express is returned from Zealand, and has brought me the Minute of the answer the States of that Province intend to make to my Memorial. ·This Minute I shall endeavour to get adopted as a report from the Secret Committee of the States, and to be sent as such to the several Provinces, whose sanction, I have little doubt, it will receive. Several weeks, however, must elapse before this can be effected, and during this space of time many incidents may arise to make the upshot of this measure of very little consequence.

LETTER FROM THE MARQUIS OF CARMARTHEN TO SIR JAMES
HARRIS.

Tunbridge Wells, July 24th, 1786.

MY DEAR SIR,—I received yesterday a copy of your despatch of the 18th, with its inclosures ; as likewise your two obliging private letters, with the papers from Berlin. You know my favourable opinion of Mr. Ewart, and consequently the attention I shall ever give to his *opinion* as well as *intelligence*. In the present instance, however, I must *pause* before I stir a step upon the grounds he has laid down for our future proceeding. My own manner of thinking with respect to Austria and Prussia remains, and probably ever will remain, unshaken : the first ought to be the *perpetual*, as it is the *natural* ally of England ; the second can, I apprehend, be but at best an *occasional* one ; and whatever conduct either foreign influence, momentary ambition, or even personal caprice, may induce those Powers to adopt, the relative situation in which they truly stand with respect to England must never be lost sight of. Could any doubt be entertained upon this situation, let any one ask his own judgment, which of those Powers can ever prove most formidable to France, and the doubt will instantly be removed.

Ewart seems to forget the circumstances which last year drove us to the necessity of even a confidential overture to Prussia. The *Electoral* Ministers had exasperated the Emperor against the King, and of course rendered the connexion between Austria and France more formidable than ever to England. In this situation the Ministers of the Crown naturally felt themselves justified in sounding the dispositions of Prussia;* though you well remember the distrust of anything like sincerity or friendship towards us from that quarter, and the declining to co-operate with us to any effect in Holland. The event of a new Sovereign in Prussia may certainly produce great and important changes in the future conduct of that Court.

In two words, I never desire a connexion with Prussia, unless Russia, and of course Denmark, are included ; and even this arrangement, in my mind, will ever be far less desirable than one in which Austria is to be united with us.

* Through Lord Cornwallis.

LETTER FROM LORD DALRYMPLE* TO SIR JAMES HARRIS.

Berlin, 25th July, 1786.

DEAR SIR,—I have received your letter, and am happy to find your Memorial is like to produce so good an effect.   I have not been able to learn precisely the sentiments of the King of Prussia with relation to it ; but I believe he is still of opinion that England should take no ostensible part in Holland.   In general, they appear to be apprehensive here lest it should increase the vigilance of France, and give fresh activity to the Opposition ; and few seem to think anything effectual can be done in the present circumstances.   I flatter myself you will prove that they are mistaken.

I am going to-morrow to Cassel, to invest the Landgrave with the Garter.   It is a commission I could readily have dispensed with.   I am, with sincere esteem,

Dear Sir, your most obedient Servant,

DALRYMPLE.

EXTRACT OF A DESPATCH FROM SIR JAMES HARRIS TO THE MARQUIS OF CARMARTHEN.

Hague, 25th July, 1786.

IN regard to the conduct of the measure which at this moment more particularly occupies my attention, I have only to say, that everything is prepared in the manner I mentioned in my last despatch of Friday ; and that unless the Faction produce some counter operation to-morrow, when the States of Holland meet, (which we do not expect,) there is every reason to hope we shall carry the answer with a high hand.

My messenger is returned from Zealand.   I have obtained the full powers for the Deputies of that Province to conclude definitively on the answer, without referring

* Lord Dalrymple was the ostensible English Minister at Berlin, Mr. Ewart the real one.

any more to their constituents for orders. The Prince and Princess continue acting in great harmony, and I experience strongly the good effects of this union.

Mons. Vander Spiegel comes hither on Thursday, and I shall concert with him our future plans of operations. He is the only man who has a head equal to the conception of great ideas, and whose energy and courage increase with the pressure and difficulties of the moment, let them be ever so great. The others require perpetual driving, and I tremble lest they should fail at the pinch.

EXTRACT OF A DESPATCH FROM SIR JAMES HARRIS TO THE MARQUIS OF CARMARTHEN.

Hague, 28th July, 1786.

THE States of Holland assembled on Wednesday. This meeting, as usual, passed in matters of form; but yesterday they voted, *ten* Towns against *nine*, that the command of the garrison of the Hague does not belong to the Stadtholder, but to them in their quality of Sovereign of the Province.

This measure, treated with so much importance by the Court, and considered by many here as the test by which the Prince was to sink or recover, never has appeared to me in the same light; and its being carried now in the way it has been (which from the beginning was clearly to be expected) does not, in my opinion, place the Stadtholder in a situation at all worse than that in which he stood before. He, on the contrary, is relieved from a state of disagreeable suspense; and this manifest attack upon one of his most incontestable privileges removes every scruple he may have hitherto had of protesting in a clear and explicit manner against the violent and unconstitutional proceedings of the ruling Faction.

It ought also to bind the two great towns of this Province more strongly to his interest, as Amsterdam and Rotterdam are both in the minority; and the insult is, perhaps, aimed as directly at them as at the Prince himself. It will likewise irritate more than ever the inhabitants of the Hague against the Patriots, as the Court is now, in a manner, for ever rendered incapable of residing here. On the whole, therefore, as things must come to a crisis before they can mend, I confess I do not see any evil from this resolution having been taken.

The Chairman of the Secret Committee, Mons. de Spaer de Hardesteyn, read to them the draft I inclosed in mine of the 18th inst.*

It was approved by all the Provinces, and would have been immediately reported, if the representative of Holland, M. de Starenberg, had not desired a delay, before he gave his opinion, till Tuesday. In this, the other members thought it proper to acquiesce, and the final conclusion on the subject now stands for that day.

The Prussian Minister called upon me very early this morning, to express his alarms and uneasiness at the resolution taken yesterday by the States of Holland relative to the command of this garrison. As he had never before opened his lips on the subject, I did not think it necessary to enter deeply with him into it; and, after hearing all he had to say, I replied, that I considered it as a vote aimed particularly at Amsterdam, and which at the same time carried with it a strong mark of inattention towards his Court, who had officially and specifically interested herself on this score. That I therefore took it for granted Amsterdam would resent this insult in a becoming manner; and that I entertained no doubt of its greatly irritating His Prussian Majesty, and convincing him of the little reliance to be placed on the moderation of the Faction, or on the assurances of Mons. de Vergennes.

I should, perhaps, have been less reserved with Mons. de Thulemeyer, if I had not the strongest reason to believe that *he* is the principal cause of the Committee's having adjourned to Tuesday, without having come to

---

* This inclosure, and many others relating to this Mission, were in a volume of the Harris Papers which is lost.

a determination ; and if I had not solid grounds for suspecting, that, rather than England should have an early and civil answer, he would forego the claim of one being made to his own memorial delivered in so long ago.

The Russian Minister has been very troublesome with his questions and misgivings of late. He infers very injudiciously, and with that hastiness very inseparable from narrow minds (from what he sees),* that I am acting in perfect concert with Mons. de Thulemeyer ; and concludes with the same unwarrantable precipitancy, that the two Courts of London and Berlin are actually entered into engagements directly opposite to the interests of the two Imperial Courts.

After having, with great patience and temper, day after day, endeavoured to do away his idle fears, I could not help telling him this morning (on his returning to the charge), that I was really tired of perpetually saying the same thing ; that his endless doubts became quite injurious, and that experience ought to have taught him, if he had any recollection, that I had never deceived him ; that, as for the rest, I really should in future be silent on the subject, and make no reply whatever to any question, directly or indirectly put to me, which tended to express a suspicion on a point I had ever been so explicit upon.

I told him I had only to add, that he was responsible for the tenour of the reports he made to his Court from hence ; and that if, in consequence of his despatches, he should mislead the Empress so far as to drive her from the natural bent of her inclination and the manifest interests of her Empire, and induce her to adopt a system in contradiction with the interests of Great Britain, the time would come when he would be *at least sorry* for what he had done, as he would be destitute of any proof in support of the doctrines he had broached. This language will, I am sure, keep Mons. de Kallitcheff in order for a month or two.

---

* A sentiment of the pure old Diplomatic school—analogous to the one which considers words as intended only to conceal our ideas.

EXTRACT OF A DESPATCH FROM SIR JAMES HARRIS TO THE
MARQUIS OF CARMARTHEN.

Hague, Tuesday, 1st August, 1786.

THE Resolution taken by the States of Holland on
Thursday, depriving the Stadtholder of the command of
the troops quartered here, engrosses the whole attention
of the Republic. The Prince of Orange, on its being told
him, betrayed neither of those symptoms I was apprehensive he might ; he received the news with great calmness,
and waits patiently at Loo (where he arrived on Saturday) the advice and opinion of his friends relative to the
conduct it best becomes him to pursue. A few days will,
probably, decide what is to be done. It has been proposed to the Patriots to suspend the effect of this Resolution, to declare it was an act of Sovereignty the States
exercised without ever intending to put it in force ; and
that, if the Stadtholder will return to the Hague, he shall,
as formerly, be left in quiet possession of the garrison.

This proposal has not been made to them (as all
former plans of reconciliation were) with an air of submission and solicitation ; but it has been told them in
very clear and explicit words, that, if it is not subscribed
to, a majority of the Provinces are determined to oppose
the irregularity of their proceedings, and to unite in their
endeavours to prevent the discord and confusion now
introducing in the government of the Republic.

The three Pensionaries, Van Berkel, Zeebergen, and Gyslaer, are *all* against anything like a composition ; but their
partisans are less violent, and almost unanimously incline
to adopt the *tempérament* proposed. France, as may be
imagined, sides with the Pensionaries ; and, indeed, it was
merely because we were out-bid by that Court at Gorcum
and Schiedam, that we lost the majority in the towns on
Thursday last. It remains to be seen to what lengths
France will go to support the Pensionaries. On this I
have only to say, that nothing will tend so effectually

to destroy their popularity as a manifest interference of France in their behalf.

Mons. Vander Spiegel is both the author and principal actor in the execution of this plan. We meet frequently (in the night), and everything which is determined upon is the result of our nocturnal conferences. If the proposal should be rejected, the *confederation* amongst the Provinces will be immediately declared, and the Prince of Orange is pledged to put himself at the head of it.

The great cities of Amsterdam and Rotterdam will protest strongly against the proceedings of Thursday; and if, either by threats or persuasions, one or more of the inferior towns can be brought over, the question will again be brought forward, and the resolution now in force be overruled.

The King of Prussia's conduct has not varied since I have been here, neither does it on the present occasion. He has (as on a similar one last year) publicly declared his disapprobation of the Memorial I have just presented, and is careful to a degree to make it appear he has no wish to serve the Stadtholder (or rather the Princess of Orange) but through the complacency of France.

LETTER FROM SIR JAMES HARRIS TO MR. EWART.

Hague, 8th August, 1786.

As I do not foresee any early opportunity of writing to you by a safe conveyance, I must employ ciphers, although they will not permit me to enter so amply into the contents of your two last private letters as I ought and could wish to do. I extracted from that by Mr. Porter such parts as seemed to me essential for His Majesty's Ministers to know; and I have the satisfaction to assure you, that in their reply they expressed the highest approbation of your zeal and abilities. As they are in possession of the important information you have been so kind as to trust me with, relative both to the actual and

probable future situation of your Court,* it remains with
them to determine the line of conduct which is to be
observed.

I, however, will tell you in confidence, and it is for
your private ear alone, that I can observe they pause, and
are unwilling, till matters are cleared up still more, to
take so decided a part in favour of Prussia as to shut the
door entirely against Austria. Many motives, which I
cannot enumerate in a letter of this kind, but for the
force of which, I flatter myself, you will give me credit,
contribute to justify this system of delay. Our future
safety, as well as future consequence, depend on our not
committing ourselves imprudently on the Continent. My
own private opinion, after what I have just said, is of
little weight : but, lest you should accuse me of having
altered it, I will repeat, that whenever it is made evident
to me, on one side, that Prussia will and *can* enter into
general and extensive connexions with England everywhere and on every political point; on the other, that
Austria is irrevocably cemented to France; I then shall
promote, to the utmost extent of my influence, the forming a Prussian connexion. This, you may recollect, has all
along been my language, and I do not see any reason
to alter it.

The favourable appearances in the Prince of Prussia,
even if supported by positive assurances, can only be considered as contingencies. *Events* alone must decide his
option when he mounts the throne, and no previous promises can or ought to bind him. England is not in a
situation to want allies; and warm as I am in wishing to
see her once more topping her part on the Continent, yet
I had rather wait for the moment (which must come
sooner or later), when, instead of seeking connexions, her
alliance shall be sought for. This seems to me to be the
system adopted by the present Cabinet, and it incontest-
ably is a wise one.

* Frederick's end was impending, and Mr. Ewart had elicited from Count
Hertzberg and the Prince of Prussia the most favourable sentiments, and
even promises respecting the future support of the Stadtholder in case
England would declare herself in his favour, and also on the project of an
Anglo-Prussian Alliance.—*Harris Papers.*

In the meantime great attention should be shown to every friendly power, particularly to the Prince of Prussia; and I flatter myself, that neither the King himself nor our Ministers will be deficient when his Uncle drops.

In short, my dear Sir, everything denotes the propriety of delay. *La poire n'est pas mûre* is a favourite word of your old King's, and we may thank him for having taught it us.

EXTRACT OF A DESPATCH FROM SIR JAMES HARRIS TO THE MARQUIS OF CARMARTHEN.

Hague, 15th August, 1786.

THE French Emissaries are harder at work than ever, and they seem, in conjunction with the leaders of the ruling Faction, determined to bring matters to as speedy a conclusion as possible; their chief instrument which they mean to employ is, as I have before said, the Free Corps. With this armed mob, devoted entirely to their service, and which they term *the majesty of the people*,* they intend to drive from the Civil Governments of the towns such Regents as are inimical to their views.

If the town of Amsterdam is wise enough to see its own interests, and bold enough to maintain itself against the popular clamour, I think still, great room is left for hope. I can venture to be responsible for the States General, and I trust for the Stadtholder; but these are not powerful enough to resist the weight of the Province of Holland supported by France. Amsterdam must, therefore, at all rates be got; and the Stadtholder will rather submit to act for a while under the protection of that city, than not obtain its voice.

* It would thus appear, that this hackneyed cant phrase originated amongst the most contemptible of all political bodies that ever existed.

DESPATCH FROM SIR JAMES HARRIS TO THE MARQUIS OF
CARMARTHEN.

Hague, Tuesday, 22nd Aug., 1786.

My Lord,—The King of Prussia fell into a state of
stupor on the night of the 16th, and died early the next
morning.

Although a Hanoverian messenger brings over to your
Lordship letters from Lord Dalrymple, I think it my duty
to communicate to you this important piece of news in as
expeditious a manner as possible, and I have in consequence given orders that an extra packet-boat should
sail immediately from Helvoet.   I shall write to-morrow
by the common post.   I have, &c.

LETTER FROM SIR JAMES HARRIS TO THE MARQUIS OF
CARMARTHEN.

Hague, 22nd Aug., 1786.

I was so eager to get away the Hanoverian messenger
this morning, that I did not think it even permitted to
detain him whilst I wrote a few private lines on the subject of the important event which took place on Thursday
last.   It must in some shape or other tend to clear off
the mist which has so long darkened our political ho-
rizon.

The King of Prussia constituted the Russian Monarchy,
and it is very doubtful whether his successor will be able
to support the same part he played with such *éclat* for so
many years.   Modest virgins have become wives of gal-
lantry, and the wisest Heirs Apparent have turned out
the weakest Kings.

EXTRACT OF A DESPATCH FROM SIR JAMES HARRIS TO THE
MARQUIS OF CARMARTHEN.

Hague, 25th Aug., 1786.

SINCE the news of the King of Prussia's death has
become public and certain (for it was not credited at
first), the Patriots have been very busy among themselves.
There has been a temporary suspension of their operations. The French persist in assuring their party that no
material alteration will take place in the conduct of the
Cabinet of Berlin.

Mons. de Verac goes so far as to pledge his Court for
the truth of what he asserts, and to declare that positive
assurances on this subject have long since been received
at Versailles. A short time must necessarily clear up
this fact, which at present is hidden under an impene-
trable veil.

EXTRACT OF A DESPATCH FROM SIR JAMES HARRIS TO THE
MARQUIS OF CARMARTHEN.

Hague, 1st Sept., 1786.

I WENT to Loo on Sunday, and returned late yesterday
morning. Nothing could be more gracious than the reception Lady Harris and myself met with; and I had only
to regret, that the indispensable necessity of not being
long absent from the Hague obliged me to refuse the
pressing invitations both from the Prince and Princess to
lengthen our stay.

The States of Gelderland were to meet the day after
at Nimeguen; and the Members were in a manner all assembled at Loo, to consult on the most proper means of
asserting their rights and maintaining their privileges.
My arrival gave them great satisfaction; and I was not
a little pleased myself to find a body of men, representing the most respectable Province of the Union, arrived at a pitch of anger and resentment to which I
have so often wished to bring the minds of our friends
and well-wishers. The Stadtholder partook strongly of

this sensation ; and he closeted me immediately after my appearance, to tell me the measures he had already taken, and those which he intended to advise the States of Gelderland to take.

In regard to the first, he had immediately ordered all the regiments of Holland out of Gelderland, and sent them to Dutch Flanders and to the Pays de la Généralité, and replaced them by others on whom he could depend. These orders were issued an hour after the news arrived, and the troops will have executed them in time for the purpose required.

In regard to the second, he told me his opinion was, that, in the Diet to be held at Nimeguen, the States should begin by declaring the towns of Elburg and Hattem as having violated the laws of the Constitution ; that the Free Corps were illegal associations, and, when employed to act against the magistracy, guilty of rebellion. That this having been the case in the two aforesaid towns, and their having refused to obey the orders of the civil authority, rendered it necessary to subdue them by force.

I shall now endeavour to transmit, as accurately as my memory will allow me to do, an abstract of the several conferences which passed between the Stadtholder and me during my three days' residence at Loo.

I passed the greatest part of the time I was at Loo either with the Prince or Princess alone, and it would be an endless task to endeavour to be an exact narrator of everything they said. The general ideas of both are perfectly the same ; and they seem entirely agreed in all great political points, with the difference that the Princess naturally inclines towards Prussia, and that the Prince is wholly and decidedly English. He, in our first conversation, in a speech of nearly an hour, delivered with the greatest precision of ideas, and most amazing accuracy of memory I ever recollect to have heard, recapitulated the whole of his conduct from the year 1778 to this day. He pointed out the various epochs in which he committed errors, and others in which he had been un-

justly accused of having erred ; and he confessed candidly, he had missed several opportunities of ameliorating
his situation, but he had been often wrongfully taxed
with neglect or inattention ; and summed up his discourse
by saying, that as on one side the weakness and defection
of his friends had discouraged him from undertaking anything great and hazardous, he was on the other hand inclined to be patient and forbearing, from the hopes that
he should by his example teach moderation to the country at large, and prevent it from hastening to its own
ruin and his downfall.   That it was from this motive he
had hitherto desisted from conversing familiarly and confidentially with me ; since, although he was fully convinced, as well from private ties of affection and gratitude
towards His Majesty, as from the interests of the United
Provinces, that their Stadtholder should ever consider the
King of Great Britain as their only real and sincere protector, yet as the Faction had fixed upon him the odious
imputation of having betrayed his country to England, he
could not be too cautious to avoid any appearances which
might tend to validate so injurious an accusation.

He then related to me what your Lordship has already
read in this despatch, and, after explaining to me in the
fullest and most confidential manner his intentions, he
went on by adverting to the consequences : these he supposed would be an immediate depriving him, on the part
of Holland, of the command of their troops, and, probably, his dismission from the Stadtholderate of their
Province.   This, he said, he expected ; and, being fully
prepared for it, should meet it with a calmness and forti-
tude his enemies were not used to.

He flattered himself the justice of the cause, and the
importance of the object, would induce Foreign Powers to
interest themselves in the fate of the Republic, which he
considered now as at stake ; and that Prussia, as well as
England, would come effectually to their support.   He
then, with very great calmness, and a most surprising
quickness, distinguished between the different motives
these two great Powers had for coming to his assistance.

Those of Prussia were *personal,* those of England were *public.* If Prussia found her account in paying her court to France, it would weigh down the inclination of the present King to support his sister; but that, if France and Austria were so closely united as they appeared from many circumstances to be, Prussia necessarily must court an alliance with England, and join most cordially with her in every measure she should think proper to take in behalf of this Republic.

This was nearly the amount of what I heard from the Prince of Orange ; and I confess, his mode of expression, his manner and energy, have given me hopes I never ventured to form before.

LETTER FROM LORD DALRYMPLE TO SIR JAMES HARRIS.

Berlin, September 2nd, 1786.

DEAR SIR,—You cannot be more surprised at receiving, than I was at being asked by Count Goertz for a letter of recommendation to you. As you have been so long, and are so well acquainted with him, it is unnecessary to give you, in the usual style of introductory letters, an account of his family, personal qualities, &c. I shall only speak to what I know of him since I came to Berlin. During that time I have always found him friendly, frequently serviceable, and uniformly, as *far as I could see,* attached to an English system ; and, while the King continues in his present disposition towards us, I think there is little danger of his changing. He is, besides, embarked with Mr. Hertzberg, and must sink or swim with him. You will learn from my official letter the state of things here, and my opinion of what is likely to follow ; but I did not choose to say then, what I tell you in the *utmost confidence,* that I suspect our people are throwing cold water upon the Prussian councils through an indirect channel ; for, as to me, I know no more what they intend or wish, than the King's Consul at Grand Cairo does.* But for

---

* Lord Carmarthen and Sir James (as has appeared) corresponded with Lord Dalrymple's Secretary, Mr. Ewart.　　　N 2

God's sake do not let this out to Goertz, or any soul where you are, though I fear that it will soon be too well known. If my conjecture is founded, the game is up : for it would be a hazardous measure for this country, uncertain of Austria and Russia, to make war against France and Holland, were she supported by England ; but alone, it would be downright Quixotism.

In my conversation with the Duke of Brunswick, he entered into the measures necessary to be taken in case force was resorted to ; and he was particularly desirous to know if an insurrection could be brought about in favour of the Prince in the Province of Holland. If it could, he was of opinion that a *sudden* and *unexpected blow*, struck immediately with a *small force*, would be more effectual than to wait till a numerous army was assembled, which would give time for both Holland and France to prepare for resistance.* Pray let me know your sentiments on the practicableness of this scheme ; but I would wish you could convey your letter into Germany, at least, by a private hand, as I have had it indirectly insinuated that our cyphers are discovered in Holland, and I would recommend that no communications of great importance should be sent by the post through Holland. You will not be surprised at the inaccuracy of this letter, when I tell you that His Serene Highness the Duke of Mecklenburg Strelitz, together with some of his Cabinet Ministers, have been sitting at my elbow during the whole time I have been writing, debating with great earnestness, whether His Highness, *who is in incognito*, should go to Court with his *riband over his waistcoat*.

Pray endeavour to find out whether my suspicion about the cyphers is founded. I fancy the information came through Mons. de Larrey.

I have shown your last letter to the Duke of Brunswick and several people here, who have expressed much satisfaction at it, and it has had considerable effect.

* The very plan which was adopted in 1787 under the Duke's direction.

EXTRACT OF A DESPATCH FROM SIR JAMES HARRIS TO THE MARQUIS OF CARMARTHEN.

Hague, 2nd September, 1786.

THE present moment is a very serious, critical, and important one, and my position equally so. I shall hope to be excused if, in these circumstances, I mix reflection with facts ; a simple narrative of what passes, without any comment, would convey but a very imperfect idea of what is going forward around me.

I begin to think Ewart has not been false in his reports ; and though his never having been anywhere but at Berlin may make him overlook several Prussian manœuvres to which I am used, yet, to say the truth, Goertz bears himself so fairly, and what he does so perfectly coincides with what he says, that, if he does deceive, he employs a species of deception the devil has hitherto reserved for his own use.

EXTRACT OF A DESPATCH FROM SIR JAMES HARRIS TO THE MARQUIS OF CARMARTHEN.

Hague, 5th Sept., 1786.

THE States of Holland, who, as I mentioned in my last, were not to take the matter into consideration till Wednesday, were, in consequence of letters from Gelderland, summoned on a sudden to meet yesterday ; and as what passed there will probably be a very memorable epoch in the annals of this country, I shall endeavour to report it to your Lordship as accurately as I possibly can.

Petitions were read, signed by several of the populace of Amsterdam, the Hague, Delft, and Rotterdam, praying the States to assist efficaciously the towns of Hattem and Elburg.

A letter, signed by six deputies of Gelderland (at the

head of which was Capel de Marschen), was afterwards
produced, stating that they had for a long time been
labouring to redress the manifold abuses which had been
introduced into the Government of their Province, and to
check the growth of an undue influence of the Stadtholder,
who, as they alleged, ought only to have a deliberative
voice in all questions of State ; that their efforts had been
fruitless ; and that, reduced in a manner to despair, they
held it their duty to address themselves to the Province of
Holland, which, from the rank it held in the Confederacy,
was more interested than any other member of the Union
to preserve the Constitution of the Republic.

After these petitions and the letter had been read,
Gyslaer got up and declared, as what he had to say was
of a very important nature, he begged, before he delivered
his sentiments, that the Act of Indemnity of the 19th
July and 3rd August, 1663, might be read.   The title of
this Act explains its meaning ; it was passed by De Witt,
" To authorize any of the members of the States of Holland to hold such language as he pleased respecting both
measures and men, whenever he thought the States in
danger, without either his own person, or those of his
children or family, being liable to be punished, at the
time or afterwards, for any expressions he might use."
This Act being stated to the Assembly, Gyslaer went on
by saying, that the cause of all the misfortunes which
had of late befallen the Republic in general, and the
several Provinces in particular, was to be found in the
personal character and conduct of the present Stadtholder, William the Fifth ; that the careless manner in
which the War had been carried on against England was
to be imputed to him ; that the machinations and internal feuds which distracted the State were his work ; that
the dread of his misusing the power lodged in his hands
was what had forced the Republic to make a Peace with
the Emperor, which rendered it contemptible in the eyes of
Europe ; that the letter William the Fifth had lately written to the States of Holland, on the subject of the command of the Hague, was a proof that he disputed their

right of Sovereignty; and that his present conduct in co-
operating with the States of Gelderland and Utrecht (which
the Pensionary of Dordt called an illegal meeting) left no
doubt of the dangerous designs he had on the liberty and
Constitution of the Republic; and that the meeting held
at Loo, on the 21st August, was with the same tyrannical views as those held formerly by the Duke d'Alva :
that therefore he moved, that a letter, drawn up in the
strongest expressions, should be written to William the
Fifth, (for so he called him all along,) forcing him to explain decisively and precisely his intentions and sentiments; and that, if his answer should not appear satisfactory, that he should immediately be suspended in the
execution of his offices as Captain-General and Stadtholder
of the Province of Holland, till such time as the States
could take into consideration, whether he should not be
entirely dismissed from them.   Gyslaer proceeded by
saying, that, till this was determined, it was indispensably
necessary to write to the different Commanders of the
regiments belonging to their Province to receive no orders
but from the States, and that they should hold themselves
in readiness to defend their Provinces, which he considered as threatened with an invasion.

This speech, the most inflammatory one ever pronounced in that Assembly, was followed by one conceived in more gentle terms, but tending to the same
end, from Zeebergen.   On the question being put, fourteen towns voted for it, four and the Corps des Nobles*
against it ; and, as amongst these four was Amsterdam,
the States did not think proper to come to an immediate
resolution, and the business now stands postponed till to-
morrow.

I took the liberty of remonstrating to the Stadtholder,
when I had the honour of seeing him the other day, that
his person was not sufficiently guarded in times like
these ; and he has since ordered a company of foot and a
squadron of horse to do duty at Loo.   This caution was
the more necessary, as I have reason to believe that the

---

* The nobles had one vote in the States General.

detachment of the Free Corps which went from hence
would have made an attempt on that palace, if it had not
been better defended than when I was there, when the
Prince had only a few halberdiers and a serjeant's guard.

EXTRACT OF A DESPATCH FROM SIR JAMES HARRIS TO THE
MARQUIS OF CARMARTHEN.

Hague, 8th Sept., 1786.

THE corps under the command of General Spengelar*
got before the last of these towns† about one o'clock on
Tuesday. He immediately sent a messenger belonging to
the States to summon the town in their name to open its
gates, and to deliver into the hands of the civil power
such of its inhabitants as stood accused of disobedience
to the established Government of the Province. He gave
them three hours to consider of an answer; and declared,
that, if in that space of time they did not submit, he
should bombard the town. Their answer was, that they
would defend it to the last extremity, and set fire to it,
rather than deliver it into his hands.

General Spengelar on this began his approaches, and
the burghers from within, on his first movement, to fire
upon his corps from some small cannon they had on the
walls; which they continued to do for near two hours,
without any other effect than killing a drummer. The
general's cannon being then near enough to bear, he discharged a volley in the air, and flung two shells into the
town. The Free Corps on this immediately quitted the
ramparts, and fled over a bridge on the Yssel; and one
of the burghers came forward to General Spengelar to
declare that the town had surrendered. As soon as this
news was received at Elburg, the Free Corps there, without waiting to be attacked, evacuated it, and a company
of infantry took possession of the place.

* Commander of the Stadtholder's forces.
† Elburg and Hattem.

The circumstances attending this event are so very humiliating for the Faction, and at the same time prove so evidently the determined character of the Province of Gelderland, that although the Patriots abate in nothing of their violence, yet it is now tempered with a great degree of fear.

The States of Holland have been sitting almost constantly since I last wrote, and, as they administered an oath of secrecy to each of their members, it is not possible to obtain an exact knowledge of what is passing. Enough, however, has transpired for us to be assured that they have already suspended the Stadtholder in his office of Captain-General of this Province,* and taken upon themselves to dispense the several regiments in their Department from the oath of allegiance they took to the States General and the Prince of Orange. The consequences of this step are, indeed, equal to an entire subversion of the Government, and amount virtually to a dissolution of the Union.

As I before said, there is a great mixture of apprehension with the violence of the Faction ; and, accustomed hitherto to carry their point by intrigue and cabal, they are driven from their bias when matters are to be decided by force of arms. It is from this principle that they have assumed the dispensing power above-mentioned, in order to send for such regiments as belong to their division from Breda, Maestricht, and other garrison towns in the Pays de Généralité, to defend their own Province, which they consider in danger, and more particularly the town of Utrecht, which they expect will be immediately attacked. Their plan is to send the Rhingrave of Salm with his corps to the defence of that city, and to place strong garrisons in the two fortresses of Woerden and Naerden, which command the avenues into this Province on its northern limits.

It is a matter of great doubt whether the commanding officers of the several regiments will obey these orders, or admit the legality of the dispensing power ; and, if even

* Province of Holland.

these do, whether the Governors of the frontier towns will suffer them to march.

I have given it as my opinion to several military men who have called upon me to-day and yesterday, that, if they consider it as valid, they will be liable on some future day *to be shot;* and that for their honour, as well as for their security, they should carry the order they have received to the President of the week, for him to lay it before the States General, in whom alone such authority is vested.

EXTRACT OF A DESPATCH FROM SIR JAMES HARRIS TO THE
MARQUIS OF CARMARTHEN.

Hague, 12th Sept., 1786.

I TRUST the conference between the States of Gelderland and Utrecht will terminate in a resolution to attack, without loss of time, the town of Utrecht, where the behaviour of the Free Corps betrays full as strong symptoms of fear as of an intention to defend themselves. They have broken down all the bridges but two, and are assembled, as it is said, to the amount of 8,000. But, even supposing them as determined as they affect to be, the inhabitants of the town of Utrecht will force them to surrender, rather than expose their persons and effects to the risks of a formal siege.

The French and the Faction are indefatigable in the Provinces : Overyssel and Groningen are, I fear, lost. They are employing every means of seduction in Friesland, and even tampering in Zealand. I trust, however, they will not be able to make any impression on either of these.

France is profuse of her money on this occasion ; and Cotleuri, to whom this branch of the business is entrusted, has disposed of upwards of three millions of livres within these three weeks. If these disorders increase, I have no doubt France will, without waiting for any requisition from hence, throw troops into the Dutch

Settlements in the East Indies ; and, under pretence of defending them, appropriate them to herself. This is so natural an incident, that I feel the inutility of putting your Lordship on your guard on the subject.

EXTRACT OF A DESPATCH FROM SIR JAMES HARRIS TO THE
MARQUIS OF CARMARTHEN.

Hague, 15th Sept., 1786.

THE States of Holland found themselves so embarrassed by the refusal of the army to obey their orders, that they were obliged to apply to the States General to have them enforced ; and their High Mightinesses, on Wednesday last, partly by persuasion and partly by threats, were brought to consent that twelve regiments should be drawn from the Generality and quartered in the Province of Holland.

Many of our friends look on this step as a matter of triumph, as well because the States of Holland were compelled to forego their pretensions of an exclusive power over that part of the army on their own establishment, as because, instead of twenty-eight regiments, which they originally intended to call into their Province, they now will have only twelve. I do not agree with them, and consider the acquiescence of the States General to the demand as an ill-advised and weak measure, since it is not only a tacit avowal that this Province was in danger of an attack from the States of Gelderland, but also authorizes a breach of the Constitution, which directs that, in all cases of emergency, the Provinces should apply to their Stadtholder as Captain-General of the Union, not to their High Mightinesses, for military support. All these considerations, however, will now be absorbed in our attention to what may be the effects of Count Goertz's mission.

He called upon me early yesterday before he had seen any one else.

Count Goertz, after expressing his confidence that I should not entertain a jealousy of any *apparent* intimacy between him and Mons. de Verac, nor endeavour, in case France complied with His Prussian Majesty's proposal, to thwart the success of his negotiation ; and after having received from me on these points such assurances as I thought it expedient to make ; went on by saying, that it was of the utmost consequence (if France should, on this occasion, either prevaricate or refuse positively to act) for his Master to know what kind of assistance he could expect from England, and how far we were inclined to go in support of this Republic : for, added the Count, he considered the existence of the Republic as an independent Power, as well as the particular interest of the House of Orange, as now at stake. He begged me to speak to him freely and openly on this point, and urged me to be ingenuous, by the strongest expressions he could use to convince me that the King of Prussia's first object was to connect himself by the closest alliance to England.

I referred him to the two Memorials I presented since I have been here, for our sentiments relative to the situation of this country, and for the line of conduct we had laid down relative to it. He might see there, I observed, how sincerely we were interested in its fate, and how ready we should be, when called upon, to contribute to restore the ancient system.

The King of Prussia did not, he said, ask any specific support, in order to reduce this country to good order and obedience. He only wanted to know with certainty that England would not remain *passive*, if, in consequence of any active measures the Court of Berlin might pursue, she should be attacked by France and Austria.

I rejoined, though this question would have come more properly through Count Lusi, or Lord Dalrymple, yet as he spoke in virtue of direct orders from the King, his Master, I certainly would make an exact report of what he said to your Lordship, and wait your orders on the subject. These, of course, I shall expect with no small degree of impatience.

Count Goertz went from me to the French Ambassador, and returned to my house in the evening to give me an account of what had passed between them. He expressed himself in very clear terms to Mons. de Verac, and told him he was sent to examine the conduct of the Patriots, relative to the House of Orange, with temper and calmness, and to endeavour, if possible, to reconcile the different parties which distracted the Republic : that he had orders to solicit his concurrence on this occasion, which he hoped the Court of Versailles would think it advisable to grant, as the consequences of a refusal would be very serious, since he would not conceal from him, that, if moderate measures had no effect, the King, his Master, was determined not to commit his dignity by suffering the first ostensible measure he had adopted on his mounting the throne (and that on such just and honourable grounds) to fail in its execution, from want of firmness and resolution.

Mons. de Verac replied to him, that he had no other answer to give him than the one he had just received by a courier :

"Que le Roi de France ne voulait pas s'immiscer lui-même dans le Gouvernement intérieur de la République, mais étant devenu son allié, il était garant de sa Liberté, de son Indépendance, et de sa Constitution, aussi bien que de ses possessions."

Count Goertz said that this language implied something more than a refusal, and he apprehended from it that his first conference with his Excellency would be his last.

The Ambassador replied, he hoped not ; that he expected his son-in-law, Mons. de la Coste, on Sunday, and that he, probably, might bring him some further instructions.

Mons. de Verac then went into a short discussion on the deplorable situation of this country, which he imputed solely to the Prince, who, he said, besides being utterly incapable of government, had now drawn upon himself the hatred of the nation ; that 60,000 men in the heart of the Republic were in arms against him.

The new Prussian Minister replied, that he was fully informed to what the distressed state of the Republic was to be ascribed, and that at a proper time he should speak freely on this subject; on which, till he was positively assured what part the Court of France meant to take, he had nothing to say to Mons. de Verac.

Their conference here ended, and I relate it not only from Count Goertz himself, but from the report given of it by the French Ambassador, who, in mentioning it, said he had been treated with an arrogance, and in an overbearing manner, he did not well know how to brook.

EXTRACTS OF A LETTER FROM SIR JAMES HARRIS TO LORD DALRYMPLE.

Hague, Sept. 18, 1786.

THE return of Mons. de Gensau affords me a safe opportunity of thanking you for your kind letter of the 2nd instant by Count Goertz.

The description you give of the character, talents, and disposition of that Minister tallies perfectly with the opinion I have ever entertained of him; and the manner in which he has conducted himself towards me since he has arrived here, fully answers the hopes I had formed that he would treat me with confidence, and without reserve.

France, underhand, encourages, assists, and foments vehement measures; and I have never said a word relative to the behaviour of that Court which the event has not fully justified.

Their ostensible language (and it is insulting to common sense, as the other is repugnant to every principle of decency) is, that His Most Christian Majesty *ne s'immisce de rien dans l'intérieur de la République, mais, qu'étant devenue son alliée, elle s'est rendue par là, garant de la liberté de sa Constitution.* Such was the language held by Mons. de Verac to Count Goertz on their first meeting.

It remains now to say a word or two on what may, or

ought to be, the conduct of such Powers as from their position or interests are more or less connected with the fate of Holland.

It is to be presumed Prussia will not retract. The King's dignity is at stake, and the reputation which is to determine the character of his reign will be fixed by the manner in which he carries through this first and important measure he has undertaken.

If there is no secret understanding between France and Austria, and if an exchange of Bavaria is not somehow or other agreed on, and to be purchased by the Emperor by delivering Holland over to France, France is acting a weak and dangerous part. But, if this secret understanding exists, the danger, not the weakness, is made over to Prussia ; and before she moves forward she must fully and explicitly open herself to England, the *only Power* who, either by a political or by a military assistance, can bear her safely through the hazardous enterprise in which she will be embarked.

In regard to the sentiments of England, I really cannot take upon myself to pronounce decisively ; but this I will be bold to say, that if His Prussian Majesty comes openly and confidentially to St. James's, and in a clear and confidential declaration of his situation, sentiments, and wishes, tells us he has renounced all those leanings towards a French connexion which marked every period of the late reign, and that he is ready to enter into an extensive and cordial alliance with us,—I say, if His Prussian Majesty will say all this, *in a proper way* and through *a proper person*, I have in my own mind not the least doubt but that he will be listened to with pleasure, and a plan of concert be very soon agreed on, which may not only tend to bring his operations here to a successful issue, but contribute to make the first actions of his reign a security for its future glory and tranquillity.

These, which are really my sentiments, may serve as an answer to that very material part of your letter which you wrote in the *utmost confidence*, and of which, till I read it there, I had no idea.[*]

[*] Vide page 179.

EXTRACT OF A DESPATCH FROM SIR JAMES HARRIS TO THE
MARQUIS OF CARMARTHEN.

Hague, 19th Sept., 1786.

On Saturday, several of the towns were not ready with
their votes, and it was held necessary, for *form's sake*,
(for they were certain as to the instruction which would
be received,) to wait for orders from their principals.   It
was, however, agreed that, in the mean while, a letter
should be written to the Prince of Orange, directing him
not to exercise any act of military authority, because (said
Gyslaer) every hour, nay, every minute, while this power
remained in his hands, the State was in danger.

In the evening, the States General received the Prince's
answer to their letter, directing him to order the twelve
regiments to march into this Province.   It was drawn up
with great dignity and good sense.   He bowed down to
their commands (he said) as coming from the Sovereigns
of the State, but he could not but express his deep concern that the last orders he should probably issue as
Captain-General of Holland would be to serve to kindle
a war between the Confederated Provinces.   He added,
that he thought it a duty he owed both to their High
Mightinesses and to himself to declare, that he was no
longer responsible for the defence of the frontier towns ;
and that, weakened as their garrisons would now be, it
remained for their High Mightinesses to provide for their
security.

An extraordinary assembly was held on the reception
of this letter on Sunday ; and though it furnished the best
and most constitutional grounds for stopping the orders
they had forced the Prince to give, and though, previous
to their meeting, almost every member of the States
General declared to me individually that the safety of
the public required that they should be stopped, yet, by
a fatality which surpasses all belief, when they came to
act collectively, the question passed with a single negative voice, and the orders were actually despatched the

same evening.   This is the third time in the space of
ten days that the Faction owe their triumph, not to their
own superior abilities, but to the weakness and timidity
of their adversaries.

Had these twelve regiments been denied them, they
would have been stopped in their career, and would not
have felt themselves strong enough to commit all the excesses they have in contemplation ; and three times it has
been in the power of the States General to put a negative
on the measure.   I scarce now see a ray of hope left
within the country itself, or any Province where we can
depend on a systematic conduct, except that of Gelderland.

Groningen and Overyssel are irrevocably gone, and the
spirit of disorder which prevails in the latter is not to
be described.   Colonel Bentinck was very near being a
victim to the fury of the mob, and owed his life, perhaps,
to the swiftness of his horse.

Utrecht, from its distressed state, promises fairly; but,
from my knowledge of the general temper of the leading
men in that Province, I am satisfied they will remain
attached to the Stadtholder no longer than they want
him.

In Friesland the contest runs very high ; but letters,
just come in from thence, seem to announce that the
majority of the States are unfavourably disposed.

Even Zealand has swerved from her allegiance.   Mons.
Vander Spiegel being too ill to attend to business, the
direction of the Province devolved on the first Secretary,
Van Beveren (a rank Patriot) ; and his activity, assisted by
a considerable quantity of louis-d'ors, opportunely distributed at *Flushing*, Ter Veere, and Zurickzee, has
turned the scale against the Prince in a Province where,
two months ago, he had every voice in his favour.   I
heard this news yesterday, and sent immediately an express to Mons. Vander Spiegel for information (if he is in
a situation to give it me) to what this unexpected change
is to be attributed ; whether there has been mismanagement as well as treachery, and whether things are lost

beyond redemption.   It is of immense importance to preserve Zealand ; since, whilst that Province is friendly,
France, as a maritime Power at least, gains little or
nothing by being in possession of the other six Provinces.

EXTRACT OF A DESPATCH FROM SIR JAMES HARRIS TO THE
MARQUIS OF CARMARTHEN.

Hague, 26th Sept., 1786.

On Sunday a meeting of the leaders of the Faction
was held at the French Ambassador's; and there is every
reason to believe that they have it in contemplation to
declare the Stadtholder an enemy to the Republic, and
not only to deprive him of his high Office, but to declare
it no longer Hereditary in his family.* Mons. de la
Coste said almost as much to Count Goertz, and held a
language which has filled him with indignation. He
confirmed everything this Minister had before heard from
Mons. de Verac and his Secretary, Le Sieur Caillard; and
far from taking any pains to disguise the intentions of
France, or to modify his expressions, Mons. de la Coste
seemed purposely to choose such as he knew must be the
most offensive to the Prussian Minister. He called the
Prince of Orange Mons. de Nassau, and said that an hereditary Stadtholder was of too new a creation to have
acquired a constitutional sanction ; that it never had the
approbation of the whole Republic, and, as it was brought
about by a revolution, might be destroyed in the same
manner.

Count Goertz was justly irritated at this indecent language, and has reported it to his Court in its full force.

---

* The Stadtholder was suspended from his authority by the States of
Holland on the 22nd of September ; and the resolution of 1706, which gave
him the nomination to the military promotions, was rescinded.   The
Equestrian Order, and the town of Hoorn, were the only two voices in his
favour.   Delft did not vote at all.—*Harris Papers.*

EXTRACT OF A DESPATCH FROM THE MARQUIS OF CARMARTHEN
TO SIR JAMES HARRIS.

Whitehall, 26th Sept., 1786.

WHATEVER eagerness Count Goertz may manifest for a
closer connexion between the two Courts, at present it is
impossible for us to throw ourselves headlong into any
engagement which might ultimately involve this country
in the most embarrassing circumstances, such as must in-
fallibly be the case, supposing England and Prussia were
committed with France, and possibly Austria, and no
other Power whatever engaged to support them. A connexion which might produce such an effect, is, I trust,
neither expected nor desired by His Prussian Majesty.

With respect to the Stadtholder, I do not see, in the
present moment, a possibility of serving him by any steps
within the Provinces, where those on whose support he
had apparent reason to rely, seem to have adopted, in the
moment of necessity, that pusillanimity and weakness
they had so often condemned in him. France, it seems,
must now decide whether the House of Orange is to be
sacrificed, or not, to gratify the vengeance rather than
contribute to the security of its persecutors, who owe
their power as well as consequence to her support. At
all events, England cannot be accused with justice of having deserted those who have appeared almost as unwilling
as unable to direct the necessary steps for their own preservation.

The time may come when the King's Mediation may
be as much the object of desire to the Republic itself as
to those actually engaged in its dissensions ; as it will in-
disputably be a source of advantage to this country, and
by any other than a cautious system, for the present, this
expectation on our part must be defeated.

Under such circumstances, it is impossible to give a
full and direct answer to Count Goertz's eager inquiries
respecting the conduct England may observe in case
France should refuse to co-operate with the Court of

o 2

Berlin, and the latter should, in consequence of pursuing active measures in Holland, be attacked by France and Austria. His Majesty's great wish is to preserve the advantages of peace, so essential to his dominions. Anxious as he is for the independence and real interests of the Republic, *he cannot risk committing himself in measures which might lead to immediate war.*

EXTRACT OF A LETTER FROM SIR JAMES HARRIS TO THE MARQUIS OF CARMARTHEN.

Hague, 3rd Oct., 1786.

It will be but mercy to write you a very short private letter to-day, after having given you the trouble of perusing a public one as long and as dull as a sermon ; but I cannot delay thanking you for yours of the 26th inst., which contains a great deal of most admirable matter, both on men and things.

I trust, whatever may be Goertz's intentions and designs, that in the end he will not have found me to have been his dupe. I understand full well how far he may be trusted ; and with better reason than the old Dane, I can say, as he did to the tide, " Thus far shalt thou go, and no further."

To commit France and Prussia in a military quarrel is my first wish ; my second, to encourage him in a political one ;—England, in both cases, to remain quiet. This I presume not to be contrary to your wishes in particular, or to the interests of England in general. I presume, also, that you would not feel yourself displeased, or England humbled, if you were to see a Prussian Minister come to London to court our alliance and friendship; and that, in case such an event were to happen, you would not suppose we were sunk or sinking in the eyes of Europe. To effect something like all this is the end of my endeavours, for the Republic comes round the moment *a system is formed.*

EXTRACT OF A DESPATCH FROM SIR JAMES HARRIS TO THE
MARQUIS OF CARMARTHEN.

Hague, 10th Oct., 1786.

THE whole tenour of the conduct of the French and
Patriots leaves not a doubt that the principal object they
aim at, is to throw the whole weight of the Belgic Confederacy into the hands of the Province of Holland.   Holland is to be Mistress of the Republic, and France is to
govern Holland.   It is with this view that they are
labouring to wrest the frontier towns from the jurisdiction of the Union, and place them under that of Holland ;
and I am sorry to say the means they employ promise
them every hope of success.

The Rhingrave of Salm, with numberless French officers, is now destroying what the Free Corps and Burghers
have done, and putting the fortifications into a regular
state of defence.   They have already erected a strong
battery on the side towards Gelderland.   The Rhingrave's corps is destined to be quartered within the town,
from which it is now only a few leagues distant.   The
moment this happens, the whole Province may be considered as having passed under the dominion of Holland ;
and every attempt to recover it, otherwise than by a
superior force, will become idle and ineffectual.

This mode of proceeding on the part of the Faction is
so notorious, and their designs are so palpable, that a
serious alarm is spread amongst the other Provinces ; and
they begin to perceive what they ought to have felt long
ago, that, by their opposition to the Stadtholder, they
have been preparing for themselves a much more oppressive form of Government than that which he ever could
or would have exercised over them.   Friesland has given
strong proofs of this conversion ; Gelderland also continues steady and determined ; and I have the best assurances from Mons. Vander Spiegel, that the defection of
Zealand was only temporary, and to be imputed to causes
which no longer exist.   It is certain, with these three

Provinces a great deal might still be done ; at least, if they unite under the same banner, the operations of the rest of the Republic will be so fettered as to render them neither useful to their friends nor dangerous to their enemies.   It is, therefore, of the utmost consequence (as the last hope remaining) to keep them together ; and I presume your Lordship will not disapprove my endeavours on this subject, in which I shall act *quite single*, independent both of the Prussian and Stadtholderian interest.

Next to recovering the Republic for England, the rendering it a useless friend to France is, I presume, the principal object of my residence here.   I have said I shall act single on this occasion, because the arrival of Goertz has evinced to me that no Prussian party can exist here, but that an English one can and certainly does exist.   The friends to the Stadtholderian Government all come to me before they go to him, and, if I was to express my disapprobation of their seeing him, would, I am persuaded, whenever I desired it, refuse him their assistance, and withhold their information from him.   They feel that England is, and has been *at all times*, and under all circumstances, deeply interested in the preservation of the Republic ; while Prussia never took any share in its concerns till such time as a Princess of the House of Brandenberg was married to the Stadtholder.

EXTRACT OF A LETTER FROM SIR JAMES HARRIS TO THE
MARQUIS OF CARMARTHEN.

Hague, 10th Oct., 1786.

I HAVE written so freely in my official letter to-day, that there is nothing left for a private one.   I am sure you have already made the same remark I have, and lament, for the sake of his own glory and consideration, that His new Prussian Majesty should have begun his reign by an ostensible measure, without having adverted to its consequences, or without appearing to have been prepared, *in any case*, to have given further instructions for carrying it through.

The French party at Berlin, from my intimate knowledge of several of its component parts, beats the other
hollow in point of talents and abilities. I do not mean
to say by this that Count Finck is not greatly inferior to
Mons. de Hertzberg, or that the Duke of Brunswick is not
at least equal to Prince Henry ; but we have on our side
no Möllendorffs, no Kniphausens, no Schulenbergs, and
various others, who, though not commanders, are to be
reckoned among the staff-officers of the French party.

EXTRACT OF A DESPATCH FROM THE MARQUIS OF CARMAR-
THEN TO SIR JAMES HARRIS.

Whitehall, 13th October, 1786.

I RECEIVED this morning your despatches, and have laid
them before the King. The keeping up a party in the
Republic well disposed towards Great Britain, is undoubtedly a most desirable object, as far as it can be done
without risk of interrupting our present tranquillity, and,
at the same time, without committing us to the performance of any engagements inconsistent with our present
pacific system. In order to promote a party of this
friendly description, I trust you will rather make use of
arguments than assurances ; as otherwise we might be
reduced to the unpleasant alternative of either deserting
a handful of friends, or of provoking a host of enemies.*

EXTRACT OF A DESPATCH FROM SIR JAMES HARRIS TO THE
MARQUIS OF CARMARTHEN.

Hague, 20th Oct., 1786.

EITHER a division in the Prussian Cabinet, or a wavering in the mind of His Prussian Majesty himself, has
completely defeated the end of Count Goertz's mission,
if it was set on foot with a view to serve the House

* By this and former despatches it will be observed that Sir James
Harris's more active views met with very little encouragement from his
Government.

of Orange and maintain the present Constitution of this country.

From what I can observe, the Court of Berlin is now much more anxious how to save its own dignity, than to resent the insults which have been offered to the Stadtholder, and Count Finckenstein (who writes to Count Goertz in the King's absence) seems to confine his whole wishes to this sole object. Count Goertz either really is, or affects to be, greatly hurt and angered at this want of firmness in his Court, and assures me that to-day he means to ask his recall, unless he should receive letters from the King, who is at Breslaw, written in a different style from those of his Minister Count Finckenstein.

EXTRACT OF A LETTER FROM SIR JAMES HARRIS TO THE MARQUIS OF CARMARTHEN.

Hague, 24th Oct., 1786.

THE letters which Count Goertz has received both from His Prussian Majesty himself and from the Prussian Ministry for these last three posts, far from bringing him any fresh instructions to proceed with energy in his negotiation, clearly demonstrate that there exists a very strong desire in the Court of Berlin to *extricate* itself with honour from the step it has taken in this country, and the whole of Count Goertz's conduct convinces me that this is now become the sole object of his mission.

I have not, however, the smallest reason for impeaching this Minister with having dealt unfairly by me. He has communicated to me the letters he writes and receives, and it is from having perused these with attention that I venture to speak positively on the subject.

The King of Prussia, who writes from Breslaw, on the 12th Oct., says, " J'approuve vos efforts pour établir un accommodement pour ma sœur sur des conditions *raisonnables et supportables,* mais je ne peux ni ne dois entreprendre quelque chose qui pourrait troubler la paix de mon Royaume."

Mons. de Hertzberg writes from the same place, and under the same date, nearly to the same effect : he adds, " On dit, Mons. le Comte, que vous négligez l'Ambassadeur de France et le Grand Pensionnaire, et ne vivez qu'avec le Ministre d'Angleterre et le parti Anglais. Le Roi est persuadé que ce n'est qu'un bruit suscité par vos ennemis. Il vous charge de remercier le Chevalier Harris de la communication que ce Ministre vous a faite, qui lui fait grand plaisir. Il vous charge de plus de demander au Chevalier Harris la permission de dire à l'Ambassadeur de France que vous avez des assurances que la Cour de Londres ne traversera pas votre négociation, et, s'il vous la donne, vous vous en servirez pour prouver à Mons. de Verac avec combien peu de fondement on a accusé le Ministre d'Angleterre d'avoir suscité l'affaire d'Elbourg et de Hattem."

When Count Goertz read this part of his letter to me on Saturday, I told him it was not in my power to grant him the permission he asked ; and that, even supposing I could grant it, it appeared to me perfectly useless to attempt to convince France of the injustice of an accusation, which she knew better than any one else to be a notorious falsehood, since it was France herself who was at the bottom of the troubles of Elburg and Hattem, and the efficient cause of what passed afterwards in consequence of them.

To attempt to undo what has been done, to rectify the evils which have been produced by the phrensy of a Faction, by the want of a judicious administration on the part of the Stadtholder, and by the ill-timed feeble intervention of Prussia ; I say, to attempt this now, directly, or avowedly, without a fixed intention of carrying our operation through by dint of force and violence if required, would be only an idle sacrifice of our friends here, and a gratuitous committing of our own dignity and consequence.

My opinion, indeed, is now what it has been all along, that, till France is ready, *nothing will provoke* her to quarrel with us ; and that, when she is ready, *nothing will prevent* it : of course, that she would not go to war for the sake of this country ; and that, if England was to threaten (and to threaten seriously), France would shrink from the challenge. But, though your Lordship's indulgence towards me may perhaps allow me to fling this out as an opinion, I by no means presume to intrude it as advice. On the contrary, I understand perfectly from your Lordship's late despatches the *prudent* line of conduct I am to pursue, and from which I neither have, nor shall deviate, until I am commanded so to do. It is, therefore, in conformity to this, that I lay aside every idea of intimidating our adversaries ; and, dismissing from my mind all thoughts of rescuing this country from the hands of its oppressors by coercive means, or regaining it as an immediate friend, I confine my endeavours for the present to prevent its becoming a dangerous enemy. This can only be brought about by forming an opposition in the Republic, by keeping up that spirit of dissatisfaction which reigns in the Provinces, by clogging the operations of the predominant party, and by preventing an unanimity of votes in the States General.

It is my duty to search for every means by which this country may be saved from sinking into a state of entire dependence on France, and it is for your Lordship's superior judgment to pronounce on their propriety or impropriety.

EXTRACT OF A DESPATCH FROM SIR JAMES HARRIS TO THE
MARQUIS OF CARMARTHEN.

Hague, 31st Oct., 1786.

THE letters written by the King of Prussia since his return from Silesia to Count Goertz denote, if possible, a still *greater repugnance* to afford anything like active assistance to the Stadtholder than before ; and His Majesty has, in very hasty and severe terms, reprimanded this Minister for having made use of stronger expressions than his instructions authorized him to employ.

Count Goertz is hurt and mortified to a degree at this censure, and foresees with concern as well the inutility

of his Mission (as far as it relates to the affairs of this
country), as the impression of weakness the manner in
which it has been conducted is likely to give of the new
reign in Prussia. The triumph of the French Faction is
complete, and they are not of a temper to be likely to
enjoy it with moderation or forbearance.

EXTRACT OF A DESPATCH FROM SIR JAMES HARRIS TO THE
MARQUIS OF CARMARTHEN.

Hague, 10th Nov., 1786.

COUNT GOERTZ had his expected meeting with the
Pensionaries yesterday evening. Van Berkel, Zeebergen,
Gyslaer, and a Burgomaster of Haerlem (Casteele), were
present ; it lasted an hour and a half. He has just read
to me the report he has made of this conference to the
King, from which it should appear that they received
him as Roman Senators would have done the Deputy of a
Tributary Province. On his exposing to them the purport of the Mediation of His Prussian Majesty, and
making them a tender of it (to settle equitable conditions for the Prince, and restore concord and order in
the Republic), they replied, that, by their exertions, concord and good order did exist, and that they were determined by the same exertions to maintain it. That it
did not become Sovereigns to enter into a discussion of
conditions with *their servant;* that the Prince had, by an
excessive abuse of power, by constant encroachments on
the liberties of the people, and by setting at defiance
their orders, brought on himself all that had happened to
him. That if he would recognize his errors, express his
repentance for what he had done, and give assurances for
his future conduct, he might return hither when he
would ; but that he must not expect to have restored to
him any of those Prerogatives taken from him by an act
of their States.

That, in short, the whole government must be new-
modelled ; and they told him (Count Goertz), if he really

interested himself for the welfare of the Prince, he would do well to advise him not to oppose or attempt to delay the Revolution they intended, since he had no time to lose, and that if they could not carry their point quietly, they would employ *force*. They called the Stadtholder Mons. le Prince ; Gyslaer said, " Mons. le Prince avoit une conduite abominable."

The *nobility* of Gelderland they styled his *domestics ;* and his representative in Zealand, his *valet*. Nothing, in a word, could exceed their arrogance and audacity, and never was the Minister of a Great King exposed to hear such insolent and overbearing language. Count Goertz was sufficiently hurt at it; but, as he acted in consequence of direct orders from the King (which he showed me this morning), he says he feels he has no reason for reproaching himself for what he has done.

Why His Prussian Majesty thought proper to commit himself thus gratuitously to the impertinence of these rough, ill-mannered Dictators, I confess I cannot guess. It was morally impossible any credit could result to him, or advantage to the Stadtholder.

LETTER FROM SIR JAMES HARRIS TO THE MARQUIS OF CARMARTHEN.

Hague, 21st Nov., 1786.

MY DEAR LORD,—Through a private but authorized channel I learn, that in a few days His Prussian Majesty will have a declared Mistress ; her name is De Voss, Maid of Honour to the Queen Dowager, niece to the Mareschal de la Cour of the late Princess of Prussia, and daughter to a person known at Berlin by the name of Mons. de Voss et de Havelberg. She was a favourite during the life of the late King, and all the ordinary means of seduction employed to lead her astray. Too wise, too cold, or too virtuous to give way to them, she, by repeated refusals, has worked up a passion to its height, and an offer has been made to make her the *Pompadour* of Berlin. Some hesitation, from a difference of opinion among her relations, has shown itself ; but, as the Lady *now* is on the yielding side, and as His Majesty is bent on success, there is little doubt of this event very soon taking place. She is a niece of Count Finck's, and of course may raise his sinking influence. She is more handsome than clever, probably more artful than either.

A Madame de Pompadour, or even a Madame de Barri, will never effectually diminish or hurt the Grandeur of the French Monarchy, which is settled on a foundation beyond the reach of the follies of the Court* to shake : but at Potzdam the case is widely different ; the whole mass of power is concentrated in the person of the *King*, and, if his shoulders are unequal to bear the burden, the edifice falls. I scarce know whether I wish this fact to be public. His Prussian Majesty certainly does lean towards England, and if circumstances or necessity drive us into an Alliance with him, why the fewer of his faults we are acquainted with the better.

EXTRACT OF A DESPATCH FROM THE MARQUIS OF CARMARTHEN
TO SIR JAMES HARRIS.

Whitehall, 21st Nov., 1786.

Mons. de Rayneval's journey is of course an interesting circumstance in the present moment.

I am fully persuaded, Sir, that you will omit no attention to Mons. de Rayneval, or to the object of his journey to Holland ; and I own, I shall be anxious to know not only the general purport of his instructions as far as they can be learnt, but the manner in which he will conduct himself towards you, and the sort of language he may think proper to hold in any conversation you may have with him.

* This curious remark of Sir J. Harris is another proof (if such were wanting) of the total blindness in which even the most intelligent and experienced men were wrapt at this period regarding the social and political state of France. The days of her ancient monarchy were at this date numbered to three years.

Mons. de Rayneval is, however, sufficiently known to you, I believe, to render any hint from me for your conduct towards him totally unnecessary and superfluous. Knowing his character and abilities, and considering the circumstances of the moment in which it is judged expedient by his Court to make use of them in Holland, it is, I own, a pleasing reflection to me, that you, Sir, are upon the spot; being convinced that, at so critical a moment, His Majesty's service requires a person of consummate penetration as well as superior abilities, to prevent the absolute completion of the views of France ultimately directed against this country, though in the first instance only apparently affecting the interests of that devoted Republic where you reside.

EXTRACT OF A DESPATCH FROM SIR JAMES HARRIS TO THE
MARQUIS OF CARMARTHEN.

Hague, 28th Nov., 1786.

THE Prince of Orange is not disposed to send any one hither to treat with Mons. de Rayneval, till he is more fully informed of the grounds on which a Treaty is to be set on foot.

Your Lordship may depend on my observing with the strictest attention every step Mons. de Rayneval takes; but I cannot flatter myself, either by a close observation of his conduct, or by any readiness I may show to obtain his friendship and good-will, that I shall be able to procure any real advantage to the public. He is too well versed in the habits of business to be out-negotiated, too well acquainted with the interests of his Court to mistake their object, and too calm and dispassionate to be driven from his purpose by flattery.

He is certainly a more respectable and estimable antagonist than those with whom I have had hitherto to cope, but he is at the same time an infinitely more dangerous one.

If I can stir up a spirit of opposition in the Provinces,

and find myself possessed of the means to support it, I may still perhaps be able to obstruct and delay the operations of the French; if not, I see nothing which can prevent an absolute completion of their views, which, as your Lordship very justly remarks, are ultimately directed against England.

[Lord Carmarthen having fallen ill, Sir James Harris took the opportunity of his absence from the Foreign Office, to address Mr. Pitt in person, and lay before him his opinions upon the state of the Dutch Republic.]

LETTER FROM SIR JAMES HARRIS TO MR. PITT.

Hague, Nov. 28, 1786.

DEAR SIR,—I am sure no apology is necessary, when the motive for troubling you relates to the public. You have also so often done me the honour to converse confidentially with me on Foreign Affairs, that I know them not to be indifferent to you, and that you consider them as making a very material part of your system of Government. In addition to this plea, and to justify still more the liberty I am taking, I have further to urge that Lord Carmarthen's illness deprives me of his support and assistance, and that, as long as I hear that he is unrecovered, I feel a reluctance in troubling him on a subject little calculated to restore health and spirits to a sick man, and on which it also seems to me expedient that we should come to an immediate resolution.

By a series of intrigue, dexterous management, and fortunate events, the French have carried their influence here to its greatest height; and the moment is now come when they are likely to fix it immoveably, by introducing a new form of Government in the Republic.

It is superfluous to examine whether, on this occasion, France will allow the Stadtholder a shade of power more or less, or whether he is or is not satisfied with the portion of authority to be left in his hands. It is evident, if this reform be the work of the French, it will tend solely to their advantage ; and that, in all future operations, the *political direction* of this country will belong to *them*. The immediate consequences of its sinking into a French Province are so disagreeable, and the remoter ones so dangerous to England, that I am certain I need not state them.   They apply also in great measure to the Republic as well as to us; and the only hope I retain of preventing the absolute completion of the views of France, with all its destructive consequences, is, by forming, encouraging, and assisting an opposition in the country itself.

My constant endeavours have uniformly tended to this object, and I have not been unsuccessful in my attempt to revive a Party here the late war had got near to annihilate, and to unite many very respectable individuals in support of the ancient system.   I have hitherto been able to keep them together by such general assurances as my instructions empowered me to make ; but the pressure of the moment is now become so great, that I am called upon for more substantial and solid proofs of our friendship, and I find myself reduced to the unpleasant dilemma either of abandoning them entirely, and, with them, all hopes of reclaiming this country, or else to amuse them (which would be both unjust and cruel) by promises I am not sure of being able to perform.

Thus circumstanced, you will, I flatter myself, forgive me if I address myself directly to you to know how I am to proceed.   Did I consult my own ease alone, I could go on enjoying, quietly and comfortably, the fruits of a lucrative and honourable Mission ; but I hope you will give me credit for serving on a much more liberal principle, and believe that these very considerations make it painful to me, unless I can be employed in it with, at least, a prospect of utility to the public.

If you will be troubled to peruse my despatches of this year, you will see the nature and extent of the assistance required, and the advantages to be obtained by it.   It does not belong to me to decide on what ought or ought not to be done ; but it is my duty to say, that if the rescuing this country from a dependence on France, and preventing that Court from employing against us in a future war the wealth, influence, and strength of this Republic be really a matter of importance, it only can be attempted in the manner I now mention. If I continue here in a state of political *inactivity,* and deprived of the means to support efficaciously the plan adopted by the friends to the ancient system, they will immediately disperse, and each of them make the best terms he can for himself, without waiting to fall a sacrifice to the animosity of the adverse party.

I may perhaps have taken the alarm too soon ; perhaps, also, I may be too anxious in the exercise of my profession ; but it appears to me, that France is making everywhere such amazing strides, and her influence becoming so great in every Court of Europe, (even in those where, till now, we had so much to say,) that *we cannot be too active in our opposition to her,* or too attentive to get a footing on the Continent, in order to be prepared to resist that weight of power she certainly means to direct against us whenever she feels herself prepared for war. She already presumes to treat us here as a Power from whom she has little to fear; and it is in consequence of her positive and repeated injunctions, and against the opinion of the majority of the States General, that the two friendly Memorials I have presented since my residence here have remained till now unanswered. But I am deviating from my subject, to which I now return, by entreating you to favour me with your intentions relative to it, and to forgive my having trespassed so long and so officiously on your time.

EXTRACT OF A LETTER FROM THE MARQUIS OF CARMARTHEN
TO SIR JAMES HARRIS.

Grosvenor Square, Dec. 5th, 1786.

My dear Sir,—Mr. Pitt called upon me to-day, and communicated to me your private letter; we had a most comfortable and confidential conversation upon the subject of Holland. He feels (as I knew he would do, when *properly stated,*) the great and serious importance of the subject; and his only difficulty appears to consist in keeping up a party without committing ourselves, till we are fully able to abide the consequence of openly declaring our sentiments.

The moment that I found his apprehensions were only respecting the *means,* rather than the *measure,* of eventually combating the French influence, and that he never would sacrifice to a consideration of *pecuniary* expense what I thought he must consider as politically necessary for this country, I own I felt the greatest pleasure and satisfaction. He will answer your letter by a few lines to-night. He has been so good as to propose a Cabinet Council, when and where I may think most convenient, in order to discuss the subject, and is perfectly and sincerely interested in doing everything for the attainment of the main object.*

LETTER FROM MR. PITT TO SIR JAMES HARRIS.

Downing Street, Dec. 5th, 1786.

Dear Sir,—I received the favour of your letter of the 28th of November, the subject of which is of great im-

---

* Lord Carmarthen had, from the commencement of Sir James Harris's mission, entered into his views respecting the part England ought to take in Dutch affairs, but on this question he then stood almost alone in the Cabinet; the Duke of Richmond being the only member of it who agreed with him. The King was brooding over his lost American Colonies, and averse to interference; and Pitt at first showed little interest in the matter. Lord Carmarthen's *private* letters all urge on Sir James Harris in the course he had adopted.—*Harris Papers.*

portance, and, I fear, of at least as much difficulty. I hope we shall be able to send you a messenger in a few days, and that you will then receive more particular and official instructions. At present I can only state to you in a few words the outline of my private sentiments on the present state of Holland.

I conceive it impossible to think of taking any step that can commit this country to the risk of extremities. Of course it follows, that we cannot encourage any party in the Republic *to incur risks in which we cannot support them;* nor would it, I conceive, be desirable that, under such circumstances, the strength of the parties opposed to each other should be brought to a test. The great object now seems to be that to which I conceive you point, *to endeavour to keep together a party which may act with advantage, both for their own country and for us, on some future day, if it should arrive.* But they must in a manner lie by for the present ; and any support from us, which too openly or actively avowed itself, would commit the honour of this country without doing good, and might, perhaps, force on a crisis, which would either lead us to a war, or make the state of the Republic, and particularly of our friends there, still more desperate. The sort of plan you suggest is, therefore, what I should like best, if it could be made practicable and effectual. At all events, I see much difficulty how the money wanted could be found here ; but what is most essential is, that, if public measures or ostensible security are necessary, we should be led into the very risks we wish to avoid.

I hardly see how any security could be held out for the loan to Friesland, without going to Parliament, which would both commit that country and expose this. If any way could be found of pledging the private credit of Government to individual merchants, and making them the ostensible security in Holland, the difficulty of furnishing the money (great as it is) might perhaps be overcome. But (if this were possible) I should be particularly anxious to have it understood, that our plan is solely to *keep together* a party for a day of more necessity, or better fitted for exertion, and that we wish to commit ourselves as little as possible at present. Lord Carmarthen is much recovered, though he does not mend so fast as I wish. I am, with great regard, dear Sir,

Your most obedient and faithful servant,

W. PITT.

If you can suggest any facilities as to the mode of what is proposed, I shall wish to hear it as soon as possible.

EXTRACT OF A DESPATCH FROM SIR JAMES HARRIS TO THE MARQUIS OF CARMARTHEN.

Hague, 5th Dec., 1786.

In Zealand, as I before said, much money has been employed; but Mons. de Rayneval was taking the most effectual way of getting it over, by declaring that the Pensionary Mons. Vander Spiegel was the only person with whom he could talk on the part of the Province.

As soon as ever this information reached me, I sent an express to Middlebourg, desiring him *not to come*; being satisfied, from numberless circumstances needless to relate, that the Faction have so artfully conducted their intrigues in Zealand, and prepared their plans so well, that the moment Mr. Vander Spiegel absents himself from the Province it is lost.

Your Lordship will observe from what I have written, that the only difference between Mons. de Rayneval's mode of acting, and that of those he has superseded, is, that he acts like a man of business, ability, and experience, whilst they behaved more like incendiaries than negotiators. I should deceive your Lordship if I was to say I thought the evil in the least diminished by the arrival of this new negotiator. The danger is certainly increased, since the catastrophe is drawing nearer and nearer; and all I can possibly effect (circumstanced as I am), is to avert the coup-de-grace as long as possible ; but this *can be* only a few weeks, and *may be* only a few days.

As for Prussia, Count Goertz remains without any instructions whatever, and I presume there can be no possible doubt but that every idea of relief or assistance from thence is given up. But, whatever may be His Prussian Majesty's intentions, they pass through the hands of his Minister at Paris.

EXTRACT OF A LETTER FROM SIR JAMES HARRIS TO THE MARQUIS OF CARMARTHEN.

Hague, 8th Dec., 1786.

IF the motives for your having been put out of sorts on the day you exerted yourself to carry the apologizing Portuguese are such as I suspect them to be, they will not greatly increase my good opinion of a certain person's feelings and sensibility, which were not very great before ; this personage—for it is a personage, not a person,—is, I take it, composed of very hard materials, and that there enters a good deal of marble into his composition.* God and your Lordship forgive me for the freedom of my observation !—If this should be the reason, and the only one, which I certainly hope it is, I am persuaded your *velléité* to resign lasted no longer than the first impressions of *humeur* which naturally were given by this ungracious conduct ; and that, before you eat your flounder, it had occurred to you, that, though you had a right to be displeased, you had none to be surprised, and that the gentleman acted as much in character as Dutch ladies do, when, on *certain* occasions, they amuse themselves in eating apples.

---

* Mr. Pitt obliged Lord Carmarthen, though very ill, to present at Court the Portuguese Minister ; and the annoyance he felt inclined him to offer his resignation. Sir James Harris's private correspondence of this date would show that Mr. Pitt's "hauteur" rendered him personally unpopular with many of his colleagues and followers. His great qualities were not yet known to them.

No letter I ever received from you, and I have in the course of my life been favoured with many very pleasant ones, ever gave me more real pleasure than that of the 5th instant. The same mail which came on yesterday brought me one from Mr. Pitt, which kept pace with yours. I have written one to him to-day, more explanatory of the subsidiary support wanted as well in Friesland and Zealand as in general here, which he desired me to do.

I have threatened him with a much longer letter soon, as the warmth with which he seems to enter into foreign politics has set my zeal afloat, and I am working like a dull poet who has just got an invitation (to dinner) from his Right Honourable patron. I shall wait, however, till I hear from you ; since, if you object to my sending it to him, I will suppress it entirely, which is more than the aforesaid poet would do with his verses.

LETTER FROM THE MARQUIS OF CARMARTHEN TO SIR JAMES HARRIS.

Grosvenor Square, Dec. 12th, 1786.

MY DEAR SIR,—I sincerely wish your conjecture was altogether right about my suffering since Wednesday se'n-night, mais soyez sûr que je connois mon homme* trop bien pour être sensiblement touché d'aucun accueil bon ou mauvais de sa part.

Your writing again to Pitt, and a more detailed letter, meets with my warmest approbation. Now we have *raised* his attention to the important object in question, we must, by all means, endeavour to *keep it up*, and not suffer Holland to be sacrificed either to lawn or cambric.

You know my sentiments respecting Prussia. With Russia and Denmark it might be well worth our while to secure her friendship ; and, if we cannot get the Eagle with *two* heads to make part of the system, I trust we may get that with only *one* (according to strict justice) at *half price*.

* Mr. Pitt.

EXTRACT OF A LETTER FROM SIR JAMES HARRIS TO THE
MARQUIS OF CARMARTHEN.

Hague, 12th Dec., 1786.

I AM afraid that the French will have time to complete
their work before we shall be ready with an opposition.
They seem to me determined to consummate, at all
events ; and I am left to choose between Eden's want of
sense or want of probity, when I read, under his hand,
that I shall find in Mons. de Rayneval a man of *temper,
forbearance, and tractability.* Eighteen years' experience
have brought me to admit, in its whole force, a truth inculcated into *John Bull* with his mother's milk—namely,
that France is a natural enemy ; and that she will remain
so as long as envy and jealousy are attributes inseparable
from the human mind, I am fully persuaded.

I am very apprehensive that our delay will be attended
with the greatest inconvenience. It is, perhaps, some comfort to reflect, that, from the texture of this country, as
much as from that of our own, it has been inevitable. I am
puzzled what I am to do, if the French carry matters to
extremities. By lifting up a finger I can raise an insurrection, and light up a civil war ; but, besides the inefficacy
of this kind of struggle, I feel an invincible repugnance
to carry my friends into risks and dangers of which I am
not to partake, and in which I cannot promise them any
certain assistance. On the other side, if I remain perfectly
quiet, the whole fire will extinguish, and the cause be
irretrievably lost. To steer, therefore, between avowed
encouragement and a total defection and neglect, seems
to be the line of conduct I am to pursue ; and it is so like
dancing on a rope, that I almost despair of performing
the task with any degree of effect or ability, or without
falling to the right or left.

You receive a very extraordinary despatch to-day from
Berlin. The late King had Solomon's *wisdom ;* this seems
disposed to have only his *concubines.* It is a singular

transition from Atheism to Illuminé. The French say, *C'est un Garçon Roi. Nous pouvons l'avoir quand nous le voulons, mais nous ne pouvons avoir la Hollande qu'à present.* This phrase, which is in the mouth of his valet-de-chambre, is, in fact, the sense of the Cabinet of Versailles.

EXTRACT OF A DESPATCH FROM SIR JAMES HARRIS TO THE MARQUIS OF CARMARTHEN.

Hague, 15th Dec., 1786.

I MENTIONED to your Lordship in my last, that both the Prince and Princess of Orange considered the proposals carried to Nimeguen by the Count Goertz as absolutely inadmissible. I have since been informed that the Princess despatched a messenger, unknown to this gentleman, on Sunday, in which she explains the motives of this refusal to the King her brother, and, after thanking His Prussian Majesty for what he has attempted in favour of her House, and lamenting its inefficacy, intimated a wish that Count Goertz should be recalled, rather than remain here in the manner he now does.

The French party are discomposed at this opinionative conduct in the Stadtholder, which they were in hopes Count Goertz would have been able to temperate. Mons. de Rayneval has been uncommonly busy since yesterday, and has been shut up almost the whole time with either one or more of the factious Pensionaries. They seem to hesitate how to proceed, and to pause before they attempt to enforce by violence what they cannot effectuate by negotiation. The eyes of people open every day more and more. The number of our friends increases ; and, provided we could procrastinate and keep things just where they are till the spring, I would almost take upon me to assure you that an opposition strong enough to stem the torrent would be ready by that time.

LETTER FROM THE MARQUIS OF CARMARTHEN TO SIR JAMES
HARRIS.

Hendon, Dec. 18th, 1786.

MY DEAR SIR,—By the accounts contained in your
letter of the 12th, it should seem there was scarce time
left for six or seven Cabinets, during the interval perhaps
of half as many weeks, to prevent Holland affording her
more than equal quota towards the complete triumph of
France. I mean, for the present; for as we shall doubtless
grow wiser, as well as the other powers, whose interest it
is to check the growth of French influence in time, I flatter
myself that Fortune will deduct something from the scale
of France in future, in order to keep up that decency of appearance so necessary in every female of reputation, and
which even the loss of sight in the aforesaid Goddess
cannot much longer preserve for her; as, had she been
only deprived of sight, blind-man's buff would have
proved the same person is not always favoured without a
secret understanding between the parties.

I have no doubt in my own mind (to speak seriously)
of the *necessity* (for propriety and expediency, perhaps,
would now be called upon too late for effect) of stopping
the French influence if possible, at all hazards, *coute qui
coute.* As to "the mischief of the measure, and the *justice of an injured country*," throw it all upon me; and, if
we can but bring those fellows the French to the gallows,
(vide Beggar's Opera,) I shall die contented. I think it
might now be so contrived that the supposed security of
France might operate to the ultimate defeat of her purposes. An insurrection *well-timed* and pretty *sharply
seasoned* might oblige us to come to a decisive conduct
respecting Holland, without leaving it to humanity alone
whether we should assist a distressed neighbour or not.
If something of this sort does not effectually awaken us,
I know we shall be so long preparing for the conflict, or
rather recruiting ourselves in order to *prepare*, when
France chooses to *begin* the conflict, that everything wor-

thy the attention of England in your *grenouillerie* will be totally out of our reach.

Hague, 22nd Dec.; 1786.

MONS. DE THULEMEYER, who since Count Goertz's absence has often seen Mons. de Rayneval, boasts of having obtained better conditions for the Stadtholder than those Count Goertz carried with him to Nimeguen, and that they are such as the Prince of Orange may consent to. If we may credit what he says, they were sent to the Stadtholder yesterday.

The conduct of the Stadtholder is at this moment everything his friends can wish, and it would be doing him great injustice not to mention with due applause his spirit, firmness, and temper at the present critical conjuncture.

LETTER FROM MR. PITT TO SIR JAMES HARRIS.

Downing Street, Dec. 26th, 1786.

DEAR SIR,—I am much obliged to you for your letter of the 23rd, which I received yesterday. The general scheme you suggest is undoubtedly desirable for this country; but I own myself not sanguine, as yet, as to the means of attaining it, though difficulties ought not to deter an attempt for which there may appear any opening. The situation of the United Provinces seems by your latter despatches to open every day more and more a prospect of our being able to cultivate an useful party there, which may at least fetter the operations of France whenever that Court takes a hostile turn, and which, in the mean time, may neither commit *us* nor *itself*. *Within that limit,* such a party cannot be too much encouraged ; but we cannot go beyond it with prudence towards ourselves, or with honesty towards them.

If you continue to think that, without departing from this caution, any secret means can be found of our giving pecuniary assistance either in Friesland or elsewhere, and that the prospect of success makes it worth the trial, I shall be inclined to do everything possible towards finding the means. It will, however, be necessary, on that supposition, that you should state in a secret letter to Lord Carmarthen, as distinctly *as possible in such a case*, the extent of the assistance wanted, the channels through which it can be afforded, without breaking through the line laid down, and the grounds for thinking it may be useful. I am very sure you will not be inclined to embark in anything of this sort without having these points cleared up to yourself. It will, after all, not be easy for us to judge them here ; but we wish, before a step of this sort is taken, to have all the considerations which relate to it fully before us.

I am, dear Sir, your most obedient and faithful servant,

W. PITT.

EXTRACT OF A DESPATCH FROM SIR JAMES HARRIS TO THE MARQUIS OF CARMARTHEN.

Hague, Tuesday, Dec. 26th, 1786.

THE conditions Mons. de Thulemeyer boasted to have obtained from Mons. de Rayneval were (as I guessed) in substance precisely the *same* as those carried to the Stadtholder by Count Goertz, and have, very deservedly, met with the same reception from His Highness.

This firm and manly conduct on his part procures him many new friends, and gives courage and spirits to his old ones ; while, on the other side, the intemperate behaviour of the leaders of the Faction, and the violence with which France seems determined to support their, or rather *her* views, raises a great and just alarm, and begins to open the eyes of the nation to a sense of the danger with which its liberties and its constitution are threatened. The Faction, however, are too far advanced to retire. If

they bend, they are instantly broken ; and they cannot
maintain their ground otherwise than by proceeding to
extremities.

EXTRACT OF A DESPATCH FROM SIR JAMES HARRIS TO THE
MARQUIS OF CARMARTHEN.

Hague, 29th Dec. 1786.

THE expression I took notice of in my other despatch
of this date, as used in the last instructions sent to Mons.
de Rayneval from Versailles, and which I have the best
reason to think is authentic, viz. *That it was become
necessary to bring the business here to a speedy and certain conclusion, for the better execution of plans equally
if not more important to France,* affords matter for very
serious and anxious reflection.   I cannot presume that
my information, further than as it relates to this particular spot, can be of any great value ; yet, such as it is, I
think it my duty to transmit it to your Lordship.

Letters from Cleves say that His Prussian Majesty has
forbid the writer of the Gazette of that town inserting in
his paper anything injurious to France.   They, moreover,
add, that Prince Henry's influence increases daily at Berlin ; and that, either directly or through his dependents,
it is expected that he will be soon able to overset Mons.
de Hertzberg, and establish the King, his nephew, in a
system of French politics : that Count Mirabeau has
been at Paris, charged with a special commission from
Prince Henry to Mons. de Vergennes ; and that, since his
return to Berlin, he is more with that Prince than ever.

The result of all this information leads to an opinion
that the Exchange of Bavaria is again coming forward in
quite a new shape ; that *France approves it,* and that
Mirabeau and Hohenfels are sent with some proposals of
aggrandizement to His Prussian Majesty, (what they are
cannot be guessed,) which may induce him not to oppose
it.   All this may be, and very probably is, idle conjecture ; and the manœuvres of France may have a direct

contrary tendency at Berlin from that of inducing the King of Prussia to gratify the Emperor in his favourite plan. The only certain fact is, that France is manœuvring there, and this alone ought to claim our utmost attention.*

EXTRACT OF A DESPATCH FROM SIR JAMES HARRIS TO THE MARQUIS OF CARMARTHEN.

Hague, Tuesday, 2nd Jan , 1787.

THE following is an extract of a letter which I received from Nimeguen on Sunday.

" Nos nouvelles finales de Berlin sont arrivées aujourd'hui (le 30 Décembre). *On* conseille des accommodemens. *On* craint des guerres civiles, et encore d'avantage de se mêler énergiquement de nos affaires. Le fait est que le Roi de Prusse voit partout l'Empereur; que la France alimente adroitement cette crainte, et fait entrevoir des secours qu'elle sauroit bien éluder dans le cas. Enfin *on* a des intérêts majeurs. Mais si on ne veut pas nous faire du bien, il faut espérer qu'on ne nous fera pas du mal.

" Nous restons fermes ici comme un roc, tandis que les ennemis se plaisent à répandre qu'il y a de la désunion entre les deux principaux Personnages sur la matière en question. Ce qui est complètement faux.

" Comptez que quoiqu'il arrive, cette fermeté sera soutenue jusqu'au bout.

" Le Prince aime mieux succomber avec honneur que de se maintenir avec ignominie."

I was interrupted by a note, giving me an account that the messenger from Count Goertz to M. de Rayneval is this moment arrived. I shall again, with your Lordship's leave, copy the note itself.

" Le contenu de la lettre du Comte de Goertz à Monsieur de Rayneval porte *un refus net*.

* Mirabeau, in his " Cour de Berlin," says, the Emperor at this time offered His Prussian Majesty to help him to the rest of Poland if he would not oppose his claims to Bavaria.

" Les instances et les réprésentations de la Princesse auprès du Roi ne lui ont valu, de la part de son frère, que des conseils froids de céder aux circonstances, de faire les sacrifices inadmissibles qu'on demandait, et *de ne pas compter sur lui.*

" Elle lui a déjà écrit, et elle lui écrira encore demain (2me Janvier), que n'ayant à choisir qu'entre la perte de l'honneur, (avec laquelle les conditions étaient inséparables,) et le danger de succomber peut-être, mais de succomber injustement, ni elle ni le Prince ne balançaient pas de donner la préférence au dernier ; et tout ce qui lui restait, c'était de prier le Roi de faire finir, au plutôt, toute négociation entre Monsieur de Goertz, Monsieur de Rayneval, et Monsieur de Thulemeyer."

These, my Lord, are Count Goertz's own words, as the person who sent me the intelligence has copied them from a letter he writes on this occasion to his secretary.

EXTRACT OF A LETTER FROM SIR JAMES HARRIS TO THE MARQUIS OF CARMARTHEN.

Hague, 3rd Jan., 1787.

As to the indefinite and unspecified charges I have lumped together at 6,000*l.* annually, they may be much less ; but I know how your hands are tied up in the office, and I cannot but think it is better to give you elbow-room. I trust I shall not be deemed as a *public defaulter,* if I apply some very small portion of this sum to the extraordinary dinners I shall be forced to give, if (as I shall be if our plans succeed) I am to become a *Chef de parti.* Hospitality is the life and soul of a party here, and an able cook goes as far, if not further, than an able secretary.

Nothing gives me so much serious and anxious concern as the immense progress of French influence on every side ; and I am sure *you* will not think me departing from my duty in endeavouring to call as much as possible the attention of Ministry to this point, on which our very existence depends. I am the more eager, as I think I see *somewhere or other* a propensity to admit the possibility of France being sincere in her assurances, or an inclination to believe that we are acute enough to outwit France. The first never can be ; and, as to the second point, I should scorn an Englishman who would wish to maintain the greatness and dignity of his country by cunning and artifice—by *playing at cups and balls* better than the French. I always apply to England those fine verses of Virgil, who, after enumerating the superior skilfulness and dexterity of the Greeks, says, —

> " Tu regere imperio populos, Romane, memento :
> (Hæ tibi erunt artes) pacisque imponere morem,
> Parcere subjectis, et debellare superbos."

E——, who is not the *Romane* in these verses, is, I find, gone back to Paris ; where, as you will observe in my official letters of to-day, I suspect Rayneval will soon go and meet him. I confess, notwithstanding the instructions sent me by this great commercial negotiator (E——), I feel more satisfaction in having contributed perhaps my mite towards driving away this Functionary *re infectâ*, than if by obsequiousness and flattery I had obtained from him the unflattering title (especially in the mouth of a Frenchman addressed to an Englishman) *" d'un homme très doux, fort raisonnable, et d'une grande facilité dans les affaires."*

EXTRACT OF A LETTER FROM THE MARQUIS OF CARMARTHEN
TO SIR JAMES HARRIS.

Hendon, 8th Jan., 1787.

My dear Sir,—I write from my Hermitage, (where, by the by, you will, I hope, be hung in effigy over my parlour chimney in a few days,) and consequently begin by thanking you most sincerely for your letter of the 5th. I feel its friendly contents, and mean to regulate myself by them as far as possible.

Your letter (with its enclosure) of the 2nd,* I received likewise to-day, and am infinitely obliged to you for it. The person whom you do not venture to answer for is *not* of the Cabinet : we are at present *sine pulvere*, and, from what I can judge from a letter I received to-day from *Windsor*, are likely to remain equally *sine palmâ*. I own I am equally hurt, and (if I might say it) angry at the answer I received from thence to my letter of yester-day.† The disgraceful conduct of this country in respect to America is quoted ; the *supposed* idea of being the Drawcansir of Europe *properly* reprobated ; a future hope, by means of some years' peace, held out as likely to restore the country to its former situation, suggested ; and the event (not barely the attempt) of acting, or indeed realizing that part, regarded as *destructive* at present. So much for the sublime !

Now in plain language, and strictly speaking in the vulgar tongue, what the devil can I do ? You know my sentiments respecting Holland are, to be effectually active at all events, with every degree of caution and prudence possible ; but not even to sacrifice to the terrors of a rupture with France the seeing the Republic becoming an absolute dependent province of hers. I stated the *Convocation des Notables* as an instance that France was not ripe for extremities ; and humbly submitted my opinion that the surest method of preserving the public tranquillity was, by taking such measures as would prevent France from finding it her *interest* to interrupt it.

---

* Sir J. Harris in this letter continued to urge more active measures in favour of the Stadtholder, with the quotation "non sine pulvere palma."

† From the King, who harped to the end of his life on the loss of our American Colonies, and who was at this time thoroughly disgusted with the results of the last war.

EXTRACT OF A DESPATCH FROM SIR JAMES HARRIS TO THE
MARQUIS OF CARMARTHEN.

Hague, 9th Jan., 1787.

MONSIEUR DE RAYNEVAL (to use his own words) is determined to make a third and last attempt, before he
leaves the Hague, to prevail on the Stadtholder to enter
upon a conciliatory negotiation. He says, he hopes
His Highness will not, for the sake of a few useless privileges (des prérogatifs stériles), expose the Republic to the
horrors of a civil war ; and he has authorized the Baron
Thulemeyer by a written note to say, *en cas que le
Stadthouder veuille faire quelques démonstrations, lui
(Monsieur de Rayneval) est prêt à les écouter.*

These are the words of his note, which Monsieur de
Rayneval sent on Sunday to Monsieur de Thulemeyer
without a signature, and allowed him to take a copy of it,
provided he returned the original. Monsieur de Rayneval has written in the meanwhile to Monsieur de
Vergennes to this effect : That having now reconciled the
opinions of the two Courts of Versailles and Berlin (les
ayant mis d'accord) relative to the affairs of this country,
he considered himself as having succeeded in the primary
and most essential object of his Mission ; that, in regard
to the bringing about a reconciliation between the two
parties, he is convinced, from what he has seen, of its impossibility under the present circumstances ; and that, if
Monsieur de Vergennes seriously wishes that this should
be effected, France must either employ force, or else consent to take up the negotiation afresh, and on quite new
principles.

The Patriots are strongly for the idea of forcing the
Stadtholder to terms; and, if they are divided in opinion,
it is only in respect to the greater or less degree of violence to be employed.

If I were not used to the timid and irresolute character
of those who compose the party with which I am acting,
I should be almost driven to renounce all hopes of effect-

ing any great purpose with such feeble instruments, from the fear they express on the present occasion, and from their extreme caution of appearing ostensibly to assert their rights and privileges. But I reckon, as the danger draws nearer, their timidity will diminish ; and as their apprehensions are not *personal*, but for their houses and property, that, although they may now hold back lest their windows should be broken, they will yet be bold enough when they see their habitations tottering about their ears.

Could I but once accomplish the great point of uniting them, everything would go smoothly ; but, in attempting this, I find the most unaccountable and most unreasonable difficulties.

Monsieur Boers, Secretary and Advocate to the Dutch East India Company, gave notice to the Court of Directors, on Thursday last, of his intention to give up his employment.

The motives he assigned do him the greatest honour. He declared he considered the Company as following the impulse of a *foreign* influence ; that the measures they were adopting would necessarily lead to its ruin ; and, not having weight enough to oppose the effect of this influence, he could not prevail on himself to take any share in the carrying through measures so contrary to his opinion and principles.

By this resignation he loses two-thirds of his income, and is reduced to a very narrow fortune.

EXTRACT OF A DESPATCH FROM SIR JAMES HARRIS TO THE MARQUIS OF CARMARTHEN.

Hague, 12th Jan., 1787.

MONSIEUR DE RAYNEVAL has received orders to return to Versailles, and his servants are preparing everything for his departure on Tuesday next.

I am inclined to think that it is settled that they shall not proceed against the Stadtholder until Monsieur de Rayneval is fairly out of the country ; and that, till this event takes place, we shall not see clearly into their intentions.

Your Lordship may recollect that this gentleman was presented, when he arrived here, with a rich service of plate. I understand one of equal value (14,000f.) is preparing for him on his taking leave.

By different means, unnecessary to detail to your Lordship, we have raised a noble spirit of opposition in the town of Rotterdam, and have drawn up an address and remonstrance to the State of Holland against the proceeding of the Patriots in that town, which is already signed by 8,000 people, amongst which are many of the first inhabitants, and all the clergy except two.

I have written to the principal English houses there, recommending to them also strongly to put their names to this paper ; for, however cautious I am not to commit my countrymen in any political measure which might be detrimental to their commercial interests, or affect their credit as traders ; yet, as these are naturalized at Rotterdam, and have to every intent and purpose the same concern that good order and tranquillity should be maintained in that city as any of its Dutch inhabitants, I cannot see the remotest reason why they should not concur in a measure which has declaredly only this object in view.

They compose the most considerable and most respectable part of the citizens of Rotterdam, and their concurrence will probably decide the effect of the Petition.

Hague, 16th Jan., 1787.

THE Stadtholder, in return to Monsieur de Rayneval's last overture, has replied in the same manner as to the two preceding ones, by again declaring that neither his duty towards his country, that towards his family, nor his own honour (notwithstanding his ardent desire of putting an end to the present troubles), allow him to yield to any concessions, so long as he remains suspended as Captain-General of Holland, and deprived of the command of the garrison of the Hague, and till he has received complete and ample satisfaction for these two unjust stigmas put on his Administration and conduct.

LETTER FROM THE MARQUIS OF CARMARTHEN TO SIR
JAMES HARRIS.

Grosvenor Square, Jan. 19th, 1787.

MY DEAR SIR,—I have nothing of sufficient importance to communicate to you to render an official despatch necessary to-night, and therefore confine myself to private correspondence.

According to appearances, I flatter myself the proposals you have mentioned respecting Friesland and Zealand have met with a favourable reception. That of the latter Province appears more difficult in its execution than the one respecting the former. The characters of *our friends* in the Republic, though not precisely what I could have wished them to be, are by no means of a nature to slacken my zeal in endeavouring to keep up a party sufficient to thwart the views of France.

The King appears perfectly to agree with you respecting the conduct of the English merchants at Rotterdam. I did not (as you may suppose) endeavour to throw cold water upon the Royal ardour, which, literally speaking, was strongly and manfully, as well as properly displayed upon the subject, but sincerely wished to *have spread it further, but* —— !

My birthday dinner went off tolerably well.

Remember me kindly to Lady Harris, and my best respects to the venerable and worthy Greffier.

EXTRACT OF A DESPATCH FROM SIR JAMES HARRIS TO THE MARQUIS OF CARMARTHEN.

Hague, 23rd Jan., 1787.

THE Stadtholderate has from the earliest period of its existence been the work of the people, and it is through the people alone that it can be restored.

I receive very satisfactory intelligence from Nimeguen. I cannot do better than convey it to your Lordship in the Princess of Orange's own words.

" On vous a bien informé touchant la dernière tentative de Mons. de Rayneval ; nous y avons répondu selon les principes de la première réponse, et cela en est resté là. Il a prétendu n'y trouver aucune base, que ses ordres étaient trop précis pour s'en écarter, et qu'il devait partir au temps marqué.

" J'espère que les liens d'union entre les Provinces se formeront de plus en plus, et que l'activité accroîtra en proportion. Plus la crise devient forte, plus la sagesse et l'énergie doivent augmenter, et je doute fort que dans le fond nos adversaires soient fort à leur aise."

It is evident from this letter, written with Her Royal Highness's own hand, that she entirely approves the conduct of the Stadtholder, and that she gave her full consent to his repeated refusals of the French proposals. It also follows that she wishes to encourage and promote the *Association*,* and that she considers it as the only

---

* Sir James Harris advised that an Association should be formed, the members of which were to sign their names and pledge themselves to the Stadtholderian party. Mr. Vander Spiegel was to have the direction of the project.

means for restoring the Stadtholder and saving the commonwealth.

In support of the last passage in the Princess's letter, I may add the sentiments of the Pensionary Vander Spiegel, who, in writing to me since M. Rayneval's departure, says, "Si, comme vous croyez, les Patriotes prétendent pousser les affaires par la violence, soyez assuré qu'ils creusent leur propre tombeau."

I hope by next post to inform your Lordship that the *Association* has begun to take shape. Besides the concurrence of the Provinces, I am not without hope of getting round, if proper measures are employed, some of the towns in Holland itself.

EXTRACT OF A DESPATCH FROM SIR JAMES HARRIS TO THE MARQUIS OF CARMARTHEN.

Hague, 30th Jan., 1787.

I CAN now give your Lordship a much better account of the internal situation of affairs here than at any time since my arrival. I received yesterday accounts from Monsieur Vander Spiegel, that the project of Association was actually signed in Zealand by all the first people of the Province, and that they were determined to abide by its principles to the last extremity.

In consequence of this very satisfactory intelligence, I immediately communicated it to our friends in Gelderland, urging them not to lose a moment in following this example; and on Friday next I expect one of the leading men of that Province here, with a long list of very respectable names.

The same measures will be taken with regard to Friesland; and the other three Provinces of Utrecht, Overyssel, and Groningen will not be neglected.

The great object is to make *all* sign *at once*, and to complete the operation before our adversaries are aware that it is on the anvil.

I am so entirely occupied in endeavouring to effect

this, and I have such a number of people perpetually coming in (whom I must see), that I have scarcely leisure to give your Lordship a detail of what is going forward.

If we succeed in forming this Association, and do not afterwards fail in the direction of it, I shall entertain great hopes of success.

EXTRACT OF A DESPATCH FROM SIR JAMES HARRIS TO THE MARQUIS OF CARMARTHEN.

Hague, 2nd Feb., 1787.

Two of the principal British merchants at Rotterdam, Mr. Pillans and Mr. Littledale, waited upon me on Wednesday morning, to explain the strong motives they had for not subscribing to the Address.

They alleged their having hitherto kept themselves religiously free from all political controversy ; that their connexions are with men of all descriptions ; and that, if they took any share on this occasion, it would not only greatly affect their mercantile situation, but their domestic comfort also ; that justice, which is in the hands of the Patriots, would be denied them, and that they should be perpetually exposed to the insults of the armed mob. That, moreover, they are convinced in their own minds, that the ten or twelve names which would be added to the list by their consenting to sign the Address, would by no means be a weight in the scale ; on the contrary, it would give it the odium of appearing an English measure, and revive the clamours against the English cabal.

As I found most of *their* reasons were of a personal nature, and as all *mine* were of a public one, I felt it absolutely useless to combat their arguments; and I thought it better to give up the point quietly, than to indispose them by entering into a needless altercation with them.   I contented myself, therefore, with desiring them to stay to dinner with me ; telling them that I had asked, for the purpose of meeting them, five or six of the principal Regents of Rotterdam, and that for my sake as well as for their own, I wished they would repeat to those gentlemen the reasons they had just given to me for declining the proposal I had made them : this they did, and we all separated on very friendly terms.

I enclose the Act of Association signed in Zealand. It is an amplification of the Three Points* I sent to your Lordship so long ago, and, both in its style and substance, is a masterly performance.

To-day I expect my friends from the Provinces ; and to-morrow I have a select dinner, for the purpose of forwarding this very essential measure of Union, on which everything depends.

Young Count Bentinck, better known by the name of Rhoon, under which his grandfather brought about the Revolution in 1747, is one of my most active and useful friends. He has (at my request) set on foot a meeting of the Members of this Province only, every Thursday evening, in order to concert a plan of opposition to be pursued in the States of Holland ; and the Deputies of Rotterdam, the Brille, Delft, Enkhuysen, and Medenblyk, already constantly attend.

This, with the Equestrian Order, insures us six votes. My constant language to them all is, " union and a preconcerted plan." If this can be obtained, and our conduct followed up with common sense and common firmness, I am satisfied our enemies must ultimately sink before us.

————

EXTRACTS OF A LETTER FROM SIR JAMES HARRIS TO MR. EWART.

Hague, Feb. 3rd., 1787.

I HAVE often expressed to you my wish that the Court of Berlin would have done either more or less in behalf

* The three points were,

1. To preserve and defend the Constitution.

2. To resist all foreign subjection, and maintain the independence of the States.

3. Mutually to aid, sustain, and indemnify one another for all losses incurred in carrying out their plan.

of the Prince of Orange. The event seems to justify my having done so. France has, by her artful and insidious language, lulled your Court into a persuasion that the Stadtholder is in the wrong ; and their party here, the Prussian *épouvantail* being removed, will proceed with an insolence equal to their confidence.

The only remaining resource the Republic now has, must be sought for within itself ; and when we look back, and consider the situations of danger and distress from which by vigorous and unexpected exertions it has in former periods extricated itself, I do not think it doing justice to the character and spirit of the Dutch nation to declare its doom irrevocably fixed. A degree of alarm is so spread, that the Provinces seem already disposed to forget their separate and distinct interests in order to form an union of measures to protect and defend those of the Constitution in general.

In regard to general politics, I have very little to say worthy your attention. My speculations on the subject were more pleasant six months ago than now; and, unless some unforeseen convulsion produces a sudden revolution amongst the Continental Powers, I think we shall all remain in the same awkward and disjointed state in which we now stand, for many years more,—at least, till such time as France thinks it a favourable opportunity, either to gratify her ambition or promote her interests, to disturb the public tranquillity. This event, whenever it happens, may jumble us into a system. Till then England has nothing to do but to prepare herself for it by every precaution of self-defence ; and to wait patiently till France, by throwing off the mask, discovers the double game she has been playing.

EXTRACTS OF A DESPATCH FROM SIR JAMES HARRIS TO THE
MARQUIS OF CARMARTHEN.

Hague, 6th Feb., 1787.

MY dinner on Saturday answered in a great measure
the purpose for which it was intended.

The Association will be signed in Gelderland by almost
the whole body of the States, and I trust in Utrecht by
far the majority of them.

Friesland wavers. The Diet is assembled there without
my having, as yet, been able to give them that kind of
support they asked for ; our enemies avail themselves of
this disposition, and already boast of having brought back
that Province to its line of duty, as they call it.

In Zealand the Association is so popular a measure that
the success it meets with is even more than could be
wished for, since it has led the people to express their
joy by excesses which may be censured.

Monsieur Vander Spiegel did all in his power to check
this popular ardour ; but he could not prevent the people
breaking the windows of the Patriots at Ter-goes, and
forcing them to wear orange-coloured ribbons.

I consider it my duty to stay up our interest in this
country, till such time as I am *distinctly* ordered to
abandon it entirely.

I confess, my Lord, I am on this point very often reduced to a great dilemma, for though my instructions, as
well as my general knowledge of the sentiments of my
Court, forbid my entirely quashing the hopes of our
friends here, yet I by no means feel myself empowered to
give them anything like positive assurances ; and, thus
circumstanced, it would be as contrary to those principles
of *political honour* on which England ever acted, as to
my *own private feelings*, if I were to amuse them with
fair words, or buoy up their expectations by specious
promises, which I was not certain in the event we meant
to, or even could, perform.

LETTER FROM THE MARQUIS OF CARMARTHEN TO SIR
JAMES HARRIS.

Whitehall, Feb. 16, 1787.

MY DEAR SIR,—I am not quite sure whether your despatch this day received is precisely worded as I could
have wished it to have been, as I am afraid it may be in-
terpreted, by *those* * whose opinions *we* must manage with
address, into a sort of complaint of not receiving proper
support from hence, in the prosecution of a plan which
all must wish to see successful, but which, if painted too
strongly, may from its glare alarm those whose eyes are
weak enough to be dazzled with any greater degree of
light than might be derived from the modest unpre-
tending glimmer of a farthing candle. In short, I can
only add, what there is no occasion for you to learn, that
we must deal with people according to what they *are,*
and not conduct ourselves upon the idea of what they
ought to be.

EXTRACT OF A DESPATCH FROM SIR JAMES HARRIS TO THE
MARQUIS OF CARMARTHEN.

Hague, 20th Feb., 1787.

THE slighting manner in which the French Ambas-
sador mentioned the name of the Prince of Orange, was
taken notice of by their High Mightinesses ; and the
Greffier Fagel was ordered by them to signify to the
Marquis de Verac, " that it was not customary in a
Ministerial Note † to name His Highness by the title of
Prince de Nassau, and that they hoped he would change
it to that of Prince Stadtholder."

The French Ambassador answered, that he had received
the Note in the very words in which it was conceived, and
that it was not in his power to make any alteration
whatever.

---

* The non-interference members, and, in fact, the majority in the Cabinet.
† This Note is lost in the missing volume before mentioned.

The Prince of Orange himself resents highly this slight put upon him, but still more the expression of *demi-confidence*, and has written a letter, which will be read to the States this day, saying, " that he never has, or wished to conceal any part of his public conduct from their High Mightinesses ; but that, not having copies of the letters the French Court now think proper to publish, it was not in his power to communicate them."

I was misinformed when I observed that the Princess of Orange was mentioned with disrespect. Your Lordship will perceive that Her Royal Highness is not named in the Note ; but, in conversing with the Pensionary, the French Ambassador said, " she took rather too much on herself, and talked in the style of *Gouvernante des Sept Provinces.*"

This Note has occasioned more sensation than any which has been presented since my arrival. The public feel the indignity offered to their Stadtholder reaches them ; and it has raised in every description of people a degree of resentment against the French which cannot fail of producing good effects.

The debates in the States of Holland ran very high on Saturday, and the conduct of the Patriots was a mixture of indecency, violence, and fear.

The whole garrison of the Hague, but particularly the regiment of Dutch Guards, are greatly offended at the idea of the Rhingrave's corps being to be quartered here ; and I expect, if the design does take place, that the most serious consequences may ensue.

This respectable regiment was grossly insulted the other night by some one who painted in their colours, over the Arms of this Province, a gallows.

The Patriots say it is an insult offered the States of Holland, and tax the regiment with having done it to show their disrespect for the arms of their Sovereign. The regiment, on the other side, considered it as having been done by the Patriots themselves, for the purpose of drawing down on them the anger of the States, and to furnish an additional pretext for bringing the Rhingrave's corps to the Hague. I have no doubt whatever that this is the fact ; and I have advised several of the officers, who have been talking to me on the subject, to spare neither pains nor expense to discover the author.

The crisis is certainly hastening on very fast ; and I should see it approach not only with great tranquillity, but even with great impatience and satisfaction, if the energy and union of one party kept pace with the violence and confusion of the other. Sorry I am to say this is not the case, and that neither my efforts nor persuasions are sufficient to rally the courage of our friends, or to call forth in them that degree of spirit which, properly exerted, would lead them to infallible success.

EXTRACT OF A DESPATCH FROM SIR JAMES HARRIS TO THE
MARQUIS OF CARMARTHEN.

Hague, 23rd Feb., 1787.

I HAVE got accounts from Amsterdam that everything there is in a state of great fermentation. That the *Patriotic Association*, in their last meeting (on Wednesday), have actually signed a *formal convention with France*, and a solemn abjuration of the House of Orange. These are the words of my letter, but to what extent they are to be understood I cannot pretend to say. That the burghers, or rather tribunes of the people, have held what they call *a council of war*,—that is, an assembly in their military capacity as guards of the town,—and declared their approbation of the conduct of Haerlem and Dordt ; that the burgomaster Hoeuft, the Sieur Alleman, and the other chiefs of the Democratical Party, are stirring up the people to a revolt, and dispersing money for this purpose without either shame or reserve. On the other side, that our friends (if they deserve that name) are hesitating what to do, and, from the dread of restoring to the Stadtholder a shadow of power, are inclined to refuse the support of twenty thousand men who work in the dockyards, and are armed with hatchets, and four times as many who would immediately rally on being called upon in the name of the House of Orange.

EXTRACT OF A DESPATCH FROM SIR JAMES HARRIS TO THE MARQUIS OF CARMARTHEN.

Hague, 2nd March, 1787.

AFTER people's minds being kept in suspense and doubt till the very last moment, the States of Holland voted on Wednesday, 10 to 9, against the Rhingrave of Salm's corps coming to the Hague.

The Patriots, though disappointed, are not dismayed at this check, and are preparing to return to the charge with redoubled vigour and activity.

To prevent this, it is of the last consequence for the well-disposed party not to deem themselves too sure, nor to think that, having done a little, they have done all ; but to take advantage of the temper of the towns while it lasts, and to follow up with perseverance, spirit, and method this first gleaming of victory.

It is for this purpose that I have, ever since this unexpected turn in our favour, been indefatigable in my endeavours to impress on the minds of our friends the indispensable necessity of observing a systematic line of conduct ; and, in concert with some of the most confidential of them, have drawn up a string of proposals to be submitted to them as a basis on which they may form their plan of operations.

It consists of five points.

1. To break the legion of Salm.

2. Not to re-admit the towns of Dordt and Haerlem to the Assembly of the States till they have given satisfaction for their irregular and indecent conduct in withdrawing from their meetings ; and that the advisers of this conduct (Gyslaer and Zeebergen) should be disqualified for ever sitting as deputies in the States.

3. That a committee should be appointed to suppress and abolish the Free Corps in every part of this Province.

4. That the commission, composed of five persons, to act as Captain-General (under the suspension of the Prince of Orange), should be broken, and the office vested in the States.

5. That the Act of Suspension should be taken off, and both the post of Captain-General and Command of the Hague be restored to the Stadtholder.

These proposals, preceded by a proper preamble, were read last night to nineteen deputies of this Province, and approved by them all ; and they have engaged to use their endeavours to get them adopted by the Regents of the towns they represent.

In regard to the other Provinces, I have to-morrow near forty of the deputies or members of the different governments to dine with me ; and I hope, when they are collected, it will appear evident to them all, the necessity of immediately signing the Association. It is an Herculean labour to make them feel they are all members of one State, threatened all with one common danger.

The Prince of Orange continues to persevere in a very manly and steady behaviour, and I am confident will never submit to any dishonourable or disgraceful terms.

EXTRACT OF A LETTER FROM SIR JAMES HARRIS
TO W. FRASER, ESQ.

Hague, 20th March, 1787.

I ENCLOSE you a letter I received yesterday from Hake.* I await your orders ; my own opinion is, that the intention is not to get or give intelligence, but to get money If you knew how stupid, heavy, and interested the Hakes are, you would be convinced no good could come from that quarter.

* Hake, father and son, were soi-disant English spies in France ; and, according to Sir J. Harris's opinion, were dear at the money they received.

Strange rumours are gone abroad, relative to the conduct of England in regard to foreign politics, without being contradicted ; if they are true, I see shortly an end to my mission, for I will never again write a despatch if I am ordered to please, to approve, or to co-operate with France.

Sed mihi vel Tellus optem prius ima dehiscat,
Vel Pater omnipotens adigat me fulmine ad umbras,
Pallentes umbras Erebi, noctemque profundam,
Ante—*I become French.*

EXTRACT OF A DESPATCH FROM SIR JAMES HARRIS TO THE MARQUIS OF CARMARTHEN.

Hague, 23rd March, 1787.

THE question which was to have come on in the States of Holland this morning was postponed.

I have this moment (12 o'clock at night) received a letter from Nimeguen.

Monsieur de Thulemeyer has been received very coolly. When my letter came away yesterday morning, he had not made any direct proposal ; but it is expected that he will make one to-day on the part of France, the basis of which is, to use the words of my correspondent, " *l'éloignement de ceux qu'on suspecte ne pas être inclinés à adopter les mesures de la France.*" On which the Prince of Orange observed, " *Monsieur Thulemeyer, veut-il que j'abandonne les honnêtes gens afin de me livrer aux misérables ?*"

EXTRACTS OF A DESPATCH FROM SIR JAMES HARRIS TO THE MARQUIS OF CARMARTHEN.

Hague, 27th March, 1787.

I HAVE from the beginning never once varied in my opinion that France knows no medium between these two extremes, and that she is bent either on subduing or on destroying this country : the methods she employs may alter according to circumstances, according to the character of her Ministers, or according to that of those on whom she means to impose ; but her object is uniformly the same, and nothing but necessity will ever force her to subscribe to a system short of this plan, at which she has been so long working, and to effectuate which she has been at such an enormous expense.

It is for this reason that no sincere proposal for an accommodation on fair and equitable terms has, or ever will, come from the Court of Versailles ; and I every day receive fresh proofs, and such as carry the strongest conviction to the mind, that Monsieur de Rayneval was sent hither *not to negotiate, but to observe;* not with a wish to terminate the dissensions of the Republic, but solely to examine how they could be best applied to the completion of the views of his Court.

I have received this morning in the strictest confidence from Nimeguen a copy of some proposals the Baron Thulemeyer laid on Saturday last before the Prince and Princess of Orange, so distinctly marked with the features I have just described, that they almost unavoidably led me to express what I so strongly feel.

These proposals were rejected as soon as heard.

EXTRACTS OF A DESPATCH FROM SIR JAMES HARRIS TO THE MARQUIS OF CARMARTHEN.

Hague, 6th April, 1787.

THE fermentation at Amsterdam has again subsided without producing any good whatever. The same pusillanimity which directed the conduct of the magistrates in February prevailed again now, and, after a very feeble resistance, they gave way on Wednesday to a mob inferior both in numbers and consideration to that from which (if they had thought proper) they might have derived the most effectual support.

They consented that day to recall and change their

present deputies to the States of Holland, to reprove them for having voted against the sentiments of the Patriots in the choice of the Commissioners to ascertain the rights of the people ; and finally, the magistrates pledged themselves to declare their intention of keeping up the Rhingrave of Salm's legion.

Every part of this engagement has been since fulfilled. Their deputies (who were men of respectable character) are recalled and reprimanded.

It seems, however, indeed certain that the imperious and despotic conduct of the French faction on this occasion has raised a great degree of resentment and indignation.

Whether it will operate to this effect at Amsterdam, and whether the Regency of that city (after having so often failed in their resolution) will at last assume spirit enough to adhere to the promises they now make, I can by no means take upon me to say. With people otherwise constituted than these Amsterdamers, I should have no scruple to pronounce in the affirmative ; since their civil liberty, their personal safety, and the security of their property are at stake.

I am well aware that, in addition to this want of firmness and judgment inherent to their natural character, they are also withheld from accepting the offer of assistance held out to them in the terms it is proposed, lest they should be instrumental in restoring too great a degree of power to the Stadtholder.

The invariable principle of even our best friends at Amsterdam is, to curtail and diminish this power as much as possible, from the very false idea that the weight and consideration of that city rises in proportion as this sinks.

This maxim, the original cause of all the present discussions, was the road through which the French influence first introduced itself into the Republic ; and it was in conformity to this maxim, and in perfect concert with all the wishes of Amsterdam, that the Court of Versailles acted, till such time as its party had acquired strength and power enough to stand alone. It then shook off an associate with whom it was to divide its authority; and who, though sufficiently hostile to a Stadtholderian form of government, was by no means disposed to adopt measures tending to overset the Constitution, or to gratify the designs of France by throwing the Republic into its arms.

Before I quit this subject, I shall observe that my advice has been asked from Amsterdam ; and that I have answered, that, " if they mean anything, and have a system, they have nothing to do but to imitate the other towns, in this Province, which act in defence of their liberties against the French Faction."

EXTRACTS OF A LETTER FROM SIR JAMES HARRIS TO THE MARQUIS OF CARMARTHEN.

Hague, 6th April, 1787.

I CAN with a safe conscience say, I have not spent a single shilling at Gorcum, nor ever used with any one of the members of that Regency any other mode of corruption than fair words and civil speeches.   I may therefore safely set at defiance the libel from Amsterdam ; and, if the newspapers get impertinent, it may as safely be resented.

Amongst various arguments used against me personally, the Patriots have lately thought proper to tax me as acting without instructions, and from my own head. Silly and impossible as this accusation is, you cannot conceive how it has gained belief here, or what I have to do to persuade people that, although you are my very good friend, and endowed with the largest share of good-nature, you would long since have recalled and disgraced me, had this been the case.

I confess, my dear Lord, it is a very arduous task to keep our party together ; and that, if either from some interior or foreign event we are not led to form a system relative to this country, it must soon disperse, and every hope of recovering Holland be lost as far as relates to *us*.

I have a great deal *to say* on this subject, but I do not think it becoming for me to *write* it ; and one of my reasons for wishing to pass a few weeks with you this summer is, to discuss very fully the importance of this country, and the risks which ought, or not, to be run to reclaim it, with the table of chances pro and con.

EXTRACTS OF A DESPATCH FROM SIR JAMES HARRIS TO THE MARQUIS OF CARMARTHEN.

Hague, 13th April, 1787.

I SHALL pay the strictest attention to every word set forth in your Lordship's despatch. It conveys the truest and most striking picture of the situation of Europe, and I shall exert myself to the utmost in my endeavours to act up to instructions so important in themselves, and so entirely consonant to my own principles and feelings.

France, I am convinced, confides more in her cunning than in her force ; and, if we assume address enough to counteract the first, we have no reason to fear the latter.

Though her operations extend on all sides, yet their *central point* is undoubtedly to be found in this country. The preserving the ascendancy she has usurped over it, and the being able to dispose of it in any way she may think proper against England, are her primary objects.

I feel this so forcibly myself, that it is with the greatest pleasure I read in the excellent despatch I am now answering, that it is your Lordship's opinion, " that we cannot be too attentive to every measure which may tend towards the accomplishment of the designs of France, and that it becomes us to counteract them by a firm and decisive conduct ; and that, at all events, we must prevent their ultimate and complete success."

I consider this as such sound and salutary policy, that it will redouble the zeal, assiduity, and (if I may say so) the affection with which I serve my Royal Master.

I mentioned to your Lordship in my last, that overtures were preparing on the part of the principal Regents of Amsterdam for uniting their interests with those of the Stadtholder.

The general principles on which this coalition is to rest, are, that the Stadtholder is to have the Suspension taken off,—the command of this garrison restored to him *unconditionally*,—and a tacit agreement is to be made to dismiss Van Berkel from the office of Pensionary. This last I suggested, and I trust it will be complied with.

On the other hand, His Highness is to give up the point of recommending to the different civil offices in the towns of this Province, and to reduce his military jurisdiction to the same degree of authority as that under which it was held by William the Third.

These articles once settled, the Prince's party at Amsterdam undertake to support the Regents against the democratical mob, and to oppose force by force, if required.

Monsieur Lutek, whom I mentioned in my last, is at the head of 2,200 armed sailors and ship-carpenters; and Mr. Bryin has nearly twice as many of the burghers under his command. These are ready, and will be immediately brought into action, if the French Faction, headed by Hooft and Abbema, should again attempt to take possession of the Stadthouse with their mob, and direct the deliberations of the Council.

In this Council, provided the coalition takes place, I am told our friends will be twenty-five, and our adversaries eleven.

The secret of our proceedings was so well kept, that it was not till Monday last that the French Ambassador took the alarm. On Tuesday, early, a meeting of the leading Patriots was held at his house; and in the evening Paludanus was despatched to Amsterdam, Gyslaer to Gorcum and Dordt, and Wassenaer Staremberg to Schiedam, with full power to give the strongest assurances that *France would support her party to the utmost;* and to these assurances, which *I know* the French Ambassador took upon himself to make in the strongest *Ministerial* manner, was added a still more powerful incentive,—fifty thousand French crowns to be distributed as these chiefs of the Faction thought most advisable for their purpose.

I trust, my Lord, that, situated as I am, I have left nothing undone which in a moment like this I could attempt with prudence.

I have contributed to the support of two friendly newspapers, one published at Bommel, the other at the Brille ; and I have had written a pamphlet to prove that all the evils which now beset the Republic arise from their alliance with France and disunion with England.

I have likewise encouraged the institution of *anti-patriotic meetings* in the several towns of this Province, particularly at Delft, Rotterdam, Gouda, and the Hague.

The great view in this was to make it appear that it was *not the voice of the people* that went with the Patriots, but that of a mercenary and armed mob ; that the people themselves continue in the same sentiments they have ever professed, and are firmly attached to the House of Orange.

These meetings have succeeded beyond our most sanguine expectations, and are become so much more numerous than the *Patriotic Associations*, that we shall hear of no more popular petitions or remonstrances to the States of Holland, where nothing of any consequence passed either to-day or yesterday.

My attention has never slackened concerning anything that passes here in any degree connected with the operations of the French in the East Indies, and your Lordship may rest assured I shall endeavour to let nothing escape unobserved or unnoticed which may relate to so important an object.

The main object of the French here seems to be, to increase the number of European troops they may dispose of in the East Indies, and for this purpose (exclusive of the 2,000 Wurtembergers I mentioned long ago) there never sails a ship on account of the Dutch Company which is not crowded with recruits.

Monsieur de Vergennes has agents employed at Amsterdam for no other purpose than to find out persons who had been accustomed to India, who knew the language and habits of the country ; and, wherever they could be discovered, they were engaged at almost any price ; and I am told there is scarcely an Indian Prince who has not a French emissary at his court.

The Faction here, in pursuance of the repeated request of France, are indefatigable in attempting to get the direction of the Company into their own hands, and every possible means (to my certain knowledge) has been employed to corrupt the present Court of Directors.

Hitherto they have not carried their point, and their success will now depend on the general turn affairs may take.

EXTRACT OF A DESPATCH FROM SIR JAMES HARRIS TO THE
MARQUIS OF CARMARTHEN.

Hague, Tuesday, 17th April, 1787.

I HAVE now the satisfaction to acquaint your Lordship, that the conferences at Nimeguen have been attended with great success ; and that a junction of interests, and a plan of co-operation between the town of Amsterdam and the Stadtholder, were agreed upon, precisely on the terms I stated in my letter.   Monsieur Reygersman returned with this news on Sunday, and the same day Mr. Caleven reached Amsterdam.

A convention specifying these conditions (which I do not repeat, from the supposition that they are fresh in your Lordship's memory) was to be signed between the chiefs of the two parties, and, immediately after, they were to be carried into execution.

The earliest day was to be fixed for calling together the Council of the city of Amsterdam, in order to appoint new deputies to the States, with instructions to propose the taking off the suspension and restoring the command.

Four thousand men selected from the ship-carpenters,

&c., were to protect the Council, and to insure the freedom of debate, with strict orders to commit no outrage of any kind, unless some act of violence should be first attempted on the other side.

Besides the inferior leaders already mentioned, the Captains Byland and Vaillant of the navy, two officers of rank and tried characters, and M. de Haren of Amsterdam, are to head them, to direct their conduct, as well when moderation and forbearance, as when courage and action, may be deemed requisite.

Things thus circumstanced, and from a pre-knowledge that the Regency of Amsterdam would readily ratify the terms their agent, Mr. Caleven, had subscribed to for them, everything was considered as settled, and to-morrow, the 18th, was fixed in our minds for the day of action. But the people of the dockyards, &c., have been so accustomed to see the Prince of Orange overreached and deceived, and are so diffident of the sincerity and sentiment of the Regency, that they positively refused, on their part, to sign the convention, unless they should previously receive an order for so doing under the sign-manual of the Prince. They even insisted that the conditions were not favourable enough ; and that the Constitution, as established in 1747 and 1766, ought to be restored, without any saving clause whatever.

I hope, however, the gentlemen above named will make them hear reason on this point, and teach them to feel that the cessions the Stadtholder makes are not his *legal prerogatives*, but encroachments which necessarily followed the great influence belonging to his post, and which (whatever stipulations he may *now* make) will undoubtedly return to him the moment he enjoys his full authority.

On the first they are perfectly untractable, and declare in the most positive manner, that nothing short of a letter from the Prince himself, or his appearance in person, will satisfy them.

For this reason, which though it is the strongest indication both of courage and zeal, yet as it leads to delays, and exposes the whole plan to the imminent danger of a premature discovery, it was agreed this morning that Monsieur Reygersman should proceed to Amsterdam, and my friend Monsieur de Nagel to Nimeguen : that the first should use his endeavours to assure the *Bijlties* (the name belonging to the men at the dockyards) that they may rely on the good-faith of the Regency of their town, &c. ; while the other, younger and more active, is to get to his destination early to-morrow morning, obtain from the Stadtholder the letter the Bijlties require, and be with it at Amsterdam by to-morrow evening.

This will, I hope, be effectuated ; and this untimely hitch to the proceeding, from the best of motives, be got over without producing any of those bad consequences which the loss of twenty-four hours commonly occasions in matters of this kind.

I need not, I am sure, remark, that everything I write in this letter is a most profound secret ; known solely to those who are actors in the business, and who are playing so deep a game, that, if it fails, their heads are in danger.

EXTRACT OF A DESPATCH FROM SIR JAMES HARRIS TO THE MARQUIS OF CARMARTHEN.

Hague, 20th April, 1787.

THE Stadtholder lost no time in giving to Monsieur de Nagel the letter the Bijlties required of him, and he arrived at Amsterdam with it on the evening of Wednesday. On his arrival he learnt from Monsieur Reygersman, that no persuasions of his, or arguments he could suggest, could prevail upon the Bijlties to agree to lend themselves to a plan which consented to any cession whatever on the part of the Stadtholder.

The Anti-Patriotic Associations increase on all sides, and it will very soon become evident, that what has hitherto been deemed the voice of the people, has not consisted of one-twentieth part of the inhabitants of the Republic.

The violent conduct of the Patriots had produced this effect, as yesterday the Faction had required that not only the keys of the Arsenal, but those of the City and Guildhall, should be delivered up to them ; and, on being refused, they had it in contemplation to take them by force.

Two companies of armed Burghers, (or rather, Free Corps,) headed by one Hogen Dorp and Bastard, are under arms before the Stadthouse, and have actually two six-pounders, which are supposed to have been given them from some French ship.

The fermentation is at its greatest height, and I scarcely conceive it possible that a week can pass over without some violent event.

The Hôtel de France is a scene of great confusion and disorder.

Monsieur de Verac is by no means equal to the pressure of the moment, and is pushed so hard both by his friends and his opponents, that he is perplexed to a degree ; the more so, as he is without instructions from his Court.

EXTRACT OF A DESPATCH FROM SIR JAMES HARRIS TO THE MARQUIS OF CARMARTHEN.

Hague, 24th April, 1787.

EVERY effort has proved ineffectual to unite the aristocracy and the Bijlties.

Monsieur Reygersman left Amsterdam on Saturday morning, and gave me on Sunday a very circumstantial account of his whole negotiation. He seems to have omitted nothing which could have contributed to reconcile the opinions of the two parties ; and, after hearing his relation, it is, I confess, impossible for me to determine on which of the parties the accusation of obstinacy is to be fixed with the greater justice.

The Patriotic Faction at Amsterdam took the earliest opportunity of availing themselves of the want of agreement between the other two parties.

On Saturday evening they filled the streets with their partisans, took possession of the Stadthouse, and compelled the Regents to dismiss from their body nine of the principal persons they considered as disaffected to their cause.

DESPATCH FROM SIR JAMES HARRIS TO THE MARQUIS OF CARMARTHEN.

Hague, 1st May, 1787.

MY LORD,—The accounts the French Ambassador sent home about a fortnight ago represented their party here in so critical a position, and the probability of its being overthrown as so very likely, that nothing remained for the Court of Versailles to do but to advise and support the violent measures we have lately seen. This produced the unexpected return of the Rhingrave of Salm; and, what was still more pernicious to our cause than the presence of this enterprising adventurer, a permission to spend money to almost any amount; and I can assure your Lordship I keep greatly within the mark when I declare, that in this period of time (a fortnight) France has expended at least a million of livres.

The consenting to such an enormous expense, when her finances are in so ruinous a state, substantiates but too fully the justness of a fear with which my mind has been continually impressed from the hour of my arrival in Holland; namely, " that the reduction of this country is the primary object of the political solicitude of France; and that she considers it as the main instrument with which she is to act in all her hostile views against England." I must, in justice to the Dutch, acknowledge that the scene which has just passed, and is still passing, does not go by unfelt by the nation. The uncorrupted and thinking part of it are indignant at the acts of oppression exercised by the Faction, and at the notoriety of the means by which it is supported ; but they know not whither to turn for protection ; they have no chief at home under whose banner they can fight, no foreign Power who seems interested in their existence. Their antagonists have both ; and, thus circumstanced, the contest becomes very unequal.

Would it lead to any good, or did I foresee the remotest prospect of success, I could, by lifting up a finger, raise a popular insurrection. More than half the body of Burghers in this Province, and the whole body of peasants, are ripe for revolt ; but it would be leading them to certain slaughter and destruction, without any possible advantage resulting from the attempt.

To oppose our antagonists with any prospect of effect, our friends must possess the same means of defence as they do. Besides a concurrence of measures preconcerted here, and moving under the orders of a chief, *foreign assistance is requisite, and some Great Power must be found who may not only think it worth their while to afford pecuniary supplies, but who may consider themselves as interested enough in preserving the Republic from becoming a French province to declare, that if, in consequence of an opposition to the ruling Faction, France should invade it, the step will not be seen with indifference.* Without such a security it would be as dishonest as it would be useless to stimulate our friends to action ; and I am confident I shall not incur the displeasure of my Royal Master by shrinking from any proposal which might tend to involve a number of individuals in the calamities and distresses of the public, without any possible benefit being the consequence of such a sacrifice.

Had our plan of coalition succeeded at Amsterdam, and the *coup de main* been struck at the time it was intended, all the succours and assurances which have since come from France would have arrived too late ; and the situation of our party would have been so favourable as to have made it worth while to have stood the risk of a contest, however deep the stake, or hazardous the enterprise.

But this having not only failed, but its discovery having added strength to the Faction and redoubled its vigilance, I am free to declare, I do not conceive there is a possibility to concert within the country itself any plan, or to form any party, equal to resist the pressure, or to prevent the immediate and irrecoverable completion of the schemes of France in their whole extent, *unless the kind of foreign support and interference* I have just now intimated can be found ; and *with* this I should be almost as confident of success, as *without* it I am certain of miscarriage.

I am conscious, my Lord, I appear to trespass beyond the limits of a despatch ; but besides its being my duty at a moment like this, and on a matter admitted on all sides to be of such a magnitude, to speak out, I have done little more than relate the substance of several very long and very serious conferences I have had since my last with persons of this country, on whose judgment, honour, and integrity I can rely ; and, having said thus much, my Lord, I hope I shall be forgiven if I go a step further, and say that *England is the only power they look up to ;* that it is *from England alone they hope for relief,* and their hope is founded as well on its national character as on its political principles.

Before I end this despatch, my Lord, (every line of which, perhaps, wants an apology,) I trust I shall be forgiven if I say a few words relative to myself.

Though so hard pressed, at times, as to have been accused of want of sincerity and attachment to the cause, I have never been induced to pronounce a syllable by which my Court may be committed ; nor, in the many meetings I have had with people of every description, have I ever pledged myself for a conduct different from that I was prescribed. A due submission to my instructions, as well as a regard to my own character, withheld me from buoying up my friends by false hopes. My endeavours have all tended to two points : the first, to do away and efface those impressions of animosity, rancour, and ill-will which the remembrance of the last war had left here against England, and which, on my arrival, were so universal as to leave me for several months without a person who would listen to me, or even consort with me ; the second, a natural consequence of the first, to collect and rally a party, to unite the friends of the old system, and to root out from the minds of the Stadtholderian Court that fatal and pernicious doctrine inculcated by the late King of Prussia, that the best way for the Prince of Orange to preserve his authority and power was by acts of complaisance and deference to France.

In these points I have completely succeeded. All the impressions of anger and resentment left by the rupture have disappeared ; and I believe I may venture to say, that in the best of times the house of no English Minister was ever so universally and so constantly frequented by people of the country as mine now is. A party in point of numbers and of persons of consideration greatly superior to that of France is formed, and ready to act under my orders ; and the Prince and Princess of Orange have made a formal abjuration of all their former political errors.

Nothing can be further from my meaning by saying all this than to be my own panegyrist, or to rate as essential services favourable alterations which circumstances much more than anything else have brought about. I only mean to state facts, which, though perhaps already sufficiently constituted, it was necessary for me to resume before I came to that with which I shall conclude this letter, by humbly entreating your Lordship to instruct me how I am to proceed.

I should deceive your Lordship, and betray the trust reposed in me, if I were to say I was equal to keep up matters here in their present state, or that I saw a possibility by procrastination or indirect encouragement to gain time, ward off the crisis, and to keep a party together in expectation of a more propitious moment.

The French are too wary and too alert to suffer this ;

and the position of our friends would become so perilous by their continuing to remain in it, that it cannot be required of them without giving them some security for the consequences. It would, as I said before, be useless and dishonourable to attempt it. Of course it would be a conduct impossible for an English Minister to advise or follow.

I submit therefore to your Lordship's wisdom whether it be not become incumbent to declare to our friends here, either that they must not hope for any support or assistance whatever, directly or indirectly, secret or avowed, from England, but that they must trust solely to their own resources, and to Providence, to extricate them from their misfortunes; or, if His Majesty's confidential servants should deem a contrary line of conduct advisable, and consider the entire subjection of this country to France as a more likely means of restoring the debilitated credit of that nation, than the operations of the most able financier,—whether, if that should be their opinion, a moment should be lost in devising a plan of vigorous and systematic measures, and, by closing with our party while it is yet time, to ensure ourselves their support in all our operations that may be intended.

If this should be the result of His Majesty's councils, I am well aware it will be expedient to be much more explicit in the minute and component parts of the plan than I have yet been. I am fully prepared on the subject; but as objections will naturally arise, and elucidations be required in its discussion, I submit it to your Lordship's decision whether it would not be advisable, as well for the sake of gaining time, as on account of greater precision, for me to go over for a few days to England.

I must entreat your Lordship to read this despatch with indulgence, to be persuaded I do not mean to intrude my opinion, or to do anything more than to perform my duty towards my Royal Master, and towards my country, to the utmost of my power.

LETTER FROM SIR JAMES HARRIS TO THE MARQUIS OF
CARMARTHEN.

Hague, 1st May, 1787.

My dear Lord,—If my to-day's despatch should produce my recall, let me still hope for a continuation of
your personal friendship. I write as I think and as I feel.
Were I to do otherwise, I had better never write at all.

If we lose this country, France will acquire what she
has always considered as the climax of her power. The
Low Countries must immediately after fall into her
clutches, and it is with this view that she is fomenting
the troubles which are beginning to appear there. There
is *good stuff* enough here to vanquish twice the strength
of our opponents; and, if we will be *bold* enough to assume
the style and tone which belong to us, *I will pledge my
head on the event.* I have mentioned my going over to
England *officially* before I knew your sentiments on this
point, from the extreme pressure of the moment. There
is no time to be lost; and what would be perhaps an easy
operation now, will become an impossible one a few
months hence.

It will perhaps be thought at home that I have caught
the infection of *party*, that I see through the medium of
faction and animosity. It is not so; I am perfectly dispassionate on the subject, and my opinion is formed on
the most sedate and cool reflection. It does not belong
to me to calculate the various inconveniences to which
our being too active in the concerns of Holland may
expose us. I can only speak to *one* point, and on that
my political creed is as much made up as that of the
most bigoted devotee. If, after all, it should be agreed
on at home that no attention should be paid to what I
have written, let me premise in time, that though I shall
most certainly acquiesce in the opinion of my superiors,
and continue to act up to those orders to the best of my
abilities, yet I shall neither have the same means of information, nor the same influence on business I have now.

I shall dwindle into a common Foreign Minister, and my despatches will be only fit to be put under pie-crust.

LETTER FROM SIR JAMES HARRIS TO THE MARQUIS OF CARMARTHEN.

Hague, 5th May, 1787.

MY DEAR LORD,—I am so full of my subject, so penetrated with the truth and importance of what I wrote Tuesday and to-day, that I wait with the most impatient anxiety the result of your deliberations. *This country may be saved and redeemed,* if we desire to become its saviour and redeemer ; and I am certain, if we begin to roar, France will shrink before us. I have not expressed half strong enough in my despatches the unconditional terms on which two-thirds of the Republic fling themselves into my arms, or how certain I am of moulding them into any shape, if you will give me Carte Blanche.

Should you disapprove or dislike my coming home (which for reasons unknown to me may be the case), will you allow me to send over to you one or more persons of rank or character to attest for the truth of all I write, and who will vouch for the fidelity and attachment of their countrymen to the old cause ? If, after all, a different system should prevail, and one which to the minds of His Majesty's Ministers may bring more benefits to our good Island than the recovery of this country, at least let me have the consolation to know that it is thought I have done my duty, and, if I stopped short of it, it was not from flagging, or from want of blood, but from obedience to the bridle.

[In consequence of the foregoing letters, Sir James Harris was recalled on the 19th of May to communicate with the Cabinet in person. Having persuaded the Government of the expediency of our taking a more active and decided part in Holland, he returned to the Hague on the 1st of June to prosecute his plan. Our Ministers at Versailles and Berlin were directed to co-operate with him, and the Orange party saw his return with the greatest joy and increased confidence.]

Hague, Friday, 11th May, 1787.

I SHALL obey with the greatest pleasure His Majesty's commands, and on this day se'nnight be on my road, so as to be able to kiss *His* hands on the Monday following. I shall with greater pleasure receive those which may authorize me to return *armed with Jove's thunder;* or at least with that kind of thunder he employed to enjoy Danaë.

The Faction rely solely on our passiveness, and they will, I am confident, retire as we advance ; but, as a few days will place me in Grosvenor Square, I will not anticipate what I have to say.

A *poor lady in great distress* has desired me to enclose you the petition which comes with this. She will know how to rate your acquiescence in her prayer if you grant it, and my gratitude will keep pace with hers.

The storm thickens here very fast, and I scarcely know whether it will be safe for me to have a meeting with the Princess (which I much wish before I go), as the villages between this and Nimeguen are in commotion, and detachments of the Free Corps are guarding the dykes. I, however, am tempted to try, as it is essential for me to keep up her courage.

(Inclosure.)

Nimègue, ce 19, 1787.

Sire,—Si quelque chose peut relever nos espérances
dans les circonstances fâcheuses où nous nous trouvons,
c'est sans doute l'intérêt que Votre Majesté daigne prendre
aux malheurs de la République, et à ceux de ma famille,
intimement liée au sort de cet état. Mons. le Chevalier
Harris vient de nous en renouveller les flatteuses assurances. Remplie de confiance dans la magnanimité qui la
caractérise, j'ose concevoir l'espoir que Votre Majesté
voudra être le protecteur et l'appui de notre juste cause,
et prévenir ainsi la perte totale de la République.

Personne n'est plus en état que Mons. Harris de lui
tracer un fidèle tableau de la situation de ce pays, par les
connaissances qu'il a sçu en acquérir depuis qu'il s'y trouve;
il y jouit de l'estime et de la bienveillance générale; tous
les honnêtes gens lui rendent cette justice. Votre Majesté verra dans le tableau qu'il pourra lui donner les
tristes effets de la discorde et de l'intrigue, mais en même
temps il ne lui échappera pas que le moment est venu où
toute la saine partie de la Nation souffre impatiemment le
joug de la Cabale dominante et désire de s'en voir dé-
livrer. Votre Majesté, en devenant son libérateur, vivi-
fiera de plus en plus les sentiments de reconnaissance,
d'attachement et de respect que je lui ai toujours porté,
et avec lesquels je fais gloire de me dire,

Sire, de Votre Majesté, la très humble et très obéissante
Cousine et Servante
(Signé)   Wilhelmine.

CONSIDERATIONS TO BE EMPLOYED WITH MINISTERS TO PREVAIL
ON THEM TO SUPPORT THE REPUBLIC OF HOLLAND.

May 19th, 1787.

1. To state its importance to England, whether from its utility as a friend, or from its power of injuring us as an enemy.

2. France feels this; and it is from this conviction that she (circumstanced as her finances now are) spares neither expense nor intrigue to carry her point.

3. She has succeeded but too well from different causes; from operating on a permanent opposition, which has existed from the first period of the Republic, to a Stadtholder; from the mismanagement of the Stadtholder himself; and, above all, from applying to the passions of individuals by bribery, flattery, and menaces.

4. The evil greater than we suppose; the remedy less difficult.

5. The Dutch begin to be awake to their situation, to recover from their prejudices against us, to see through the designs of France; four Provinces avowedly of this opinion, and one-third of the States of Holland. But the French party have managed to get the reins of government so entirely in their hands, and to maintain them with such a strong armed force, that the well-meaning part of the Republic, however numerous and respectable, are not in a situation to wrest them out of their hands alone, and from within themselves. They want subsidiary assistance for the moment, security for the future, and, above all, a leader. These three points would be found in the foreign Power who would do for them what France does for the Patriots. The expense to such a power would be less, and the security required be never called for, as success would be almost the certain result.

The interference of such a Power would be efficacious, because France would certainly not venture to risk a war for the sake of a country she is endeavouring to obtain before she can venture on war; and, secondly, because the moment the good Party here are sure of support, they would come forth in number, power, and with an energy and indignation which must bear down their antagonists.

This encouragement can be made manifest by a declaration to France relative to her intentions on this Republic, and also to the Republic, saying, that His Majesty cannot see any longer her Constitution overset.

Minutes of Cabinet, May 23rd, 1787.

(Dinner at the Lord Chancellor's.)

Present—Mr. Pitt   Duke of Richmond
        Lord Carmarthen   Lord Stafford
        Lord Sydney   Sir James Harris.
        The Lord Chancellor

Subject,—The State of Affairs in Holland.

Question,—Whether England should abandon them entirely to France, or interpose?

The Chancellor took the lead. Started objections merely to obviate them—expressed doubt on the importance of Holland—questioned, even if France carried her point now, if her ascendancy would be so permanently and solidly established as to enable her to give the Republic any political direction she pleased. He soon, however, as he went along, did away his own doubts, and then, in the most forcible terms that could be employed, declared against all half-measures; said, if we moved at all, we must make up our minds at once to go to war; that our preparations for war should go *pari passu* with our Declaration to France, or else it would avail nothing; that, if we acted short of this, we should do as we did by America— lose our object by the very ends we employed to attain it. That, to his mind on the present occasion, if we stirred at all, everything *short of war* was to be set down as clear gain : the means he proposed were, to subsidize German troops immediately, and to raise a German army in support of our friends equal to oppose that which France might march to the assistance of hers.

Duke of Richmond.—Combated the idea of Holland's being of little importance ; as well as the supposition, that, if France prevailed now, there still would remain enough of an English party there to fetter her operations. Agreed entirely in the wisdom of preparing for extremities, whatever might be the event ; talked on military operations—called for a map of Germany—traced the marches from Cassel and Hanover to Holland, and also from *Givet to Maestricht.*

Mr. Pitt.—Admitted the *immense* consequence of Holland being preserved as an Independent State ; that it was an object of the greatest magnitude ; that he had no hesitation on what ought to be done, if we did *anything ;* and that we must make up our account on the first instance to go to war as a possible, though not a probable, event. The question he said was, Which risk was the greatest, that of attempting to stop France in the progress of her preparatory designs now, or to wait to resist the execution of them when she was ready to attack us ? This was so intricate a one, and so difficult to be solved, that it required time and reflection, and could not be pronounced on at the first meeting. He asked Sir James Harris what kind of succours the well-meaning party in the Republic required ?

Sir James Harris.—Said, pecuniary relief for the present, and assurances of support for the future ; that the money was wanted by the Province of Gelderland to take into their pay the troops disbanded by Holland, and that the assurances were required to insure them against a French army.

The Chancellor.—Inquired whether Sir James Harris thought the party, *if supported* by England in the way required, would be strong enough to resist the other, or if, *not* supported, it would fail entirely ? To both these questions Sir James replied in the affirmative.

The conversation then turned on the general propriety of England's interference, or not ; and the danger of doing nothing was opposed to that of embarking in a war.

Sir James Harris contended France was not in a state to quarrel ; that her ultimate end was not to fight for the possession of Holland, but to fight in concert with Holland against England. That she had neither an army, revenue, nor ministry ; of course, a more favourable moment could not present itself for England holding a high and becoming language to France.

Lord Stafford here interposed, and said, " And if England lets this moment go by unnoticed, and suffers France to carry her points with impunity, what then will be the consequence, what effect will such a tame and inattentive conduct have on the minds of the other Powers of Europe ?"

Mr. Pitt assented to all this ; admitted the whole truth of both what Sir James Harris and Lord Stafford said; but added, that although, in the upshot of the present business, war was only a *possible*, not a *probable* event, yet it being a *possible one* was sufficient to make it necessary for England to reflect before she stirred ; to weigh maturely whether anything could repay the disturbing that state of growing affluence and prosperity in which she now was, and whether this was not increasing so fast as not to make her equal to resist any force France could collect some years hence.

Sir James Harris represented in strong colours the force France *would* by that time have collected ; the impression our inaction could have on Europe, &c. He also turned the medal, and showed to how great a pitch of glory it would raise England to have checked France in her career, and to have saved Holland. This, which was to his mind the *probable* chance, surely deserved consideration.

The Chancellor asked how long France would be able to keep Holland.

Sir James said, for as long a term as was necessary to complete her designs ; that if he, or any of the Cabinet, wished for further information, he must refer them to paper.

Lord Carmarthen then began to read these papers ; but, as they were in French, it was agreed they had better circulate.

The Cabinet broke up at twelve ; fixed for the 25th, at half-past eight in the evening.

May, 24th.

With Mr. Pitt.   He questioned me on the *detail* of Holland ; went nearly over the same ground as in the Cabinet, but with more precision ; felt strongly the importance of the object ; asked what Provinces I could depend on ; desired me to give him my ideas on what should be done respecting France ;* sent for a map of Holland ; made me show him the situation of the Provinces, &c.   I proposed a squadron of frigates at Flushing : he did not object to it : talked on the money : how to be applied, and through whom.

Minute of Cabinet, Whitehall, May 26th, 1787.

Present—The Lord Chancellor   Lord Privy Seal
                Duke of Richmond   Lord Viscount Howe
                Lord Sydney   Right Hon. Wm. Pitt.
                Lord Carmarthen

" It is humbly submitted to your Majesty, that, in consequence of the representations made by Sir James Harris, and the information received subsequent to his departure, of the actual measures and avowed disposition of the States of Guelderland, Utrecht, and Zealand, as well as of the prevailing party in Friesland, of the divisions in Holland, and the probability of a favourable impression in Groningen and Overyssel, and also of the firm determination of the Prince of Orange to resist the en-

* Sir James Harris proposed that a verbal Insinuation should be made to France (which he drew up for Mr. Pitt) inviting her to explain suitably and satisfactorily the preparations she was making near Givet, which rumour attributed to an intention of intervening in Holland.—*Harris Papers.*

croachments of Holland, and of the prospect that many officers and troops in the pay of Holland would enlist, or remain in the service of the other States, if means can be furnished for paying them ; it appears that a pecuniary assistance may have the effect of enabling the well-disposed Provinces to maintain a sufficient force to counteract the immediate efforts of the Province of Holland.

" That the great objects of attention, in the present moment, appear to be, to provide for the pay of such officers and troops as may quit the service of Holland, and enter into that of the other States ; and to establish activity and concord among the States who are inclined to act collectively, as well as among those who may be disposed to resist the prevailing party in the different towns of Holland.

" That, on these grounds, it is with all humility submitted to your Majesty, that it would be expedient to advance a sum not exceeding 20,000*l*. by way of loan, or otherwise, if it should be found necessary, for these immediate objects.

" That the consideration of any other measures to be taken must necessarily depend upon the effects produced by the internal exertions of the Provinces thus assisted, and on the various events which may follow."

" I, the underwritten James Harris, attended the several meetings of the Cabinet, when this Minute was agreed to, and requested a copy of it as a voucher for my conduct.

" JAMES HARRIS."

" May 28th, 1787."

COPY OF MR. EWART'S LETTER TO THE MARQUIS OF
CARMARTHEN.

Berlin, 29th May, 1787.

THREE days ago an Estafette arrived from Nimeguen
with the Princess of Orange's answer to the negative
reply the King returned to her request for a supply of
cannon and ammunition from Wesel. As Her Highness's
letter to her brother on this occasion is more remarkable
than any of her former ones, both on account of the
nature of its contents, and of the declaration which accompanied it, "that it was the last effort, and that, whatever might happen, her future conduct (in regard to His
Prussian Majesty) should be regulated by his reply," I
think it right to communicate the most interesting parts
of it to your Lordship.

The Princess begins with observing, " that the cannon
they had occasion for were at Wesel ; but, as she supposed
from the style of her brother's answer that he was averse
to grant them, she should take care, however great the
necessity might be, not to make his officers do what was
disagreeable to him, though she only asked for that indirect assistance against the most unjust attack." Her
Royal Highness next represents, " that having no reproach to make to herself, and having done everything
in her power to prevent things from proceeding to extremities, she waited with resignation the result of the
present contest ; but that she *never* would give her consent to an humiliating accommodation, which could only
serve to deliver up into the hands of France the country,
her own family, and so many brave people who were
determined to risk everything in support of the good
cause. That the cause was now become that of the
whole Nation ; and that, while the different colleagues of
the States General stood forth so nobly in defence of the
Constitution, while the army remained faithful, and while
the whole country was in commotion, she could never
think of renewing a negotiation with France, as was pro-

posed. *That everything now depended on the fate of arms,* and that there was no longer any room to hesitate." She concluded with thanking His Majesty for deigning to offer his good wishes for her, which she hoped would be listened to by Heaven, should she be destitute of every other assistance.

Nothing is yet known of the impression which this letter has made on the King ; but Mons. Hertzberg intends renewing his representations to-day, to entreat His Majesty to offer the Princess whatever indirect assistance she may require, either in money or warlike stores.

EXTRACT OF A DESPATCH FROM SIR JAMES HARRIS TO THE MARQUIS OF CARMARTHEN.

Hague, 1st June, 1787.

To-day, in the morning, the States General came to a resolution (by a majority composed of the four Provinces of Gelderland, Zealand, Utrecht, and Friesland) to order the Council of State to write to all the officers Holland has lately suspended, for having kept their *general* rather than their *Provincial* oath, to resume their commissions, and exercise their military functions as before. Their High Mightinesses have, at the same time, concluded, in the name of the Generality, that all officers obeying the orders of Holland in preference to theirs, should be suspended. They have also caused circular letters to be sent to every regiment, warning them not to suffer themselves to be disarmed, and to respect no orders but such as come to them either from the Council of State or from their High Mightinesses themselves.

When this resolution was reported, as is usual, at two o'clock, to the States of Holland, the town of Dordt immediately proposed (through Gyslaer, its Pensionary), that since, from this resolution, it appeared that four Provinces were attempting to get the whole power of the Union into their hands, it became highly expedient for Holland not to be subdued, and particularly to ensure the fidelity of its troops ; consequently, that notice should be issued to their *Cordon* not to obey, under pain of incurring the indignation of their Noble Mightinesses, any orders coming from the States General ; and also to appoint a committee to determine if, after such a conduct on the part of four of the Confederate States, who are manifestly entering into a conspiracy against that of Holland, it is either safe to deliberate with them, or decent to suffer them to carry on their deliberations on the territory of the States of Holland.

This Resolution was carried in the States by eleven to three.

This is by far the most decisive step that has been yet taken. It sets the States General and the States of Holland at open defiance of each other. The whole will turn on the conduct of the army, and which order they will respect the most ; and my coming at this critical moment may, perhaps, not a little influence its decision.

EXTRACT OF A DESPATCH FROM SIR JAMES HARRIS TO THE MARQUIS OF CARMARTHEN.

Hague, 8th June, 1787.

ALTHOUGH nothing has passed since Tuesday to make me more sanguine than I was then, yet I shall hold it my duty to proceed as if I were sure of my exertions being attended with success.

I continue to persist in endeavouring to carry into execution the plan I have laid down in my own mind, and which the experience I have acquired of the country, and everything which is passing under my eyes, convince me to be the only one that can possibly restore the Republic to that situation in which we wish to see it placed.

The four friendly Provinces must be formed into a solid and permanent union ; the army must be brought over; and a strong opposition must be kept up in Holland, as well to leave us a footing in this Province, as to fetter and harass the operations of the Faction. Any measures short of these will avail nothing ; but, as they cannot be effected without bringing matters to a crisis, we must not shrink from the dangers attendant on a moment of this kind. If the well-disposed Members of the Government, and such as called so loudly on me for assistance, think the game too deep a one to play, after the support I have held out to them, it will be fruitless to make any further attempts to serve them.

LETTER FROM THE MARQUIS OF CARMARTHEN TO SIR JAMES HARRIS.

Whitehall, June 8th, 1787.

My DEAR SIR,—You will, I fear, think we are unreasonable in the length as well as the frequency of our official despatches, and yet, if I am not mistaken, the warmth with which the business is at last taken up will prove a sufficient excuse on that head. I answered for you to-day that you would not be offended at having some professional men of both branches of military service (wet and dry) sent into Holland. Others are sent elsewhere, so that we shall not be wanting, I trust, in respect to every degree of useful as well as necessary information.

Both the Duke of Richmond and Pitt were lamenting to-day the situation of such a foreign Minister as yourself, whose activity was perpetually liable to interruptions of official duty, and who, when willing and able to turn every moment to advantage, was obliged to sacrifice hours in such times to the setting down what was already done for the information of his Court. I shall now conclude this hasty scrawl with the sincerest hope that you will *go on and prosper*, and this is the sentiment of us all. Dr. Jackson spoilt one of my best table-cloths to-day by a bumper to the said effect. Adieu, my dear Harris! Believe me, at all times, your truly sincere and affectionate friend.

EXTRACT OF A DESPATCH FROM THE MARQUIS OF CARMARTHEN TO SIR JAMES HARRIS.

Whitehall, 12th June, 1787.

THE communication made to the King of Prussia by the Princess of Orange can certainly in no degree pledge His Majesty, and perhaps it may be attended with advantage, if the general idea that this country may possibly take some share in the events now depending is conveyed in this manner to the French Court. At the same time His Majesty's servants think that the expressions, particularly the concluding part of the last paragraph, " qu'elle y prend intérêt, que son discours au Parlement le prouve, *et qu'elle le montrera dans l'occasion*," seem to imply that His Majesty had given some positive assurances that there might exist an occasion on which His Majesty had already determined to take part by open interference, if the Constitution and independence of the Republic were in danger. I am persuaded you did not, and I hope the Princess did not, consider them as carrying this meaning.

Upon the whole, there seems no reason to believe that the King of Prussia entertains an idea of interfering in any way that can be effectual in favour of the Republic, or that any communication with him on the subject can produce any good consequences ; at all events, His Majesty's servants wish that this country should not be at all involved in any intercourse which may take place under the present circumstances between the Princess of Orange and that Court.

Hague, June 13th, 1787.

MY DEAR LORD,—Although worn to the stumps, and
that my tongue cleaves to my mouth with talking and
arguing, yet I will employ the little strength I have left
to thank you for your kind letter of the 8th, and still
more for your excellent despatches, which fill me with joy,
zeal, and courage : I wish I could add *hope*, but that must
come from this side of the water, where joy, zeal, and
courage are not known.

I am highly sensible of the Duke of Richmond's and
Mr. Pitt's kind feelings for me. I, really, barely suffice
corporeally for the exercise of my duty ; and mentally I
fear you will sometimes find me below par, as I am forced
to snatch every five minutes of quiet to write, and my
reports are without method or perspicuity.

I hope your Lordship will approve my having written
directly to Pitt, to intreat him to make me prompt payment, as I am at a dead lock without a very considerable
remittance.

EXTRACT OF A DESPATCH FROM SIR JAMES HARRIS TO THE
MARQUIS OF CARMARTHEN.

Hague, 15th June, 1787.

BEFORE I enter upon it, I must beg your Lordship to be
assured that I stated in very clear and unambiguous
terms that England must be left to act for herself in case
of the open interference of France ; that Mons. de Nagel,
who was charged by me to explain the event of my journey to England to the Stadtholder, was equally guarded
in his expressions ; and that to the repeated and pressing
solicitations which have been since made to me, I have
invariably replied in the same language.

Having said this, I must add that I find it a very difficult, not to say an impossible, task to prevent an impression contrary to that we wish to avoid giving, being

received. His Majesty's confidential servants may recollect, that when I was permitted to lay before them what appeared to me to be the situation of the Party here and its wishes, that I said, besides pecuniary support, our friends required a specific promise of avowed assistance from England in case of an attack from France; and although I was at the time, and still am, very ready to admit that it was as unreasonable in them to expect it as it would have been injudicious in us to grant it, yet it was my duty to state their opinions (not mine), and to say then, "that I was fearful the success of my endeavours, without such an assurance as they asked for being given, would be very precarious."

I am now again from the same motive compelled to say, that I clearly perceive, notwithstanding all the caution I can use, that the manner in which I have declared myself on this point has not been satisfactory to the majority of them, and that there are many who are led to believe from it that England will in *no case* interfere in their favour.

Matters in the meanwhile get so very serious here that a crisis cannot be at a great distance.

The Faction has prevailed. Holland, Groningen and Overyssel, joined by the Deputies who have usurped the representation of Utrecht, have rescinded the Resolution* I took so much pains to get passed on Sunday; and the President of the week, in defiance of every principle on which the Union of Utrecht rests, gave the question in their favour.

This point gained, they immediately ordered, by virtue of the same illegal majority, that letters should be written to the Prince as Captain-General of the Union, not to march a single soldier out of the Pays de la Généralité; and to the Council of State, not to grant cannon or mili-

---

* At an extraordinary Assembly of the States General, held on Sunday June 10, two Resolutions were passed. Their object was to give the army a legal authority to leave the territory of Holland, and put themselves under the protection of the Union; and, as an additional motive to encourage them, their High Mightinesses stigmatized and suspended Gen. Van Ryssel, and took from him the command of the Cordon.—*Harris Papers.*

tary stores, to any Province whatever without their express orders.

SECRET NOTE FROM THE PRINCESS OF ORANGE TO SIR JAMES
HARRIS.

Ce 18 Juin, 1787.

LA situation devient si critique, et si dangereuse que je suis extrèmement embarrassée dans ma correspondance avec Mons. de N——,* n'ayant pas de chiffre avec lui. C'est ce qui me fait prendre le parti de vous prier de l'entretenir de ma part, et de lui faire la confidence comme je vous la fais de même sous la sceau du secret ; que je viens de recevoir deux lettres, l'une du Comte de Goertz, l'autre de Mons. de Rh——.† Ils désirent et conseillent l'un et l'autre, que Mr. H——‡ put être engagé à représenter chez lui que la seul moyen de sauver la République ce seroit d'engager Sa Majesté Britannique de dire au Roi de Prusse.—"Joignez vous à moi pour dégager la République de ses fers, et prévenir sa ruine totale. Si vous ne prenez pas ce parti, il sera impossible que la ligue Germanique subsiste, et je me trouverais dans l'impossibilité de concourir à son maintien." Les deux amis ci-dessus jugent l'un et l'autre séparément, qu'une démarche pareille feroit immanquablement son effet sur Sa Majesté Prussienne.

Mons. ——§ est par conséquent prié de donner cette ouverture sous le sceau du secret à Mr. H——et de me mettre en état de répondre à —— de la résolution que Mr. H—— prendra à cet égard.

* Nagel.   † Rhoon.   ‡ Mr. Harris.   § Mr. Hogendorp.

EXTRACT OF A DESPATCH FROM SIR JAMES HARRIS TO THE
MARQUIS OF CARMARTHEN.

Hague, 19th June, 1787.

In regard to the question asked by the Princess of
Orange, on subsidiary foreign troops, I have answered,
" Que le Roi ne serait peut-être pas éloigné de faire faire
l'insinuation que Son Altesse Royale demande ; mais
qu'avant de s'y prêter, il est essentiel que Sa Majesté soit
instruite à qui, et au nom de qui, la réquisition doit être
faite, le nombre de troupes qu'elle comprendera, et les
fonds assignés pour en fournir les frais." I hope in saying
this I have not mistaken your Lordship's meaning, (in
case this measure should be adopted,) which I confess
after all I much fear cannot be done on any good ground,
and with any prospect of utility arising from it, in the
present unhinged state of the Provinces. I retain my
opinion, and indeed I am every day more and more convinced from Mons. Thulemeyer's conduct being suffered to
go on unnoticed and uncensured by his Court, that this
Minister actually has it in his instructions to prevent any
settlement taking place in the affairs of the Republic
without the interference of his Royal Master. It was
with this impression on my mind, that I flung out the
idea of the friendly Provinces rejecting all conciliatory
plans coming from without, in which England was not
included. *Their* saying this is not the same as if *we*
said it ; it will go to prove their attachment to England,
and to the old system, but will not involve England
deeper in the concerns of this country, than it may be
expedient for her afterwards to go.

Mine, of June 15th, I hope will acquaint your Lordship with the check we received in the States General
on that day, and the probability there then existed
of all our measures being overthrown by the Province
of Utrecht being allowed to give its vote by deputies
forced into the Assembly by the Faction. Finding it
was next to impossible to operate on the minds of the

friendly Deputies, (whom I described but too faithfully when I said they were abashed and disconcerted with what had passed, and their imaginations frightened with what was still to happen,) there remained nothing to be done but to endeavour to prevail on the Council of State, (who are charged with the execution of the orders of their High Mightinesses,) to declare that they could not consider the resolution of Thursday, which admitted the new commissioner from Utrecht, and that of Friday which was carried by their vote, as having passed according to the forms prescribed by the Union, and that it was incompatible with their duty to the Confederate States to carry them into execution.

I shall not trouble your Lordship with an account of the means I employed to effect this point, or describe how difficult a task I found it, in so short a time as passed between the breaking up of the Assembly on Friday night, and at its re-meeting on Saturday at noon, to determine the minds of men, naturally slow and timid, to consent to adopt so new and so vigorous a measure. By the assistance of my friends, and by the availing ourselves of the constitutional ground on which we stood, we, however, prevailed on the members of the Council of State to admit our arguments, and to prepare a letter, addressed to their High Mightinesses.

When they met, therefore, on Saturday instead of confirming their proceedings of Friday, and of finally rescinding the favourable resolutions of the 1st, 2nd, and 10th, and of substituting as many of a directly contrary tendency in their place, their whole plan was stopped by this letter, and by another to a similar effect written by the Chamber of Accounts, who, on their side, also declared they could not issue any money under such irregular orders. Their meeting was tumultuous to a degree, and, after breaking up in the morning without coming to any conclusion, they assembled again in the evening. Most of the friendly Deputies dined with me, and I spared no pains to keep up their spirits, and to make them feel that the danger of yielding was much greater than that of resisting. My great wish was to get through the week without any conclusion whatever, and to wait till this began, when not only a less hostile Deputy presides, but because I was in hopes, that the messengers would be returned from Friesland.

The Assembly on Saturday night was still more tumultuous than that in the morning; a complete disorder and confusion reigned, and the disputes ran so high that swords were drawn, and the Baron de Zuylen, a man of great honour and spirit and one of the legal Deputies of Utrecht, not being able to brook the impertinence of Mons. d'Averhont, one of the illegal ones, held so high a language to him, that a duel was fought on Sunday morning, which, however, to my great satisfaction, ended without any personal injury to either of the parties, and much to the honour of Mons. de Zuylen, and I must in justice add without derogating from that of Mons. d'Averhont. The Assembly broke up at eight o'clock, P.M., without a possibility of coming to a conclusion, and adjourned till Monday. This was the great point I wished to obtain.

When the States met yesterday, and four additional deputies, in order to strengthen their party, appeared with their commissions, signed by the meeting at Utrecht, they were refused to be admitted; the right of voting was taken from Mons. d'Averhont and the others, who had, if I may use the word, been smuggled into the Assembly on Friday, and the old and real Deputies were reinstated in their right of voting.

To-day nothing of any consequence whatever has passed in the States General, and in the few resolutions of mere form which were taken, the legal Deputies of Utrecht voted, and the intruders were set aside. The right wing of the Cordon is almost wholly come over to us. As soon as I found, from having sounded the temper of the Council of State, that we should stop (for, at least, twenty-four hours) the execution of the resolution taken on Friday, I despatched two officers on whom I can rely to Gorcum, and instructed them to use their utmost

influence to prevail on that garrison to march into Gelderland immediately and without a moment's loss of time.
They succeeded most effectually. On Sunday, at four in
the morning, the town was evacuated as well as the
fortress on the opposite shore, called Wercum, and the
regiment of Salm Marinier, that of Waldeck, with the
whole body of officers, and a company of artillery, before
ten, arrived at Dalem, the first town or rather village in
in Gelderland, where they immediately took the oath of
allegiance to that Province. The left wing, though certainly well-disposed and ripe for defection also, are not
yet in movement.

If the defection in the Cordon continues, and if the
military people we have placed about the Prince at
Amersfort, know how to take due advantage of it, the
army under Mons. Vander Hoop* will, in point of numbers, be very soon greatly superior to that of Holland.
Should this happen, and should we, on the other side, be
able to establish a plurality in the States General, I submit it to your Lordship's judgment, whether (during a
week when the President can be depended upon), it would
not be advisable that I should go to Nimeguen; that I
should there fully, and to the bottom, discuss the whole
plan of operations with the Prince and Princess of Orange;
hear in what theirs agrees with, or in what it may differ
from, that we have laid down here; and if our ideas meet,
whether it would not be in that case expedient to send
Col. Drummond to Amesfort, to examine and inspect the
state of General Vander Hoop's army, as well as to its
effective force, as to its discipline and disposition ; and,
after he has made his observations on it, to inquire of the
General himself, the various articles of which he is in
want, in order that it should be well appointed in every
respect, and supposing everything he asked for were
granted, what he then would undertake to attempt with
a fair probability of success.

This will lead to a question nobody has yet solved to
my satisfaction, whether it is possible to take Utrecht or

---

* General commanding the Stadtholder's army.

not. If it be, and General Vander Hoop is only withheld from the enterprise for want of the proper military
means, such as artillery, bombs, &c., I think these should,
at all events and at all rates, be immediately procured
for him, and he be encouraged to proceed. The town of
Utrecht is in open rebellion, and as long as it is declared
so by four of the Confederate States, it is not only no infraction of the Union, but even the duty of the Stadtholder
to reduce it.

EXTRACT OF A DESPATCH FROM SIR JAMES HARRIS TO THE
MARQUIS OF CARMARTHEN.

Hague, 22nd June, 1787.

THE French Ambassador protracted his stay at Amsterdam till yesterday evening. I had his motions watched
minutely, and your Lordship may rely, that he and the
chiefs of the Faction there are reciprocally dissatisfied
with each other. His object was to encourage and revive
the spirit of his party at a time when it is hard pressed ;
but on being asked by Abbema, Bekker, and Hooft, whether if they proceeded to extremities, and were in a
situation of distress and danger, France would come with
troops to their support, he replied (after endeavouring to
avoid the question,) that he had no authority to say she
would ; and on being pushed still harder, he attempted to
palliate the refusal by trying to persuade them it would
be a measure more hurtful than beneficial to them, since
it would certainly lead to a quarrel with other Powers,
and create a general war in Europe, in which they could
possibly find no advantage. This reasoning was not admitted, and the three days Mons. de Verac passed at
Amsterdam were spent in bickerings and altercations
between him and his friends. He was for proving the
Party was strong enough of itself and wanted no exterior
support. They, that without such assistance, they had
no security, and could not venture to undertake any of
the measures which had been adopted.

I am called out of my bed by an express from Amsterdam, by which I learn the following important intelligence. That, in consequence of a courier the French Ambassador met here on his return yesterday, Mons. de la Coste was immediately re-dispatched to Amsterdam, where he came in time last night to call a meeting of the confidential managers of the Faction. The particulars of what passed at this meeting my informer does not pretend to have discovered accurately, but he says that this morning it was resolved by the Regency of that city, assembled in Council, to instruct their Deputies in the States of Holland to propose that a formal demand should be immediately made to France to grant her Mediation in the present troubles.

This paper (and this is the most material part of the intelligence) was evidently prepared originally in French, and translated hastily into Dutch, and goes to prove that France is actually ready to act as Mediatrix.

My informer adds, that this resolution, taken by the Council, was immediately ordered to be sent to the Hague; and that he supposes it will be drawn up and prepared in time for the Deputy of Amsterdam, certainly, to make the proposal in the States of Holland to-morrow.

EXTRACT OF A DESPATCH FROM SIR JAMES HARRIS TO THE
MARQUIS OF CARMARTHEN.

Hague, 25th June, 1787.

THE States met at half-past ten. The proposal was made, but the piece I mentioned in my last not produced. It was, as I suggested, taken *ad referendum* by the eight votes of the minority, and its future discussion put off till Tuesday.

A flat rejection of it is a measure not calculated for the tame and timorous minds of our party ; besides, supposing I could work up the temper of our friends in Gelderland, Utrecht, and Zealand, to such a pitch of vigour as is requisite to take so decided a step, I am certain I could not operate on those of Friesland, who begin to waver ; and, if not managed with great delicacy, care, and caution, may desert us, and carry the majority into the other scale.

My idea therefore is, and I conceive it nearly meets the sentiments of His Majesty's confidential servants, to endeavour to prevail on the four friendly Provinces, in the first instance, to take it *ad referendum*, (this will gain us ten days,) and afterwards, when the matter comes to be finally deliberated upon, to say they are not averse to the Mediation of France, *provided other great Powers*, fully as much concerned as France to preserve the Constitution and maintain the independence of the Republic, should be *also* called upon to act as Mediators ; and, if they should be pressed to declare whom they mean by these Powers, to name the three great monarchies which (besides France) surround the Republic—England, the Emperor, and Prussia.

The naming England singly would appear *a party measure*, and tend to renew the unfavourable impressions made by the last war, and open a wound barely healed.

The naming it with Prussia alone might imply a disposition to give Prussia the lead in the negotiation ; but the joining her to the other two would not only avoid either of these constructions being put on their conduct, but indicate also a real and sincere desire of terminating the dispute cordially and impartially.

On Saturday, in the afternoon, a person of confidence (Mr. Charles Hogendorp) was sent from Amersfort by the Princess of Orange, to acquaint Messrs. Nagel, Reygersman, Royer, and myself, that, seeing the languor of the States General, and the want of vigour, union, and activity which marked all their proceedings, she was determined to come immediately to the Hague, and *put herself at the head of the party.* That the Prince had given his consent ; and that she should bring letters from him to the States General and the States of Holland, empowering her to act, or negotiate, as circumstances might require. She had no doubt, she said, *that* her person would be respected ; that, at all events, she felt it was a risk which, from the magnitude of the object at stake, it was a duty she owed her family to run, and her mind was perfectly at ease as to any consequences to which she might be exposed. After explaining these her intentions, she ordered Mons. Hogendorp to say, that she only waited for our sanction to put them into immediate execution.

Mons. Nagel, Reygersman, and Royer did not hesitate an instant in giving it their approbation ; and, though I perhaps saw room at least for reflection, I felt it out of my power to refuse mine to a measure of such uncommon magnanimity and spirit. I only begged that Mons. Hogendorp would return directly to Amersfort and state to Her Royal Highness the true and faithful situation of things here ; that he would not depreciate her adversaries, or overrate the abilities of her friends ; and if, after giving this a patient hearing, Her Royal Highness still remained in the same opinion, it would be impossible for her to doubt of our straining every nerve to assist her at a moment when she filled us with admiration and respect.

An express, in reply to this, returned an hour ago, bringing no other answer than to order relays on the road, and an apartment to be prepared for her at the *Maison du Bois* for Thursday next.

Our first care now is to ensure the safe arrival of this great and respectable Princess ; to prevent her being either insulted on the way, or exposed to any danger here ; and it is for this purpose that to-night scouts are sent out on every side to find out the passages from Gelderland into Holland which are not occupied by detachments of the Free Corps. I sincerely hope this may be effected. The secret is most profoundly kept, and the first news of Her Royal Highness's arrival will be notified to the States General.

As it is impossible to foresee to what consequences it

may lead, I must beg your Lordship, in answer to this, to instruct me how I should behave if the French party should be daring and brutal enough to commit any act of violence on Her Royal Highness.

LETTER FROM THE MARQUIS OF CARMARTHEN TO SIR JAMES HARRIS.

Whitehall, June 26th, 1787.

MY DEAR HARRIS,—You will find by the despatch of to-day that we by no means relax in attention to the affairs of Holland. You are, as you deserve to be, in high favour with us all, and I was much pleased at the anxiety of the Cabinet to have some personal compliment paid to you in the despatch on the subject of the Utrecht Deputies; which, probably, without you, would have remained in the way our enemies could have wished.

For God's sake bring the well-disposed Dutch to some plan of active operation, if possible, without delay! The present moment seems to be precisely that in which the decisive stroke must be hazarded.

EXTRACT OF A LETTER FROM SIR JAMES HARRIS TO THE MARQUIS OF CARMARTHEN.

Hague, June 26th, 1787.

MY DEAR LORD,—The experiment which is going to be made by Her Royal Highness does undoubtedly infinite honour to her courage and spirit, but I am not at all at my ease as to the effect it may produce. From a turn I have in me to chivalry, (though I am not sentimental,) I feel a most strong disposition to support and defend her; for, let what will be the success, she deserves support.

You see we again stand on high ground in the Generality ; and if the Princess of Orange can, by her presence, give Their High Mightinesses what God has, I fear, refused them, and make them act like men, I will adore her as an angel.

I have been up till three these last four nights writing. I am forced to sacrifice the day to audiences, and to going from house to house. I regret no labours whilst I see you so much in earnest at home ; but, if I die in harness, do not give me to the hounds.

EXTRACT OF A DESPATCH FROM SIR JAMES HARRIS TO THE MARQUIS OF CARMARTHEN.

Hague, 29th June, 1787.

THE apprehensions I expressed in my last were but too well founded. The Princess of Orange was stopped yesterday evening on her road to this place at a village called Haestricht, near Gonda, by a detachment of Free Corps belonging to that town, assisted by some troopers who had deserted from the regiment of Hesse Phillipsdahl. The reason on which they grounded their proceedings was an order from the Commission of Five* to prevent all suspected persons from coming into the Province of Holland. They carried Her Royal Highness to a farm-house adjoining ; whence, after keeping her for some time in confinement, they allowed her, at her particular request, to go under a strong guard to a small town called Schoonhoven, where she now is. The Princess of Orange left Nimeguen early in the morning : her suite was composed of one maid of honour (Mad^lle Starenberg), Colonel Rudolph Bentinck, Count George Randwyck (one of her Chamberlains), and a Prussian officer, about the young Princes, called Stampfort ; these are all kept under arrest as well as Her Royal Highness. She has written letters from Schoonhoven to the Great Pensionary, and to the Greffier Fagel,

---

* The Commission of Woerden, also called the Commission of Five, was appointed by the Patriots to conduct their military affairs. They put the Rhingrave of Salm at the head of their army.

acquainting them with what has happened, and to declare
that her sole motive for coming to the Hague was to promote a conciliation, as far as should be in her power, between the contending parties, and to express her surprise
and concern that she was not allowed to proceed without
interruption.   In her letter to the Pensionary, she dwells
with becoming dignity on this point, will not allow herself a doubt that the conduct of the Commission will be
disavowed by the States of Holland, and that she shall
immediately receive their consent to continue her journey,
and come to the Hague.

I am forced to write down events as they arise ; this
makes my despatches long : but it is impossible for me to
expect to have leisure to digest and class them in any
order, if I were to wait till within a few hours of the post
going out.   The first news of this ill-timed and unfortunate incident came here about eleven last night, but no
certain account till between one and two this morning.
All those in the secret but myself were waiting, with the
greatest anxiety, from nine till this hour at the House in
the Wood.   I excused myself from going thither, to avoid
the natural inferences which would be drawn from it, and
which would be equally pernicious to the Princess and
myself.   To avoid appearances I supped yesterday at the
French Ambassador's ; and I confess, when I returned
home, and found no accounts of Her Royal Highness, I
forestalled the unpleasant news I received soon after.   It
was debated immediately what was to be done.   I advised
waking the President of the week (Count Welderen) ; insisting on his calling instantly an assembly of the States
General, to require ample and full reparation of the States
of Holland for the insult offered to the person of Her Royal
Highness ; and, if this was refused, to come to two resolutions, one to send 1500 men of this garrison immediately
to rescue the Princess, the other to authorize the Prince
of Orange to march directly with the troops of Utrecht
and Gelderland into the Province, to revenge in a becoming manner the indignity offered to his family.   The
idea was relished and adopted readily by the few people

who were present ; but it was not calculated for the timid temper of the States, and still less for the doubtful character of the President.

The night was passed in debate and deliberation, and the minds of those who ought to have come forward on this occasion were so wrought upon by idle apprehensions of every kind, that it was impossible to bring them to anything like a fixed plan. Towards eight, the two letters from the Princess I mentioned above arrived ; but as these, and everything else, came through the hands of the Patriots, they neither made us acquainted with the real state of the fact, nor with the real wishes and intentions of the Princess. At ten (and not sooner), owing to the cause already mentioned, their High Mightinesses met ; and although there was a general expression of strong disapprobation of what had happened, yet they broke up by declaring that they would take no resolution on the subject until they were informed of what had passed in the States of Holland, as it was possible Their High Mightinesses might of themselves repair the injury, and suffer Her Royal Highness still to proceed on her journey hither.

There is something so unmanly and spiritless in this indifference, that I could hardly treat, with decent patience, several of the deputies who came to announce to me their disgraceful inactivity.

What passes in the States of Holland will scarcely be known till towards six ; in the meanwhile, my great uneasiness is, lest the common people and Bourgeoisie of the Hague, who are of a directly contrary character to the deputies, should be led to express their indignation at this insult offered the Princess, in a manner which, from its inefficacy, would be hurtful to the cause and fatal to themselves.

Mons. de Rhoon (whom I have some difficulty to contain) himself, and other leaders of the people, promise me they shall be kept in order. It would indeed be the summit of madness in them to rise ; the Hague is full of horse and foot patrol, and no four or five people can speak together in the streets without being immediately liable to be dispersed.

My mind was never so anxiously occupied as at this present moment. The event which has just happened oversets our whole plan; and the conduct of the States General exposes to me such a wretched prospect of what is to be expected from them in the hour of trial, that almost every hope vanishes.

This, my Lord, to my mind, is the great evil which arises from the present mischance. When considered simply as an attempt which has failed, various means of reparation present themselves to our minds; but when we see that by its consequences it has discovered the extreme pusillanimity and torpitude of those we are to call friends, and laid open to the full view of the public the inefficiency of our means to oppose, I greatly fear we must look upon the disease as incurable, and confess our party here to be struck with a political palsy from which no assistance we can afford will be equal to recover it.

6 o'clock.

The States of Holland broke up an hour ago. The Equestrian Order proposed sending a Deputation of Excuse for what had been done, and to request Her Royal Highness to continue her route. This was overruled, and, instead of it, the orders given by the Commission of Five to stop her, approved, and the Great Pensionary directed to reply to her letter, that, as it was impossible to come to any resolution on its contents to-day, it was expedient for everything to remain *in statu quo* till the States had taken the sense of their towns upon it. This amounts to a full confirmation of her detention; and, unless Her Royal Highness can find means of returning to Gelderland (from which Schoonhoven is only a few miles distant), it gives me the greatest uneasiness, lest she should be sent into the hands of the Rhingrave of Salm, and be carried to Utrecht.

I am highly sensible of the approbation which my conduct has met with; but this sensation has its alloy, when I reflect on the little utility which has been produced from the recovery of our ground in the States General.

I have only to add, that a person of confidence (Kinckel)
is gone this moment at my request to try whether he can
get access to the Princess; and, if he succeeds, to entreat
Her Royal Highness to try every means to return to
Gelderland, and get out of the hands of her adversaries,
unless she has reason to hope for assistance which is to
come from other quarters than the Hague.

EXTRACT OF A LETTER FROM SIR JAMES HARRIS TO THE
MARQUIS OF CARMARTHEN.

Hague, June 29th, 1787.

MY DEAR LORD,—*Check to the Queen*, and in a move or
two check mate is, I fear, the state of our game. Politics
have often vexed me, but they never angered me till now.
Notwithstanding the importance of the object, and the
situation of distress in which the first woman in the
Republic was placed, not a single Deputy would leave
their beds before the usual hour, and, when they did rise,
it was to prove that they were as inactive and spiritless
when awake as when asleep.

I have, perhaps, given a too free scope to my ill-hu-
mour in my despatches ; but my bile runs through the
pores at the ends of my fingers, and mixes with the ink as
I write.   Your kind praises for what I did to recover our
lost ground in the States General was very grateful to
me, my dear Lord : I hope you and your colleagues will
not ultimately measure my merits by my success ; if you
do, I may end my days in the Tower.

LETTER FROM THE MARQUIS OF CARMARTHEN TO SIR JAMES
HARRIS.

Whitehall, July 3rd, 1787.

MY DEAR HARRIS,—Don't be so disheartened by a check
to the Queen ; let her be covered by the Knight, and all's

safe. Seriously, I am sorry for anything so unpleasant happening to the Princess, whose character so highly deserves a better fate ; the event, however, may still be productive of good. If the King her brother is not the dirtiest and shabbiest of Kings, he must resent it, *coute qui coute.* I long to see Hartsink, as he will be able to tell me much concerning the Van Thompsons at Amsterdam. What in the name of common sense are our friends about, that they do not stir, now the army is so well disposed ? Do they choose to be starved, rather than fight with advantage on their side ? The whole seems incomprehensible. I told Luci that I took for granted a strong detachment from Wesel would, of course, receive orders to march the moment the news of the Princess's being stopped arrived at Berlin ; and in truth, unless the Prussian Monarch is sold to France, they ought. You see, the French give out great preparations as being ordered. Only take care of Maestricht, and never mind the twenty-five battalions at Givet.

[The insult offered to the Princess of Orange eventually proved the most fortunate occurrence for the Stadtholder's party, as it confirmed the new King of Prussia in the Anti-French feelings which Mr. Ewart had been inculcating for the last two years. William, King of Prussia, was the weakest of men, and his whole reign a course of tergiversation and folly.]

EXTRACT OF A DESPATCH FROM SIR JAMES HARRIS TO THE
MARQUIS OF CARMARTHEN.

Hague, 3rd July, 1787.

It is with great pleasure that I can inform your Lordship of the safe arrival of the Princess of Orange at Nimeguen. She was allowed to depart from Schoonhoven on Saturday, at six in the morning ; and though she said at that place that she would remain at Leerdam till she was informed of the definite resolution of the States of Holland relative to the treatment she had met with, yet, as she met there Kinckel, who expressed to Her Royal Highness my strong desire of seeing her safe in Gelderland, she proceeded without stopping, or without any molestation, to Nimeguen, where she got about ten o'clock on Saturday.

I have every reason to be satisfied with the advice I gave, as the Rhingrave of Salm was actually advanced as far as Woerden with a corps of 300 horse ; and I have little doubt, if Her Royal Highness had remained either at Schoonhoven or Leerdam, would have endeavoured to have got possession of her person.

Mons. Thulemeyer, who remained perfectly inactive Friday, Saturday, and Sunday, and who even was unguarded enough to attempt joking with me on what has happened to the sister of the Sovereign he serves, presented yesterday a Memorial to their High Mightinesses. The only answer he got to it was the *passport* he asked for.

A resolution was taken yesterday in consequence of an address from the people to the Council of Amsterdam to prohibit the territory of Holland, not only to the Prince and Princess of Orange, but to all persons dependent on them, as long as the present troubles last. It passed in the Council, and to-day will probably be carried up to the States of Holland. In Gelderland everything goes on tolerably. The Free Corps are disarmed on all sides ; they made some resistance at Arnheim, and two houses were pillaged and destroyed before they could be brought to submit.

EXTRACT OF A DESPATCH FROM SIR JAMES HARRIS TO THE MARQUIS OF CARMARTHEN.

Hague, 6th July, 1787.

NOTHING of any consequence has passed in the States General this week. They seem to meet for no other purpose than to be tame spectators of the different acts of oppression and violence exercised by those of Holland.

These on Wednesday and yesterday came to several

resolutions, all tending to enforce their authority, without the least regard to the freedom of the subject, or the fundamental laws of the Constitution.

They forbid any address, petition, or remonstrance to be brought up to them, not perfectly analogous to their sentiments and intentions; a preposterous order, which, in fact, puts an end to all petitions whatever.

They prohibited, under pain of imprisonment and correction, the singing or *whistling* certain tunes made in former times in honour of the House of Orange; and they permitted to be brought up to them the enclosed Declarations from the chiefs of the Free Corps, which they have since made public.* It is the most extraordinary performance that was ever allowed to make its appearance in any country under the regulation of a Civil Government, since it declares in substance that a body of men unknown to the Constitution set themselves above the law, menace the administrators of justice, and signify in clear and unequivocal terms their intention of exercising a sovereign authority whenever they think themselves injured or offended.

A body of Free Corps, to the amount of about 200 men, came into the Hague this evening. To prevent any disorder, the whole garrison was under arms from three till eight o'clock.

LETTER FROM SIR JAMES HARRIS TO MR. EWART.

(In juice, and without signature.)

Hague, July 6th, 1787.

An absolute want of leisure is the real and only cause of my silence.

If the King of Prussia is seriously in earnest to assist the Republic, and to co-operate with England, he must say so, explicitly and clearly, at St. James's. After what has passed, no overture ought, or will, originate on our side. The situation of this country calls aloud for immediate and effective support; and it is on this point, not on

* Lost in the missing volume.

one of negotiation, that the Courts of London and Berlin should concur.

The conduct of Thulemeyer is infamous. If he has the smallest ground for it, it is idle to suppose any good can ever come from your quarter.

EXTRACT FROM MR. EWART'S LETTER TO THE MARQUIS OF CARMARTHEN.

7th July, 1787.

THE contents of the Princess's letter, and of the King's answer both to her and to the Prince, are entirely unknown to both the Cabinet Ministers here ; but I am assured from good authority, that His Majesty, on receiving the first advices (during the night of the 3rd), not only despatched the instructions for the orders to be sent to the Hague and to Versailles, but likewise wrote himself to General Gaudi at Wesel, and to two Generals commanding the regiments of cavalry quartered nearest to Westphalia, to hold themselves in readiness for marching ; and His Majesty at the same time declared, that he was determined to have complete satisfaction for the insult offered to his sister, whatever it might cost him to obtain it.

What I have related passed on the 3rd at midnight, when the King despatched the above-mentioned orders ; but next day His Majesty received a piece of intelligence which disconcerted him extremely, and has, I understand, occupied his whole attention ever since.

My authority is Mons. de Bishopswerder, who is at present the only person here that possesses the entire confidence of the King relative to Foreign Affairs. I was informed by this gentleman of the King's having received advice that the Court of London was actually determined not to interfere at all in Dutch affairs, in consequence of representations made by Mr. Pitt against it.* His Ma-

* Atroce mensonge de ce faquin Thulemeyer, Ministre de Sa Majesté Prussienne à la Haye, mais dévoué à la France.—*Original Note.*

jesty had been much discouraged by the intelligence, especially as it contradicted all that the Princess of Orange had written relative to the intentions of England ; and he (Mons. de Bishopswerder) therefore wished to know from me, privately, whether I had received any information on the subject.

EXTRACT OF A DESPATCH FROM SIR JAMES HARRIS TO THE MARQUIS OF CARMARTHEN.

Hague, 10th July, 1787.

AMSTERDAM is at the absolute disposal of the mob. They have elected two new Burgomasters, and they set at defiance those who, a few weeks ago, were their leaders. Your Lordship may suppose how the trade and credit of that great city sunk.

A detachment of 300 men, supported by one of 1400, from the Prince's army, took possession on Saturday morning of the town of Wyk Le Duerstede. It surrendered on the first summons, without firing a gun. There were about 400 Free Corps in it, who abandoned it on the appearance of the troops. I understand some of the leaders are taken ; particularly a Dissenting clergyman named Van der Kemp, famous for being the original institutor of the Free Corps.

This trifling success has animated the soldiery ; and what tends more to keep up their spirits is, that the Rhingrave, at the head of 600 horse and 2000 foot, made a sally with a view of repairing this loss, but, as he came near the lines at Zeyst, he found the army in such good order that he returned with great precipitation to Utrecht.

Mr. Thulemeyer had orders to express himself in strong and explicit terms to the Pensionary and Greffier, which I am told he did ; and I presume he had also orders to wait on the French Ambassador, as he went to him before he saw either of the Dutch Ministers.

He appeared last night embarrassed and vexed to a

degree, and not without reason, as he had been heedless enough to assure the Faction that the manner in which he had drawn up his reports was such as would prevent his Royal Master from taking any umbrage at what has passed.

LETTER FROM SIR JAMES HARRIS TO THE MARQUIS OF CARMARTHEN.

Hague, July 10th, 1787.

MY DEAR LORD,—I have been so unwell for these last ten days, that I have at times been afraid I should knock up; as long, however, as I have a fibre which holds, I will stick to the stuff. The event* in the Low Countries, and the wrath of Prussia, are great incidents, which in their consequences may bring *both* the German Powers at our feet, and leave us the choice of either of them for our helpmate here. It is for this reason that I should be cautious of embarking hastily, or too far, with either of them, till we see which can offer the best bargain.

I think I foresee the anger of His Prussian Majesty dwindle gradually away, and that it will end in his saying his sister was ill-advised in attempting to come to the Hague, *et qu'il ne veut pas déranger ses propres affaires pour arranger celles d'autrui*; a memorable phrase in his mouth, which, if my pen was likely to make a lasting impression, should hand him down to posterity with the reputation he deserves.

Though my despatch of to-day wears a more promising aspect than those of this day se'nnight, yet I confess I have no hopes of anything which can be done within the compass of my profession; and that, before any good can be effected, our *black* coats must be dyed *red*. Many thanks for your kind letter of the 3d July. My head aches too much for me to write more, but my heart is well enough to feel and return your friendship.

* A temporary revolt in the Low Countries in consequence of some unconstitutional Edicts of the Emperor.

LETTER FROM SIR JAMES HARRIS TO MR. EWART.

Hague, 13th July, 1787.

THULEMEYER'S Memorials have not had any great effect, but perhaps the march of troops may give them weight : nothing short of this will ; and, even then, I believe the Faction absurd and haughty enough to resist.   Why does not your Court, if really sincere, apply to ours ?   I am certain we should agree in a few conferences ; but, after what has passed, England cannot take the *first* step.

Thulemeyer (whose whole conduct is shameful to a degree) has, as I understand, written home that Mr. Pitt would resign rather than assist the Dutch.   I beg you will contradict this as an *untruth*, which he was prompted to advance by the French Embassy, to whom he always goes for instructions.   England, on the contrary, you may be assured, never will suffer France to subdue this country, and is preparing to prove this to be her intention.   The Republic *can* only be saved by support from without.   Matters are gone too far to be reconciled from within ; and the ferment is at such a height that nothing short of compulsion can set it to rights.   I must beg pardon for not writing oftener.   You are the last person on the Continent to whom I should wish to seem neglectful, but it is impossible for me to describe to you how wholly my time is employed.

EXTRACT OF A DESPATCH FROM SIR JAMES HARRIS TO THE MARQUIS OF CARMARTHEN.

Hague, 13th July, 1787.

YOUR Lordship may be assured I shall make no other use of the confidential communication of the several papers inclosed to me by His Majesty's command, which have passed between the Courts of London and Versailles, than such as your Lordship prescribes.

Before I enter more deeply on the subject, I must repeat what I have already said, that it is impossible for me to reconcile the language held by the French Minister at Versailles to the conduct the French Ambassador holds here. They are in perfect contradiction with each other, not only in respect to their intentions in this Republic, and to the means they are disposed to employ, but also in their language with regard to England; for while Mons. de Montmorin,* in his conversation with Mr. Eden, appears to act under the apprehension that England has it in contemplation to take an active share in the concerns of the Republic, Mons. de Verac and his followers assert with the greatest confidence that nothing of the kind will happen, and that they are perfectly sure of England's remaining a passive spectator of what will take place.

I remain, however, firm in opinion, that unless there be a concerted plan with some other Power, of which I am totally ignorant, France, after having tried the whole effect of menace, will not proceed to extremities, but condescend to settle the degree of influence she is to retain in this Republic by negotiation; for the great object in dispute, as I take it, is not so much how this country is to be governed, but whether France shall, by the exercise of undue influence, get the direction of the Republic wholly into her own hands; or whether it shall be restored to a state of independence, and at liberty either to return to the ancient system, or to form such political connexions as may appear the most suitable to its interests. The attainment of the first point is the end France pursues; that of the second, is the object of England; and on this the whole of the negotiation is to rest.

Were it merely a question of right, and could it be supposed that the two Courts had no other interest in the disputes than to determine dispassionately what was the legal Constitution of the country, the matter could not admit of a doubt. The Constitution was settled by the unanimous voice of the nation in 1747, and confirmed as unanimously in 1766.

A perpetual Stadtholder was then given to the Republic by a concurrent vote of the several federate States,

* French Minister for Foreign Affairs.

and the office made hereditary in the House of Orange.
The powers and privileges with which he was vested are
clearly and explicitly stated ; and it is an abuse of terms,
and in perfect contradiction to the opinion of the ablest
lawyers of this country to call him (as Mons. Montmorin,
after Mons. de Rayneval, does,) *un Serviteur, ou un Offi-
cier de la République.* He is an inherent part of the
supreme Government of the country, partakes as such of
the Sovereign authority, stands at least on the same line
with the other members who compose this sovereign body ;
and France, by proposing to thrust him in the first instance out of this line, aims at carrying her great point at
the very outset of the negotiation.

Your Lordship will observe, that the source of the present troubles are innovations introduced since 1747.   If
the Constitution then established was legal (and it was
admitted as such for upwards of thirty years), those innovations are illegal.   They are the work of the French
party.

To simplify negotiation as much as possible, it is my
opinion that the form of Government, as established in
1747, should be taken up as the basis of the negotiation,
without any further retrospect ; and that the discussion
should turn on the reform of such abuses as may have
been since introduced, either by a misinterpretation of
the power given to the Stadtholder, or by any vice in his
administration.

If France does not consent to this, it is positive that
she has her views to an entire subversion of the Stadtholderate ; and it seems as if Mons. Montmorin hinted at
this, when, writing to Mr. Eden on the Government of this
country, he says, " *Supposant que le Stadthoudérat en
fut une partie nécessaire.*"   Now, if France supposes it
not to be a necessary part of the Government, it will, I
presume, be very difficult for our ideas to meet.   But if
France, either from motives of moderation or prudence,
should be brought to consent to negotiate on the principles laid down in 1747, the first proposals must in my
mind originate from her, as it is her party that are con-

tending for a change in the Government, while ours is only wishing to preserve it as it now stands.

Mons. Thulemeyer, in virtue of further orders he received by the post from Berlin yesterday, enforced, by a visit to the Minister of the Republic this morning, the demand set forth in the two memorials he presented on Tuesday last. He read to them a despatch from His Prussian Majesty, wherein it is said, " *Si on ne lui donne une réponse prompte et satisfaisante, il pourrait prendre d'autres mesures.*"

Mons. Thulemeyer was asked by the Greffier and by the Pensionary whether it was true that a body of Prussians had received orders to hold themselves in readiness to march ; his answer was, " *qu'il n'en était pas instruit.*" But the fact is, certainly, that such orders are given.

The inclosed letter from the Baron de Spaar, who resides occasionally at Cleves, leaves no doubt on the subject, and it is confirmed to me by the Princess of Orange herself.

EXTRACTS OF A DESPATCH FROM SIR JAMES HARRIS TO THE
MARQUIS OF CARMARTHEN.

Hague, 17th July, 1787.

THE States of Holland on Saturday morning resolved on making the answer to Mons. Thulemeyer's Memorial. It is drawn up very artfully, but is far from giving the satisfaction His Prussian Majesty requires, and much less does it signify any intention of punishing the persons who were employed in stopping the Princess of Orange, or those who gave the order.

He said, however, not a word more than he was obliged to say, and suppressed the strongest part of his Instructions, which enjoined him to say, that His Prussian Majesty considered the treatment his Sister had met with as a personal insult offered to himself, and a manifest infraction of the law of nations ; and, on the whole, has conducted himself on this occasion in so lax, remiss, and

lukewarm a manner, that it is evident to me he is either
under the firm persuasion that the King, his Master, is not
in earnest, or that he has a certainty of being provided
for in case he should incur the displeasure and disgrace of
his Sovereign. Letters from Cleves and the adjacent
parts confirm the idea of the march of troops.

LETTER FROM SIR JAMES HARRIS TO THE PRINCESS OF
ORANGE, NIMEGUEN.

La Haye, ce 20 Juillet, 1787.

MADAME,—J'espère que Votre Altesse Royale ne désap-
prouvera pas la démarche que ma Cour va faire* à celle
de Berlin, et dont j'ai prié Mons. de Nagel de faire un
détail plus exact que le temps ne me permet de faire
aujourd'hui.

J'ai travaillé, depuis l'indignité outrageante offerte à
Votre Altesse Royale près de Schoonhoven, à déterminer
le Roi, mon Maître, à faire cette démarche ; mais je me
suis abstenu d'en parler. C'est par des faits, et pas par
des paroles, que je désire la servir. C'est la manière la
plus analogue aux circonstances, et surtout à ce zélé et
respectueux attachement avec lequel, &c.

EXTRACTS OF A LETTER FROM SIR JAMES HARRIS TO
MR. EWART.

Hague, 20th July, 1787.

THERE can be nothing for me to add to the despatches
Major brings you.† They serve as a full confirmation of

* It was with great difficulty that Sir James Harris prevailed on the
English Government to move as actively in this matter as he wished ; but
at last Ministers made the most of the insult to the Princess of Orange, to
induce her brother to take those decisive measures which he afterwards
adopted, guaranteed by a promise of support against France.

† Major took out the guarantee of England to support Prussia, should
France declare war in consequence of her military intervention. We promised
to back the Duke of Brunswick's advance by a demonstration of forty ships
of the line.

the few sentences I lately have troubled you with. I have for some time past been working to bring this measure to bear, and it cannot fall into better hands than yours. The Faction here are really mad ; and the assurances France gives them that Prussia will do nothing, joined to those they receive from Mons. Thulemeyer, "that he has given and will continue to give such a turn to the insult offered the Princess as to prevent its having any consequences," gives them an audacious security that is unaccountable.

I beg you will let me hear by the first post of the safe arrival of Major, for which I am very anxious. Your letters to the office, of the 14th instant, are just come in, and I like very much their contents ; push them to come forward where you are, and you will not find us retire before the proposal.

COPY OF PART OF MR. EWART'S LETTER TO THE MARQUIS OF CARMARTHEN.

July 21, 1787.

YESTERDAY Count Finckenstein informed me officially, that His Prussian Majesty had issued effective orders on the 18th for the march of twenty-three battalions of infantry, two regiments of heavy cavalry, one regiment of dragoons, ten squadrons of hussars, and a corps of jägers, accompanied with a strong train of artillery, consisting of forty-eight pieces of heavy cannon, and about fifty field-pieces of six and three-pounders. The whole force is estimated at about 25,000 men, of which the cavalry makes 5000 ; and I was acquainted that this army was destined to repair with all possible expedition to the frontiers of Holland, in order to support and enforce His Majesty's demand of satisfaction for the insult offered to the Princess of Orange. The King has written to the Duke of Brunswick, to know if it be agreeable to him to take the command ; but I understand General Möllendorff expects it will devolve on him.

EXTRACTS OF A DESPATCH FROM SIR JAMES HARRIS TO THE
MARQUIS OF CARMARTHEN.

Hague, 24th July, 1787.

I HAD the honour of receiving your Lordship's despatch, of the 20th instant, on Sunday. I am happy to find that I have been so fortunate as to anticipate the instructions it contains, and that the conduct I have observed since the memorial communicated to your Lordship by Mons. Barthelemi,* and given in here by the French Ambassador, has been such as your Lordship prescribes me. I think I may venture to say, that nothing that comes from *France* will alter the fixed resolution of the four Provinces to reject the single Mediation of that Court, and indeed all Mediation whatever, unless the other neighbouring Powers are called upon in the way I have already mentioned to accede to it. The menaces, insinuations, and promises of the French Faction have had no weight with them, and they remain more determined on this point than on any which has of late come under their deliberation. I trust the steps taken by M. Thulemeyer yesterday, *Ministerially*, will not stagger their resolution. I shall endeavour to relate them to your Lordship as exactly as possible.

This Minister received a courier on Sunday about six o'clock ; at nine he went to the French Hotel, and remained there till eleven. Early the next morning he waited upon the Pensionary, and upon the Greffier. He was a long time with the former, and I am ignorant of what passed between them ; but to the latter he said, that the King, his Master, continued to insist on a complete and full satisfaction for the affront put on his Sister, and that he (M. Thulemeyer) little doubted that this would be granted, since he knew the Court of France highly disapproved the answer given by the Netherland Minister

---

* Barthelemi was French Minister in London ; his memorial conveyed only friendly sentiments, but no promise of positive assistance to the Patriots.

to the King of Prussia, and that Mons. de Verac had promised him to lend him his influence to get it re-scinded, and a favourable one substituted in its place. From this subject he passed to that of the Mediation, ob-serving that he had it in command to say, that it would be very agreeable to His Prussian Majesty if the Provinces would invite him, as Holland had done France, to inter-pose his good offices, in order to terminate the disputes of the Republic.

That it was his (the King of Prussia's) wish, that the arrangement of these disputes should be left to France and Prussia alone; and his opinion, " *qu'il ne convenait pas d'inviter l'Angleterre de se joindre à la Médiation at-tendu qu'elle n'avoit pas les mêmes Relations avec la Ré-publique que les Cours de Berlin et de Versailles;*" these words he read out of a despatch he took from his pocket.

After he had explained himself in this manner, and dwelt forcibly and repeatedly on the expediency of *ex-cluding England*, he desired the Greffier to report what he had said to the States General, as it was of great import-ance for them to be on their guard on this occasion.

Mons. Fagel positively declined this commission, unless the Sieur Thulemeyer would give it in to him in writing. This he refused to do ; but said, since the Greffier would not undertake it, he would himself go round to the first Deputy of each Province, and acquaint them with the opinions and wishes of his Court.

This he did in the course of yesterday ; and I find, though the substance of what he said to these gentlemen was perfectly correspondent with what passed between him and the Greffier, yet that he made use of expressions more or less strong, according to the character of the per-son with whom he spoke.

As I had early notice of his intentions, I was before-hand with him in some of his visits, and close at his heels in all. I found all the Deputies quite open and sincere in avowing to me what he had said ; and I must, also, in justice to them declare, that they seem to see through the danger of the proposal, and to remain firm in their inten-

tion of having at least England added to the Mediation.
I could perceive, however, that the Sieur Thulemeyer's
visit had awakened in their minds ideas I have been so
long endeavouring to suppress, and left suspicions unfavourable to our general principles and intentions which it
is highly essential should not be suffered to take root.

It is with a view to prevent this, that I have invited
them all to dine with me to-morrow, when I hope to keep
them to their present principles, and to prevent their
being led astray either by their own weakness, or by the
insidious language of the Prussian Minister—a language
to me perfectly inexplicable, after reading the last letters
which came from Berlin (those of the 17th); since, though
it appears indeed that His Prussian Majesty does not
decline a conjoint Mediation with France, yet he couples
to his consent such conditions relative to this Republic as
he must know France never will hear of, unless forced
into them by England's uniting her efforts with those of
Prussia.   At the same time, that a Foreign Minister
should be daring enough, when speaking to the Minister
of the Court where he resides, to read from a despatch
words which were *not to be found* in it, or venture, in
order to answer the ends *for which he is undoubtedly
paid by the Patriots*, to commit his Court, and pledge his
Master for a falsehood, which a very short period must
discover to be such, is a degree of profligacy and folly
which seldom unite in the same person ; yet, either this
must be the case, or the language of the Prussian Minister
to Mr. Ewart is perfectly insincere and insidious.   Time
alone can clear up this mystery.

DESPATCH FROM SIR J. HARRIS TO MR. EWART AND
SIR ROBERT KEITH.

Hague, July 24, 1787.

It is impossible to bring a description of the affairs of
this country within the means of a ciphered letter.   The
first cause of the confusion is lost sight of : instead of an

Opposition to the Stadtholderate by a few aristocratical leaders, a Democratical faction now is working at an entire subversion of the Constitution. France has armed them ; and they have attained such a degree of power and strength, that I much doubt her ability at keeping them in order. Hitherto she has encouraged their excesses, but if she turns her thoughts towards negotiation (as I believe she will be forced to do), it will be expedient for her to change her conduct ; and in this case I should not be surprised to see the mob change sides and act against her.

There is no manner of doubt that the troubles in the Low Countries are closely connected with those which prevail here, that they are instigated by France, and that notwithstanding the Flemish consent to send Deputies to Vienna, that they are by no means yet in a way to subside.

This ought to make the King of Prussia perfectly at ease as to his operations here ; and the fear of the Emperor ought not even to furnish him with a pretext for listening to France, or to desist from giving a full scope to the vengeance he is disposed to take for the insult offered his sister.

The Emperor has written with his own hand a very civil letter to the Stadtholder, wherein, besides entirely approving his conduct, he appears sincerely interested in his success.

TO SIR ROBERT KEITH ALONE.

You may assure the Austrian Minister that two of the leading Patriots have been at Brussels to propose to the States of Brabant to unite with Holland in one common cause of independence, and to apply to France for assistance. They moreover have offered them money and munitions ; these were accepted, but the idea of applying to France was not immediately closed with, though far from rejected. I see nothing of the Imperial Chargé des Affaires here ; he continues to live with the Patriots.

EXTRACT OF A DESPATCH FROM THE MARQUIS OF
CARMARTHEN TO SIR JAMES HARRIS.

Whitehall, 27th July, 1787.

THE conduct of His Prussian Majesty is evidently of a
great importance with a view to negotiation, and still
more so with a view to any other measures which might
possibly be adopted, if the negotiation should fail, and
France proceed to extremities. While the troops of the
Republic are employed in the Prince of Orange's cordon,
in the Province of Utrecht, to watch the motions of the
Free Corps in the Province of Holland, the frontier towns
remain without a garrison sufficient to prevent a corps of
French troops from taking possession of any of them,
without the ceremony of a regular siege ; and, should
the corps thought of for Givet assemble there, they would
be so situated with respect to distance as to be able to
strike such a blow before almost any German army, even
if previous arrangements were taken for their immediately
marching, could possibly arrive to protect them. To
prevent this, there appears no means but the Prussian
troops from Wesel and Cleves, which are still nearer than
those of France, being ready to move upon the first certain information of those of France having quitted their
own territories. This support is however very uncertain
at present.

DESPATCH FROM MR. EWART TO SIR JAMES HARRIS.

Berlin, 28th July, 1787.

MAJOR arrived on the 25th, without having met with
the least interruption, and I hope to be able to despatch
him to-morrow night. He came at the *most critical
moment*, when an infamous intrigue was on the point of
overthrowing everything at Potzdam in favour of France ;
but, with the victorious arms I have now put into the
hands of our friends, I trust the cabal will be overpowered,
and the weapons turned against themselves.

Count Finckenstein, one of the chief abettors, is seized

with a panic, and in a long conference I had with him yesterday, not only admitted all the points I insisted on, but made his rapport conformable, so that I hope to have a suitable ministerial answer.

EXTRACT OF A DESPATCH FROM SIR JAMES HARRIS TO THE MARQUIS OF CARMARTHEN.

Hague, Tuesday, July 31st, 1787.

LETTERS from Amersfort give an account of an attack made, in the night of the 28th instant, by five hundred Free Corps and some Hussars on a palace belonging to the Prince of Orange, in the Province of Utrecht, called Soesdyk.   One hundred and fifty men of the regiment of Hesse Cassel were quartered there, and the assailants were repulsed with a considerable loss.   The number of the killed and wounded is uncertain, and the accounts vary from two hundred to forty.   It is however a fact, that very few of the Free Corps are returned to Utrecht, from whence the sally was made ; and it is probable that, not having succeeded in their attempt, they are dispersed, and gone back to their respective habitations.

EXTRACTS OF A DESPATCH FROM SIR JAMES HARRIS TO THE MARQUIS OF CARMARTHEN.

Hague, Tuesday, 7th Aug., 1787.

MY LORD,—Baron Thulemeyer gave in the two inclosed Memorials yesterday.*   He passed some time with the Great Pensionary, and probably entered with him more minutely into the terms on which the King, his Master, expects satisfaction than with the Greffier, to whom he spoke vaguely.   He took again notice to both these Ministers, that one of the motives for His Prussian Majesty assembling an army near Cleves was to enforce the demand set forth in the Memorial.   After he had said the little he thought proper to say to Mons. de Fagel

* They were in the missing volume of the Harris Papers.

on the subject of the affront offered to the Princess of Orange, he told him, that he had now received the King of Prussia's special command to declare that it was his wish to see Great Britain annexed to the Mediation, from a full persuasion that the sentiments of His Britannic Majesty corresponded perfectly with his on the affairs of this country, and that His Majesty's intervention would greatly contribute to induce France to subscribe to the only conditions which could be accepted by the Stadtholder.

I do not as yet find that he has held a similar language to the Deputies. Yet, after what he said to them last week, he will execute the spirit of his orders imperfectly, if he does not express to them, as well as to the Greffier, *this alteration* in his Master's opinion ; for, after the authentic information I received from Nimeguen, there can be no doubt that it is an alteration produced in consequence of the well-timed instructions carried to Berlin by Major, and that in the beginning the King of Prussia was really disinclined to the admittance of England ; and though the Declaration made by the Prussian Ministry to Mr. Ewart, as matters now stand, is perfectly sufficient, yet it certainly was not sincere as to the principle on which they pretended it to be grounded.

The Princess of Orange has acted on this occasion with the same uprightness and honour as on all others. She immediately wrote, in her own hand, to the Greffier, and to the principal Deputy of each Province, to inform them that Mons. Thulemeyer had *mis-stated* the sentiments of his Court, and that the King her brother, far from wishing to exclude England from the Mediation, was anxiously desirous that England should be invited to join in it ; and in a letter intended for me to see she says—" La manière franche et ouverte dont votre Cour s'est expliquée à Berlin a fait le plus grand effet, et je ne saurai assez vous en témoigner ma reconnaissance." These letters all came to hand Saturday, three days before Mr. Thulemeyer spoke on the subject.

The Duke of Brunswick was expected at Wesel yesterday ; and to-day or to-morrow at Nimeguen.

EXTRACTS OF A DESPATCH FROM SIR JAMES HARRIS TO THE
MARQUIS OF CARMARTHEN.

Hague, Friday, 10th Aug., 1787

My Lord,—The Memorials given in on the 6th inst.
by the Prussian Minister seem to have increased rather
than put a check to the intemperance of the Patriotic
faction.

The States of Holland yesterday said they were not
ready with their answer ; but, as if they always mean to
treat everything which came from Berlin with contempt,
the Suspension of the Prince of Orange as Stadtholder of
this Province was brought forward by Haarlem. A majority of the towns appeared to be agreed as to the general propriety of the measure ; but they differed so widely
as to the mode of carrying it into execution, that they
were not able to come to any conclusion.

France continues to encourage them in all these acts
of violence, in the underhand way I mentioned in my
last, and assures them they have nothing to apprehend
from Prussia. The French Ambassador himself went so
far as to say yesterday, that the march of the Prussian
troops would certainly be countermanded ; and Mons. de
la Coste pledges himself to them that, if they should come
with hostile intentions, His Most Christian Majesty will
not desert his friends in the Republic. I trust His
Prussian Majesty will not suffer himself to be led to engage in a *paper war* with these Patriots. He would be
as much *their* inferior in such a contest as they would be
his, if it was to be brought to decision of arms.

EXTRACTS OF A LETTER FROM THE MARQUIS OF CARMARTHEN
TO SIR JAMES HARRIS.

Whitehall, 10th Aug., 1787.

My dear Sir,—I have many thanks to return for your
kind private letter received by to-day's mail. Grenville,

I can assure you, mentions your kind and confidential behaviour to him in the highest terms. I long to know how he will find *les esprits disposés à Nimègue.* The Duke of Brunswick was, I think, to arrive there on Wednesday last.

The King does not approve of the hints contained in the Princess's paper respecting the Duke of Brunswick. His Majesty told me to-day, "We are upon very good terms; and he has expressed himself as much obliged to me for having given his son a higher rank in the Hanoverian service than he had asked for."

Could you find any way of getting at the Duke, directly or indirectly; I have always wished him to be more than a *brother-in-law to us.* He is surely at all times worth being well with, and more than usually so at present, as, perhaps, the whole line of conduct which Prussia may adopt respecting Holland, in either event of war or reconciliation, may depend on him.

We have sent a copy of the Memorial you are to present to the States General, to be communicated to France, together with some reports respecting provisions bought up for a fleet, camps on the frontiers, preparations at Cherbourg, Dutch transports at Dunkirk, &c., sufficient to disturb Eden's sleep, whatever effect they may produce on Montmorin's or Rayneval's repose.

If Prussia is sincere, the Province of Holland must become the seat of war after the declaration of the *Corps Francs.* Why it has not been so already I know not.

EXTRACT OF A DESPATCH FROM SIR JAMES HARRIS TO THE MARQUIS OF CARMARTHEN.

Hague, Aug. 14th, 1787.

MY LORD,—I received on Saturday an anonymous note expressing the strong desire of a person deeply interested in the affairs of this country to have an interview with me, and fixing the hour and place for that purpose. As

the rendezvous was at the house of a very respectable and
well-disposed burgher, I made no difficulty in going to
the appointment, and I was not a little surprised to find
there Mr. Remfner, the Prussian Minister's Secretary.
He bears a very good character; but I had seen him so
seldom, that I scarce could reckon him amongst my acquaintance.

Having made an apology for the trouble he gave me,
and stating the reasons which obliged him to see me in
private, he said, his attachment to the interests of the
House of Orange and the extreme pressure of the moment
convinced him of the necessity that a kind of communication should be established between the British and Prussian Missions at the Hague; and being well aware that it
was very difficult for me to repose any confidence in Mr.
Thulemeyer, whose character and principles he would not
attempt to defend, he (Mr. Remfner) had determined to
solicit this interview with me himself.

After a great deal of prefatory discourse on the situation of this country, and of the means necessary to restore peace and good order, and all of which (though his
ideas were perfectly just and rational) I heard without
giving any opinion of my own, he told me, that France
was actually disposed to consent to the six points sent
from Berlin to Versailles, as the basis of a negotiation,
insisting however on the march of the Prussian troops
being countermanded. A courier, which left Versailles
on the 3rd of August, he said, carried despatches written in a very high and peremptory tone on this last
point; but that a *second* followed him on the 6th, in
whose despatches this tone was abated, and the halt of
the troops no longer enforced by menace, but asked as a
favour. News to this effect, he said, had been received
here on Saturday morning, the 11th, from Baron Goltz;
and this, he observed, was to account for the French Ambassador's having so positively asserted that no Prussian
army would approach the frontiers of the Republic. Mr.
Remfner confessed his great uneasiness lest this in the
end should prove true; and that it was to express his

apprehension to me on this subject, and to give me time
for preparing other measures, that he had wished so much
to see me.   He reasoned very justly on the fatal consequence of a counter-order, and on the art and duplicity
of France in proposing it should be given, &c. &c.

I expressed myself much obliged to him for the confidence he placed in me, applauded his zeal in the good
cause, encouraged him to continue his intercourse with
me, by telling him as much of what is passing between
the Courts of London and Berlin as he may report to
his principal without any harm arising from it.   We
agreed on meeting again occasionally, but I left with him
the means of settling these meetings, as I do not hold it
necessary to make him acquainted with anything I wish
to keep secret, till I have had time to be satisfied as to
the real motive of his drawing towards me in so singular
a manner.

I confess, my lord, I am at a loss how to account for
it, from his intimating to me in the course of his conversation (though he never attempted to vindicate Mr. Thulemeyer) how much he wished that it was possible for me
to be, at least in appearance, on friendly terms with him,
and from his repeatedly declaring that this Minister
would be overjoyed if I was to shew him any civilities or
attentions : it occurred to me at times, that the interview
had been suggested by Mr. Thulemeyer himself, in consequence of the appearance of an approaching intimacy
between the two Courts, and which, if it leads to a co-
operation of measures between them relative to the affairs
of the Republic, may, if he does not change his principles
and conduct, be the cause of his disgrace as well as his
recall.   My mind was so prepossessed with this idea, that
I was more reserved with Mr. Remfner than I should
otherwise have been ; and perhaps very unjustly gave
him less credit for his good intentions than he deserves.
The truth of the information he gave me will be the test
of his sincerity.

EXTRACTS OF A DESPATCH FROM SIR JAMES HARRIS TO THE
MARQUIS OF CARMARTHEN.

Hague, Wednesday, Aug. 15, 1787.

I SUBMIT it to your Lordship, whether it would not be
advisable, in order to keep his Prussian Majesty attached
towards England, to enter without loss of time with him
into a discussion of the six preliminary points, which
though they are substantially good, yet were evidently
drawn up in a hasty and crude manner, and by a person
neither well informed as to the first cause of the disputes,
nor deeply versed in the Government of this country; and
it will be highly necessary that the sense these six fundamental points are meant to convey should be perfectly
and clearly understood, before they can be trusted as the
grounds of a negotiation to be carried on with so able and
so artful an opponent as France.

It is impossible for me, straitened as I am this morning for time, to enter fully into this intricate subject;
but I cannot avoid remarking that it is singular, that
Count Finck should be so adverse to the Constitution of
1766, and so partial to that of 1747. The one is simply a renewal of the other, without any alteration or new
insertion whatever, but a recital of the same Acts, word
for word; and the only reason for my always preferring
1766 to 1747, was, because it was a moment of *general
peace*, and no pretence could be alleged for calling it an
involuntary measure, or one deriving from the circumstances of the times.

[This letter alludes to the secret convention now agreed
upon, and afterwards signed Oct. 2, 1787, between England and Prussia for the defence of the States. The
articles were to this effect:]

1. Not to act as Mediators but after the following
plan, unless by mutual consent.
2. To resist all Foreign interference to their co-operation.

3. To disarm and dissolve the Free Corps. To permit the Provinces to settle their complaints with the Stadt-holder after the forms of the Constitution. To restore the Prince of Orange to all his rights as Stadtholder and Captain-General according to the Constitution of 1747. To cancel all innovations introduced by force. To restore the dismissed magistrates to the free exercise of their duties.

4. To march a Prussian army into Holland ; England to prepare forty ships of the line to support it.

5. In the event of any Power disapproving the above stipulations, and taking hostile measures against either of the Contracting Parties, to defend each other and accomplish their object by force of arms.

EXTRACTS OF A LETTER FROM SIR JAMES HARRIS TO THE PRINCESS OF ORANGE, AT NIMEGUEN.

La Haye, ce 16 Aôut, 1787.

MADAME,—Quoique je ne doute nullement que Votre Altesse Royale ne soit parfaitement instruite par le retour du Colonel Stampfort,* de ce que mon dernier courier, arrivé Mardi au soir, m'a rapporté de Berlin, cependant comme Mons. Aylau a eu la bonté de m'avertir qu'il se présente une occasion sûre pour écrire aujourd'hui à Nimègue, je crois qu'il est de mon devoir d'en profiter.

Sans entrer dans des détails qui ne seront qu'autant de répétitions pour Votre Altesse Royale, il suffit de re-marquer, que le ton que nous avons pris vis-à-vis de la Cour de Versailles depuis mon dernier voyage à Londres, et que nous continuons toujours de prendre, doit la met-tre indispensablement dans le cas ou de se déclarer ouvertement en faveur de son parti ici, ou de se prêter à un accommodement, qui, en sauvant son honneur, l'obli-gera d'abandonner ses vues.

Il ne s'agit que de profiter de ces circonstances, d'accé-

---

* Stampfort, who was tutor to the Prince of Orange's sons, was sent to Berlin by the Princess of Orange to urge her brother to assist her. He continued to waver to the last moment.

lérer l'exécution et de ne pas laisser à la Cour de Versailles le loisir de combler la mesure de ses intrigues, déjà trop avancées ici, ou d'en enfanter des nouvelles ailleurs. C'est ce qu'elle cherche évidemment à faire, en voulant gagner le temps, et en trainant les affaires en longueur. Je me flatte qu'on portera le même jugement à Berlin, et que sans s'arrêter aux démarches ultérieures de la France, Sa Majesté Prussienne poursuivra *jusqu'au bout* le système énergique qu'elle paroit avoir adopté.

Sa Majesté peut être assurée de *notre entier concours.* Nous ferons fort de *tenir la France en bride pendant que Sa Majesté agit;* et avec de cettes dispositions, quand même la France *s'émanciperait,* l'exécution sans être plus difficile, n'en sera que plus glorieuse.

EXTRACTS OF A DESPATCH FROM SIR JAMES HARRIS TO THE
MARQUIS OF CARMARTHEN.

Hague, Monday, Aug. 20th, 1787.

I HAVE reason to think Mons. Thulemeyer received to-day by the post the first very severe reprimand he has had, and at the same time an intimation of his recall.

Verbal accounts which I have received from Nimeguen say, that the Princess of Orange went on Saturday to Cleves, to have an interview with the Duke of Brunswick to regulate the final plan of execution, for which she considered herself as vested with sufficient powers by the last letters she received from Berlin, which were of the 11th.

Without knowing precisely what this plan is, I have ventured, by a person in whom I can confide, who is going to-day to Nimeguen, to urge the necessity of acting with the *greatest expedition;* and I am sure, when your Lordship reads my other letter of this day, you will admit that I cannot express this too strongly.

I have a strong additional motive for despatching an extra packet, besides that of conveying Shaw in as expeditious a manner as possible to England. Saturday, a few hours after my letters were sent away, advices were received here that a body of Free Corps, the number of which was differently reported, had raised their camp near Woerden, and were in march towards the Hague.

The States of Holland having broken up till Wednesday, the Deputy Committee was immediately assembled, and orders given to the whole garrison to be under arms, and to oppose by force the entrance of any armed corps into the Hague. Picquets were placed in every part of the town, and the different avenues to it strongly guarded; and advanced posts were stationed all round it, at the distance of a mile.

Late in the evening accounts were brought that 700 men, with four pieces of cannon and several baggage-waggons, were arrived at Vorschoot, a considerable village, about two miles from Leyden, and five from hence. They halted there all yesterday, when their numbers were increased by detachments from Leyden and the neighbourhood, to make them in all about 1200 or 1400 men strong. They produced patents from the Commission of Woerden for their march thus far; and others in blank, from the same Commission, which enables them to go where they please. The Deputy Committee, in consequence of this information, ordered a camp of half the picquets to be formed at the entrance of the wood close to the town; and one, of the remaining half, at Ryswick, at the distance of a mile.

These dispositions are certainly fully sufficient to protect the Hague from any surprise or insult, *provided* they are confirmed by the States of Holland, who, in consequence of this event, are summoned to assemble extraordinary to-day. It is with me a great matter of doubt whether they will not revoke them, and, instead of treating the approach of the Free Corps as an event of alarm, consider it as a desirable circumstance. If this should take place, I cannot be responsible for the consequences, as I am convinced neither the garrison nor the well-disposed burghers will suffer them to take possession of the Hague.

It is under this supposition that I have sent by Shaw all my public papers to England, which I entreat your Lordship's leave to allow to remain in the office ; that I destroyed all the cyphers but the last new ones, which are also prepared to be burnt at a moment's warning ; that I have not left a single scrap of paper in my house that can either commit my Court or my friends here, who have been in correspondence with me.

This precaution may, perhaps, appear superfluous ; but I hope I shall be considered as having erred on the right side, when it is recollected what kind of people these Free Corps are, and the little chance of any respect being paid to the houses of people in a public character, in a popular conflict between two parties exasperated as they are. This, however, is the only precaution I have taken, as I hold it beneath the respectable character with which I am invested to allow it to appear that I suppose it for a moment possible that any set of men will be so daring as to presume to offer it any insult or outrage. I have supplied money towards arming *all our friends* here, and, besides the garrison, they amount to near 2500 ; but they are in want of cannon, and, if Delft is surprised, they will be in want of powder.

I just learn, while I am writing, that the corps of Vorschoot is under march towards Voorbourg, about a mile from hence, and as far from Delft, where they intend to encamp. They are increased by 100 horse : 300 hussars, it is said, belonging to Salm's legion, are expected ; and I am assured there are upwards of 300 French among them.

Everything rests, in my mind, on what passes to-day in the States of Holland. I, however, dare not detain my messenger till then, as I fear the communication between this place and Delft will be stopped before the evening, and my papers then be not safe. I have, however, a blank order for a Scheveling fishing-boat, which I shall send away to-night, if anything of sufficient importance should occur. I write in great haste, and under perpetual but necessary interruption.

DESPATCH FROM SIR JAMES HARRIS TO THE MARQUIS OF
CARMARTHEN.

Hague, Tuesday, 21st Aug., 1787.

My Lord,—The Princess of Orange has sent a person
she can trust to acquaint me with the result of what
passed between Her Royal Highness and the Duke of
Brunswick on Friday ; also in general of her ideas on
the present situation of affairs.   The object of her last
interview with the Duke of Brunswick (which took place
at Cleves) was to explain herself to him on the nature
of the *Satisfaction* she required, which Her Royal Highness had been authorized, by her last letters from Berlin,
to do.

The Duke of Brunswick perfectly acquiesced in these
conditions, and a courier was despatched with them the
same day to His Prussian Majesty.   There is little doubt,
after what Mr. Ewart has written, that His Majesty will
approve them ; and the courier will be back by the 2nd
of September, the day when it is expected the whole
force which is to compose the army in Westphalia will
be assembled.   The Duke of Brunswick (however pressing the circumstance) does not think it prudent to attempt anything till then, or to strike a stroke which is
not sure of succeeding.   Then, that is, the first week in
September, the Prussian Minister is to present a third
Memorial ; which, if it does not instantly produce the
satisfaction required, will be followed by an invasion of
this Province by the Prussian army.

Yesterday, during the whole day, the number of the
Free Corps were continually augmenting by detachments
which came from all sides.   In the evening they committed several outrages at Voorbourg, where they were
encamped, insomuch so that the States of Holland were
summoned at eleven at night, and sat till two.   But notwithstanding these outrages were proved in the clearest
manner by several persons who declared on oath their
houses had been broken open and pillaged, yet the Patriotic Faction in the States would neither suffer any

succours to be sent to Voorbourg, nor any order issued to check the excesses of the Free Corps ; and their meeting passed in wrangling and violent altercation.

To-day, at nine o'clock, the Free Corps were advanced to the gates of Delft. They planted their cannon against the walls of the town, and at twelve took possession of it without any resistance. They immediately assembled the body of magistrates, dismissed eleven Regents who were not of their party, and appointed others in their place. This done, they made themselves masters of the Arsenal, the largest in the Republic, and the magazine of powder, both belonging to the Generality, and under the immediate protection of the Council of State. Though timely notice was given of this event to the States of Holland, they positively refused sending any succours, or even to give orders to the few troops who were in the town to defend the magazines of the Union. It became impracticable to carry into execution my plan of sending three hundred men there from amongst these Burghers ; too much time was lost in deliberation ; and besides, at this moment, the alarm is so great here, and so well founded, that it would be imprudent to diminish the number of the well-disposed inhabitants.

I never was more perplexed in any period of my public life, to know what advice to give my friends, or what kind of language to hold to them, than at the present conjuncture. If I did not think I saw a fair prospect of everything being set right in the course of a month, and that even the very excesses now committing by the Free Corps tend to insure rather than render doubtful this event, I own I should not hesitate to encourage them to strike a desperate blow ; and though inferior in number, in arms, and in discipline, prefer a spirited resistance to the serving submissively under the yoke of these tyrants. But with these expectations, and with the doubtful chance of success if the issue was to rest on a trial of force so much against them, I am lead to endeavour to inspire them with patience and resignation, and to induce them to submit to lesser evils, rather than expose themselves to almost certain destruction. This language ill suits the character of many of them, and, as I cannot explain to them my motives, I am at times accused (though very unjustly) of being a lukewarm, and even timid supporter. In regard to myself, I have had frequent admonitions and intimations to be personally on my guard, and that I should do well to leave the Hague *in time.* Till, however, I have His Majesty's orders, nothing but actual compulsion shall induce me to stir ; my public papers are all safe, I have no part of my family with me, and of course no motive of uneasiness or anxiety, let the event be what it will.

I shall keep this despatch open till to-morrow morning, and end it for the present by observing, that there is no doubt of the French being at the bottom of everything that is going forward ; that it is part of a plan sketched out at Paris by Mons. de Rayneval, and moulded into shape here by Mons. de la Coste and the Rhingrave of Salm. French soldiers continue pouring into the country, and no less than forty artillery-men passed through Gertruydenberg on Sunday last ; and my courier, Brooks, in returning from Helvoet this morning, at two o'clock, says that he was stopped three times between Delft and this place, by the outposts of the Free Corps, and that each time the officer who questioned him was French. I shall send him to-morrow by a cross-road, with which he is acquainted, or, if on reconnoitring he should find it invested, by a Scheveling fishing-boat.

Wednesday Morning, Seven o'clock.

This night has passed over without any event ; but it seems only to be deferred, not dismissed. I have employed the greatest part of it in persuading our friends to be temperate and cool. I have employed such people as I know have most weight with the Burghers, to make them feel the difference between real courage and rashness, and that my advising them to forbearance does not proceed either from apprehension or disregard, but from my being in a situation to judge more dispassionately than they can, and from my better knowledge of all the circumstances. I have talked this language to the Magis-

trates of the Hague, and I trust have brought the people
at large to allow the justness of my reasoning. They,
however, are determined to defend themselves if attacked,
and against this I did not even pretend to start a single
objection.

EXTRACT OF A LETTER FROM SIR JAMES HARRIS TO THE
MARQUIS OF CARMARTHEN.

Hague, 21st Aug., 1787.

My dear Lord,—Matters have got very serious indeed,
and I cannot sufficiently applaud myself for having sent
away my papers when I did ; two hours later all the
avenues to Helvoet were stopped, and they would probably have fallen into the hands of the Free Corps. We
are besieged on every side, and have neither walls nor
cannon to defend ourselves. I expect every day, almost
every hour, to hear of an attempt on the part of the
Free Corps to come into the Hague, and this will inevitably lead to a scene of destruction which will know no
bounds. I await patiently orders for what I am to do,
for although I am sufficiently apprized, and fully admit
the danger to which I am exposed in staying in the
Hague, yet its being a residence of personal danger is not
a motive for me to quit it, and I must have some better
reason for leaving it, before I can prevail on myself to
stir. If I am *De-Witted* don't let me be *out-witted*, but
revenge me.

The infamy and profligacy of the French make me long
to change my profession, and to fight them with a
sharper instrument than a pen. It must be with these
(not our pens, but our swords,) that we must carry the
Mediation through, if we mean it should be attended with
any success. There are strong reports of a popular insurrection in France. Si Dieu voudroit les punir par où
ils ont péché, comme j'admirerois la justice divine.*

---

* Curious invocation of the Revolution of 1789, two years after this date.

EXTRACT OF A DESPATCH FROM SIR JAMES HARRIS TO THE
MARQUIS OF CARMARTHEN.

Hague, 24th August, 1787.

THE last resource of our friends if pushed to extremities, is to go to the Brille. This place is well fortified,
difficult of access, and, if the communication is kept open
with Helvoet, succours may easily be thrown into it.
The Swiss regiment in garrison there, I have reason to
believe, will not stir, unless by a direct order from the
States General. The magazines are well filled, and they
are putting the cannon on the ramparts. The Free Corps
must receive a very considerable reinforcement before
they can venture to attack it, but they will find batter-
ing cannon and ammunition sufficient in the arsenal at
Delft.

EXTRACTS OF A DESPATCH FROM SIR JAMES HARRIS TO THE
MARQUIS OF CARMARTHEN.

Hague, Tuesday, 28th August, 1787.

I SUBMIT to your Lordship's judgment to decide,
whether it would not be expedient to express to France
our wish, that she should signify to the States of Holland,
that it is her express desire that England should be one
of the co-mediating Powers, and that she expects of their
Noble Mightinesses that they would conform to the opinion of the other Provinces. The Court of Versailles,
notwithstanding what has been declared both at London
and Berlin, has hitherto been silent on this point ; the
Patriots profess themselves perfectly ignorant that France
has ever consented to have any Co-mediators, and say,
that, till they are officially informed of it by the French
Ambassador, they shall persist in their first opinion of
annexing no other Power to the Mediation.

I also submit to your Lordship, whether it would not
contribute to the forwarding our views, if it could be so
managed, that the French Ambassador here (whoever he

may be) was ordered to communicate with me on this subject. The least appearance of an understanding between us would fill the minds of the Patriots with doubts and suspicions, while our friends are too well convinced of our sincerity and uprightness to entertain any such misgivings. Mons. de Verac is recalled, and Mons. de la Coste returned to Paris on a sudden; whether he was ordered to return to give an account of his conduct, or whether he is gone to try to revoke the recall of his father-in-law, I cannot precisely discover. From the consternation, however, I observe in the family, I rather suspect it is from the first of these motives. They are fearful he will be exposed to some very heavy disgrace. He has, as I have often mentioned to your Lordship, of late, been the instigator of all the violences committed by the Free Corps; and though I know enough of the good sense and sound judgment of Mons. de la Coste to be satisfied he did not act without authority, yet it is by no means a new thing in France to reprimand and even punish those who have only executed orders.

I mentioned to your Lordship on Friday, that the Brille was the place of refuge our friends could resort to in case the Patriotic party here should carry matters to extremities. I have with this view taken every step consistent with my situation for putting that place in a state of defence, and for keeping up the spirits and good dispositions of its Regents. There are about 900 Swiss in it, and 300 well-affected armed Burghers.

A committee of three persons from amongst its Magistrates is appointed to direct all the necessary operations. The chief of these, the reigning Burgomaster of the town, was with me yesterday morning. He declared himself responsible both for himself and co-Regents, that they would hold out the town to the last moment, provided they were sure of not being abandoned by England.

I thought myself authorized as well by the circumstances here, as by the general tenor of your Lordship's late despatches, to give him strong indirect encouragement on this point, without pledging myself by any explicit assurance, or committing any part of the secret improper for him to know. I promised him pecuniary and other supplies ; and, after calculating the state of the finances of the town, which are very low, and the probable expenses likely to occur, we found that with 30,000 florins it could subsist for two months, the pay of the garrison included.

We likewise endeavoured to concert means to convey into the Brille the quantity of powder your Lordship mentions as being ready at Harwich. If we once can get it safe to the Brille, it may easily be brought in small quantities here by Scheveling fishing-boats, who can land it in the night near this place. I say in small quantities, since from the precarious situation of the Hague, if we supplied it too largely at once, it might in the end be employed against us.

LETTER FROM MR. EWART TO SIR JAMES HARRIS.

28th August, 1787.

I CANNOT express how much I was disappointed in not hearing from you by the last post.

I fear some insinuation in the Duke of Brunswick's letter with relation to the expediency of keeping on good terms with France, may do mischief ; and I am sure I need not entreat you to employ *every means to encourage the Duke to proceed*, and to procure for the King of Prussia the most decisive explanations from England relative to the effective support he may be sure of. Without such powerful incitements there is no saying what may happen if the Duke wavers.

LETTER FROM SIR JAMES HARRIS TO THE PRINCESS OF
ORANGE, NIMEGUEN.

La Haye, ce 29 Août, 1787.

MADAME, — Le motif qui m'engage à dépêcher un courier à Nimègue, est pour faire part à Votre Altesse Royale des nouvelles que j'ai reçues de ma Cour, qui me paroissent aussi satisfaisantes qu'intéressantes.

Elle a déclarée en termes très nets et précis, à celle de Versailles, que le Roi sent très vivement l'insulte faite à Votre Altesse Royale ; que la Satisfaction doit être sans aucune restriction et proportionnée à l'affront. Sa Majesté applaudit hautement la conduite du Roi de Prusse, approuve entièrement l'assemblement d'un corps d'armée dans le pays de Cleves, et n'hésite pas de dire, que si la France s'avise d'en assembler un à Givet, ou ailleurs, elle se verra dans le cas de prendre incessamment des mesures qui peuvent mener à des suites très désagréables. De plus elle a dit à la France que si elle porte des obstacles, soit indirectement, soit ouvertement, à la Satisfaction, l'Angleterre ne sauroit le considérer que comme un indice qu'elle ne pense pas sincèrement à la Médiation. Qu'il est parfaitement illusoire de sa part de prétendre qu'une alliance défensive, conclue avec la République entière, l'oblige de soutenir un parti dont les principes sont condamnés par la pluralité des confédérés, avec laquelle cette alliance est contractée.

Mr. Eden a ordre de dire que l'Angleterre se flatte que la France, tant dans ses écrits, que dans ses conférences, voudroit user de plus de ménagement en parlant sur la conduite de Monseigneur le Prince Stadthouder. Que celle-ci a été dès le commencement sans reproche, et que d'ailleurs la France ne doit pas oublier les liens du sang qui unissent Son Altesse Sereine avec sa Majesté Britannique.

Cette pièce finit par un petit mot pour prouver que le Prince Stadthouder n'est pas Serviteur de la République, mais partie primitive et intégrante de la Souveraineté, et toute au moins fait pour négocier sur la même ligne que les Etats.

Je demande pardon à Votre Altesse Royale si je rends imparfaitement le contenu de cette pièce, mais je tâche de faire saisir le sens à Votre Altesse Royale, sans l'ennuyer par des longueurs. Elle a été communiquée en entier à Berlin, accompagnée par une dépêche dans laquelle nous nous déclarons *prêts à entrer dans un plan de concert avec Sa Majesté Prussienne sur tous les objets relatifs à ce pays, et décidés à les soutenir de toutes les manières.*

EXTRACTS OF A DESPATCH FROM SIR JAMES HARRIS TO THE MARQUIS OF CARMARTHEN.

Hague, Friday, 31st Aug., 1787.

THE alarm here increases ; it is difficult to determine which is most feared, the arrival or the retreat of the Prussian army. If it comes forward and attempts to penetrate into this Province, our friends think they have everything to apprehend from the despair and violence of the Free Corps ; and if it stops short, or retrogrades, they foresee, and with very great reason, that the whole government of the country will fall into the hands of their adversaries. In the first case, they think their property and persons exposed to destruction ; in the second, they have to expect loss of place, influence, patronage, and consideration. Your Lordship will perceive in the course of this despatch on what these apprehensions are grounded.

I shall say nothing relative to the military dispositions of the Free Corps ; they continue to be formed upon the same plan, though their execution is less expeditious than it was supposed it would be.

The bad weather, and some forward movements of the Prince's army near Utrecht, probably occasion this delay. The ground was become so wet near Delft, that they broke up their camp yesterday, and removed it to a drier spot near Ryswick, which brings them still nearer the Hague. Fifty of them have taken possession of Hounslaerdyk, a palace belonging to the Prince of Orange, and put into confinement the steward and bailiff.

I have seen to-day a letter from a French officer at Dinant, in the Bishoprick of Liege, who, mistaking the principles of the person he knows here, writes him word, —" Daignez me recommander à Messrs. Blyswick et Gyslaer pour tâcher d'obtenir la grace de lever un corps Français qui sera recruté *en secret* dans les soldats du Régiment Royal Comptois, où je sais qu'ils m'ont proposé jusqu'au nombre de 600 hommes qui se détacheront déguisés, et se réuniront en Hollande sans que cela compromette la France." (Signé Baron de Bosce, de la date du 15 Août.)

This evening Mons. Thulemeyer has again called upon me ; he is full of excuses for his past conduct, and assurances of his openness and sincerity. I however detected him as deficient in this last point ; for, though he mentioned to me the heads on which the satisfaction is to be grounded, he suppressed the conditions annexed to it, of which I know he is informed since this morning from his secretary, with whom I am in constant intelligence, and whose confidence, I flatter myself, I have obtained.

The recall of Mons. de Verac is not yet public, though it is certain. Mons. de St. Priest is to be his successor.

Mons. Bourgoin remains Chargé des Affaires. It should appear that Mons. de Rayneval had resolved on operating M. de Verac's recall when he left the Hague, and that M. de Verac's friends, who are numerous, and high in rank, had hitherto saved him ; but that M. de Maillebois, who got to Paris about three weeks ago, effected the point by describing his conduct in, I believe, a very unfair and uncandid manner. His friends say he is to go to Switzerland, and Mons. de la Coste to Bonn ; others, that they will be both disgraced.

I find there is no immediate want of powder at the Brille, and the getting it in there is so difficult, that our friends have not as yet been able to tell me how it can come over without great risks. We have contrived to bring a supply in here sufficient to answer the purpose of the moment, and I gave my reasons why I do not wish to have too large a store deposited in the Hague.

I have taken the proper steps that the money I mentioned in my last should be conveyed in a safe and unsuspected manner to the Brille, as soon as any remittances from the Treasury are made to me. These measures of precaution become more and more necessary, as your Lordship will perceive, from the accounts I give to-day in my other letters, of the conduct and declared intentions of the Free Corps.

EXTRACT OF A DESPATCH FROM SIR JAMES HARRIS TO THE
MARQUIS OF CARMARTHEN.

Hague, Tuesday, 4th Sept., 1787.

THE nomination of Mons. de la Coste to Deuxponts, and the promise Mons. de Verac has received of having the first vacant blue ribbon and the Swiss embassy, have done away in a great measure the impressions of discouragement his sudden recall had made on the Patriotic party here.

LETTER FROM THE DUKE OF BRUNSWICK TO SIR JAMES HARRIS.

MONSIEUR.—Je suis chargé par M. le Général Fawcet de vous faire parvenir l'incluse ;* et, comme il m'a porté une lettre de Sa Majesté Britannique, je prends la liberté de vous prier de faire passer la réponse au Roi. Quoique je désire que toutes ces affaires de la République puissent se déterminer sans notre intervention, je crains beaucoup que cela ne sera pas possible. Je vous recommande les environs de Givet. Si les Français ne nous troublent point, je me flatte que notre opération ne sera pas de bien longue durée.

J'ai l'honneur d'être, avec les sentimens les plus distingués, Monsieur,

Votre très humble et très obéissant Serviteur,

CHARLES GRAND DUC DE BROUNSVIC LUNEBOURG.

A Wesel, ce 6 de Septembre, 1787.

* Missing.

EXTRACT OF A DESPATCH FROM SIR JAMES HARRIS TO THE
MARQUIS OF CARMARTHEN.

Hague, Friday, 7th Sept., 1787.

THE accounts received this morning from Friesland continue to be far from very pleasing.   The Free Corps have
taken possession of the coast from Hardlinguen to Worcum,
and increase in force in the interior of the Province.   They
perpetually receive fresh supplies from Amsterdam ; and
two or three armed vessels, which guard the coasts, interrupt everything which is sent to the assistance of the
States of the Province, sitting at Leewarden.   The mal-
contents are flush of money, and receive, per man, four
florins a week.

DESPATCH FROM SIR JAMES HARRIS TO THE MARQUIS OF
CARMARTHEN.

Hague, Monday, 10th Sept., 1787.

I AM informed, through a secret but good channel,
that Paulus, who is now at Paris, is to give every necessary information relative to the soundings and bearings
of the coast of that Province, which his post enables him
to do with great exactness.

It is intended, says my informer, to be a *coup de main*,
and to be effected by an embarkation in the night from
Dunkirk.   Three frigates and a fifty-gun ship would prevent any attempt of the kind, and effectually secure the
Province.   Our ships might lie in the road of Flushing,
without any reason being assigned for their being there ;
the officer who commands directs his operations in concert
with the Pensionary and our friends, as circumstances
may require.

This information seems to me of a nature to be communicated with the greatest expedition : it is for this
reason that I have determined to despatch a pink from
Scheveling ; and, as the wind is fair, I hope it will reach
your Lordship to-morrow.   I continue to take every

necessary precaution at the Brille ; and, by way of encouragement, have allowed each soldier twelve pence a week in addition to his pay.

I have, on my private account, borrowed 30,000 florins to be deposited there ; and I must entreat your Lordship to press the immediate payment of 20,000*l.* into my banker's hands, otherwise the army in Utrecht will disband for want of pay.

Mons. de Thulemeyer, in consequence of a courier which came on Sunday night, received orders to declare that His Prussian Majesty expected that in a few days' time the *Satisfaction* should be given him for the insult offered the Princess of Orange near Schoonhoven.

His Prussian Majesty requires that this satisfaction should consist of a " Letter of excuse and disavowal, of a Rescission of the resolutions taken by the States of Holland on the occasion of Her Royal Highness's detention, a punishment of those who stopped and insulted her—an Invitation of Her Royal Highness to come to the Hague, and an assurance that no fresh attack should be made on the rights and privileges of the Prince."

The Prussian Minister conveyed these conditions to the States of Holland by a " note verbale," and to the States General by a memorial.   Their High Mightinesses came to a resolution immediately to exhort Holland to cement measures, and declared they would not consider themselves as responsible for the consequences of a contrary conduct.   The States of Holland were assembled and divided.   Van Berkel, on the part of Amsterdam, was violent to a degree.

The Prussian Manifesto is ready.   I have the honour to enclose it ; it will not appear till the army is in march. The consternation amongst the Patriotic party is very visible, and is not a little increased by the news received this morning by letters from Vienna of the 30th August, that the Porte has declared war on Russia, and Mons. Bulgakoff is in the Seven Towers.

EXTRACTS OF A DESPATCH FROM SIR JAMES HARRIS TO THE
MARQUIS OF CARMARTHEN.

Hague, 11th Sept., 1787.

On Saturday the States of Holland again took into
consideration the subject of the Satisfaction.

I mentioned to your Lordship yesterday the conduct
observed by the States General ; it was friendly and proper. The resolution to exhort Their Noble Mightinesses
to be attentive to the consequences, if they persist in
their refusal of .giving *Satisfaction*, was made known to
them to-day by their own deputies in the States General,
and not by letter.

The deliberation on the *notes verbales* in the States
of Holland rested on the question, whether the matter
should become an immediate object of debate, or be postponed till Wednesday. The result was, its being postponed ; and a resolution taken in the mean time to send
a messenger to Paris, to acquaint His Most Christian Majesty with the violent conduct of Prussia, and to entreat
his support and assistance. This proposition was made
by Mr. Van Berkel ; his expressions were, " Que la Note
de la part du Roi de Prusse étoit si insultante, que tout
vrai Patriote ne pouvoit y répondre que par le plus souve-
rain mépris ; et qu'il devoit tout souffrir, et tout attendre
de la justice de sa cause et du secours de Dieu, plutôt que
de souscrire à de pareilles conditions. Que les suites
fâcheuses devoient retomber sur la tête de ceux qui, sous
main, envenimoient les choses, et attiroient les maux à
leur Patrie. La conduite des Etats vis-à-vis Mad^me la
Princesse avoit été irréprochable, et n'avoit pu être dirigée
autrement ; qu'il falloit donc incessamment donner connoissance au Roi de France de la conduite despotique et
tyrannique du Roi de Prusse, en faisant part à Sa Majesté
Très Chrétienne des deux Notes, et en requérant son
secours."

All the towns which compose the majority agreed with
him as to the propriety of an immediate application to

France, but they were divided as to fixing a day for resuming business ; some were for to-day, others for tomorrow, and, on voting, these last prevailed. The conclusion, therefore, of their assembly was, that the business should stand over till Wednesday, and a courier be immediately despatched to Versailles ; and this courier went away last night at eleven o'clock.

The Great Pensionary, in the course of the deliberation, repeatedly reminded the assembly that the time was limited, that His Prussian Majesty had explained himself in the clearest terms, and that war would be the certain consequence of their deferring their conclusion beyond the fixed term, which expired Wednesday at midnight.

The Patriotic leaders remain, however, firm in their opinion ; and though they were evidently abashed and alarmed, endeavour to keep up the appearance of steadiness and tranquillity. Your Lordship may easily conceive the kind of sensation this interesting and anxious moment produces on the minds of the Nation at large ; and it is considered by them all as one which, in the event, is to determine the nature of their existence as a political State. I am using my utmost endeavours to prevail on our friends to take a due advantage of it, by coming forward with addresses and remonstrances, which would tend to increase the embarrassment of the Faction, and open the eyes of the Nation.

It is evident that the French have not only entirely lost their popularity with the nation at large, but that even the leaders of the party doubt either the will or capacity of the Court of France to assist them, notwithstanding the strong assurances to the contrary Mons. de Verac continued to give to the very last moment of his stay.

EXTRACTS OF A DESPATCH FROM SIR JAMES HARRIS TO THE
MARQUIS OF CARMARTHEN.

Hague, Wednesday, 12th Sept., 1787.

In addition to what I have written in my other letters
of yesterday's date, I have now to inform your Lordship
that yesterday, on the States of Holland resuming, according to their usual custom, the subject of debate of the
preceding day, the Sieur Van Berkel declared that Amsterdam was determined not even to *deliberate* on the
Prussian *notes verbales*, which they considered as insulting and injurious to the dignity and Sovereign character
with which Their Noble Mightinesses were invested.

The Sieur Gyslaer, on the part of Dordt, expressed the
same sentiments, though in a less offensive manner ; but
his colleague, Roo de Westmaes, declared, " *Qu'un Souve-
rain ne pourroit jamais faire des excuses à la femme de
son premier Serviteur.*"

Zeebergen (for Haarlem) declared his town to be of a
similar opinion, " *et que quand on ne pourroit plus ré-
sister, alors on regarderoit le procès comme perdu avec
dépens,*" a singular, and, I hope, prophetic expression.

Such being the opinion of the three leading Pensionaries, it is to be presumed that the satisfaction required
will be refused, and of course the Prussian troops march.

The herd of Free Corps still remain in the neighbourhood of the Hague ; they continue to commit the most notorious acts of injustice, and to keep the inhabitants in a
perpetual alarm.

As your Lordship will naturally be anxious to have the
earliest information of the event of to-day's deliberation,
I despatch a Scheveling boat with a copy of the Resolution taken to-day by the States of Holland, delivered
an hour ago by the Grand Pensionary to Mons. de Thulemeyer.

In the assembly, the leading towns, in debating on
this subject, did not, in any point, depart from the principles they laid down yesterday morning ; their language

was high, insolent, and menacing ; and they insisted, in the most pointed manner, that the only motive they had in voting for the deputation, was to elucidate His Prussian Majesty on a point on which he had been so maliciously and grossly misinformed. This measure of Their Noble Mightinesses is so very wide of the terms the Prussian Minister had it in command to require, that it is to be supposed that the Duke of Brunswick will not admit it, as in any degree coming up to the spirit of his instructions; and we may expect that immediately after the reception of it, the troops under his command will march. Such at least seems to be the general opinion, and we may expect by Friday or Saturday to hear that the attack has begun.

EXTRACTS OF A DESPATCH FROM SIR JAMES HARRIS TO THE MARQUIS OF CARMARTHEN.

Hague, 14th Sept., 1787.

THE two sixteen-pound howitzers, with their carriages, 500 charges, and everything belonging to them, which the Frieslanders want to be sent to Leewarden, are to be conveyed there in the following manner.

A vessel well known in England by the name of a Groninguen Tjalk, must be hired ; the guns, &c., put in the hold, and covered with a cargo of rape-seed. The ship must not exceed 100 tons, or be more than fifteen feet in breadth. The bills of lading must mention *rapeseed*, to the order of Syds, Peeters, and Son, at Leewarden. The vessel must direct its course by the Amelander gate, and from thence to the Dokkamer Nieuw Zylen. It is important to observe these directions, in order to avoid the cruisers on the Zuyder Zee.

Count Charles Bentinck was the person who was so good as to undertake the journey to the Brille. He put the Regency on their guard against what is passing in the States of Holland, and took such precautions as I hope will prevent the success of our adversaries' plans on that town. The 30,000 florins I have advanced are safely arrived, concealed under a package of iron. The entrance of the Meuse towards the Brille at low water is *eight feet and a half.*

The idea of moving the States General from the Hague has from the day of my return from England, in May, been my primary and favourite object ; and I have sunk in my despatches a great deal I have said and done to bring this to bear, because I have said and done it with inutility. I have of late been not less anxious of joining to the four friendly Provinces the minority in Holland and the deposed Regents, and, if I have laboured with more than common pains on any one point, it has been on this. My labours, however, I have before said, have been vain ; those personal motives to which your Lordship refers, added to an extreme irresolution and weakness of character, prevail over every other consideration.

At this moment their retreat is become impossible ; the avenues of the Province are stopped upon every side. The Free Corps who guard those avenues would certainly not suffer any of the well-disposed Deputies, either single or in a body, to pass ; and the danger of their leaving the Hague is full as great as that of their staying in it. It is indeed probable, as your Lordship will perceive from my other despatch, that the States of Holland may banish the Deputies of Gelderland and Utrecht from their Province ; in which case it is to be supposed they will send them away with a safe-guard. This event, if it happens, will be a virtual dissolution of the assembly of the States General, and will put the Foreign Ministers residing here in a very singular position. From the instructions I already have, and from my general knowledge of His Majesty's sentiments, I should hold myself, under such circumstances, fully authorized to quit the Hague ; but as there are other circumstances of a still superior nature, and as the very incident which gives rise to this expulsion may make my presence here absolutely necessary, I do not mean to remove unless compelled to it by a total subversion of all government, in which case I must proceed to Helvoet as the only free passage, and from thence get as well as I can to the Generality through Zealand.

An additional motive for my staying here is, the degree of confidence my presence gives the well-disposed party. They think the danger less from my being disposed to share it with them ; for they reckon, (and perhaps very truly,) that our antagonists, if driven to despair, will not pay any great respect to the immunities due to a Foreign Minister. I can only repeat, on this point, that, as for myself, I only consider the menaces of the Free Corps as the vapourings of a disorderly and profligate mob, calculated to operate on weak minds.

To satisfy them, however, and in order to have nothing to reproach myself with, I despatched an express last night to the Princess, suggesting to her the idea of inserting at the end of the Manifesto, in consequence of the declarations which have appeared at Delft and elsewhere, an article to express that, if any act of cruelty and violence should be exercised by the Free Corps or others on the persons or property of the inhabitants of the Republic in consequence of the march of the Prussian troops, the authors of such outrages will be afterwards punished with the utmost severity.

EXTRACTS OF A DESPATCH FROM SIR JAMES HARRIS TO THE MARQUIS OF CARMARTHEN.

Hague, Tuesday, 18th Sept., 1787.

I AM happy to have a great deal of important and satisfactory intelligence to communicate to your Lordship. I shall endeavour to class it as methodically as the subject will admit, but I write at the moment of an apparent Revolution, which, though greatly advanced, is still pending, and in which I am too deeply interested not to be exposed to perpetual and necessary interruptions. The last article in my last letter was to acquaint your Lordship with the march of the Prussian army in three columns ; it since has passed the frontiers of this Province, and made itself master of Gorcum, Dordt, and Schoonhoven, and several other of the principal towns of South Holland.

On Sunday morning news was received that the Rhingrave of Salm had evacuated Utrecht, nailed up 140 pieces of cannon he was obliged to leave behind him, destroyed, as far as he was able, powder and other stores, and retired with what he could collect of the garrison in great disorder towards Amsterdam and Naerden. The same morning the Prince of Orange took possession of the town, and the same day Montfort, the Vaart ; and the whole Province of Utrecht surrendered itself into his hands. These two events, viz., the rapid and successful invasion of the Prussian troops, and the reduction of Utrecht, produced the strongest sensation here.

Both the States of Holland and the States General were immediately convoked (Sunday morning) to deliberate on what was to be done under such very serious circumstances. The consternation amongst the Patriotic Faction was great. In the States of Holland the debates turned on moving their Assembly to Amsterdam, and on sending this garrison to the defence of Gorcum, not then taken. Neither Van Berkel, Gyslaer, nor Zeebergen ventured to attend, and the sentiments of their respective towns were delivered in writing, and went to the two points I have just mentioned.

The Constitution of the Province presented various invincible arguments for not suffering the States to leave the Hague, and they were made a good use of. To prevent the garrison from quitting this place, and leaving it at the mercy of the Free Corps (who, on Sunday, were very insolent and overbearing), after having given notice to such of my friends as I could depend upon in the States General, I proposed to the Foreign Ministers, my colleagues, to present a Note to the President of the Week, founded on that we had given in above ten days ago. This, after a short discussion with the Spanish Minister, was unanimously agreed to. I have the honour to enclose it as it was given in yesterday by the Russian

and Danish Ministers, together with the answer Their
High Mightinesses immediately made to it.* This had the
desired effect. The removal of the garrison was dropped
in the States of Holland ; and, if it had not been given up,
I had so far animated the States General, that they were
pledged to take upon themselves the command of the troops
here, and insist on their remaining if those of Holland
had judged proper to order them out of the Hague.

The carrying this point led to two other very essential
ones. The Hague was immediately ordered, by the preponderance of the friendly party in the States General,
and by that it began to gain in Holland, to be put into
a state of defence : picquets, patroles, advanced posts, &c.,
composed of the troops of the Union, were immediately
ordered ; and the body of Free Corps belonging to this
town, and who were so loud in their threats on Sunday,
broke up their guard last night, leaving behind two pieces
of cannon. Some left the Hague, and others retired to
their respective dwellings. These circumstances were too
favourable to let slip. I assembled some of our select
friends, whose names are well known to your Lordship,
yesterday evening ; I pressed, in the strongest manner,
the expediency of striking a blow while the panic lasted,
and of forcing a victory by bringing back the Prince of
Orange to the Hague, invested with all the authority
given him in 1747 and 1766.

Most of the Patriotic families, and particularly those
persons who have taken an active part in the Faction,
are fled ; and the panic is so great, that several of them,
after having made a formal recantation of their principles,
have requested of me to take their effects under my protection ; and I have, from one person alone, bonds and
papers to the amount of near 50,000 florins besides
jewels.

In the moment I am writing, the populace of the
Hague have disarmed such of the Free Corps as did not
escape this night ; and several hundreds of people, much
against my will, but without my having it in my power

* Both these are lost in the missing volume.

to prevent them, have brought their muskets, and discharged them, by way of a compliment, before the door of my house. They have also taken their standard, and torn it to pieces under my windows.

I understand Mons. de St. Priest, the new French Ambassador, left Paris on Monday, and that he may be expected here in a day or two.

Half-past eleven, Tuesday night.

The States of Holland, who broke up about half an hour ago, have agreed to the proposal made by the Equestrian order without any alteration or addition, and I think I can now venture to congratulate your Lordship that the Revolution in this country is as complete as it was in 1747. I wish it may be as lasting.

Your Lordship reading this letter will, I am sure, consider its contents as incredible, and I confess I scarce can bring myself to believe what has passed. I had no idea that our success could have been so rapid and complete when I began ; and *it was only as I went along*, that I perceived that there was a possibility of going to the lengths we have gone, and *that it was worth the trial*.

I confess it gives me on every account the greatest satisfaction that their Noble Mightinesses judged proper to consent to the proposal to-night, as measures were taken for compelling them to-morrow, which might have led to very serious consequences.

As it is, the spirit of party, suddenly triumphing over an antagonist who has acted with oppression, has led the populace to commit excesses with which I could have wished this memorable day not to have been sullied. They have broken windows, destroyed several houses belonging to the Patriots, and it is impossible, heated as they are with liquor, and flushed with success, to keep them within bounds.

LETTER FROM SIR JAMES HARRIS TO THE MARQUIS OF
CARMARTHEN.

Hague, Sept. 18th, 1787.

MY DEAR LORD,—I hope you will be satisfied with
what I am about now.   I am astonished myself at what
is passing; and when I consider that a week ago I expected to be driven out of the Hague, and that at this
hour I could drive all the Patriots before me with a nod,
I confess it appears like enchantment—too much so, I
fear sometimes, to be real or lasting.

I am writing at a most anxious moment; while the
States are sitting to deliberate on the *great point*,* as
they think it.   Do not be surprised that my next letter
may treat of riots and commotions, but riots and commotions we durst not fly from.

You cannot conceive the mad extravagance of the
populace; my house is besieged with huzzas and acclamations; and I confess that it might as well not have
happened, though I was gratified with the sight of the
tearing the colours of the Free Corps before my eyes,
and to see that the inhabitants of the Hague consider
me as their friend and advocate.   If St. Priest† comes
soon, he must enter the Hague decorated with Orange-
coloured ribbons, or else he will not be suffered to enter
it at all.

The Garrisons are as extravagant as the Burghers in
their expressions of joy, and, if necessary, might be led
any lengths.   In short, the work of yesterday and to-
day has compensated for months of plague and crosses;
and, if I carry my point to-night, I shall sleep in a
Political Paradise.

* Vide page 335.   † The French Minister.

EXTRACTS OF A DESPATCH FROM SIR JAMES HARRIS TO THE MARQUIS OF CARMARTHEN.

Hague, Thursday, 20th Sept., 1787.

I DESPATCH an Extraordinary Packet with the very agreeable and satisfactory intelligence, that His Serene Highness the Prince of Orange came to the Hague amidst the acclamations of the people to-day at two P.M.

His horses were taken from his carriage at a mile from the town, and he was drawn into the town by the Corps of Orange Burghers. The streets through which he passed were lined with the troops of the garrison, and he was literally borne on the shoulders of the people when he arrived at the Stadtholderian palace.

I met His Serene Highness at the bottom of the stairs, and I cannot express to your Lordship how much I felt on the occasion. I retired with him in private for a very few minutes, but it was not a time to enter on business.

A Deputation from the States General, attended by their Greffier and President of the Week, another from the States of Holland, the Council of State, the Equestrian Orders, the Gecommitteeraden, the Courts of Justice, and all the different Colleges, waited on him, each in a body, and he was invested by them all with every right and privilege which had been suspended or taken from him. All the Foreign Ministers, except the French, Spanish, and American, went in the course of the day to compliment His Highness, as well as the Clergy and Magistracy of the Hague. In short, no single point was wanting to make his reception as complete as possible.

I have this evening been with the Prince alone for half an hour, and His Serene Highness, in the strongest terms words could express, repeatedly charged me to say, he considered he owed everything which had passed to His Majesty's support and protection, and that nothing should ever efface this obligation from his memory.

z 2

It was difficult to discourse on business with any precision. The multitude of objects which presented themselves, the situation of mind in which the Prince as well
as myself naturally were, made it impossible to bring our
ideas into any order. We, however, passed cursorily
over the most material points, and His Highness seems
in all of them to be exactly of the opinion his friends
here had laid down; to take every advantage of the
present circumstances, to compel Amsterdam to reasonable terms, if that town continues (as it seems probable
it will) to refuse to join with the others, to send immediate assistance to Friesland, to dismiss all the officers
appointed by the Commission of Woerden, and to reinstate all those dismissed by this Commission; to declare
the Rhingrave of Salm a traitor and a rebel, to engage
the States of Utrecht to sign the Règlement of 1674, to
force the town of Groningen to join with the Amme-
landers, to call to account the Judiciary proceeding of
the Gecommitteeraden, since it has taken the Administra-
tration of Justice out of the hands of the Courts of Holland, and, in short, to rectify all the *allures* the French
faction have introduced into the Republic within these
last seven years.

Amsterdam has written a very violent and insolent
letter to them, declaring that she considers all their
present proceedings as illegal and unconstitutional. It
is in my mind very immaterial whether this is attended
to or not, as it is impossible that even France can pretend to consider the two or three towns which meet
there as the *legal* Assembly of the States of Holland.

In order, however, to deprive France of every shadow
of a title to interfere in the concerns of this Province, I
have proposed to my friends in the States of Holland to
bring forward to-morrow a Resolution to declare to the
Court of Versailles, that His Serene Highness the Prince
of Orange is reinstated in all his rights and privileges as
Stadtholder of the Union, and of this Provence; that
Their High Mightinesses determined to grant to His
Prussian Majesty the satisfaction required ; and, of

course, no subject of dispute remaining between them and the Stadtholder, or the Princess of Orange, they were agreed to rescind their Resolution of the 9th, in which they had applied to His Most Christian Majesty for assistance.

If this passes, and no pains shall be spared on my side to carry it through, the march of a French army, should France persist in her determination to grant assistance to the Faction, will become an act of hostility committed against the nation at large, and the blame and consequences of a wanton interruption of the peace of Europe remain with France.   But, if she chooses to retract her determination, it furnishes her with a very fair plea for so doing, and saves her honour from any imputation of having broken her word with the Province of Holland.

LETTER FROM SIR JAMES HARRIS TO THE MARQUIS OF CARMARTHEN.

Hague, Sept. 21st., 1787.

I CANNOT describe to you, my dear Lord, my feelings on to-day, certainly the most glorious one I shall ever see.   Never were politics and sentiment so intimately connected, neither is it possible to suppose a public event which can influence more powerfully on the private sensations of individuals.

The acclamations and benedictions which follow me whenever I appear in the streets; the gratitude of those who compose the uppermost class of the people, and the attachment the Garrison has shewn me on this occasion, have been all so strongly expressed, that they really have overpowered me; and, although unused to the melting mood, I could not keep my eyes from watering when I met the Prince at the bottom of the stairs.

The situation and temper at the Hague is indescribable.   I have entreated the Prince to double the vedettes, as the whole garrison is drunk; and I should not be surprised if some of the Rhingrave's corps were to attempt a *coup de main*. I have also desired the Prince, and I am sure you will approve it, to join the good old Greffier's grandson* to the office of Greffier, and that that Office should not go out of the family. I also shall desire that Nagel, (who has been my right hand,) may be sent to England, to thank His Majesty; (and, if he is sent,) treat him as you would me, if you think I deserve to be well treated.

LETTER FROM SIR JAMES HARRIS TO THE DUKE OF BRUNSWICK, AT GOUDA.

La Haye, 22 Sept., 1787.

MONSEIGNEUR,—L'incertitude si mes lettres parviendront en sûreté à Votre Altesse Sereine est la seule cause qui m'a fait tarder de joindre jusqu'à présent mes expressions de joie et de reconnaissance à celles de toute la Nation Batave, sur la manière prompte, sage, et glorieuse dont elle l'a délivré du joug d'oppression sous lequel elle gémissoit.

Vous êtes, Monseigneur, son Libérateur. C'est sous l'abri de votre protection que les amis de la Patrie ont dirigé leurs opérations; et comme leur succès jusqu'à présent n'est dû qu'à Votre Altesse seule, ainsi la confection et la consolidation de l'ouvrage salutaire si heureusement commencé dépendra de la continuation de son appui.

Il s'écroulera infailliblement si le repliement des troupes sous ses ordres se fait avant que le nouvel ordre de choses produit par leur approche soit plus solidement établi.

Amsterdam, le foyer de la Cabale, et où tous ceux qui ont commis l'attentat contre l'auguste personne de Son Altesse Royale, Madame la Princesse d'Orange, se sent réfugiés, continue de protester et de s'inscrire en faux

* Baron Fagel.—He was Dutch Minister in London in 1827.

contre toutes les résolutions prises dans ce moment par Leurs Nobles et Grandes Puissances; et bien qu'elle ne se trouve secondée dans son avis que par la ville d'Alckmaer seule, elle fait cependant une partie trop essentielle de cette Province, pour que son aveu ne soit indispensable pour rendre la satisfaction dûe à Son Altesse Royale complète et permanente.

Vous daignerez me pardonner, Monseigneur, si j'ose écrire avec franchise; mais les ordres de ma Cour me portent à lui tout communiquer, et je ne connois pas de meilleure manière de les remplir que celle de m'ouvrir sans réserve.

Je dois, avant de conclure cette lettre, faire part à Votre Altesse Sereine, que Mons. de Montmorin, dans une conférence qu'il eut avec Mr. Eden le 14me du mois, (après qu'on avoit reçu à Versailles la résolution des Etats de Hollande du 9me pour demander du secours de Sa Majesté Très Chrétienne) s'est exprimé sur un ton très fort, et a déclaré " que le Roi de France se verrait obligé d'accorder l'assistance réquise."

M. de Barthelemi, le Chargé des Affaires de France à Londres, a parlé sur le même ton le 17me à Lord Carmarthen; et bien que d'après la manière vague et obscure dans laquelle la France s'est exprimée, tant à Versailles qu'à Londres, il n'y ait point de doute que ce langage menaçant n'aboutira à rien, cependant le Roi a donné incessamment des ordres à Mons. le Général Fawcett* de presser la conclusion de la besogne dont il est chargé, et en même temps d'accélérer l'équipement d'une flotte très considérable.

Cette démonstration jointe à une réponse ferme et énergique, faite à la Cour de France le 18me, dans laquelle Sa Majesté fait voir d'une manière nette et claire que son intention est de satisfaire en tout aux assurances de Co-opération qu'elle a données à Sa Majesté Prus-

---

* General Fawcett was sent to Berlin to conclude with His Prussian Majesty respecting the reciprocal contingents of troops to be furnished by England and Prussia, in case France should take hostile steps. England was to furnish 15,000 from Great Britain, 10,000 from Hanover, and 10,000 Hessians.

sienne, et à celle de protection qu'elle a promise à la République des Provinces Uniés, seront suffisantes selon toutes les apparences pour contenir la France, et doivent nous tranquilliser parfaitement sur le parti qu'elle prendra dans cette occasion.

EXTRACTS OF A DESPATCH FROM SIR JAMES HARRIS TO THE MARQUIS OF CARMARTHEN.

Hague, Tuesday, 25th Sept., 1787.

THE States of Holland agreed on Saturday to write a letter to Her Royal Highness the Princess of Orange, inviting her to return to the Hague, and expressive of " their earnest desire to grant Her Royal Highness the satisfaction for the insult offered her near Schoonhoven, in the manner insisted on by His Prussian Majesty." In consequence of this letter, Her Royal Highness came here from Utrecht yesterday, about three o'clock. She was received with the same acclamations as the Prince; the horses were taken from her carriage, and she was drawn through the principal streets by a number of women, amidst the shouts of an immense multitude.

Peace and good order also begin to be re-established, and I trust the joys of to-night will not induce the mob to commit acts of riot and depredation we have taken such immense pains to suppress, although, I am sorry to say, not always with the success I could wish.

The Duke of Brunswick removed his head-quarters on Saturday from Gouda' to Alphen. Yesterday he went to reconnoitre Amsterdam, and the advanced posts of his division moved forward as far as Amstelsween and Oudekerke, while the column under the command of General Gourde was drawing near it by Wesep and Minden. The Duke's plan is to get between the town and the two principal batteries which defend it; the one at the Halfweg Sluys between Haarlem and Amsterdam, the other on the opposite side of Diemen. He approaches on the banks of the Amstel, which river is defended by four or five gun-boats; but which can by no means essentially impede his march. I wrote to His Highness on Saturday, and again this morning; the contents of both my letters went to prove the necessity of coercing Amsterdam, and that the satisfaction would neither be complete nor solid till this city had subscribed to the resolution taken by Their Noble Mightinesses, &c.

He answered me in a few words, that he felt the necessity of what I said, and was determined to try.

The progress in the political part of the Revolution just effected keeps pace with the military operations, and every hour serves to prove how happy the Nation is to be delivered from the French yoke. I spare neither pains nor entreaties to forward my friends in the great work of disarming the Free Corps, both in the towns and villages: 1500 stand of arms have been brought in from the Westland. At Rotterdam, Delft, the Brille, Dordt, Gouda, Schoonhoven, and Gorcum, the Regents had forced them to deliver up their arms; and I hope to-morrow or next day to get a resolution passed by Their High Mightinesses to break and cashier them throughout the whole Province. The immense preparations they had got together, both of offensive and defensive weapons, is not to be conceived, and leaves us no doubt of the atrociousness of their designs, and the imminent danger to which the Statholderian party would have been exposed if Providence had not prevented it by producing the event which has just happened.

LETTER FROM THE MARQUIS OF CARMARTHEN TO
SIR J. HARRIS.

Whitehall, Sept. 25th., 1787.

MY DEAR SIR,—I scarce know in what terms to express my congratulations on the glorious events of the

last week.   In addition to the public advantages which
I trust will result from them, the part you have acted in
this great and memorable contest, and the share you
have had in the conducting it to the present happy issue
will render your name immortal; and you will do me
the justice to be persuaded of the additional satisfaction
I feel at the *personal* as well as official merit you have
manifested throughout, and which the world at. large
must ever acknowledge.   I must not omit my father's
congratulations; his expression is, " Pray when you
write to good Sir James, tell him I feel still greater
satisfaction at his having been the great instrument of
this glorious work."

France appears sulky; Montmorin chooses to forget, or
appears to forget, his Court having declared a resolution
of supporting their friends in Holland, in the event of the
Prussian troops entering the Republic.   I have just seen
a letter from Helvoet, mentioning its being reported at
your house last Friday, that Amsterdam had surrendered to six hundred hussars, who had been admitted into
the town by the Jews, and adding, that Tuesday last
had been fixed upon for a general massacre of the
Prince's friends.

I am extremely glad at the resolution of the States of
Holland respecting assistance from France, and particularly happy to find the good town of Dordt so active in
the *good* cause.

Believe me, ever most faithfully
and affectionately yours,
CARMARTHEN.

P.S., 4 P.M.—I have this moment heard from Amsterdam that the adjacent country is inundated, and that
the Patriots are erecting batteries, to make, at least,
a show of defence; probably for the purpose of a Capitulation.

LETTER FROM THE DUKE OF BRUNSWICK TO SIR JAMES HARRIS.

MONSIEUR,—Je prends la liberté de vous informer que je me rendrai demain, incognito, à la Haye pour parler au Prince et à la Princesse sur les affaires d'Amsterdam. S'il est possible je m'estimerais très heureux de vous entretenir un instant. Je compte de repartir tout de suite, afin de ne point perdre de temps inutilement. J'ai l'honneur d'être, avec les sentiments les plus distingués,

Monsieur, votre très humble

et très ob. Serviteur.

CHARLES G^d DUC DE B.

A Le Muyde, ce 27 de Septembre, 1787.

LETTER FROM MR. PITT TO SIR JAMES HARRIS.

Downing-Street, Friday Night, Sept. 28, 1787.

DEAR SIR,—Though I have not half the time to say anything like half what I feel on the late happy events, I cannot help troubling you with a single line to congratulate and to thank you for myself, and still more for the public, on a success so much owing to your zeal and exertions. I should have done so before this time, if I could have found any leisure when our messengers were setting out. The work seems so near completed, that it is almost out of the reach of accident. We must, however, continue all our exertions till everything is absolutely secure. There seems but one opinion in this country on the propriety of our efforts; and if the struggle had become necessary, I believe, we should have had nothing to regret or to fear from it.

I am, with great truth and regard, dear Sir,

Your obedient and faithful servant,

W. PITT.

EXTRACTS OF A DESPATCH FROM SIR JAMES HARRIS TO
THE MARQUIS OF CARMARTHEN.

Hague, 28th Sept., 1787.

THE seventeen towns which now meet in the States of
Holland are all perfectly agreed; but Amsterdam, as I
before observed, still refuses to join the Assembly, and
continues to protest against every thing that passes.
The Province of Holland, they say, is conquered by the
Prussian troops, and thus circumstanced the deliberations of the States cannot be free, or the resolutions they
take binding.   As long as this city, the centre of the
Faction, and where all its chiefs have taken refuge,
persists in this conduct, the Satisfaction cannot be
deemed complete, and much less the Restoration of the
Stadtholder permanent and secure.   The near approach
of the Duke's army to its gates has not yet produced
the effect expected.

The Duke of Brunswick wrote me a letter last night,
to say he would come this morning *incognito* to the
Hague, and desired me to be present at the conferences
he wished to hold on this occasion.   The Stadtholder,
the Princess of Orange, Messrs. Vander Spiegel, Royer,
Vansitters, Reiggersman, Tollins, and myself, assembled
this morning at ten o'clock, (the hour of the Duke's
arrival,) in Her Royal Highness's dressing-room, and
we remained together till four.   The great object to be
discussed was, " Whether Amsterdam should be carried
or not."   The Duke, who had himself been to reconnoitre the avenues of the town to the foot of the
batteries which defend it, and exposed his person to
dangers he ought to avoid, stated the various difficulties
of carrying on an offensive war in a country like that
round Amsterdam; but he stated them not with a view
to shrink from the enterprise, but merely to urge a
quick decision, as the change of the weather to rain,
and the approach of the autumn, made the probability
of success to rest on expedition.   An attempt to pro-

duce better terms and to open a negotiation *by threats* was proposed by some; an idea of investing it still closer, and making the mercantile part of its inhabitants feel the inconveniences of a blockade, was proposed by others; and some again were for prolonging the truce, (established since Tuesday, which expires tomorrow,) and attempting in the meanwhile to send emissaries into the town to ferment division, and form a party within its walls, who would be disposed to deliver it upon the first summons. To all these expedients taken separately I ventured to object. I proposed comparing the two papers given by Mr. Abbema to the Duke, with the last memorial presented by the Baron de Thulemeyer, and to see in what they differed. The commission the Duke of Brunswick holds under His Prussian Majesty, I took the liberty to observe, is clear and explicit. It was to obtain the Satisfaction in the precise terms set forth in the above Memorial, and in case this should be refused, to employ *force;* it was on this principle His Serene Highness had hitherto acted, and to depart from it in favour of a city, where the aggressors had taken refuge, and which was itself the principal aggressor, would not only defeat everything which had hitherto been done, but throw a cloud over the military part of the transaction, which would be highly injurious to the glory of the Prussian arms, and to that of the great general who commanded them.

As to the idea of not exposing a populous and opulent city to the events of a siege, it was a consideration well worthy attention, but it was one which ought to opetate much more powerfully on those within the walls of the town than on the besiegers, and induce them to be less daring and opinionative; and that the consequences, whatever they may be, as well as the whole blame, would rest on those eight or ten factious leaders who exposed it, from the most unjustifiable of all motives, to the fate of war; that my opinion, therefore, was, that His Serene Highness should, immedi-

ately on the expiration of the truce, make his approaches towards Amsterdam, summon it to submit,
and on a refusal *attack it instantaneously;* and in the
meanwhile emissaries should be sent from hence with
authority to insinuate on the Exchange at Amsterdam,
and to the populace at large, that neither His Prussian
Majesty nor Her Royal Highness, nor any one else,
had the most distant wish of inflicting personal punishment on the offenders; that it was an *apology,* not
revenge, that was sought for, and this obtained, the
authors of the insult were at liberty to retire when and
where they pleased; their persons and property would
be secure, and they even might remain in the country,
provided they would renounce all claim whatever to be
employed in future, either in the Regency of Amsterdam
or that of any other town or province of the Republic.

This opinion, after some discussion, prevailed, and
the Duke left the Hague between four and five, determined to carry it into execution. The letters His
Highness received from Berlin to-day, the intelligence I
gave him of the disposition of England, and the wavering contradictory conduct of France, seemed to leave no
doubt in his mind, that it was such a one as ought to
be pursued.

I had some private conversation with the Duke of
Brunswick, with which I think it material for your
Lordship to be acquainted.

His Highness is persuaded that when France is fully
informed of what is passing here, and when she finds
a fixed resolution in the Courts of Berlin and London
to support each other in the principles they have laid
down, that she will retract all she has said, and submit
to the terms proposed, in which case he gives it as his
opinion, that the way should be smoothed for her, and
the operatino concluded as little at the expense of her
pride and vanity as possible. The event in itself will
be sufficiently humiliating.

His Highness, in great confidence, entrusted me with
his plan of attack on Amsterdam. His head-quarter is

now at Leymuyden, on the Haarlem lake. He intends, as the country is in a manner impracticable for the moving of artillery, to embark a strong detachment at Alsmeer, and to land it at the back of the battery, at the half-way Sluys, between Haarlem and Amsterdam. If he succeeds, he gets upon a paved causeway, eighty feet broad. He commands this attack himself, and takes with him four howitzers, with 200 shells. Three other attacks will be made at the same time from Ouderkerke, Abkoude, and Diemendam. He does not intend to suffer any of his troops to enter the town in case of success.

I talked a great deal with him on the necessity of his not withdrawing his troops too soon. He admitted the utility of their remaining here, and promised me that their retreat out of the Province should be as slow as their entrance into it was rapid.

The Duke of Brunswick told me that His Prussian Majesty, if France carried matters to extremities, intended to come himself into the Duchy of Cleves, and to increase his army there to 65,000 men. That this, added to those in His Majesty's pay, would make nearly a corps of 100,000 men, which he (the Duke) should advise to be divided into two armies, the one to cover this country, the other to attack France in her own dominions.

LETTER FROM THE MARQUIS OF CARMARTHEN TO SIR JAMES HARRIS.

Whitehall, 28th Sept., 1787.

MY DEAR HARRIS,—I was literally ordered by the King to let you know that Count Lynden* had expressed his joy at the late Revolution to the Duke of Richmond and myself. His Majesty said, " I am sure Harris will enjoy it." Lynden talked to me yesterday for above a quarter of an hour on the subject, how happy it was to

* The Patriot Ex-Ambassador in London.

see everything restored to tranquillity without bloodshed, and only hoped the Constitution would be preserved agreeable to the settlements of 1747 and 1766, &c. With, I believe, *equal sincerity,* he assured me of his alarms for the safety of *sa chère femme* during the late troubles.

Depuis le plus grand, jusqu'au plus petit, on chante vos éloges, et je me flatte bientôt de pouvoir vous informer que vous ne serez pas quitte pour le chant.

Pray take Amsterdam soon, if it is not already taken, that I may not go to the ball at Windsor on Monday, *Re infectâ.*

The French Ministers say, that had their friends in Holland behaved better, and made a decent resistance, they should have been obliged, though *with regret,* to have afforded them assistance. Pray take care that this new instance of French protection and good faith may be known among their unfortunate Dutch dependants.

LETTER FROM THE DUKE OF BRUNSWICK TO SIR JAMES HARRIS.

MONSIEUR,—Votre courier m'a trouvé ici à Kuttelsdorf. Les troupes du Roi de Prusse, ayant fait aujourd'hui un mouvement en avant vers Amsterdam, Abbema et Golt m'ont suivis; je leur ai donné la note ci-jointe, et demain à la pointe du jour on poussera leur postes jusqu'à Amsterdam, en attaquant et Muyde et l'Écluse de Halfweg. Comptez sur mon zèle, et sur un désir extrême de bien finir ceci. Les nouvelles de Mr. Grenville* que vous avez eu la complaisance de me communiquer sont bien consolantes, et servent à me rassurer infiniment; s'il y a quelque chose d'intéressant dans ces contrées demain, ou après demain, j'enverrai Mr. Murray. Gordon est extrêmement zélé; il veut nous rendre des services très essentiels. Je n'ai que le temps de

* From Paris.

vous assurer que rien n'égale la haute considération
avec laquelle j'ai l'honneur d'être, Monsieur,

Votre très humble et très obéissant Serviteur,

CHARLES G DUC DE BRONSVIC LUNEBOURG.

A Kuttelsdorf, ce 30 Septembre, 1787.

REPONSE DONNE AUX DEPUTES D'AMSTERDAM.

Le 30 Septembre, à 11 heures avant Midi.

JE regarde la Trève comme expirée dès ce soir entre
les sept et huit heures, temps que Messieurs les
Députés pourront être de retour à Amsterdam. Je suis
fermement résolu d'aller en avant et d'exécuter mes
ordres, à moins que je ne reçois de Son Altesse Royale
Mme la Princesse d'Orange une lettre, par laquelle Elle me
marque qu'elle ne désire plus d'autre satisfaction, et in-
tercède pour m'engager à replier les troupes.

EXTRACT OF A DESPATCH FROM SIR JAMES HARRIS TO THE MARQUIS OF CARMARTHEN.

Hague, Tuesday, 2nd Oct., 1787.

ON the 29th September, a Deputation waited on the
Princess with the proposal from the city of Amsterdam.
Your Lordship will observe that the substance of
what Amsterdam offers here is the same as that of the
Resolution of Their Noble Mightinesses of the 8th September, very artfully concealed under other words, and
that nothing is conceded but a simple apology.

The Deputies at first were disposed to assume a high
tone, but the dignified and spirited manner in which
His Royal Highness answered them, soon brought them
to their proper level.   They returned the same evening
without going to the Assembly of the States.

I was with the Princess immediately before and after

they left her, and it was agreed that a messenger should be sent without loss of time to the Duke, to inform him of what had passed, and to recommend him not to prolong the truce.

Messrs. Abbema and Golt expected to find him at Leymunden, but he had moved forward as far as Kuydersteert, two leagues nearer Amsterdam, to which place they followed him on foot. He refused to see them alone, and spoke to them in the midst of his officers, and on the march. He sent them back *blindfolded* under a strong guard to the outposts of their city, by way of retaliation for their party having done the same by a Prussian officer who had summoned Naerden.

Yesterday, early, His Serene Highness attacked one of the principal posts at Amsterdam, and carried it, and several small batteries dependent on it, with the loss of about 150 men killed and wounded, and 3 officers. He also took the battery at Half-weg Sluys. This made him master of the whole district between the Amstel and the Haarlem lake, and his advanced posts are now at Overtoom, within a mile and a half of the gates of the city.

At noon, yesterday, the same Deputies again returned to him, their tone humbled, and greatly agitated, entreating him to grant a truce of two days, and assuring him that during this time their town would prepare a Resolution, which would give entire satisfaction to the Princess of Orange. This His Serene Highness granted.

At eleven last night a letter from the town, arrived here for the Princess of Orange, inclosing a Resolution to the same effect. But the whole fell to the ground by the deputies from Amsterdam refusing to acknowledge the legality of the Assembly, and the validity of the Resolutions taken by it since the 17th. The instructions they produced were also still very wide of the concessions required, inasmuch as they would not hear of the removal of the magistrates intruded in the

Regency by force, or of disarming the Free Corps. The Assembly, therefore, broke up without any business whatever being done.

Mr. Tollins will be despatched to-night to the Duke, declaring it to be the unanimous opinion of the friends to the good cause that his army should march against Amsterdam, and begin an attack on the town, unless it sent Deputies to the States of Holland to avow their legality, and to ratify every act which had passed in them since the restoration of the Stadtholder. This goes to the root of the evil; it grants the Satisfaction in its whole extent; it confirms the re-integration of the Stadtholderate, and works at once an effectual cure. There is little doubt that His Serene Highness will readily subscribe to our opinions; for, besides these, I have reason to believe the letters he got to-day from Berlin told him expressly that nothing short of the submission of Amsterdam would satisfy His Prussian Majesty; intimating at the same time, that he had appeared rather too lax and cool on this point. In addition to this, the factious leaders have personally offended him by an indirect attempt to corrupt him.

EXTRACTS OF A DESPATCH FROM SIR JAMES HARRIS TO THE MARQUIS OF CARMARTHEN.

Hague, Friday, 5th Oct., 1787.

THREE days were granted by the Duke for the purpose of negotiation. On a nearer view, however, of the business, and on entering into a discussion with the Deputies sent here, the concessions made by Amsterdam were still found to be wide of the mark; and from the manner in which they have been brought forward, there is every reason to suppose that the great object of those who defend Amsterdam, is to delay and procrastinate, in hopes that the advanced season of the spring-tide

A A 2

may so much increase the difficulties of the approaches to the town as to force the Duke to retire.

A gentleman who was sent to me from Amsterdam yesterday morning, and who spoke the language of all the principal houses of trade, said that they are unanimous in their wishes to see the town in the possession of the Prussians. He was certain the inhabitants would force the Free Corps to open the gates on the first summons. I, however, am not quite so sanguine as he is; and I confess, from what I hear from officers who are daily coming to me from the headquarters, I am not without great uneasiness, if the weather should change to rain, that the Duke will find it equally difficult to attack the town, or to retire from before it. I gave my informant much greater credit for veracity when he described the interior of Amsterdam as a scene of confusion and disorder not to be conceived.

EXTRACT OF A LETTER FROM SIR JAMES HARRIS TO THE
MARQUIS OF CARMARTHEN.

Hague, Sunday, 7th Oct., 1787.

BEFORE the truce expired yesterday, the Deputies of Amsterdam came to the Assembly of the States of Holland, acknowledged its legality, and agreed, unconditionally, to all the Resolutions which have been passed since the 18th September, that of the 22nd, in which they made their last stand, inclusively. In consequence of this compliance, a deputation of Their Noble Mightinesses waited at noon on Her Royal Highness the Princess of Orange, to express, in the name of the States, their deep concern at what had happened on the 28th June, and to ask Her Royal Highness what kind of satisfaction she required. The Princess replied to them by a compliment, declaring she would give them her answer in writing on Monday. This, as she has just done me the honour to acquaint me, will be in perfect conformity to the points set forth in His Prussian Majesty's last Memorial, except that Her Royal Highness intends to require a rescission of all the Resolutions which were passed to justify the conduct of the Commission of Woerden before the 18th September, and that the Commission of Defence for the town of Amsterdam, consisting of four of the most violent Patriots, should be included amongst the guilty persons. She consents to remit any punishment as far as may regard the insult offered her, on condition the offenders (whom Her Royal Highness will afterwards be called upon to name) are immediately dismissed from their employments, and pronounced incapable of ever serving the Republic in any capacity whatever; but she declares she cannot pledge herself for their not being proceeded against in the course of law, if they have been guilty of any crimes against the State. I particularly desired her to insert this last article, and I trust it will meet your Lordship's approbation. It is necessary to hold a rod of terror over the heads of these factious leaders, though it may, perhaps, not be to make use of it. This entire submission of Amsterdam looks like a termination of the whole business; but it must not be considered as completely at an end till these terms are carried into execution.

EXTRACT OF A DESPATCH FROM SIR JAMES HARRIS TO THE
MARQUIS OF CARMARTHEN.

Hague, Tuesday, 9th Oct., 1787.

ACCOUNTS, received from the Duke of Brunswick this evening, say, that the Amsterdammers have abandoned all their out-posts; that Muyden has surrendered; that he is in possession of their posts at Overtoom and Diemerbrok, and that he surrounds the town completely close to its walls on the land side. It is hoped that to-morrow we shall hear of its having consented to receive either a Prussian or a Dutch garrison, on which its

safety, as well as the final decision of the dispute in
favour of the present system, depends.

Hague, Friday, 12th Oct., 1787.

I INFORMED your Lordship in my last, that the out-
posts were abandoned, and that on the 8th the Duke
was master of the whole suburbs.   On the 9th, in the
morning, His Highness made his dispositions for bom-
barding the town, and shells would have been thrown
into it at noon, if a deputation had not waited on him to
acquaint him with the steps which had been taken at
the Hague (stated in mine, 2nd Oct.) and entreating
His Highness to name the conditions to which he wished
the town to subscribe.   On the next morning, Wednesday, he signed the capitulation, and in consequence of
it, took possession in the evening of the principal gate
of the town.   The greatest order was observed in the
town while the Prussians took possession of its gate;
and when the Burgomaster Bokker came to deliver up
the keys to the Duke of Brunswick, His Highness, after
giving the strongest assurances that the strictest discipline should be observed by his troops, declared, at the
same time, that he would make the town responsible for
any insult that should be offered to any of the Prussian
officers or soldiers who might appear in the streets under
the protection of one of his passports.

The same day the Magistrates, who had been forced
on the town by the Free Corps, were dismissed, the
former ones (amongst whom were Messrs. Dedel and
Beels) were restored to their offices without any disorder or resistance on the part either of the armed or
unarmed mob.

This morning the Burgomaster and Council of the
town have written a letter to Colonel Bentinck, as

Quarter-Master-General, desiring him to request of the Stadtholder to order immediately troops of the Union, to the amount of not less than 2000 men, amongst which a regiment of horse, to be sent to garrison the town. This last measure, to effectuate which in the way it has taken place, has been the great object of our endeavours, for several days past, not only completes the entire submission of Amsterdam for the moment, but insures its good behaviour for a long while, and is what neither William II. could effect by force, nor any of the other Stadtholders by influence and persuasion.

The disarming of the Free Corps goes on very quietly; many fled before the Prussians came into the town, and the others readily gave up a cause whose pecuniary sources were stopped. There was a trifling riot between some of them and a mob of Jews (extremely zealous in the Prince's favour,) in which it is said two of the latter were killed.

It is uncertain what is become of Van Berkel; he was not to be found yesterday in Amsterdam, and it is supposed he has absconded. Abbema is fled to France, and the Rhingrave of Salm was heard of on his way through Mentz about ten days ago, declaiming loudly against the treachery and perfidiousness of the Court of Versailles, to whose promises of support he said he had fallen a victim.

EXTRACT OF A DESPATCH FROM SIR JAMES HARRIS TO THE MARQUIS OF CARMARTHEN.

Hague, Tuesday, 26th Oct., 1787.

THE Princess of Orange sent for me early yesterday morning, to inform me that the Duke of Brunswick had that moment written her word, that he had received the preceding evening a letter from the King of Prussia, declaring it to be His Majesty's intention that Amsterdam should be laid under contribution, and forced to pay the expenses of this expedition, from the time his troops left Wesel till their return into the Duchy of Cleves.*

His Serene Highness expressed himself greatly perplexed with these instructions, which he could not execute without a breach of the capitulation he had signed on the 9th with the Amsterdammers, and which were also in contradiction to the assurances given in the Manifesto which His Prussian Majesty had published when his troops first entered the Republic. Besides these reasons, the Duke of Brunswick declared himself strongly against the measure, taken in a political light. He said it would sully the glory of the Prussian arms, and terminate an expedition which had been undertaken on the most liberal of motives, in a manner very unbecoming a great Monarch; that it would, instead of procuring to His Prussian Majesty the friendship and alliance of the Republic, tend to make it his irreconcilable enemy, and undoubtedly would spread an alarm and jealousy throughout Europe which might lead to very serious consequences. After dwelling with great feeling on these considerations, His Serene Highness ended his letter by entreating the Princess to state them immediately in their strongest colours to His Prussian Majesty, to represent to him that Amsterdam having consented to subscribe *unconditionally* to all the Resolutions taken by its co-members in the States of Holland since the 18th September, the coming upon it now with this after-demand, would raise a fermentation which might undo everything that has been done. He also requested His Royal Highness to write at the same time to Mons. de Hertzberg, pointing out to this Minister how ill-judged and ill-timed such a step would be, and that it was as indefensible in its principles as difficult in its execution.

His Serene Highness said, if Her Royal Highness would undertake this, he would write to the same effect, and notwithstanding his orders were positive, delay

---

* This demand of His Prussian Majesty is highly characteristic of the man, whose whole reign was a course of broken promises and mean actions.

executing them till the return of the messenger from Berlin. I found the Princess greatly embarrassed, and even agitated; the more so, as the day before she received a letter from the King her brother, dated the 9th, in which he declared, that he had laid aside all thoughts of levying any contributions in the Province of Holland, and *authorized her to say so.* This letter Her Royal Highness had shewn to me, and I could not but agree with her in considering it in every respect as a very favourable circumstance. It was so difficult to reconcile the orders sent to the Duke of Brunswick with this Declaration, particularly as they must have been within a few hours' date of one another, that I found myself greatly perplexed what answer to make to Her Royal Highness, when she did me the honour to tell me she had sent for me to ask my advice, and to say it was a business of a nature she could confide to me alone, since the very idea, if it got abroad, and was known to the people of the country, however well disposed, would fill them with alarms and misgivings.

Our conversation ended in determining that Her Royal Highness should write nearly in the terms the Duke desired, qualifying, however, any expressions which might seem too strong, by laying it down as an axiom, that His Prussian Majesty, having no other view in what he has done than to obtain the Satisfaction, certainly could not wish to adopt measures which might overthrow the good consequences which were likely to follow from his success. I suggested to the Princess whether it would not have its effect to contrast His Prussian Majesty's conduct on this occasion with that of the Emperor at the end of his disputes with this country in 1785, who certainly did not add to his reputation by having laid it for some years under a kind of annual tribute. Her Royal Highness, I believe, availed herself of this hint, as it seemed to strike her, and she despatched at three o'clock P.M. an estafette to Berlin, by whom I also sent a full account of this awkward business to Mr. Ewart.

LETTER FROM THE DUKE OF BRUNSWICK TO SIR JAMES HARRIS.

MONSIEUR,—J'ai reçu avec bien de la reconnaissance les nouvelles très intéressantes que vous avez bien voulu me communiquer, et je vois avec beaucoup de satisfaction que nous devons à l'Angleterre seule l'heureuse tournure que les affaires prennent.* Je vous avoue que je souhaite que les Etats Généraux voulussent prendre au plus tôt des troupes en subside, afin que ce détachment des troupes Prussiennes qui va rester ici, puisse retourner avant l'hiver dans le pays de Cleves; quand on a tant fait, que le Roi, il est fâcheux de l'exposer à des pourparlors avec la France sur des objets qui n'en valent pas la peine et uniquement parceque l'on ne sait jamais se résoudre à temps dans ce pays-ci.

Je vous prie de dire dans l'occasion, que le Roi ne donneroit jamais ses troupes en subside, et qu'outre plusieurs autres raisons qui l'empêchent, le Roi ne souffrirait jamais que ses troupes prêtassent serment à une Puissance étrangère, et que ses officiers fussent soumis aux Bourguemaîtres des villes dans lesquelles on les metteroit en garnison. Je n'ai pas le temps d'écrire à Madame la Princesse, d'ailleurs je lui ai envoyé ce matin, Mons. Tollins, pour l'entretenir sur plusieurs objets qui concèrnent le conseil de guerre de la ville d'Amsterdam. Tout sera fini demain, 23. Le Magistrat enverra des Députés à la Haye, pour marquer qu'il a satisfait à tout, et j'enverrai le 25 les témoignages authentiques du désarmement et de tout ce qui y a rapport à Madame la Princesse, après quoi je regarde ma commission comme terminée. Je compte attendre cependant une lettre de Madame la Princesse, par laquelle elle me dise, que la satisfaction étant complète, elle s'attend que les troupes du Roi quitteront le territoire de la République. J'ai fait proposer au Sieur Dedel d'envoyer les armes que les

---

* The question was " What troops should be subsidized by the Stadtholder."

Bourgeois ont réunis à Muyden, mais je n'en ai point encore réponse. Sûr est il qu'il y a un très grand nombre d'armes chez les armuriers de la ville, et que malgré les armes délivrées, la Bourgeoisie pourroit aisément en trouver de nouvelles. Il me semble que le grand point sera maintenant de faire que les Etats autorisent le Prince de changer les Régences. Ce point de gagné et Mr. Vander Spiegel crée Pensionnaire, je crois que l'on osera tout espérer pour le bien de ce Pays-ci, et pour les arrangemens à prendre relativement aux alliances.

Pardonnez que je vous parle de choses que vous savez infiniment mieux que moi; je ne désire que de trouver bientôt l'occasion de vous prouver, Monsieur, que rien n'égale les sentimens de la haute considération avec laquelle j'ai l'honneur d'être, Monsieur,

Votre très humble et très obéissant Serviteur,

CHARLES.

A Küttelsdorf, ce 23 Octobre, 1787.

P.S.—Si l'Angleterre pouvoit céder 4000 Hessois à la Hollande, l'affaire seroit faite d'abord, et ils seroient ici en six semaines.

EXTRACT OF A DESPATCH FROM SIR JAMES HARRIS TO THE MARQUIS OF CARMARTHEN.

Hague, Friday, 26th Oct., 1787.

His Prussian Majesty has given up entirely the idea of raising a large contribution, either at Amsterdam, or on the towns of this Province, taken collectively, to pay the expenses of his expedition; but he still insists on a gratification of 400,000 florins being given to his troops, and the Duke of Brunswick writes word that his orders on the point are positive. Mons. de Thulemeyer has, in consequence, prepared a note which he thinks of presenting to the States of Holland. He has not communicated or spoken to me on the subject, but I know such to be his intentions. It is greatly to be wished that His

Prussian Majesty could have been induced to forego this claim wholly, which will take away so much merit from his conduct; and, on whatever principles it may be founded, be considered by every class of people here, as an exaction and act of oppression.

In order to prevent the very disagreeable constructions which would undoubtedly be put if it came forward in the form of a Ministerial demand, I have been endeavouring this morning to induce the Prince and Princess of Orange to try to prevail on the States of Holland to offer the sum required gratuitously, as a present they are desirous of bestowing on the Prussian troops for the service His Prussian Majesty has done the Republic; and if their Highnesses find this method likely to be adopted by Their Noble Mightinesses, they will send for Mr. Thulemeyer and prevent his giving in the note. I am not certain of success; but the gratification, if it is to come, will be much more honourable both to those who give it, and those who receive it, by being a spontaneous act of the donors, than if in consequence of the Prussian memorial, which, under the present circumstances, would be considered as a mandate.

I had, this morning, a long conversation with Mr. Vander Spiegel (who came last night) on this subject, and it gave me no small pleasure to find that we were perfectly agreed on every point. He has, after no small persuasion, consented to accept the office of Grand Pensionary, on condition that the Stadtholder will engage himself to do business in a regular and methodical manner. The Duke of Brunswick considers his commission as finished, and will, I believe, be here on Sunday.

EXTRACT OF A DESPATCH FROM SIR JAMES HARRIS TO THE MARQUIS OF CARMARTHEN.

Hague, Tuesday, 30th Oct., 1787.

His Serene Highness the Duke of Brunswick came here on Sunday, accompanied by the Duke of Saxe-

Weimar, the Prince of Anhalt, and several officers of rank and distinction.

Yesterday the Palace, called the old Court, was magnificently illuminated, and after a brilliant evening and drawing-room, a very splendid supper was given by the Prince Stadtholder in honour of His Serene Highness.

The plan I proposed to prevent the unpleasant consequences of a ministerial requisition on the part of His Prussian Majesty, for a pecuniary gratification for his troops, will be adopted, and I hope carried.

Mr. Vander Spiegel has contented himself with receiving the strongest verbal assurances from the Prince of Orange of his determination to establish in the different departments, under his direction, a regular and methodical mode of doing business. His Serene Highness did not like the idea of being bound down by a solemn deed to do what in itself seemed so reasonable and proper, and I found that if it had been forced upon him, he would never have acted cordially with the new Great Pensionary.

I have talked very fully to him on the subject of the Alliance;* and after his starting a few difficulties, chiefly in consequence of his having been absent from the Hague for these last three months, and not exactly informed of what had passed, we were perfectly agreed on all its points, and he promised to assist me with all his weight to carry it through.

The vote for taking a body of foreign troops into pay will probably pass this week; I strongly recommend 8000 men, but the majority of the Provinces incline for 5000; the difference is not of sufficient consequence to employ on this occasion a stretch of influence, which I may want for a more important purpose.

I had a long conversation on all these subjects with His Serene Highness the Duke of Brunswick yesterday evening at my house (where he preferred I should see him), and I was happy to find my ideas met his on most of them. I urged His Highness not to withdraw his

---

* Between England, Prussia, and Holland.

troops from around Amsterdam till that town had voted both for the Alliance and the Special Commission, and I entreated him to insist on these steps being immediately taken. He assured me his retreat should be as slow as possible.

EXTRACT OF A DESPATCH FROM SIR JAMES HARRIS TO THE MARQUIS OF CARMARTHEN.

Hague, Friday, 2nd Nov. 1787.

THE Great Pensionary Blyswick will give up his post on this day se'ennight, and immediately afterwards the nomination of Mr. Vander Spiegel take place. It was my wish that Mr. Blyswick should have been stigmatized with some public mark of disgrace, or at least that he should have been called upon to give an account of his Administration.

The same motives which prevent the Great Pensionary's being dismissed with censure apply to the dismission of Paulus; and this Minister, who has avowedly been the bitterest enemy of the Stadtholderate, is suffered to remain in office till he chooses to resign.

This moderation and forbearance, far from producing the effect intended, is considered by the Patriots as a symptom of instability and irresolution in the present Government; and encourages them to keep their hopes of recovering their ground still alive.[*]

This appears in a very unpleasant manner at Amsterdam, where the remnants of the French Faction are moving Heaven and earth to breed dissensions between the troops in garrison there and the citizens; and they have so far succeeded as to have raised something very like a mutiny in the Horse Guards.

I received a messenger from the Duke of Dorset[†] and

---

[*] Lord Carmarthen strongly recommends Sir James Harris to insist on lenity and forbearance towards the defeated Patriots, and if possible to abstain from personal punishments.

[†] English Ambassador at Paris.

Mr. Eden on Wednesday, with an account of the signature of the Declarations for disarming, executed between the Courts of London and Versailles, on the 27th October; and yesterday Major brought me your Lordship's letter, with the same account.

It gives great satisfaction here, and conveys the most convincing proof of the will and ability of Great Britain to assist and support the Republic, while it gives a directly contrary impression of the sentiments and faculties of France.

EXTRACT OF A LETTER FROM SIR JAMES HARRIS TO THE
MARQUIS OF CARMARTHEN.

Hague, Nov. 16th, 1787.

My DEAR LORD,—The Duke of Saxe-Weimar, who remains here for some days longer, called upon me this evening, and entered into a very long political conversation. I had been informed he was not disposed to promote a connexion between England and Prussia. I was, of course, on my guard, and more of a hearer than a speaker. He, however, entered very fairly on the subject; and after stating several reasons which might make a French alliance more advantageous to His Prussian Majesty than an English one, he concluded by agreeing that under the present circumstances they were not applicable, and that nothing was left for the Court of Berlin but to form, without loss of time, the closest connexion with that of Great Britain. The Duke of Brunswick held precisely the same language.

I do not vouch for the sincerity of either of them; and as far as Mr. Ewart's reports go, at the very moment they are talking in this manner to me, their letters, particularly those of the Duke of Brunswick to His Prussian Majesty, are drawn up in a directly contrary sense. Ewart enters very fully into this subject to me in a private letter, dated the 9th November, and presses very strongly the absolute necessity of now im-

mediately, and without loss of time, bringing forward
the proposal of an Alliance at Berlin, if any such idea
is formed, and if we wish it should succeed.

Ewart, therefore, recommends pushing things, and sees
the greatest danger in delay.   As I am persuaded he is
too diffident to hold this language himself to you, either
in a private or official letter, I think it part of my duty
to convey his sentiments to you, which I do with the
less scruple, as there is every reason to have confidence
in his judgment and discernment.   He says he no
longer fears the machinations of Goertz and Thulemeyer, or the intrigues of the subaltern antagonists ;
but that he is apprehensive the danger may come from
much more dangerous sources, — from the Dukes of
Brunswick* and Weimar, and Colonel Stein.

I shall endeavour to see as much of the Duke of
Weimar as possible.   He was, I am convinced, sent to
me to-day by order of the King of Prussia, with whom
he is a great favourite; and the whole of his language
was prepared, and tending to draw from me matter for
a despatch.

As to the Duke of Brunswick, the last thing he said
to me was, " Il ne reste autre chose à faire pour la
Prusse, que de se jeter entre les bras de l'Angleterre."
And he went so far as to tell me, that I should move
Heaven and earth to remove Thulemeyer, since he could
assure me, that, in spite of his instructions, he was
acting against the Alliances, and had very lately (at
the time when he was full to me of his assurances of
confidence and support) sent a laboured Memorial to
Berlin, to prove how greatly it was against the interest
of Prussia to enter into a political system with the
maritime powers.   It was for this reason that I persuaded the Princess of Orange to ask for Goertz; and
I have written with the same view to Ewart.

If I might venture to add my own opinion, there

* Mr. Ewart warns Sir James Harris to be aware of the Duke of Brunswick's tricks, and that he had learned from Frederick that the perfection of
sound policy was deceit.   Colonel Stein was a French partisan.—*Harris
Papers.*

remains at present no other part for us to take but to *close with Prussia.*

Hague, Nov. 29th, 1787.

A THOUSAND thanks, my dear Lord, for your kind and friendly letter of the 25th, and as many for the very grateful compliment from your most respectable father. Pray return it in the way it is felt. Believe me, my dear Lord, when I say your partial encomiums give me as much pleasure as the event itself.

I had on Thursday between three and four hundred people at supper, at the head of which were the Prince and Princess. I made it as like a fête as possible, by illuminations, dancing, music, &c. The whole Hague were assembled round my house; and I did not conceive the faculty of noise and shouting to belong so perfectly to this nation. We separated at five. At nine, on Friday, the Duke of Brunswick arrived. From ten to four yesterday morning I was in conference with him; and if you will turn your eyes on what I have since written you, you will not suppose I have had any time for rest. The doing business, and giving fêtes is too much at once; and nothing but such an occasion could have given me mental or bodily health for the purpose.

The idea of a massacre of the Prince's friends is far from being an idle conjecture. There is every reason to think it was intended, even after the incursion of the Prussian troops; and this induced me to press on the Revolution, which, if I had not effected by fair means, I was determined to have attempted by force, and to *vaincre ou mourir;* but, as I before said, this must be matter of conversation, or at least the present sensation be left to subside before I send it to you on paper.

[Sir James Harris had now to conduct the Treaty between England and Holland. During the war we had taken Negapatnam, in the East Indies; and the discussions concerning the restitution of this place went near to frustrate our past success. He was instructed to ask for Rhio and Trincomalee, as equivalents for Negapatnam. This, at Sir James's urgent request, was abandoned, and the Treaty signed at the Hague, April 15th, 1788.]

EXTRACT OF A DESPATCH FROM SIR JAMES HARRIS TO THE MARQUIS OF CARMARTHEN.

Hague, 4th Dec., 1787.

IN regard to the principles of the Armed Neutrality, as well as those established in the Marine Treaty of 1674, I have, without ever making them an object of ministerial discussion, uniformly held the same language, that they were utterly inadmissible by England, and never would be consented to. I have also endeavoured to impress this idea through my confidential friends, and to make the Dutch nation at large feel through them, that the principles on which we shall persist in this refusal are those of self-defence; that they cannot be departed from; and that if the Republic becomes sincerely and *bonâ fide* the friend and ally of Great Britain, the trifling advantages she would obtain by being the carriers of contraband articles to our enemies would be most abundantly compensated by the protection England would afford her trade in general, whenever she was attacked.

These reasons, I have good hope to believe, are felt by the greatest part of the nation; and I flatter myself, this delicate subject will either be not brought forward at all, or not expose us to any material hitch in the Negotiation.

I must beg your Lordship to inform me whether it will be considered as sufficient that it should pass over entirely unnoticed. England never has recognised the five points of the famous Neutral Code, adopted by most of the maritime powers. The Treaty of 1674 is annulled; and it seems to me, when nothing is expressed relative to the Neutral Trade, that it will remain with us to put our own explanation on the point, and to insist on the Dutch (supposing the case should happen, which, if the conditions of the Alliance are strictly adhered to, cannot) abiding by what was considered by all Europe as the only principles on which the trade could be carried on before the extravagant and absurd principles of the Armed Neutrality were broached.

If I am in error, and it should be deemed necessary to come to some specific explanation with the Dutch on this point, I will endeavour to make the Article pass your Lordship proposes to send me; but your Lordship is aware, if the Dutch openly, and in a treaty which will probably be soon publicly known, consent to give up the principles of the Armed Neutrality, the other members of that League will instantly accuse them of having broken their engagements, and oppose the principles of our Alliance with this country.

EXTRACT OF A DESPATCH FROM SIR JAMES HARRIS TO THE MARQUIS OF CARMARTHEN.

Hague, 18th Dec., 1787.

I HAVE had several very long conversations with Mr. Vander Spiegel, and I am sorry to say, that though we are perfectly and sincerely agreed as to the principle, yet we still differ widely as to the execution.

After enumerating various reasons, all of which he repeatedly said, he in his own mind rejected, but to which from the nature of the Government, and from the limited sphere of his influence, he was forced to listen to, as those on which he was obliged to regulate his conduct, our conversation was brought nearly to the same point where it stood when our last, and which I stated in mine, 26th Oct., ended. He went indeed a step further, and intreated me in the strongest manner to make the cession of Negapatnam an unconditional stipulation.

He said that it was universally believed here, that we required the cession of this place at the end of the last war solely because we considered the Republic at that moment as our enemy, or at least as a dangerous instrument in the hands of our enemies, and that our sole view in getting Negapatnam was to deprive the Dutch of the power of being hurtful to us in the Indies. That the position of affairs therefore now being perfectly inverted, the motive was at an end, and that the very same mode of reasoning which induced us to keep this settlement, now should induce us to restore it.

If we insisted on the equivalent, the Nation, (for it was their feelings, not his own that he was describing) would be under the idea that the reconciliation was imperfect and not sincere, and that Great Britain wished to avail herself of the consequences of a war, which both she and the Republic ought to efface entirely from their recollection at the instant of the political re-union, if it was intended that union should be permanent.

In regard to the Ninth, which was the great and sole point of our discussion, Mr. Vander Spiegel wished me to suggest the following idea to your Lordship—That the restoration of Negapatnam on the part of Great Britain should be stipulated in a distinct article, unconditionally, and the renewal of the Treaty of friendship and Alliance between the two countries stated as the equivalent.

The restoration of Negapatnam is to be separated from the abolition of the Sixth Article of Peace.

It is to be restored in an article by itself, and the Alliance to be the price of the restitution.

LETTER FROM SIR JAMES HARRIS TO THE MARQUIS OF
CARMARTHEN.

Hague, Jan. 4th, 1788.

MY DEAR LORD,—I have this moment received your kind letter of the 1st of January, and most sincerely return all the friendly wishes and congratulations it contains. I see every reason to hope that the year 1788 will go on as gloriously for England as 1787 ended; and if it does, as a labourer in the vineyard, I shall partake most feelingly of the good consequence our good Island will derive from it.

Negapatnam *shall not* be restored unconditionally, and the idea will, I trust, be broached no more. I hope the mode I propose in my long official letter of to-day will be adopted. The Article I drew up, and which I now wish to stand as one in the main Treaty, is calculated to conciliate and gratify both nations. If we wait till the Indian arrangements are concluded, before the alliance is to be signed, we risk losing both: and the conclusion of the latter will, beyond a doubt, facilitate the Negotiation for the first, which, requiring great management and coaxing, I have little hopes we shall carry through in the way we wish.

Mrs. Robinson wrote me word that you told her, some time ago, that I was appointed Ambassador; of course I am prepared for the *dignity*. While good things are showering down on my head, will none fall on that of my friend Gomm?* who wants them more than I do, and for whom I wish them much more than for myself. I do not mean by this, that I am not fully sensible of their value, but to convey my feelings on the situation of a man who has taken such a fatiguing share in my labours, and who is twenty years nearer the grave than I am. Adieu! my dear Lord.

* Secretary of Legation, and an old and faithful servant in his Department.

EXTRACT OF A LETTER FROM SIR JAMES HARRIS TO THE
RIGHT HON. WILLIAM PITT.

Hague, January 4, 1788.

DEAR SIR,—I am very much concerned to be forced
to say, that I see an utter impossibility of passing the
Alliance with the article which refers to the East India
arrangements, in the words in which alone I am instructed to give it in.   It is absolutely necessary, unless
we consent to abandon the measure entirely, to hold out,
in clear and precise terms, a disposition on our part to
restore Negapatnam, and forego the free navigation of
the Eastern Seas; and no expressions short of those I
took the liberty of sending over relative to these two
points will be sufficient to make the rest of the
treaty go down.   If, therefore, it really is considered
as a beneficial measure, it must be purchased at this
price.

An intimate acquaintance with the narrow habits and
rooted prejudices of the greater part of the Regents of
this country, made me, from the beginning, apprehensive
where the business would hitch, and it was on this
account that I have all along recommended so earnestly
(and still recommend), and, perhaps, too officiously, the
giving way, as far as it was possible, on these points.

I submit it, therefore, once more to your judgment,
whether we had not better give way, and gratify the
Dutch with a prospect of cessions, they are so pertina-
ciously bent on having than expose the whole system to
such an untimely check.   The fate of the Treaty
depends on the decision of the Cabinet on my despatch
of to-day.

The advanced state of the Prussian Treaty, and the
great facility with which the Berlin Ministry consented
to the alterations proposed by Their High Mightinesses,
forms in their minds a striking contrast.

France well knows how to avail herself of the situation
of men's minds.   She works artfully both on their fears

and hopes by different reports and insinuations; and, I confess, I dread if the Berlin Treaty is finally concluded before ours, that she will, at any price or rate, purchase the friendship of that Court, and by forming an Union here, exclude us more effectively than ever from this country.

LETTER FROM THE MARQUIS OF CARMARTHEN TO SIR JAMES HARRIS.

Whitehall, Feb. 1st, 1788.

MY DEAR SIR,—I almost thought the winds had determined to cut off all communication from Holland; they have, however, since relented, and six mails are arrived since Monday noon. I am particularly obliged to you for your private letter received by that which came this morning, and most sincerely hope that your reasoning, in respect to the Empress, may be verified by the event.* England and Prussia, by acting in concert with Holland properly disposed, may, I think, do a great deal.

The Marquis de La Luzerne is arrived; he does not appear remarkably brilliant: we have had a conference or two; he conducted himself, in general, well; full of general professions of friendship, but not disposed to enter into any particular subject which could lead further. His *début* in public was rather unfortunate, as he brought the Chevalier Ternan to Court, who certainly met with a very distinguished reception, being scarcely (if at all) spoken to by their Majesties, and not at all by myself, to whom the Ambassador presented him, or any other person, excepting foreigners. Similar attention was paid him by Lord Salisbury, Lord Southampton, and the rest of the English, one day last week at the Spanish Ambassador's, where we met him at

---

* Alluding to a wish expressed by Sir James Harris, that the Empress of Russia should join the Alliance. She chose to evince some disapprobation at the Anglo-Prussian interference in Holland.

dinner. Mons. de la Luzerne, blind as he is, must have perceived the impropriety he had been guilty of in introducing him; and I hear to-day the Chevalier does not intend to stay, or, what is more probable, will remain *incog.*

I am more displeased than surprised at what you say of Boers;* he did not improve, in my opinion, by being more known; and, perhaps, was more calculated to succeed at Bowood than either at St. James's or Whitehall. The King, speaking to him one day about Lynden, Boers seemed not to see a necessity for that Minister being recalled: for, though he had heard he was not agreeable to this Court, *yet he would not allow that to be a sufficient reason for the Republic recalling her Minister, as there might be no end to objections of that sort.*

Your account of my godson Jackson gives me great pleasure, and I beg you to remember me kindly to him, assuring him, at the same time, that he cannot hit upon a more likely method of securing my approbation than by meriting yours.

Believe me ever, my dear Sir,

Most sincerely and affectionately yours,

CARMARTHEN.

EXTRACT OF A DESPATCH FROM SIR JAMES HARRIS TO THE MARQUIS OF CARMARTHEN.

Hague, 5th Feb., 1788.

MR. VANDER SPIEGEL, in speaking on the subject of the Treaty, held the most friendly and most judicious language; he said he wished the Alliance should be so drawn up as to unite not only the two Governments, but the two Nations, in such a solid and compact manner, as to make it impossible for any intrigue, either foreign or domestic, to dissolve it; that he considered the cementing this National Union as the greatest blessing

* Boers had succeeded Lynden at the Court of St. James's

which could befall both countries, and that if it could be
got at by foregoing any advantages which, however
beneficial, might prevent its becoming sincere and permanent, he shewed they ought without hesitation to be
reciprocally sacrificed.

That, the union once formed, it was essential, in
order to consolidate and ensure their system of friendship, that the two countries should have a *continental
ally*; that on this point, from every reason, England
ought to take the lead, and it was his invariable advice
and opinion that the Republic should not fetter itself
with any engagements which might prevent it joining
with England in any continental system she might here-
after adopt.

Mr. Vander Spiegel, after discussing this subject,
in the able and friendly manner I have just mentioned
took a view of the present state of Europe in general,
and drew from it the most favourable consequences to
England and the Republic, if they followed up with
attention and assiduity their Continental interests.

He said the Sieur Caillard, French Chargé d'Affaires,
had been with him in the morning to give in M. de
Verac's letters of recall, and that his language, as well
as the accustomed Memorial presented on that occasion
to Their High Mightinesses, was *mielleux et bas*.

He condsidered that country (France) as in a state
of utter insignificancy, not because its finances and its
army were out of order, evils which in a country with
such resources could be easily retrieved under a good
Administration, but because he evidently saw that the
few men in France equal to its government were strug-
gling for power and high office, and that everything but
the gratification of their private ambition was neglected
and forgotten. That it was, therefore, highly expedient
to take advantage of this circumstance, and to act as if
we were aware it was a transient, not a lasting moment
of weakness and inactivity.

His reports from Russia, he said, agreed very much
with those I had received and communicated to him.

He thought, with good management, that the Empress might be detached from the Austrian connexion, at least, inasmuch as it drew her towards France. He agreed entirely with me in opinion, that if England, Prussia, and the Republic, were united in one and the same system, the Court of Petersburg would be more likely to join us, than before such a union was definitively concluded; and my opinion was founded on my knowledge of the Empress's character, which leaves me no doubt, that she is actuated in all her public conduct by motives of vanity alone, and that, as she well knows the most glory is likely to follow the strongest party, it is towards that she will ever incline.

LETTER FROM SIR JAMES HARRIS TO THE MARQUIS OF CARMARTHEN.

Hague, Feb. 15th, 1788.

My dear Lord,—It is certain the alarm has taken and is spreading here.* It is for this reason I have written my to-day's despatch in such clear and strong terms. Our conduct, if we mean (as we certainly do) to prevent this country from being annihilated, or from re-becoming a French province, must be framed not on *what ought to be,* but on *what is* the case, and this reasoning, the only rational one in politics, will apply to what I sent by Major on the Alliance, on Tuesday, as well as to what I wrote to you on the kind of measures it is expected by our party here we should adopt.

The King of Prussia has been so very cunning, and has smoothed so much beyond the expectations of every body the objections which were started here to the project he first sent, that if we do not gratify their whims, the Dutch will be sour and piqued, and our

---

* Alluding to our refusing to cede Negapatnam, on which point the Dutch were naturally susceptible.

Union will be without a honey-moon, which, in political treaties, lasts longer than in connubial ones.

Is the good account from Russia really true? does Kate relent? and has the Petruchio behaviour we so properly assumed tamed the Shrew of the North?

EXTRACT OF A DESPATCH FROM SIR JAMES HARRIS TO THE MARQUIS OF CARMARTHEN.

Hague, 22nd Feb., 1788.

I HAD the honour to receive your Lordship's despatch of the 17th instant, by Roworth, late in the evening of the 20th. I have passed almost the whole of the time which has since intervened with the Prince Stadtholder and Ministers of the Republic, and it would give me great and real pleasure, if it was in my power to say, that the results of my conferences were such as were likely to meet the wishes of His Majesty's servants. But His Highness the Prince Stadtholder, the Pensionary, and the Greffier, all declared in the most positive terms, that the Treaty certainly would not pass, unless an article was inserted expressing in a much more clear and positive manner a disposition on our part to forego the advantages we obtained by the last peace, than any instructions authorized me to subscribe to.

As the Prince of Orange, Mr. Vander Spiegel, and Mr. Fagel, are staunch friends to the English system, and as the influence of the first, and the official existence of the other two, is inseparably connected with the fate of the negotiation, it is impossible to suspect them of design or artifice, much less to impute to them any disinclination or ill-will towards the measure itself.

I employed all the solid and judicious reasonings with which the despatch I am now answering furnished me, and I omitted no one motive which suggested itself to me, to alter their opinions. I intimated that it was our ultimatum that they now had before their eyes, and that if it was not considered as sufficient, I was fearful the negotiation would be broken off.

The answer I received to this was, that it was not with their opinions and sentiments I had to contend; but those of the Nation at large; that with them, every thing I had said, had its due weight and force; that no doubt existed in their minds of His Majesty's friendly and good intentions; and that if the business could be determined by their voice, it would soon be brought to a short and favourable issue, but that this was not the case; and that considerable as their influence was, it was not equal to operate on the minds of men, strongly imbibed with prejudices, and actuated by doubts and suspicions.

Such was the state of the business at six this evening, when the Pensionary again desired me to call upon him; he confirmed to me all I had before heard; he said he had sounded the dispositions of the leading Deputies, as well of the towns as of the Provinces, and that he found them prejudiced and opinionative on the point in the extreme; that he was morally certain he should commit his influence in the Secret Committee, if he was to support the project as it now stood; that the Greffier would do the same, and that even the Stadtholder could not succeed in carrying it through, so rooted and inveterate were the prejudices of men's tempers on this point; that he was certainly ready, if I insisted upon it, to make the trial; that he would be responsible of the Greffier being equally ready, and he was sure the Prince of Orange would not hold back on this occasion, if I required his coming forward; that in consideration of the great obligations they were under to His Majesty, as hearty and firm friends to the cause, and (I use his expression), as friends personally attached and allied to me, they would not hesitate complying with my wishes if I insisted on it, but that their efforts would be ineffectual, and that I should only involve them in the fate of the negotiation, and give a violent and almost irrecoverable shock to their influence. He spoke with a degree of sensibility and feeling I never recollect to have seen in any person in a similar situation, and lamented in the most forcible terms, the possible failure of a system his heart was so fond of, and which he had looked upon as in a manner certain. After a good deal of discourse to this effect, (which I mention rather to shew his character than for any other purpose,) and after assuring me on his honour that I might be satisfied (however unreasonable the temper and disposition of his countrymen might seem), that the treaty would not pass with the Eleventh article.

Having now given your Lordship an exact account of this disagreeable hitch in the Negotiation, it remains for me to say, that if my opinion is of any weight, I will freely say it coincides perfectly with those I have just been stating; that I am satisfied from my having put the temper of this people so often to the test, that all that is alleged is strictly true. If the alliance fails, the influence we have recovered here will very soon drop, and the system we have taken such pains to restore be eclipsed in its dawn, and when it was on the point of being so lastingly fixed.

[On the 14th March, Sir James Harris was appointed Ambassador Extraordinary and Plenipotentiary to the States General of the United Provinces.]

EXTRACT OF A DESPATCH FROM SIR JAMES HARRIS TO THE
MARQUIS OF CARMARTHEN.

Hague, 14th March, 1788.

IN the course of yesterday and to-day the whole Hague have left their names at my door, a circumstance I should not think worth mentioning, if their earnestness to shew this mark of attention to His Majesty's Ambassador was not a proof of the extreme pleasure and satisfaction they feel at an event which they consider as a forerunner of a near and complete restoration of the ancient union and alliance between the two Nations. This sentiment was manifested in a still stronger and more convincing manner by the number of respectable Burghers and inhabitants of the city who were assembled round my carriages this morning, when I waited in ceremony on His Highness the Prince Stadtholder. The crowd was very great, and the expressions of joy and satisfaction loud and repeated. The Prince of Orange received me at the door of my carriage, and gave me the right hand; on coming into his closet he likewise gave me the place of rank, and when the doors were shut upon us, I made him the compliment your Lordship instructed me to make, and I delivered to him His Majesty's Letter of Credence. His Highness attended me on my departure to the door of my carriage, and I returned to my house in the same manner as I came. I then, though not with the same ceremony, and with only one carriage and a pair of horses waited on Her Royal Highness the Princess of Orange. The gentlemen of the Court received me at my carriage, and Her Royal Highness was waiting for me in her drawing-room. I made her a suitable compliment; took notice that she herself had laid the basis of the great work which now gave me the opportunity of paying my court to her by her magnanimity and heroic conduct ; and that while my Royal Master charged me to assure her of his sincere regard and affection, I could add the whole British nation were the greatest admirers of her virtues.

Her Royal Highness replied by the fullest expressions of her feelings for His Majesty's goodness ; that she should never forget the obligations she owed His Majesty, and that I might be satisfied she should hold it her duty to employ every means within her reach to form and cement a union between the countries. The whole of this day has been so very agreeable to me, both for the sake of the cause in which I am employed, as on account of my private and personal feelings, that I hope I may be pardoned having dwelt so long upon it.

[IN the course of a debate in the House of Commons on April 18th, 1788, a member of Opposition asked the Prime Minister what occasion there was for maintaining an Ambassador at the Hague, at so large an expense.

MR. PITT answered, it so happened that he held in his hand a paper, which he had the happiness to have received that evening in the House, the purport of which was to inform him, that the Secretary of Sir James Harris, our Minister at the Hague, had just arrived with the Treaty of Alliance concluded with the United States of Holland; and in the negotiation and effectual conclusion of which, that very able Minister had the merit of being principally instrumental. To that Minister the country was under the highest obligations, and, therefore, in the very moment of the most satisfactory conviction of the successful efforts of Sir James Harris, he hoped the honourable gentleman did not mean to state it as a matter of serious complaint, that the expense of the establishment of a Minister whose services to his country were inestimable, was too much for the public to bear, or that it was altogether unnecessary.—*Hansard's Parliamentary History*, A.D. 1788.

Sir James Harris went by the King's commands to England in May, and returned to the Hague on the 9th of June, bringing with him the following autograph letter from George III. to the Princess of Orange. Sir James was now directed to conclude a triple alliance with The States and Prussia as soon as possible. The French were actively engaged with Prince Henry of Prussia in thwarting this measure.]

LETTER FROM THE KING OF ENGLAND TO THE PRINCESS
OF ORANGE.

St. James's, ce 6 Juin, 1788.

MADAME, MA COUSINE,—Le retour du Chevalier Harris à la Haye me fournit l'occasion de vous renouveller les sentiments d'admiration que m'a inspiré votre conduite dans ces circonstances critiques. Heureusement le Traité d'Alliance avec les Provinces Uniés a rétabli un systême qui a toujours été avantageux aux deux pays, et vous me trouverez en tout temps prêt à resserrer ces liens par tout ce qu'on pourroit me proposer à cet effet qui ne seroit contraire aux intérêts de ma couronne.

Le Chevalier est mis en état de parler avec le Roi de Prusse, si Sa Majesté trouvait qu'il fut avantageux de dresser un Traité d'Alliance entre nos deux Couronnes avant que de sonder d'autres Puissances. Je vous prie d'être persuadée que je regarde l'Alliance que j'ai fait avec le Roi votre frère en ma qualité d'Electeur, comme un garant du maintien de la Constitution Germanique, et que je considèrerai une Alliance semblable entre nos deux Couronnes comme un moyen d'obliger les Cours de Vienne et de Versailles à désirer la continuation de la paix de l'Europe, et pour cet effet entre autres à travaillier à une paix en Turquie.*

Je ne cesserai, &c.

EXTRACT OF A LETTER FROM SIR JAMES HARRIS TO
MR. EWART.

Loo, 13th June, 1788.

As you have been apprised by Lord Carmarthen of the orders which I received from the King during my stay in England, you will, I am sure, not be sorry or surprised to hear that I have signed this morning the

* This letter was written by the King in the Closet, in the presence of Sir James Harris.— *Original Note.*

Prussian Contre-Projet, under the title of a " Provisional Treaty of Defensive Alliance." My instructions were *discretionary*, and they did not indeed positively prescribe to me to conclude this measure ; but I perceived the King of Prussia to be so wearied out by procrastination, so awake to suspicion, so liable to be wrought upon by persons who are enemies to our connexion, and by whom he has been, and will be surrounded, that I considered it as a matter of the last importance to put an end both to the pretext and effect of their intrigues by bringing matters to a point, and by irrevocably fixing the principles of the two Courts by a signature.

I hope you will not only approve what I have done, but that you will find it greatly contribute to facilitate the main negotiation which is still to be concluded, and the conduct of which will be entrusted entirely to you. If this had not been agreed to previous to my leaving London, I should certainly, notwithstanding the importance I attach to the measure, not have been prevailed upon to execute instructions which make me appear to have stepped in between you and the conclusion of a work solely your own.

I trust the Prussian Ministry, particularly Count Hertzberg will see it in this light, and not be induced to believe that our friend Alvensleben acted from any other motive than that of doing good.

EXTRACT OF A DESPATCH FROM SIR JAMES HARRIS TO THE MARQUIS OF CARMARTHEN.

Hague, 15th June, 1788.

I HAD the honour of acquainting your Lordship by a very few lines written in great haste on Friday last, that I had signed that day a Provisional Treaty of Alliance with his Prussian Majesty at Loo.*

* This transaction is spoken of by various writers as a masterpiece of diplomatic ability. Foreign Ministers were afterwards interdicted from

After a very long passage, under all the disagreeable circumstances of a contrary wind and rough sea, I got to the Hague on Monday the 9th instant, at four in the morning. As I found on my arrival the conduct of the French Ambassador and (particularly his Memorial on the Sixth Article of our Treaty) although it was universally disapproved, had given a kind of uneasiness, and as I was well aware of the proneness of our friends to take unreasonable alarm, I held it necessary immediately to announce my return to the President of the Week and Ministers of the Republic, to assure them of His Majesty's invariable affection for Their High Mightinesses.

I reiterated both to the Greffier and Mr. Catwyk (the President) the necessity of paying no attention whatever to the high language of France. (Mr. Vander Spiegel was gone to compliment the King of Prussia at Wesel.) I endeavoured to impress this sentiment on the very few persons whom I found at the Hague; and, after having used my best endeavours to prevent the States General from taking any false step during the absence of the Court and the Pensionary, I set out for Loo, where I arrived in the night of Tuesday the 10th, a few hours before the Prince and Princess of Orange, who had been to meet His Prussian Majesty at Cleves.

On my passage through the Hague I found that the messenger, with His Prussian Majesty's answer to your Lordship's despatch of May 14, had crossed me between Harwich and Helvoet. My Secretary, under the idea that I should be still in England on his arrival, had not taken copy of any of Mr. Ewart's principal despatches, and I could only learn from a private letter from that gentleman, and from the Ministerial answer made by the Prussian Ministry, that the King of Prussia was dissatisfied with the delay, full of doubts and suspicions, *and that there was a powerful party at Berlin, who were*

transacting business personally with the King, and when Lord Malmesbury was sent to Berlin in 1793, he went without any diplomatic rank to meet this difficulty.

employing every means to fix them on his mind, and to
indispose him against any connexion with England.

These circumstances, at least as far as related to the
unfavourable sentiments of His Prussian Majesty, and
to the intrigues of the French party at Berlin, were confirmed to me at Loo, and I learnt from the Princess of
Orange, whom I saw early on Wednesday morning, that
emissaries from France had been posted at Magdeburg,
Wesel, and Cleves; that they had been most active in
their attempts to impress His Prussian Majesty with the
most disadvantageous idea of England; and their great
aim was to persuade him, that His Royal Highness and
myself were joined in a plan to make all his measures
subservient to the purposes of England and the Republic, at the expense of his own interest and security.

Her Royal Highness added, that these persons had
been indefatigable in their pains to prejudice the King,
her brother, personally against me; that I had been described to him as a very artful and dangerous man, as
one who had always inclined to an Austrian connexion;
and they recalled to his mind my conduct at Petersburg,
to which he ought to attribute principally the very ungracious reception he met with from the Empress, and
the unsuccessful issue of his visit. The Princess of
Orange told me, that she had endeavoured to do away
the effect of these insinuations; that she was in hopes to
have succeeded to a great degree, but that she was
forced to apprize me that His Prussian Majesty was still
rather *afraid of me*, and that I had a most nice and
difficult game to play. Her Royal Highness, however,
was so highly satisfied with the instructions which I had
brought back, particularly so extremely gratified by the
letter I delivered her from His Majesty, that I was sure
of having her *whole support*, and this, notwithstanding
what I heard, encouraged me to proceed with confidence
and resolution.

His Prussian Majesty arrived at Loo at noon on Wednesday (the day after my arrival), and I employed the
very short interval which passed between my interview

with the Princess of Orange, and His Prussian Majesty's
arrival, in collecting my thoughts and preparing myself
as well as I was able under the circumstance of being
ignorant of what Mr. Ewart had written to your Lordship by his last messenger, to set my negotiation a-foot
in a right track.

Although the persons who attended the King, Bishopswerder, Bruhl, Gensaw, and Stein, were all well-disposed but the last, I was determined not to apply to any
of them for assistance or support, but address myself
directly to His Prussian Majesty; to state to him in a
plain and simple manner the substance of my instructions; to explain to him the only reasons which had produced delay; and then, if I observed that he gave credit
to what I said, to propose to him (according to my instructions) the option of either immediately signing the
Provisional Treaty, or else of postponing it till such
time as a general one on a broader basis, and to which
other Powers were to be invited to accede, could be prepared. I only desired the Princess of Orange that, before I saw the King, her brother, she would communicate
to him the letter she had received from His Majesty, as
I was certain this would go further to bring His Prussian Majesty back to a right way of thinking, than any
assistance which I might have obtained from the persons
in his suite, even supposing, which was far from being
the case, they were disposed to use their endeavours to
influence their Master in my favour. I kept my intentions a profound secret from everybody but the Princess; I resisted the repeated and urgent solicitation,
both of Mr. d'Alvensleben and several other persons at
Loo, with whom I had the habit of living in confidence;
and I appeared so entirely occupied with the festivity
which was going forward, as to make most people, as
they told me afterwards, suppose that I had no other
object in coming to Loo than to pay my court. The
only measure I took was to prevent Mr. Stein from
seeing the King *alone*, before I had my first audience,
and for this purpose I gave one hundred ducats to the

valet de chambre, who stood at the closet-door, and whom I had well known at Berlin, with a promise of as many more if he would refuse the *entrée* to Mr. Stein, under any pretence he thought proper, till the next morning.

I did not myself appear in the transaction with the King's valet de chambre, but carried it on through a person belonging to the Prince of Orange's Court, on whom I could depend, and it succeeded to my wishes, as Mr. Stein twice presented himself at the closet-door, and was twice sent away.

The whole day of the King's arrival was so taken up with receiving deputations, with festivity, balls and plays, and the Princess naturally was so happy to have the King, her brother, as much to herself as possible, that it was not till seven o'clock on Thursday morning that I could be admitted to an audience. I observed, on this occasion, precisely the plan I had laid down. I employed no art, or any words which bore the remotest reference to duplicity; I stated things precisely as they were, and after recapitulating, as well as my memory would allow me to do, all which had passed between the two Courts from the signature of the Convention on the 2nd October, 1787, to this day, I explained away, as I went along, every circumstance which could wear the appearance of delay or unwillingness on our part to unite ourselves by the closest political bonds with His Prussian Majesty.

The King of Prussia said, that what he had heard had given him the greatest pleasure; that he had always wished (and he referred to my recollection for his having said so many years ago) to see Great Britain and Prussia closely united; that since his accession, it had been his principal object; that besides political motives, which undoubtedly called for this connexion, he had such a personal respect and affection for my Royal Master as to make His Majesty's alliance, in every sense, the most desirable to him; that he did not see any reason why the two Courts should not immediately unite;

that, however, he must take some hours to reflect on what I had said, and that he would send for me when he had come to a resolution.

The day, however, was so crowded with amusements and *spectacles* of every kind, and the evening with illuminations and fireworks, that it was not till after midnight, while the Courts were dancing, that His Prussian Majesty could find a moment to speak to me by myself. He then made me walk with him behind the pavilion in the garden where the ball was, and there told me that he had revolved in his mind what I had said, that he was highly sensible of the King's confidence in leaving him the option on this occasion; and that he did not hesitate to declare, that he thought it preferable to conclude the Provisional Alliance with the Act of Guarantee for Holland, directly; and, in the mean time, to sound and consult with other Powers on the general and more extensive alliance, which, he said, had also his full and entire concurrence.

I now felt myself at liberty to speak to Mr. Alvensleben, which I immediately did, and we passed almost the whole of the remainder of the night in drawing up a full power for him (we had no Secretaries, and the King had left all his but one at Wesel), and in preparing the Secret Articles, and in having the Provisional Treaty copied out fair.

At nine the next day (Friday 13th), the King of Prussia sent for me into his closet; Mr. d'Alvensleben had laid before him the Draft of the Treaty and Secret Articles, and His Majesty said he had a remark or two to make, and a trifling alteration to propose, with which, he trusted, I should comply.

Being thus agreed as to the Articles, Mr. d'Alvensleben and myself went into my apartment in the palace; and, in presence of the Great Pensionary, Mr. Vander Spiegel, proceeded to the signature, and we entitled the Treaty, *The Provisional Treaty of Loo.*

Nothing could be greater than the satisfaction of the Prince and Princess of Orange, and the Pensionary. The

Prince, when I communicated it to him, took me in his arms, and said, " Je vous dois mon Stadthouderat et mon bonheur."

I think, my Lord, I have now nearly related to your Lordship every material circumstance which has passed. The result of the whole is this, that I found His Prussian Majesty in a very unpropitious moment, wearied out with procrastination, and awake to suspicions of every kind; a violent fresh attempt had been made by the French Cabal at Berlin to indispose him against England, which had succeeded in giving him the false impressions of our system, and the strong personal prejudices against me; that the emissaries of this Cabal had been relayed (if I may use the expression) on the road, and that one of them (Stein) had actually followed him to Loo (for I do not take notice of Mons. de Maillebois and Prince Galitzin, who had intruded themselves there for the same purpose), as it required little trouble to keep them uninformed, and at a distance. I left the King of Prussia totally and radically cured of all these misgivings, under a full conviction of the fairness of our proceedings towards him, penetrated with sentiments of grateful respect and affection for His Majesty, with the highest opinion of the integrity and abilities of his confidential servants, and determined to connect himself still closer with His Majesty than he has already done by the Treaty signed the 13th. In return, he only required that we should immediately consent to open a negotiation for the main Treaty at Berlin; and I confess, my Lord, I am particularly anxious that this should be complied with, as I have a feeling of delicacy towards Mr. Ewart, to whom the whole of the merit of this business belongs, and from whom I should be extremely sorry to take any other part of it, except such as derives from the casual circumstance of my being at Loo, and from having had it in my power to execute fortunately the instructions I received when last in England.

I shall conclude this despatch by saying, that if I had

observed a different line of conduct, if I had held off in my conferences with the King, or refused decidedly to pledge myself, that the Treaty of Alliance on a more general plan between the Courts of Berlin and London should be immediately brought forward; in short, if I had, under any pretext whatever, however well founded, evaded the signature of the Provisional Treaty, refused to pledge myself for the signature of the Definitive one, or put off the negotiation to a distant day, all the dangerous impressions our enemies have attempted to give would have fixed themselves in the mind of the King of Prussia, and every after attempt to do them away would have come too late; we should have lost the Court of Berlin, and, undoubtedly, with it (if we consider the revival of the French intrigues here, which correspond precisely with their intrigues at Berlin) our footing so lately recovered in this country, and we should have been reduced to the *same isolated situation* we stood in some time ago, with the additional aggravation of having awakened the resentment and jealousy of our vindictive, implacable, and powerful enemies.

EXTRACT OF A DESPATCH FROM MR. EWART TO SIR JAMES HARRIS.

Berlin, 18th June, 1788.

My dear Sir,—The arrival of Slater, yesterday, with your letters of the 13th, relieved me from a state of inexpressible anxiety and uneasiness, in which I had spent two sad days and nights, without having received the smallest information myself, either from England or elsewhere, relative to your negotiation; while I was overwhelmed with the reproaches of Count Hertzberg, who having got very early advices of your being provided with full powers to sign our Treaty, insisted that a plot had been laid to surprise and deceive his Prussian Majesty, contrary to his interests, as well as to the justice he owed to his own Cabinet.

When I went to him, immediately on receiving your letters, I still found him equally enraged at what he said he must ever consider as an unfair and unwarrantable proceeding, though the King had transmitted to him the preceding evening the original papers, together with his own and Alversleben's commentary, and he declared he was preparing a report to prove to His Majesty that he had been surprised. But I rejoice to inform you, that, with the assistance of your ample explanations, which I read over and over again to him, I succeeded in appeasing his resentment by working on his Patriotic feelings, in representing to him the infinite value of the measure in itself, however irregular or unfair the manner of concluding it might be, which did not at all affect the essential object. He likewise admitted that it would effectually put an end to the French intrigues about the King's person, as nothing could possibly be so mortifying to that Court as to have a Treaty directed solely against them, concluded by Prussia in Holland, and in the House of the Prince of Orange, circumstances which they would never forgive. On this occasion he expressed his surprise at the incredible change that had happened in the King's dispositions, especially in regard to the French Court, during his short stay at Loo, comparing the orders he had given at his departure, with his commentary on the Treaty.

Count Finckenstein, though extremely irritated, signed the report, only observing, that since the thing was done, there was no help for it.

EXTRACT OF A DESPATCH FROM SIR JAMES HARRIS TO
THE MARQUIS OF CARMARTHEN.

Hague, 20th June, 1788.

THE French emissaries, whom I mentioned to your Lordship in my last, as being here in great numbers, begin to disperse, and upwards of twenty of them have left the Republic within these four days. Mons. de St. Priest, who had stood out with me in a point of etiquette, has also given way, and consented to make me the first visit, as well as Madame de St. Priest to Lady Harris, on both of which I insisted. All these proceedings clearly denote that they consider their cause as desperate, and, of course, point out to us the favourable moment for consolidating the great system in which we are fortunately embarked.

The Patriots and French certainly feel as much disappointment as despair on this occasion; they had placed the greatest confidence in the success of their intrigues, and reckoned on the effects they thought themselves sure of producing on His Prussian Majesty's mind by the dexterous agents they had employed to indispose him against England. My return, and the signature of the Treaty at Loo, were so sudden, that they had no time to oppose me, and the measure was agreed on and concluded before they knew it was in agitation.

EXTRACT OF A DESPATCH FROM SIR JAMES HARRIS TO THE MARQUIS OF CARMARTHEN.

Hague, 24th June, 1788.

I HAD the honour to receive yesterday your Lordship's despatch of the 20th. It is with the greatest pleasure that I hear, that those accounts which I sent by Heslop of what passed during my stay at Loo have met His Majesty's approbation. Every information which I have been able to obtain, since my return from thence, goes to prove, that no pains had been spared by the French to indispose His Prussian Majesty against an English connexion; that they had considered their plans so well laid as made their success very probable, of which they were so sanguine, that they had committed themselves greatly by the assurances they had given to their party here; and Mons. de St. Priest was so per-

suaded that my conferences with His Prussian Majesty
would lead to nothing, that he would not believe the
fact of the Provisional Alliance being signed when it
was mentioned, and treated the Russian and Austrian
Ministers, who were the first to carry the news to him,
as credulous and misinformed; now, however, that he is
compelled to acknowledge the truth of what he heard
from them, he is embarrassed and vexed, and declares
to those about him, that, for many reasons, his Embassy
must now end. I have strong reason to believe he will
be ordered to withdraw before the Stadtholderian Court
comes back, and that only a Chargé des Affaires will be
left here.

[The defensive Treaty of Alliance between Great
Britain and Prussia was grounded on the Provisional
Treaty of Loo, and was signed at Berlin, August 13th,
1788.]

LETTER FROM MR. PITT TO SIR JAMES HARRIS.

Downing Street, Friday Night, July 17th, 1788.

MY DEAR SIR,—Mr. Fraser has this instant brought
me your despatches. Though in the midst of more business than usual, I cannot let the packet go without expressing how much I am concerned at the account of
your health, which is so interesting to us all. You have
so good a right to holidays whenever you want them,
that there cannot be a moment's difficulty as to leave
of absence, though you will easily conceive how much
we shall regret the necessity, both from the cause of it
and the effects. I am the more anxious to write these
few hasty lines, as Lord Carmarthen is out of town. A
Westminster canvass, in addition to the usual plagues of
office will account for their haste. Similar reasons, and
those only, have prevented my writing to you for some

time past on many points on which I have much wished to do it.

I am, with great truth, dear Sir,

Your obedient and faithful servant,

W. PITT.

EXTRACT OF A LETTER FROM SIR JAMES HARRIS TO THE MARQUIS OF CARMARTHEN.

July 18th, 1788.

MY DEAR LORD,—I am somewhat better, but so exhausted with the going out this morning, and with writing since, that I have scarce strength left to tell you so. I *now* hope I shall be able to weather the storm till October ; but then you must indeed let me lie in dock for a few months, or I founder.

LETTER FROM THE MARQUIS OF CARMARTHEN TO SIR JAMES HARRIS.

Whitehall, July 22, 1788.

MY DEAR SIR,—I not only sincerely lament your present indisposition, but still more the appearance of a single doubt in your mind of the possibility of your ease and convenience not being fully attended to on this side the water. I was at Tunbridge when your last letters reached me, but was very happy to find that Mr. Pitt had written to you immediately on the receipt of them. In case you do not find yourself better very soon, I could wish you would have some medical advice from hence, as, perhaps, an English physician would do more good to your constitution in a few days than the best Dutch one in double the time. I do not wish to worry you with a single word of political business, so only beg of you to keep up your spirits, and take every possible care of yourself.   Believe me, &c.

[On the 19th of September, 1788, Sir James Harris was raised to the Peerage, as the reward of his services during this Mission. Without his energy and perseverance, the utter discouragement in which he found the Stadtholder and his party, and the lukewarmness of our own Government, who looked upon the state of Holland as hopeless, must have delivered that country to the French. He had now secured to England (before isolated) two powerful allies. Under the " old order of things " our political position was immensely improved by these events; but the " old order" had but a few months to exist, and the great French Revolution of 1789 rendered all past policy nugatory.]

LETTER ADDRESSED BY THE STATES GENERAL TO THE KING OF ENGLAND, ON THE DEPARTURE OF LORD MALMESBURY.

Septembre, 1778.

SIRE,—Ce n'est pas sans regret que nous avons appris par la lettre que Votre Majesté nous a fait l'honneur de nous écrire le 20 du mois passé, qu'elle a trouvé bon d'accorder au Lord Malmesbury, son Ambassadeur Extraordinaire auprès de nous, la démission qu'il lui a demandée en cette qualité. Ce Ministre nous a donné pendant tout le cours de sa mission des preuves si signalées de ses talents et de son zèle infatigable à rétablir et à resserrer de plus en plus les nœuds de la bonne intelligence et de l'étroite union qui subsistent actuellement entre Votre Majesté et notre République, il a d'ailleurs si bien réussi par ses qualités personnelles à se concilier l'estime et l'affection générale que nous ne craignons pas d'assurer Votre Majesté, que nous partageons avec le public les regrets que son départ occasionne.

Nous ne perdrons jamais le souvenir des services essentiels que le Lord Malmesbury, pendant la durée de sa residence auprès de nous, a rendus aux deux nations;

services qui favorisés par la Providence ont contribué à rétablir la Constitution de cet Etat sur sa véritable base, à assurer le bonheur de ses habitants en rendant à la Sérénissime Maison d'Orange le libre exercise de tous ses droits, et à avancer la gloire de Votre Majesté et de son règne.

[The following letter was written to Lord Malmesbury in Switzerland, where he went to recruit his health. He returned to England, and continued to support his old friends in Parliament in accordance with the agreement he made with Mr. Pitt on going to the Hague. In consequence of the King's mental malady, the Regency Bill was brought forward by Ministers, and Lord Malmesbury voted with forty-seven Peers against it. The King recovered and the Bill was dropped.]

LETTER FROM MR. FOX TO LORD MALMESBURY.

St. James's Street, 27th Nov., 1788.

MY DEAR LORD,—I hear a messenger is going to you, and, hurried as I am at this crisis, I take the first opportunity of letting you know that I think your presence in England may be of exceeding service whatever turn affairs may take. I am sure if they take the turn which I expect, I should feel myself very much in want of your advice and assistance upon some very important points.

I am very sincerely, yours ever,

C. J. FOX.

1790.

EXTRACT OF A LETTER FROM LORD MALMESBURY TO THE DUKE OF PORTLAND.

Spring Gardens, Sunday, October 3rd, 1790.

MY DEAR LORD,—I had fully intended to have come this week to Welbeck, and am vexed that various reasons not worth entering into prevent it. Besides the pleasure I always have when I am with your Grace, I should have been happy to have talked over with you the several events which have occurred since I saw you last, and which, from their nature, are not only likely to become subject of serious discussion at home, but also in their consequence to affect materially the interests and situation of this country abroad. My reasonings are confined to Foreign politics alone; neither my information nor my habits apply to any other.

I understand that a great deal of conversation passed between us and our allies, before we could agree to the terms on which the negotiation at Reichenbach should be opened. In most points, England and Holland were of the same opinion. Peace on the Continent, through their Mediation, without any of the Belligerent Powers being losers or gainers by the war, was their object. Prussia was less moderate, and disposed to mix up views of aggrandisement with the general pacification. Thorn and Dantzic and a restoration of part of Galicia to the Poles, was a point long insisted on by the Cabinet of Berlin. This both England and the Dutch disapproved, and Prussia at last, though reluctantly, renounced it under a kind of conditional clause you will see inserted in a copy of the Treaty printed in the newspapers. The preservation of the Low Countries to the house of Austria, was a still more difficult point to carry. England *very wisely* insisted upon it; but the Dutch, still sore from the behaviour of the late Emperor* towards them, were not disposed to consider it as so necessary a measure; and several messengers past and discussions took place, before the article on this point, as it now stands in the declarations of Reichenbach could be drawn up in a way to meet the concurrence of the Allies. When, however, they were once agreed, and their pretensions made known, the King of Hungary was not in a situation to contend with them. He, therefore, almost without a struggle, consented to a peace with the Porte on the principles of the reestablishment of a strict *status quo* as before the war, with the express condition of abandoning Russia; to secure the ancient constitution of the Belgic Provinces, and not to employ coercive measures against them unless every other should fail; and the Allies (under whose guarantee the whole Treaty was to be secured) should admit force to be necessary for recovering the sovereignty of them. These are the outlines of what passed at Reichenbach. The Empress of Russia was immediately informed of it by the King of Hungary, and invited by the Mediating Powers to imitate his example of moderation and forbearance, and it was insinuated that in case of a refusal, a Prussian army would be assembled on the frontiers of Courland. Her Imperial Majesty replied, that, as the Porte had declared war on her, it ought not to be expected that she should be told the terms on which she should make peace; and she, at the same time, held the language of moderation and complaisance, particularly to England, and that her regard for the three Courts, who were ready to employ their good offices towards a general pacification, would go much further with her than menace. Her Imperial Majesty, at the same time, availed herself very ably of the early account she had of this transaction; and well aware from the King of Sweden being in Finland, that he could not be so soon informed as she was, of the upshot of the conferences at Reichen-

---

* Vide Sir J. Harris's Correspondence from the Hague, alluding to the Emperor's aggressions.

bach, she directly proposed to him Peace on the very terms she knew the Allies meant to obtain it for him. To this he very naturally consented; the terms were the very best he could expect, and it flattered his vanity much more to obtain them through himself, than under the influence of any Foreign Power. This separate Peace took us and Prussia equally unawares; it deranged the whole plan, and may very materially affect our interests.

The King of Sweden had for these last six months asked naval assistance from England, and pecuniary assistance from Prussia; and both Courts had kept him in suspense about granting what was asked of them. As, however, the object of the meeting at Reichenbach was to separate Austria and Russia, and by all possible means to distress the latter, it was at last agreed to give both. A squadron of seventeen ships was ready to sail in the Downs; and the King of Prussia had actually remitted one-half of the subsidy asked by Sweden, when the news was received that the Peace had been signed in Finland. This, as I before said, deranged the general plan, and particularly defeated our great object of insulating Russia, and of securing one of the Baltic Powers to our system. It is now *as* probable that *Sweden* will unite with Russia as with us; and that a League between the three Courts of Petersburg, Stockholm, and Copenhagen, under the name of a Family Compact (for each of them are governed by a Sovereign of the House of Holstein), will take place. The idea has been agitated before. It is, I know, apprehended here, and we are not without fears, that the King of Hungary may consider the Convention at Reichenbach a compulsory measure, to which he was forced to give way from circumstances, and break it in the same manner as Francis the First did the Treaty at Madrid, and join the Empress of Russia against Prussia, as soon as he has settled his disputes in the Netherlands, and signed his definitive Treaty with the Turks. The balance will then stand thus: the two circum-Baltic

Powers, and the two Imperial Courts against England, Prussia, and Holland,—rather an unequal war both by land and sea.

This seems to be nearly the situation of our affairs on the Continent, which, though not quite so good a one as I should wish, or could have hoped for, yet I should by no means consider it as materially a bad one.

France, too, is disposed at least to effect a fulfilling of the stipulations of the Family Compact, and to make a show of furnishing succours; but from France I fear very little, as I have the best reason for believing that country on the eve of a civil war.* I am informed that the Count d'Artois and the Prince de Condé have been for a long time preparing themselves for an attempt to effect a counter-revolution; that they have employed emissaries, and expended large sums of money in the Lyonnois, Franche Comté, les Trois, Evêchés, and Burgundy; and that they intend, on or about the 15th of October,† to enter France from the side of Turin, at the head of a considerable body of troops, partly raised by themselves, partly furnished by the King of Sardinia.   They have been entreated by the Queen and *Monsieur* to delay it, as they are not yet ready in Paris and the neighbourhood; and particularly the Queen wishes them to wait till the King of Hungary has got his army assembled in the Low Countries; but Count d'Artois will not listen to this, and is determined to proceed on the day I mention. He will probably lead his followers to certain destruction; as, besides his measures being ill-taken, and not ripe for execution, his eagerness has created a jealousy in the Queen and Monsieur, that it is for himself, *not for the King*, that he is working; and that they shall not be better off if he succeeds than under the rule of the National Assembly.   This, which is, I am almost positive, the true situation of France, puts it as a Power quite out of the line, and it is not worthy to be reckoned either as a friend or foe.   It is on the eve of becoming a

* The great French Revolution had begun the year previous.
† This project was not carried into effect.

scene of bloodshed and massacre, which it is impossible to think of without concern and sorrow, however it may serve our interests or gratify our prejudices.

I have now, my dear Lord, very much, I fear, at the expense of your patience, and very little to your edification, gone over, to the best of my knowledge, all the ground of the present dispute, and the relative situation of the other Powers of Europe to that of England. The result is, that I think we are trifling away the high situation in which this country stood; that we are going to change it from one of security, honour, and power, to one of dilemma, if not of peril; that if this happens, it will have become so from inability and neglect; from carelessness and indecision in our conduct towards our allies, and from petulance and flippancy in that towards our enemies,

I have not seen or sought either the Prince or Duke of York, though they have been both in town; neither have I heard a word about their concerns since I saw you last.

EXTRACT OF A LETTER FROM LORD MALMESBURY TO THE
DUKE OF PORTLAND.

Coblentz, October 14th, 1791.

My DEAR LORD,—I found the Duke of York—what I ever have found him when serious and important business came before him—sincere, correct, and open. Had I seen any probability of success, I should have let *him* conduct the business, and endeavoured to have given *him* the whole merit of it with the Prince.* But one day at Berlin was sufficient to shew me its impracticability. It therefore remained only for me not to expose the Prince to a refusal, and to satisfy him that the Duke of York had never lost sight of his interest, and that if anything

---

* Lord Malmesbury was earnestly requested by the Prince of Wales to endeavour to assist in negotiating a loan for him at Berlin, where the Duke of York was about to be married.

could have been done, he would have done it himself.
I was, however, very careful in my conversation with the
Duke, to avoid anything which could intimate that a
contrary idea could exist in the Prince's mind; and as I
left him completely satisfied that he possessed his brother's friendship fully and completely, I trust the Prince
will, on his side, receive the Duke when he returns to
England under the entire conviction that he deserves his
confidence and affection as much as ever. If I have
obtained this point, and prevented the Prince from gratuitously committing himself, I shall not regret the long
and disagreeable journey I have just ended.

The ceremony of the wedding was rather precipitate;
no positive news of the Great Seal being put to the King's
permission was received, and the Ratification of the articles signed by Mr. Ewart and the Prussian Ministers
was not returned. The King of Prussia had fixed the
day, and the Duke of York, and, I must say, the Duchess,
were too eager and impatient to wait. I am afraid Ewart
will be reprimanded; but the neglect and delay were on
their side, and no real blame rests with Ewart. I believe
and hope she will make him happy, and please in England. She is far from handsome, but lively, sensible, and
very tractable, and if only one tenth part of the attachment they now shew for each other remains, it will be
very sufficient to make an excellent ménage.

Both the King and Queen have written the kindest
and most affectionate letters to the Duke and Duchess
during the whole of this business, and I am sure you will
not disapprove my having prevailed on the Duke to leave
the nomination of the Ladies who are to be about the
Duchess wholly to their Majesties' choice; besides the
good effect of such an attention, it will relieve the Duke
from the embarrassment of applications, and particularly
such as might be suggested to the Prince to make him,
—which it would be difficult for him to refuse, and from
the complexion of the Prince's society, it might be by no
means advisable for him to grant—as it is of the last consequence (and of this the Duke is fully persuaded) that

the Duchess should begin well and under the most respectable impressions possible.

I believe I have said everything essential relative to
the main object of my going to Berlin, and to the Duke
of York's marriage. I shall now, in as few words as possible, state the situation in which it appears to me that
Court stands with respect to ours. I find that during
and since the negotiation at Reichenbach,* there have
been several points of disagreement between the two
Courts. It would exceed the bounds of a letter to give
a detailed account. In general, both sides seem to have
been to blame. The King of Prussia, or rather Mons.
Hertzberg for him, was perpetually forming new plans,
sometimes against the House of Austria, and sometimes
on Poland. As they are all of them plans of ambition,
they bore no reference either to our alliance, or to the
system on which it was formed, and on these grounds we
might have argued. If the King of Prussia was inconsistent in his proposals, we were equally so in our manner of treating them; we seemed to approve at one time,
at another to reprobate them, and often neglected, for
months together, taking any notice of them. On the
single point relative to the Russian Peace with the Porte,
we were agreed from the beginning, and this measure
was as much a measure of our interest as that of Potzdam. My sentiments on it are not unknown to your
Grace. I thought it at the time a measure of sound
policy, and everything I have seen since I have been on
the Continent makes me lament the weakness of our
Ministry in giving way on that occasion; we have
lost a powerful friend, and made a powerful enemy by
it.

It is foreign to the object of this letter to dwell on
the consequences it will produce on the side of Prussia.

---

* The Treaty of Reichenbach was entered into in June 1790. The British, Prussian, and Dutch Ministers assisted at the Conferences. Peace was
concluded between Austria and the Porte. Its object also embraced the
settlement of the differences between the Emperor Leopold and his subjects
in the Netherlands. Russia kept aloof from the Convention, and could not
be induced to make peace with Turkey.

As to Russia, we have for the time, if not irrevocably, lost it. Our influence, which before was all powerful, is entirely gone, and His Prussian Majesty is piqued at our desertion of him, as he calls it, and has formed a connexion with the Court of Vienna in direct opposition to our interest.

His Prussian Majesty, although as gracious, and even kind to me as possible, studiously avoided talking to me on public concerns; and he observes the same reserve with His Majesty's Minister, who, instead of being as he was a few months ago, in the whole secret, and in a manner the Director of the Prussian Cabinet, is now neither consulted nor trusted. How long this unnatural connexion with Austria may last, after the first moment of pique against us is over, I do not pretend to say. It is very unpopular at Berlin, and Bishopswerder being a foreigner, is loudly murmured against, and taxed with having sold his Master to the Emperor. In the meanwhile, however, it has broken up our continental system, and let us down from that high situation in which we stood. It appears very clear to me, from some confidential communications which were made to me, that Lord Grenville was the cause of Mr. Pitt's giving way,* and that he acted not from the reason which was given—the nation's being against it, but from its being his fixed opinion that we should not interfere at all in the affairs of the Continent.

LETTER FROM LORD MALMESBURY TO THE DUKE OF PORTLAND.

Coblentz, Oct. 20th, 1791.

MY DEAR LORD,—I promised you in my last to give you some accout of what the swarm of French, now

----

* March 30th, the King sent a Message to Parliament, recommending a Naval Armament as a check upon Russia, who at that period was pushing her conquests in Turkey to such a degree as to threaten the annihilation of the Ottoman Empire. Addresses approving the Message were carried through both Houses, but the public feeling being strong against provoking a war with Russia the plan was abandoned.

living here, are about, and what is likely, from my observation, to be the result of their operations. It is no
very easy matter to make this clearly out, or to follow,
with any degree of perspecuity, a plan conducted by
people under the influence of almost every passion which
can agitate the human mind.

The most steady and reasonable amongst them appear to be the two Princes. Monsieur eminently
deserves this character, and the Count d'Artois is very
much reclaimed from that dissipated and flighty reputation he once deserved.

The two Princes are supposed to be at the head of the
Noblesse, and they are assisted by a Council composed
of Mons. de Calone, the Marshals Broglie and Castries,
Jaucort, Haseland, and Vaudreuil, Lieutenant-Generals,
the Prince of Nassau and the Prince Xavier of Saxe,
commonly called Le Comte de Lusace.

Calonne* is the active and leading man, and all
their schemes are strongly marked with the impression
of his own imagination and sanguine character. Their
object goes to interest all the different Sovereigns of
Europe in their cause, to obtain, according to the position
or faculty of each Court, pecuniary or military assistance, and to enter France at the head of an army,
preceded by a new project of Constitution in the form
of a Manifesto.

They here consider the friendly assurances coming
from almost all the different powers of Europe, as so
many sure means of recovering their ground in France;
but they seem to have forgot, that, as yet, they have
obtained nothing but professions; that each of these
Courts is actuated by different interests; that they are
jealous of each other; that there is no coalition between
them, and no union of measures; no convention how the

---

* Monsieur de Calonne was Minister of Finance for three years subsequent to M. Neckar's dismissal in 1784; but the latter's Comte Rendu,
which had made all the financial abuses public, and the fierce opposition of
the privileged classes, who were exempted from taxation, rendered all his
plans of improvement abortive, and he was compelled to resign, and retired
to England in 1787.

assistance of each is to be given, or in what proportion: and that to bring about such a concert, so as to make it useful, requires time, and, I fear, abilities much greater than belong to any one here.

Such is the outline of their plan, as far as I can collect from the conversation of a set of people whose minds, as I before said, are agitated to the last degree. On the whole, however, they highly deserve compassion. They are in general brave and high-minded, and bring a much larger share of good humour and pleasantry into society than I believe any other nation in a similar situation would do. The two Princes, I must repeat, are the most striking instances of this truth, and it is impossible to see them, and the evenness of their temper and patience, without being anxious and interested about them. *They* are too wise to hope for immediate relief, and, I believe, think but ill of the prospect they have before them. But they consider it their duty to keep up the spirits of their followers, who amount in this town and the neighbourhood to between two and three thousand Gentlemen.

———

[The following papers are taken from a Diary which Lord Malmesbury appears to have commenced whilst travelling for his pleasure in Italy, from which country, the state of parties in England soon recalled him.]

DIARY.

Turin, May 5, 1792.

Great preparations for war—Semonville refused as Minister of the Nation by the King of Sardinia—stopped at Alessandria, and passports denied him—La Lande (Chargé des Affaires de France) instructed to say, that if these are not sent, the French shall consider it as an act of hostility—King of Sardinia persists—La Lande goes away without taking leave, May 3rd, 1792.

King of Sardinia behaves with great dignity and spirit—does business himself—sent troops to his frontiers, 6000 men to Nice, 14,000 to Chambery—his whole army, 35,000 men, militia (which are very good) included—his revenue 1,200,000—a million two hundred thousand pounds—his Minister, Mons. de Hautefort, for Foreign Affairs—Trevor's politics rather gloomy.

Florence, May 20.

Mr. Udney, Consul at Leghorn, read me a letter from a Corsican to Paoli, informing him that the Empress of Russia had certainly views on Corsica—that Tamara was at Leghorn for the purpose of effectuating them, and that her fleet, if it came into the Mediterranean, would be with this intent. Udney gave credit to this report, and he told me that in general the Empress was doing everything in her power to increase her trade and her power in the Mediterranean.

He mentioned to me an ex-Jesuit of Paraguay, whom we had, through him, taken into our pay (on the Nootka Sound business), and given 300l. a-year to, from his promising to raise a revolt in South America, if necessary

—Lord Harvey not very deep in politics, though desirous of doing well.

MANHEIM, MAY 22.

WITH Kinckel,* his bearings are not in favour of the conduct of the Aristocrats, though his principles are with them—he accuses them of having drawn an immense number of French after them by promises they cannot perform, and by spreading reports they know to be false. His idea is also that the Emperor will take Bavaria, give Alsatia and Lorraine to the Elector Palatine, Prussia to have Thorne and Dantzic and the Palatinate of Posen, and the Empress of Russia to have her influence and interest restored her in Poland.

Kinckel seems to believe that we and Prussia understood each other, and that His Prussian Majesty was in better humour with us than when I saw him at Berlin—Bishopswerder all-powerful—in Holland things do not go so well as they ought—Welderen, Lynden de Blytterswyk, and that set,† counteract the Great Pensionary, and neither the Prince nor Princess of Orange have the spirit to support him—he could not explain to me her journey to Brunswick.

The Courts of Vienna and Berlin had communicated their Alliance (signed in February, 1792) to England and Holland, with a note, saying, it was purely a connexion of friendship, &c.—The public Treaty is certainly nothing more. The Maritime Powers, Russia, and the Electorate of Saxony, are invited to accede— probably there are secret Articles—in the body of the Treaty—the French affairs are not mentioned. Kinckel said that some failure in the Court bankers at Petersburg had considerably affected Hope at Amsterdam.

---

* Kinckel was an Admiral in the Dutch service, and was also employed in the diplomatic line by the Stadtholder. He bore a high character for talent and integrity.

† Men in the French interest.

COBLENTZ, MAY 26.

THE PRINCES, since their residence in this Electorate, have received two millions of livres from the King of Prussia, two millions from the Empress, a promise of the same sum from the Emperor, but not yet paid above a half; a promise of 1,200,000 livres from Naples, 500,000 of which is paid; and a million and a half from Spain, of which the half is kept to provide for the emigrants there.

Their expenses amount yearly to 8,200,000 livres. They have 18,000 men in pay, besides others to provide for, and emigrants as they arrive. Many of the Noblesse come on foot—live in the most frugal way. This from Fancourt, who seemed to think that there was little doubt of the success of the " enterprise" formed by the Great Powers against France; but he was doubtful whether it had not a double object, and that besides the restoration of a regular Government in France, a dismemberment was not intended. This, he said, besides hurting the feelings of the Princes, would essentially hurt their future situation, and fling an odium on the whole body of emigrants—that they explained themselves very fully on this point to the different Powers—that the Court of Vienna *had* declared in express terms that she would take nothing—but that this was previous to the declaration of war by the French against the King of Hungary—and that since this event Kaunitz* was not so clear in his assurances on this subject. To avoid, however, any possibility of blame, or a charge of connivance being attributed to them, the Princes had just sent a Memorial to the Court of Vienna, to be communicated to that of Berlin, in which they entered very fully on this matter, urged their hopes that no *division* was thought of, and that it would tarnish the glory of the Intervening Powers, and defeat their (the Princes')

* Prime Minister at Vienna.

object. This Memorial, drawn up by Calonne, is, as
Fancourt assured me, a *chef-d'œuvre;* but he doubted
its effect. He seems to think it fair that the expenses
the Powers might incur by an armament should be
defrayed them, and that to this the Princes would
pledge themselves. The truth, however, seems to be,
that the Princes are not considered or treated in this
negotiation as Principals; and their great fault has,
from the beginning, been, that they have acted as
such, without the power or means. They will certainly
be comprised in the general arrangement, but be
allowed to take very little share, and to claim very
little merit, in the settling of it. With this they will
be dissatisfied and disappointed; as, besides the hopes
Mons. de Calonne and other sanguine friends of theirs
gave them, that in the event they would be restored
to a higher situation than that from which they were
driven, they also stand engaged to provide for a very
numerous body of friends, who have either followed
or accompanied them in their emigration. These
friends (a very few excepted) rate their services very
high, and expect to be amply repaid for the real or
supposed sacrifices they have made; and this it certainly will not be in the power of the Princes to do;
of course admitting the interposition of the Foreign
Powers to be attended with complete success, the
Princes will necessarily be exposed to numerous reproaches and accusations of having either originally
deceived or ultimately abandoned their followers.

I talked with *Monsieur** on this point. He did
not admit (to the extent I am satisfied he ought) that
the Foreign Powers are acting without consulting or without any concert with them; yet he could not but confess, that their communications towards them were
incomplete, and confidence far from entire. His feelings were, however, perfectly right. He said *he* had
often advised the being less liberal in promises to the
emigrants who joined them, less confident of success,

* Afterwards Louis XVIII.

and more cautious in their general language, but he had been overruled. He added, on my saying his situation was certainly ameliorated since I saw him last, that it certainly was; "but," said he, "when I hear of the success of the Austrians, and of the poltroonery of the enemy, I have a feeling which goes to my heart; car je ne saurois me dissimuler que ce sont des Français qui sont battus, des Français qui s'enfuient."

Le Comte d'Artois* talked very little to me on public affairs—indeed I saw him but for a moment. Calonne was as usual full of hopes and vapouring—he said he was very well satisfied with England. We had *officially* declared to all the Continental Powers, that we would observe the *strictest neutrality*.

He was less pleased with Spain; and he taxed Lord Gower and Lady Sutherland with strong leanings towards democracy. He spoke very slightingly of young Burke—he considered their "*procès comme gagné*"— that they should be at Paris before the winter—that he admitted that much would remain to be done when they got there.

Romanzow, who is accredited to the Princes from the Empress of Russia, was of course not disposed to be very communicative. *He* attributed the whole League in favour of the Princes to the Empress. He praised them—said their conduct was very good, and that they possessed the very difficult art of being popular, without letting themselves down—that Count d'Artois' behaviour was manly and steady. He spoke well of Madame de Balbi and of Jaucourt, and with contempt of the infamous slur flung on their character by a Corsican adventurer. He said that the Princess of Orange had gone to Brunswick through a fear that the democratical party would attack the Republic, when *he* said, the Patriots again began to become formidable. This I do not credit. He reprobated the Alliance between Prussia and Austria—said the whole Prussian force, with the King at the head of it, would be on the Rhine

* Afterwards Charles X. dethroned by the Revolution of July 1830.

about the 21st of June. I touched on the Empress's
views in Poland; but either he knew nothing of them,
or did not choose to enter on the subject. He said that
Soltikoff (who formerly was about the Grand Duke)
and Prince Repnin had the direction of the army in
the room of Potemkin—that Besberodko had asked for
his retreat, and that the Portefeuille was given to
Sabow. His father (the Marechal Romanzow) remained in the Ukraine, and certainly would not be tempted
to take ever again any share in public concerns. Galitzin, he said, had asked for his dismission, and Rosa-
monski was to succeed him as Ambassador at Vienna.
Romanzow spoke of this *with feeling*, as he always had
expected that post. He now said he should return to
Russia, and renounce the Foreign Line.

Brussels, May 29.

Everything apparently quiet—Gardiner still there,
waiting orders to go to Warsaw. Baron Galbi* called
on me. He had left Paris the 25th, without taking
leave. He said the French had drawn their advanced
post nearer Valenciennes; and that he saw no appearance of any new operations. He travelled with the
Austrian Chargé des Affaires (Blumendorff), and had
an escort.

Fernan Nunez (Spanish Ambassador at Paris) now at
Louvain, sat a morning with me. He said he had been
accused of being a Democrat; that nothing was further
from his principles; but that it was impossible for him
to approve the violence and wrong-headedness of the
Coblentz party; that it was because he wished them
well, he disapproved their conduct. He had been accused of having altered a Memorial—it was very true—
it was sent to him, drawn up in harsh terms, ill-timed,
and, as he thought, calculated to commit *his* Court, and

* Prussian Minister at Paris.

not serve that of France; that therefore he altered the words, not the sense; and it was, he thought, his right and his duty so to do. He had written to Mons. Florida de Blanca on these terms, and said that if a person of his rank and character had not this right, " qu'il feroit bien d'envoyer un Valet en Ambassade." He said the Court of Spain held back because she could not see the real system of the Intervening Powers, or their real end; that Aranda, though old (seventy-three) was still very stout and hale.

OSTEND, JUNE 1.

THIS town without a soldier—the fortifications going to decay—the few troops they had recalled on the declaration of war—this produced no stop in the trade. The French ships admitted as before, only the persons not allowed to go up the country or to Bruges.

ENGLAND.

LANDED at Dover on Saturday, June 2nd, 1792, at noon—found the proclamation of the 21st,* and the debates in consequence of it. Arrived in London by dinner, Sunday the 3rd—Chancellor going out.

Saw Prince of Wales early the 4th—he was very well pleased with what I had done at Berlin, thanked me for it, &c.—stated his affairs to me as more distressed than ever. Several executions had been in his house—Lord Rawdon had saved him from one — that his debts amounted to 370,000*l.* He said he was trying, through the Chancellor, to prevail on the King to apply to Parliament to increase his income.

---

* Issued against Seditious Writings and Associations, and aimed principally at Tom Paine's compositions.—*Editor's Note.*

On the Wednesday following I was with him again, by appointment. He repeated the same again, said that if the King would raise his revenue to 100,000*l.* a-year, he would appropriate 35,000*l.* of it to pay the interest of his debts, and establish a Sinking-fund. That if this could not be done, he must break up his establishment, reduce his income to 10,000*l.* a-year and *go abroad.* He *made a merit* of having given up the turf, and blamed the Duke of York for remaining on it. He said (which I well knew before), that his racing-stable cost him upwards of 30,000*l.* yearly. He was very anxious, and as is usual on these occasions, nervous and agitated. He said (on my asking him the question), that he did not stand so well with the King as he did some months ago, but that he was better than ever with the Queen—that *she* had advised him to press the King, through the Chancellor, to propose to Mr. Pitt to bring an increase of the Prince's income before Parliament, and that if this was done, she would use her influence to promote it.

I strongly recommended his pressing the Queen. He suggested the idea of going to Mr. Pitt *directly* through the Chancellor, &c. I doubted both the consent of the Chancellor to such a step, at the moment he was going out, and his influence and weight if he did consent to it. I took the liberty of disapproving his going abroad on any terms, and particularly under the circumstances he mentioned; said, that if he should unfortunately be reduced to the necessity of lowering his income to the degree he had mentioned, it would be much better to live in England than *out* of it. That the shewing *in* England he *could* reduce his expenses, and live economically would do him credit, prove him in earnest, and if he kept up to such a plan, would in the event be much more likely to induce the public to take his situation into consideration, than any attempts through Ministry, Opposition, or even the Queen herself.—I saw the Duke of York on the 4th of June, and the Duchess, at their own house. He mentioned, with concern and uneasi-

ness, the division in the Party.* He considered it as
a breaking up of its strength, and he was apprehensive
of the consequences to the country at large. He condemned Fox, and reprobated in the strongest terms the
conduct of Grey,† Lambton, and the Reformers. He
said the King of Prussia had for a long time not written
either to him or to the Duchess, or even answered their
letters, without his being able to assign a cause. He
said he stood very well at St. James's.

I saw the Prince again on the 7th June, at Carlton
House, as before. He repeated the same things, and
added, that if he could not obtain some assurance from
the King that he would apply to Parliament in the next
Session of Parliament, before this ended, that he should
be ruined, and *must go abroad.*—I combated again
this idea; but he appeared to have a wish and some
whim about going abroad I could not discover.—He
talked coldly and unaffectionately about the Duke and
Duchess of York, and very slightingly of the Duke of
Clarence. He asked me whether I approved his having
spoken on the Proclamation in the manner he had, and
held very right language on the subject. I told him I
was sorry his lawyers, Erskine and Pigot, went a different way from him; that this was unbecoming.—He
said he *once* had thought of dismissing them, but that,
on considering it, was inclined to believe that such a
marked measure would only give them consequence, and
do more harm than good, by bringing the subject into
more frequent conversation.

---

* The old Whig Party, of which the Duke of Portland and Mr. Fox
were the recognised leaders. When Mr. Fox declared himself favourable to
the French Revolution, and, though he condemned its cruelties, became the
apologist of its extravagances, and almost adopted its violent opinions and
mischievous principles in Parliament, the most influential members of his
party seceded from him.

† Mr. Grey moved an amendment (May 25th) to the address on the
Proclamation against wicked and seditious writings. In his speech he made
a violent attack on Mr. Pitt. Mr. Grey was at this time Member of
the Society called Friends of the People, who were supposed to be in correspondence with the Jacobin Club in Paris.

COLONEL ST. LEGER.

HE called on me on the 8th June. He said the
Prince was more attached to Mrs. Fitzherbert than
ever; that he had been living with Mrs. Crouch; that
she (Mrs. Fitzherbert) piqued him by treating this with
ridicule, and coquetted on her side. This hurt his
vanity, and brought him back; and he is now more
under her influence than ever. She dislikes the Duchess
of York, because the Duchess will not treat her " *en belle
sœur :*" it is that is the cause of the coolness between
the two brothers. He confirmed the total ruin of the
Prince, and said the Duke's affairs were in a very bad
way. He had returned to England with the highest
reputation, and might have done what he pleased with
the King, who doted on him; that he very idly has resumed several of his old habits; he plays at Brooks's,
goes to Newmarket, and loses, and neglects St. James's;
that he behaves vastly well to the Duchess, and is
happy. He accounted for the King of Prussia's displeasure towards them, by Madame Dienhoff's dislike of
the Duchess, by the reports of the Princess of Ferdi-
nand, who is in correspondence with the Duchess of
Cumberland, and by the general spirit of intrigue which
prevails at Berlin. Anthony St. Leger confirmed all
that his brother said about Mrs. Fitzherbert. He
blamed her excessively; and said she was the cause of
the two brothers being ill together. He said Lake was
the cause of the whole Newmarket story; that he had
behaved very ill towards the Prince; that the result was
good, as it had driven the Prince from the turf, though
unfortunately the Duke of York still remained on it.

JUNE 9.

DUKE OF PORTLAND, Lord Fitzwilliam, Lord Loughborough, and Burke, at Burlington House in the even-

ing—Burke declaimed on the conduct of Fox,* that his conduct had disqualified him for office—that he was tainted with French politics and principles; that he, on a late occasion, deserted his old friends, and had preferred a new set in the Party.—He set forth the principles of the Party as established on the King's accession—that their principles were those of true Whigs—that these had been always adhered to by them—that it was absolutely necessary to force Fox to a specific declaration—that Fox was a *Host*—that great harm and great good must follow him always—that a union of all the abilities, all the weight, and all the wealth of this country was necessary—the times required it, &c. He went on for an hour, during which time we were quite silent. Lord Fitzwilliam read an account of what had passed in the Association at Sheffield, and the resolution it had come to—a letter of thanks to its chairman, and of approbation from Grey. Lord Fitzwilliam, alarmed, expressed a strong wish for Government being supported in all measures which tended to strengthen the country, &c.—On Burke's going away, Lord Loughborough agreed he had said what was true, but that it *should not be said;* that it would displease and alienate Charles Fox, but that Burke's principle was a right one, and that the times called for a Junction.

When I was left alone with the Duke of Portland and Lord Fitzwilliam, we entered more deeply and more confidentially into the business. They agreed Fox's conduct had been very ill-judged, and very distressing; that to separate from him would be highly disagreeable, yet that to remain with him after what he professed, was giving their tacit approbation to the sentiments he had avowed in the House of Commons on the Parliamentary Reform, which sentiments were in direct

* Early in the session, Fox presented a petition from the Unitarians, complaining of the statutes in force, and praying for more extensive toleration. On this subject he based a motion, which Burke opposed in a magnificent speech, rebuking the wild theories of the day, and pointing out that the petitioners were not merely a religious Sect, but a political Faction aiming at the destruction of the Church.

contradiction to theirs.—The state of the times was amply discussed, and it was agreed by all of us that they called out for a Junction.

Tom Pelham* called on me on the 6th June, and after telling him what I had done at Berlin, he told me that, on the failure of the French King's escape in July last, Fox had been prevailed on, as he believes, by the Duchess of Devonshire, through Sheridan, to write letters to Barnave† and La Fayette, (under the idea they intended to try the King and Queen of France as state criminals) not to sully their conduct by condemning them to die. Fox proposed in these letters, either no notice at all, or the exiling them; as his mind was taught to suppose they would be put to death, his letters went to reprobate that idea.

Tom Pelham very wisely did not deliver these letters, but *burnt* them. Fox highly approved this on cool reflection, and it was very lucky, as Pelham was so strictly searched at Pontarlier, that they certainly would have been taken from him if he had not destroyed them.

SATURDAY, JUNE 10.

LONG tête-à-tête conversation with the Duke of Portland. He agreed that the circumstances of the times made a Coalition with Pitt a very necessary measure; that the security of the country required it, as well relative to its foreign as to its internal situation. That Pitt was of such consequence in the country, and the Prince of Wales so little respected, that we considered it as impossible for him to form an Administration of which Pitt was not to be a part; that an attempt to the contrary, in the present temper of people's minds,

---

* Afterwards Lord Chichester.
† One of the leaders of the people, and second only to Mirabeau in eloquence. He kept up relations with the Court, and was more moderate in his views than the other Jacobins.

would produce the greatest confusion, and even go
to endanger the succession. In short, the result of two
hours' discussion was, that a Coalition was so desirable
a measure, that not only every overture tending towards
one should be listened to, but even overtures made
to promote it, were it practicable.

LETTER FROM SIR GILBERT ELLIOT TO LORD MALMESBURY.

Minto, 12th June, 1792.

MY DEAR LORD MALMESBURY,—I was extremely sorry
that I could not at last welcome your return to England.
I had been in daily hopes of your arrival for some time
before I left London, but having exceeded my promise
by some weeks already, and having appointed several
days for my departure and failed in them, I was unwilling to postpone my return to Scotland again, especially as the time of your arrival did not appear to be
quite certain. I confess, however, there never was
a time when I should have been more desirous of seeing
you, and talking over the interesting topics which you
have found in agitation at your arrival. The field is
so large that there is no attempting it on paper, and yet
the matter is so important, and I am at all times
so anxious that we should think alike on any capital
points, that I own I am impatient to learn from yourself your general sentiments on those subjects which
engage the attention of our common friends at this
time. I confess that I am not apprehensive that we are
likely to differ on this occasion, and that from all I
know of your turn of mind on the present subjects of
discussion, and of your political attachments, I think it
impossible that we should not concur in every point.
With regard to Parliamentary Reform, and in general to
every other shape in which a spirit of speculative innovation may shew itself, as well as with regard to the
peculiar influence of the present times and circumstances

on these subjects, I can express my sentiments very
shortly, by saying that they are precisely the same with
the Duke of Portland's.   With regard to *politics*, I can
also describe my situation in two words by saying, that
I am of the Duke of Portland's party.

I have always understood that this was exactly the
same thing as saying that I was of the *same* party with
Fox; and a contrary opinion is so painful to me; I
revolt so strongly against the notion of a separation
in interest and party between the Duke of Portland and
Fox, that I am perhaps unable to consider as impartially as I ought many things which induce other
men, whose opinions I have long been accustomed to
revere, to think that such a situation ought to take
place, or rather has already taken place. I can only say
now, (for the subject is too large for a letter,) that I
most cordially and devoutly hope not. If I am disappointed, however, in that hope, and a choice must be
made, I have already expressed what that choice is.

The Duke will have told you what symptoms there
were before I left London of a disposition in the Ministry
to enlarge the basis of Government by some arrangement with his party.   There are public as well as
private grounds which would, no doubt, make us look to
such an event with satisfaction.   But I confess there
are other considerations which seem to render it very
improbable that, viewing all circumstances, any arrangement should be at present practicable, which we should
think either agreeable or advisable, whether on public
or party grounds.   Is it intended to include Fox? and
if it is, can he bring his mind in its present tone and
temper on the subjects which are likely to come in play,
to so sudden and so great a change of sentiment, as
to afford a reasonable prospect that the Government,
composed as this idea supposes, would not be as much
at variance as Pitt's Cabinet has hitherto been?   On
the other hand, if Fox is excluded, can a coalition
between the Duke of Portland and Pitt, founded on
a separation from Fox, be reconciled to our feelings, or

be free from that sort of disrepute in the world which would extremely counteract any service we should intend to render the public by the measure? These difficulties appear to me at present insurmountable; and I am inclined to think that the most creditable part we can take for ourselves, and the most serviceable to the country, will be, to distinguish ourselves very clearly (as, in fact, we have done) from our innovating friends in all that relates to their *mania*, and to support the Government and constitution of the country in all that relates to that subject, *out of office*. The country will, by this means, have the benefit of our weight, which by such a conduct will *deservedly* be very great. We shall place ourselves on very high ground, and if a time should come when His Majesty shall find it advisable to employ new men, both his eyes and those of the nation will naturally be turned towards our party.

It is possible that what may have passed since my departure may render all I have been now saying unnecessary, and the whole of this subject is so critical and interesting, that I must rely on your friendship for correct and particular information. I shall repeat to you what I said to the Duke, and have told distinctly to Elliot of Wells. If any resolution should be taken by the Duke of Portland, I do not mean as to arrangements with Ministry, but as to settling and arranging our own party, that should make him wish to have *his* friends about him, I will return on the first summons. On the other hand, if, contrary to my expectations, he should enter on any direct negotiation with Ministry for an arrangement, I should then wish *on my own account* to be on the spot, and will be obliged to you or the Duke for notice of such a measure. We are all in perfect health, but are not favoured at present with a Tuscan sky. Is it impossible that we should see you here this summer? It would be a great happiness to us, and a great addition to that which we expect in a visit from the Douglasses and Sir George Cornewall.

Believe me ever, my dear Lord Malmesbury, your most affectionate,   GILBERT ELLIOT.

On Tuesday, June 13th, I saw Lord Loughborough alone at Burlington House; he asked me my opinion on the present times, and gave me his, and nearly the same conversation as in over-leaf passed between us. He then told me, that as long ago as when Fox had first of all declared his opinions on a Parliamentary reform, Lord Auckland had written to him a letter purporting and affecting to believe that this conduct had entirely broken up the Party, made an irreparable breach in it, and held out proposals of a coalition with Pitt. Lord Loughborough took *no* notice of this letter. Soon after the measure of the Proclamation was agitated, Pitt consulted and communicated on it with the leaders of Opposition. The Duke of Portland went to Downing Street, and in a meeting afterwards held amongst the leaders of the Party at Burlington House, the proclamation was read, and sent back altered, which alterations were approved by Pitt.—Fox was present, but declared against it, not so much as a bad measure in itself, but as an unnecessary one; and which, by being unnecessary, might, by awakening the attention of the public to ideal dangers, be productive of real evil.—Everybody else thought it a wise and essential step to be taken. It was proposed to them by Government to attend the Privy Council, but on an objection of Lord Stormont this was not accepted. He said that it was very different the supporting a measure, and becoming responsible for it, and his objection prevailed. Lord Loughborough said, they were now sorry it had, as the meeting in this way, and on such a measure besides the good effect it naturally would have produced on the minds of the public, would have been *approaching and conciliatory*. After the debate in the House of Lords, and after the secession of the Chancellor was no longer to be doubted, Dundas first wrote and then spoke to Lord Loughborough, expressing his wish that this temporary union could become a permanent one. He held out four vacant Cabinet places, —the Chancellor (his own), the Secretary of State for Home Affairs, the President of the Council, and Privy

Seal, besides two or three Privy Councillors' places in
the House of Commons, and the Lord Lieutenancy of
Ireland; Lord Loughborough took all this *ad referendum*, and was now come to talk it over with the Duke
of Portland. I was present at this conversation, which
immediately followed that I have been writing, and
excepting the Duke's entire approbation of a Junction,
was nearly a repetition of it— it ended by agreeing it
was right to hear everything.

June 13.

Duke of Portland said he had seen Fox for two
hours. Fox, he said, was a friend to Coalition. That
he only wished it to be brought about in such a way as
it should appear they had not *acceded* to Pitt's Ministry,
but went to it on fair and even conditions to share
equally with him all the power, patronage, &c.—Duke's
idea that Pitt should not keep the Treasury, but some
neutral man be put there—the Duke of Leeds; that he
himself should not come into office, but support Government *out of employment.* This I was strongly disinclined to, but did not express it that day. I doubted
whether the King, or rather the Queen, knew of these
proposals; stated the difficulties there, and the still
greater at Carlton House.

Friday, June 15.

Two long conversations with the Duke of Portland in
the morning and evening. I strongly insisted, if any
arrangement was to take place, on the absolute necessity
of his being in a Cabinet office; that if he was to receive
any public mark of the King's favour (such as the
Garter, &c.), and although he should support Administra-

tion with the weight of all his friends, in the most
evident manner, his not being in office would always be
considered as if Fox (if he came in) or Pitt (if he remained in) wished to exclude him from the secrets of
Government; and the impression his not being in the
Cabinet would have on the minds of the public at large
would be, either that he was set aside, or that measures
were in contemplation, they (Fox and Pitt) were
ashamed or afraid to trust to him; that his being out of
office would defeat, in my mind, the great end of the
Union, since it in that case would not carry with it, to
the sense of the people, that confidence and security so
much wanted in the present moment, and on which the
very basis of the negotiation rested. This had effect
with the Duke: he confessed Lord Fitzwilliam thought
as I did, and ended by saying, that, whatever his own
feelings or opinions might be, he would do what his
friends wished and advised him to do. He related to
to me that Lord Loughborough had the night before
(Thursday, the 14th) met Pitt at Dundas's, that he
spoke with great openness and appearance of sincerity—
that on Lord Loughborough's asking him whether the
King knew it, Pitt said he did not come with the King's
command to propose a coalition, but that he would be
responsible that it would please the King *and the Queen*,
and that the only difficulty at all likely to arise was
about Fox, and that difficulty entirely owing to Fox's
conduct in Parliament during the last four months.
That *everything else* was entirely forgotten, and that he
himself did not recollect that in all their Parliamentary
altercations, a single word had ever dropped from either
of them to prevent their acting together without any
fair reproach being made of a disavowal of principles, or
an inconsistency of character. Pitt said that it *perhaps*
would not be quite easy to give Fox the Foreign Department *immediately*, but that in a few months he certainly
might have it. Dundas was in this conference very
eager for bringing about the Union, and Pitt did not
seem less so.

The Duke of Portland and myself took the matter into further consideration; we agreed on the absolute necessity of coming to a clear and explicit understanding, first with *Fox*, as to his principles and intended conduct on several great public measures in which he was involved, and then to the same clear and explicit understanding with Pitt on them. These measures were, *Parliamentary Reform, the Abolition of the Slave Trade, the Repeal of the Test Act,* and the system to be observed *relative to French politics.* That on *all* these Fox differed from us, and Pitt on several of them—that therefore till these were fairly and candidly discussed, and our opinions made in some degree to meet upon them, it would be idle to attempt to form a Cabinet. On reasoning on the various points, our minds were naturally led to the situation of this country, standing *single,* or as it relates to that of the rest of Europe; and every pending and probable event brought the strongest conviction to them of the necessity of a strong Government being formed. Any accident happening to the King of any kind, either the German Alliances being successful or otherwise in their attempts on France; Russia's overwhelming Poland; an attack on Holland; a rallying of the Reformers and their doctrines here. Such and many other events, several of which were inevitable in the course of a short time, and all probable, led us to decide that *if Pitt meant what we did* "*bona fide,*" a Coalition was a most desirable measure.

SATURDAY, JUNE 16.

DINNER at Lord Loughborough's with Fox. While Lord Loughborough was engaged with his company (which were foreigners) I talked with Fox, and afterwards carried him to Burlington House.—He had not heard of the last meeting with Pitt; he was full of doubts and misgivings, and did not make himself (as

he generally does) practicable.—He seemed *a little hurt*
at the first advance not having been made to him; but
this I collected from his manner, not from any direct
expression. He doubted Pitt's sincerity, and suspected
he had no other view than to weaken their party and
strengthen his own—that to divide the Opposition was
his great object; he doubted, also, the King's having
consented willingly to dismiss the Chancellor,* and
seemed to think it *possible* a new Administration might
be made through him, from which Pitt was to be excluded.
He contended, that it was impossible ever to suppose
Pitt would admit him to an equal share of power, and
that whatever might be his own feelings or readiness to
give way, he could not, for the sake of the honour *and
pride* of the Party, come in on any other terms. Pitt
must have the Treasury, he said, and he on his part
had friends in the House of Commons he *must* attend
to.—These friends I conceived to be Sheridan, Grey,
Erskine, and Lord Robert Spencer; after stating these
doubts and difficulties, and dwelling on them with a
degree of peevishness and obstinacy very unlike him,
he however ended by saying, that he *loved coalitions;*
that, as a party man, he thought it a good thing for
his party to come into office, were it only for a month;
and, under the particular circumstances of the country,
he thought it of very great importance that a strong
Administration should exist. He reasoned on Foreign
Politics with his usual ability, and on the same system
as formerly. When we got to Burlington House he was
not inclined to speak, and it was with great difficulty I
could lead him and the Duke of Portland into discourse.
Fox repeated merely what he had said to me on the way,
spoke *with acrimony* of Pitt, and repeatedly said " the
pride of the Party must be saved." I observed *purposely*,
that I conceived if the Duke of Portland and he were
agreed, they necessarily must lead the Party, and that *all*

---

* Lord Thurlow, who had secretly treated with the Opposition during the
King's illness, and at a later period thwarted Mr. Pitt's measures, was dismissed from office June 15, 1792, and the Great Seal was put into Commission.

their friends would follow them. The Duke seemed
to acquiesce, but Fox was silent and embarrassed, and
said, with a degree of harshness very unlike his usual
manner, that he did not believe that Pitt was sincere,
and that even if he was sincere, he did not believe any
coalition could take place. I endeavoured to bring him
to—at least, give the proposal fair play, by urging its
importance as to public concerns, which he admitted;
and I contended that he had no option as a party man,
but either of coming in now, or of waiting till public
calamity or national distress drove Pitt from office, and
that then he necessarily must come in to support the
very measures which Pitt had not been equal to carry
through for the public safety; that, therefore, it was not
unreasonable to argue, that his coming into an equal
share of power now with Pitt, was not only likely to prevent these public evils which threatened the community
at large, but to insure to him and his friends a much
more permanent and secure possession of office, than if
they waited till the King, against his will, and driven to
it by distress, was forced to take them in; that coming
in now, *his power* necessarily must increase from the
palpable good effects it would produce; that on his
coming in then, it would diminish, from perhaps an
unpopular and difficult task being put upon him, and
from his not possessing the confidence of the Crown.
This had some effect on him; I left him and the Duke
alone, and I was glad to learn that the next morning,
when he called again at Burlington House, he was more
accommodating, and less taciturn than the preceding
evening.

Sunday June 17.

Lord Loughborough called on me; he related, very
accurately, all that had passed between him, Pitt, and
Dundas, on the Thursday evening—it was nearly what
I had before heard from the Duke of Portland. Pitt,

he said, wore every appearance of sincerity and frankness; that in speaking to him, and in listening to him, he started no difficulties or objections, but assured him it was his wish to unite cordially and heartily—not in the way of bargain, but to form a strong and united Ministry. His only doubts were about Fox, and these, he said, *might* be got over. He was a little apprehensive of Fox's opinions relative to the French Revolution, and hinted that he was afraid he had gone *too far*.—That this was an objection to his coming *at once into the Foreign Department*, because it would look like a change of system. On Lord Loughborough's observing to him that, perhaps on his part, too, the strong manner in which he (Pitt) had promoted the Abolition of the Slave Trade would require some explanation, he said, certainly some concessions must be made; the King did not like the measure, and very naturally; still less the manner in which it was supported—by addresses and petitions, a method he (Pitt) also disliked, as it was a bad precedent to establish. He went over all the great depending measures, and inferring from them all the eligibility of uniting the strength and utility of the country, and of giving (said Dundas) to the natural aristocracy of the country its due weight and power. Pitt said, he hoped we were not going out of town; and on Lord Loughborough saying Lord Fitzwilliam was, he said he hoped not, as he was a most respectable and useful man.

The conference ended: leaving Lord Loughborough under a perfect conviction of Pitt's being in earnest, and with the impression that he would, after he had spoken to Lord Grenville and to the King, renew the subject.

Monday, June 18.

With Lord Fitzwilliam, in Grosvenor Square, for the purpose of discussing the subject of a coalition with him,

and of endeavouring to prevail on him to speak to Fox—
Lord Fitzwilliam's sentiments perfectly right—he said
his opposition never had been to the Constitution of the
country, but to the Government when it acted in a way
he thought contrary to the Constitution; that, therefore,
when that was in danger, he ceased to be in Opposition.
On going over the matter it became evident that the great
obstacle would arise from Fox's being too much entangled
with Grey, Lambton, and that set of men who had lately
separated themselves from the Party, in order to form a
party of their own, and who publicly professed doctrines
and opinions in direct opposition to what he and I considered to be for the good and welfare of the public.
That this would indeed be very hard and unreasonable,
that for the sake of these very men, who both in their
public and private capacity had been as inimical as possible, an arrangement should be broken off so salutary
and so advisable.   Lord Fitzwilliam and myself agreed
on every point; he, however, went beyond me in insisting on the indispensable necessity of Pitt resigning the
Treasury for another Cabinet office.   He acquiesced in
the wisdom of trying to bring Fox to be less attached to
these false friends, and said Tom Grenville was the best
man to speak to him.   Lord Fitzwilliam expressed his
dislike to Sheridan, said he might have a lucrative place,
but never could be admitted to one of trust and confidence.   On my wishing him not to leave town, he
said he could safely trust his conscience with the Duke
of Portland, and was at the same time ready to return
at the shortest notice.

TUESDAY, JUNE 19.

LORD LOUGHBOROUGH with me—he said he had heard
nothing new.   On my telling him what had passed between me and Lord Fitzwilliam, he said he really
thought it unreasonable to expect that Pitt should quit

the Treasury—that he could not, and *would not* make such a proposal—I desired him to see Lord Fitzwilliam, and he went to him from me.

THURSDAY, JUNE 21.

I MET Lord Bute (Lord Mountstuart) at the Drawing-room; he was acquainted with what had passed, from the Duke of Portland, and thought upon it just as I did—he said the day before he had been in the Closet to take leave of the King on his going to Scotland, and that on taking leave, and asking his orders, he said to His Majesty, that he left London much happier and more comfortable than he should have done a month sooner, from being informed that His Majesty had it in his contemplation to add a great strength to his Administration by joining to it some of the most respectable and considerable families in the country. The King was silent, looked down, and for a minute or two said nothing; he then asked Lord Bute, who was the person in that party he was most attached to—Lord Bute replied, the Duke of Portland; upon this, the King spoke out loudly in praise of the Duke, and spoke of him with expressions of the highest regard and esteem. —Lord Bute again repeated his wish and hopes that a Ministry composed of the united parties would be made, and the King was again silent. Lord Bute naturally inferred from this that His Majesty was fully acquainted with what had passed, but that he did not choose to commit himself, as matters were not ripe.—Lord Bute desired me to mention this to the Duke of Portland, which I did the same day.—The Duke's remarks on this conference were the same as Lord Bute's, and in a long conversation I had with the Duke afterwards, in which he related one that had passed between him and Fox, the same things were repeated I have mentioned before. —The Duke said, Fox was much more practicable, and had said, " *it was so damned right a thing*, that it must

be done."—He, however, still held out on the impossibility of his acting *under* Pitt.

FRIDAY, JUNE 22.

BURKE wished to see me, and I went to breakfast with
him.—He said he had no wish for anything himself,
that he *would* accept no office, but that for the general
good he was a most warm advocate for a coalition.　He
observed, *Mr. Fox's coach stops the way*, and with his
usual eloquence, warmth, and wit, went through the
whole of Fox's conduct, which he blamed, and concluded
by observing how very hard it was that on *his account*
an arrangement calculated to preserve the country should
be broken off ; yet he foresaw it would *be broken off*, as
there was no doing without Fox, or with him.　That,
therefore, he wished, as the least evil which could follow,
and the only good which could in such a case arise from
a negotiation having been once set afloat, that it should
be declared by the Duke of Portland, &c., as the heads
of the great Whig Party, that all systematic opposition
was at an end; that the principles broached by Grey,
&c., and *not disavowed* by Fox, had necessarily drawn a
line of division in the party, and that it was necessary
to declare this distinctly, and decidedly ; that for the
better security, and in order to give a strong and convincing mark of it to the public, Lord Loughborough
should, by being made Chancellor, represent the party
in the Cabinet, and be the link between them (the Whig
Party he meant,) and Government in order that if, on
some future day, the difficulties now arising from Fox's
character and conduct should decrease, or the distress of
the country increase, a junction might be accomplished,
in a more easy and natural manner, than even by the
beginning the whole afresh.　Burke dwelt very strongly
on ,these points, and said he wished to explain them to
me, in order that I might mention them at Burlington
House, which I did the same day; but the Duke of

Portland saw many inconveniences attending this which had escaped Burke's notice; and although he confessed all systematic opposition *was* at an end, yet he very wisely thought the saying so in express terms to Pitt, would be a very unwise and unsafe declaration.   I left town on the 23d; and on the 27th June, I received a letter from the Duke of Portland:

" DEAR LORD MALMESBURY,—There is an end of my arrangement, at least for the present; no personal or political objection on the part of Pitt, and distinctly none from any higher quarter, because it had not been mooted there; but the difficulty arises in conciliating his (Pitt's) own friends to the measure of coalescing with Fox at present.   I am much pleased and obliged by the success of your County meeting.   I hope you will dine here on Tuesday and Wednesday, and as many more days as you and we stay in town.

Yours ever,   P.

" Wednesday, 27th June, 1792."

I returned to London on Tuesday, July 3d, 1792, in the evening, and went immediately to the Duke of Portland's.   He repeated to me in fuller terms what he had said in his letter.   On talking over the subject, we agreed that it was probably more from private and personal reasons of Pitt, than from any deference on his part to the opinions of his friends, that the arrangement was at an end ; that if it was any of his friends, it was Lord Grenville and the Duke of Richmond; that, however, it was evident that it was only suspended, not *broken off*, and that it would be taken up again before the meeting of Parliament.   The Duke of Portland still persists in his idea of the necessity of Pitt's quitting the Treasury, which *I* never could, or can consider, either as quite necessary or quite reasonable.

JULY 4.

I ATTENDED the levee, with the Hampshire Address
on the Proclamation, brought up almost entirely by
members of the Opposition—the King very gracious to
us all.

JULY 5.

I MET Lord Loughborough at the drawing-room; he
told me what had passed, (at a dinner at Dundas's, on
Monday, June 25th,) when Pitt declined going further
with the arrangement, and said, Pitt spoke in such a
manner as to leave him no doubt whatever that he
meant and wished it should come forward again. Dundas repeatedly said, he could only come to opposition to
fill up some of the offices likely to be vacant, and particularly specified that of Governor-General in India.
Lord Loughborough related to me a very long conversation he had a few days before with Fox, in which he
said Fox appeared more harsh, impracticable, and opinionative, than he could have supposed him to be; that
he saw no chance of anything being done while Fox
remained in his present temper of mind. He quoted
one thing Fox said, viz., "That although it should be
the united opinion of all his friends, that he ought to
come into office, leaving Pitt in the post he now fills,
he still should maintain his own; and, although in that
case he should so far defer to theirs as not to refuse
coming into office, rather than prevent an arrangement,
yet that if that was to happen, he would go into the
House of Lords, and not remain in the House of Commons."—Lord Loughborough appeared hurt with Fox's
behaviour and manners towards him.—I endeavoured
to account for it, and believe with reason, by saying, he
had spoken with him on the eve of the day on which
he was to go out with Lord Lauderdale as second to
fight Arnold, and that this dwelt on his spirits, and
probably influenced his temper.—I dined that day at

Burlington House, but no new matter arising, our conversation was not worth putting down.—Tom Pelham
breakfasted with me every day this week. (July 4th,
5th, 6th, 7th, 8th, &c.) He said the Duke of Richmond had been remarkably civil and guarded at the
Sussex meeting, and that he afterwards went to Lord
Sheffield's, where he (Tom Pelham) was also; that he
took Lord Sheffield aside after dinner, and told him all
that had passed concerning *the arrangement;* expressed
himself in the strongest terms as an advocate for it,
and went so far as to say the country could not go on
without it; he said he saw no difficulty in arranging
Pitt and Fox (of course we cannot suppose the objections Pitt referred to came from him), and declared
that they were so put to for men, that if a Blue Ribbon became vacant, they should not know whom to be-
stow it upon.

JULY 11.

DUKE OF PORTLAND said Pitt certainly still ardently
wishes for an arrangement; that he had offered the
Governor-Generalship of India to be disposed of by Opposition, and had mentioned Lord North, Mr. Wyndham, and Tom Grenville, as three of the properest men
to be chosen from; the Duke of Portland wished for Sir
Gilbert Elliot.

July 23rd and 24th I passed at Oatlands with the
Duke and Duchess of York; he informed me of what
had passed, and ardently wishes it.

JULY 25.

AT Burlington House in the evening—Duke of Portland told me that the Duke of Leeds had, through Rol-
liston, expressed a wish to see him.—On the 26th, they

met at the Duke of Leeds's in Grosvenor Square, and
after strong expressions of his sincere wishes for an
arrangement, the Duke of Leeds offered to speak to the
King at Windsor.

JULY 27.

DUKE OF PORTLAND, although he placed no great faith
in the intervention of the Duke of Leeds, in consequence
of Fox's promoting it, acquiesced in the Duke of Leeds's
seeing the King.

FRIDAY, JULY 27.

DEAR LORD MALMESBURY,—I find that it has been
stated to Fox that the Duke of Leeds is desirous, and
thinks it necessary for him to have from me, in writing,
the outline or substance of the sentiments I stated to
him respecting the formation of a new and extended
Administration, by way of credentials for him to speak
from to the King, and that he would go into the Closet,
or find some opportunity of conversing with His Majesty
upon the subject of a new arrangement, could he go to
him with such a paper in his pocket. Considering the
channel through which this intelligence has come to Fox,
there appears great difficulty in my appearing to know
it, in such a way as to warrant my writing to the Duke.
I own, besides, to *you*, that I have no expectation of any
effect from the Duke of Leeds's intervention. But I
think the bringing about such a coalition of such importance to this country, that I should be very sorry
indeed to omit any means of doing it within my power.
Such a communication to the Duke of Leeds can do no
harm, and if you could *discover* that it was his wish that
such a one should be made to him from me—still more,
if you could be authorized by him to intimate to me
such a wish or opinion on his part, I would lose no time
in availing myself of it. But can a gentleman, a man

of the Duke of Leeds's rank, want credentials in writing for any fact he thinks fit to assert in conversation, any more in the Closet than elsewhere?

Yours ever, PORTLAND.

P.S.—You had not left town ten minutes, when I sent to communicate this intelligence to you. I shall not direct this in my own hand, or seal it with my own seal.

The Duke of Portland told me this day that the Garter had been offered to him through Lord Loughborough, which he had refused; and that the University of Oxford intended him for their Chancellor, which gave him great pleasure.

The 28th and 29th inst. I passed with the Duke of Leeds at North Mims—talked the whole matter over with him, whether he felt himself well enough with the King to venture to speak to him, &c. On his assuring me he was on a footing of *perfect confidence* since the Regency, and more particularly since his conduct on the Russian armament,* he required a letter from the Duke of Portland *as an authority* or voucher for his introducing the subject: this he had. He also wanted to know Fox's opinion, and whether he thought it advisable for him to speak with Pitt and Dundas, as well as with the King. The Duke of Leeds was in earnest; but, as he always is, carried away more by his imagination and sanguine hopes, in which his string of toadeaters encourage him, than by reason and reflection.

MONDAY, JULY 30.

I DINED with Fox at St. Anne's Hill—nobody there but Tom Grenville. He did not seem at all sanguine

---

* In the debates in the House of Lords, in May and June 1791, the Duke of Leeds supported the address in answer to the King's Message recommending a naval armament to keep Russia in check; and, on the measure being abandoned by his colleagues, he resigned the office of Secretary of State for Foreign Affairs.

as to the arrangement in general—expressed his dislike
to the manner in which it was set afloat—had Pitt been
in earnest, he would have come in a straight line to him,
or to the Duke of Portland, and not employed Dundas to
speak to Lord Loughborough—but Pitt, he argued, was
not sincere, and only wished to separate and break up
the Party. He said it was for this reason he approved
the Duke of Leeds seeing the King, and that he expected
no other good from him than that it would be evidently
proved from the King's manner, that he was in the
right. Talking of the Duke of Portland's refusal of the
Garter, he says he should not have considered the offer
(in the way it came) *as an offer*. All this was said in
great good humour. Much talk on Foreign politics: we
agreed on the general principle, but differed on particular points. His leanings about French politics are
not *quite* correct—his opinion of the King of Prussia
much too low—his partiality for a Russian connexion
very great—he said Lord North had been offered distinctly the government of India, and that he had refused
it—approved of the Duke of Leeds speaking to Dundas
and Pitt *after* he had seen the King, *not* before.—Fox
made Pitt's quitting the Treasury a *sine quâ non*, and
was so opinionative and fixed about it, that it was impossible even to reason with him on the subject.—From
St. Anne's Hill I went to Bagshot, passed through the
camp near Hartford Bridge on Tuesday, 31st, and got
that day by dinner to Durnford, with my sister Louisa,
where I remained till Saturday, August 4, when I went
to Stoneham, where I met *Francis*—he violent about
assisting the Poles*—in general very Republican. I
joked, but did not dispute with him.

* July 20th, 1792, Russia and Prussia carried into effect the second par-
tition of Poland. This unprincipled act of spoliation greatly weakened the
moral influence of the Allies during the war with the French Republic, and
received fearful retribution through the hands of Napoleon.

Durnford, Sunday, July 31st, 1792.

MY DEAR LORD,—Fox has great satisfaction from your idea of seeing the King, as he considers the success of the whole to depend on His Majesty having an arrangement in his wishes; the ascertaining that, he looks upon as a very material point, and which nothing is so likely to do as what you intend.

He has no objection to your speaking fully and without reserve to Pitt and Dundas; but he conceives that it would be highly unadvisable for you to communicate with either of them till after you had seen the King. The degree of utility to be drawn from your seeing them, he observed, would depend entirely on the more or less degree of intimacy and confidence with which you continue to live with them; and on this point your own judgment was the best and only rule to go by.

Fox repeatedly dwelt on the indispensable necessity of an alteration in the Treasury, and that, without that was admitted, nothing could be done. I fear this will be an insurmountable obstacle, although, if an arrangement takes place, with everybody belonging to it in the same views, and acting on the same principle, I still think it might be got over. I am, &c.

MALMESBURY.

His Grace the Duke of Leeds,
&c., &c., &c., &c., North Mims.

TUESDAY, DECEMBER 11.

CAME to London from Brookwood, to attend the Meeting of Parliament, called together by Proclamation for embodying the Militia, issued the 1st December; dined and passed the evening at Burlington House—Charles Fox, Duke of Devonshire, Tom Grenville, and Lord Fitzwilliam, at dinner. Conversation on the particular circumstances of the times, on the legality and wisdom of calling out the Militia, and on the truth or falsehood of the alarms which had occasioned this measure. Fox treated the alarms as totally groundless—that they were raised for particular purposes by Ministers—that there was not only no insurrection, or imminent danger of invasion (the technical words in the Act of Parliament), but no *unusual* symptoms of discontent, or proneness to complain in the people; that the whole was a trick, and as such he should oppose it.—*None* of the company agreed with him—Lord Fitzwilliam quoted what was passing at Sheffield and Leeds—he blamed Ministry for neglect and carelessness, which had reduced them to the embarrassing dilemma of calling together Parliament, he believed against the *letter of law*, though justified by the circumstances of the times—Tom Grenville said nearly the same, and the few words which fell from the Dukes of Devonshire and Portland were to the same effect. I contended, also, for the propriety of the measure, expressing my great dislike to opposing it; and although I was willing to allow much negligence and inattention to Ministers, yet what made the immediate pressure of the moment, arose from the rapid success of the French, and from the daring and desperate measures they professed in consequence of it. No one, not even Fox himself, called in doubt the *necessity* of assisting the Dutch if attacked; but *he*, and *he* only, seemed inclined to think the opening the Scheldt was not a sufficient motive, and would not even be considered as such by the Dutch themselves. He talked of it even as a bad ground to stand upon, and that he thought it would not go down with the Nation. In speaking of France and its situation, he spoke of it too favourably and too moderately, and prepared us very evidently for the motion he made the Saturday following *for acknowledging it as a Republic, and sending an Ambassador there;* his principles, too, bore the strongest marks of a leaning towards Republicanism, and he expressed them almost as strongly to us collectively, as he had done before to me alone, at St. Anne's Hill, and in St. James's Square.

WEDNESDAY, DECEMBER 12.

I DINED again at Burlington House. After dinner we had a meeting of Lords, to settle what should be done the next day—Dukes of Norfolk, Portland, and Devonshire, Lords Fitzwilliam, Carlisle, Loughborough, Porchester, Derby, Guildford, Stamford, Stormont, Rawdon, Bute, Spencer, and myself, present.

Duke of Portland opened the business by stating the peculiar circumstances of the times, and wishing to hear what his friends thought most advisable to do. After a good deal of very desultory talk, and a great many sour and peevish things from Lord Derby towards Lord Loughborough, it was agreed, in consequence of a proposal from the Duke of Norfolk, that no amendment should be proposed to the Address, nor any supported; that it should pass without a division, and be generally approved, although each Lord should reserve to himself the faculty of reasoning on any parts of it he might think exceptionable. After this meeting had broke up, and when nobody was left but the Duke of Portland, Lord Rawdon, and myself, *Fox* came in with the speech, which he had had from the Cockpit. He disapproved it highly, and on our telling him our determination, he said he should certainly advise another line of conduct in the House of Commons; and on my remonstrating, he with an oath declared *that there was no address at this moment Pitt could frame, he would not propose an amendment to, and divide the House upon.* This was putting an end to all discussion.

THURSDAY, DECEMBER 13.

THE Address was carried without a division in our House; but Lord Lansdowne proposed an amendment, and the Duke of Norfolk (notwithstanding what he had said the night before) seconded it, and voted for it. Lord Lansdowne's speech was all mischief, and that of a true *boutefeu.* In the House of Commons an amendment similar to that of Lord Lansdowne was moved by Fox, who divided, as he said he would, the House. The numbers were, 290 against it, and 50 for it. Of these 50, 21 were reformers, 4 Lord Lansdowne's members, and the rest people personally attached to Fox, and who, from this feeling, and *against their sentiments,* voted with him.

Such were Crewe, Lord Edward Bentinck, Lord George Cavendish, Lord Milton, Lionel Damer, and others. Some of them, from an excess of good nature in Lord Fitzwilliam and the Duke of Portland, voted at their particular request, in order to avoid, if possible, and as long as possible, an irreparable breach with Fox, and to leave open for him a door to return. Friday and Saturday Fox held the same violent language as on Thursday, and on Saturday he moved *to acknowledge the French Republic, and to send a Minister there.* Several of his old friends declared against him on their legs, and he did not venture to divide the House. The cry against him out of doors was excessive, and his friends were hurt beyond measure; several left London.

On Saturday I dined at York House.—The Duke very much hurt at Fox's conduct, and recommending strongly a decided separation from him.

SUNDAY, DECEMBER 16.

DINED at Burlington House with Sir Gilbert Elliot and Elliot of Wells.—After dinner we had a very serious and interesting conversation with the Duke of Portland. Sir Gilbert stated to him in the strongest manner the conduct of Fox, that it was founded on the worst of principles, on those on which the French Revolution was founded—that it went to overthrow the country, and that (whatever personal regard we still might retain for Fox, under the idea that he acted either under an error or under the influence of others, and not from design) it

was become essential for our honour and for the sake of
the country, to separate from him—that if the Duke of
Portland delayed or hesitated, he would become partaker
of his bad reputation and unpopularity; that besides
this, which was the *first consideration*, the party would
be broken up, for it was impossible for us or for many
others, not publicly and on our legs to express our entire
disapprobation of Fox's conduct and principles; that
although *we* know he was averse to them, yet his being
silent on the subject left the minds of the world at large
impressed with the conviction he was favourable to
them; that the sense of the party was supposed always
to go with him; and as his brother, Lord Edward Bentinck, and his nearest connexions had voted with Fox,
he was supposed to have adopted his principles, and we
were either to remain under the unjust stigma of adopting them also, or of passing as having deserted and
abandoned our party. This *we* knew not to be the
case; but we spoke of what alone could give weight and
consequence to the party, and by which our public conduct could *alone* be judged, viz. *the opinion of the public*.
That this would and did already pronounce him as acting a doubtful and wavering part, unbecoming his high
character, and the head of such a party,—and us, who
were amongst the leading members of it, either as having
differed with him, and, of course, become *rats* and de-
serters, or else, which would hurt us still more, as having
concurred in Fox's doctrines; that therefore we entreated him as friends, sincerely and affectionately
loving him, and attentive to his honour and reputation,
to come to a fair and short explanation with Fox, and
separate from him *amicably*, but decidedly; and not to
lend his name and commit our opinions and character
by being silent and inactive on this occasion. To all
this, strange as it may appear, the Duke of Portland replied nothing; neither would he answer a word to me
when I repeatedly, on his silence, asked him what was
to be done—what were his opinions—adding, that I
wished only to know them, in order, if possible, to

square mine to them, could I obtain a syllable of answer.
The only word we could draw forth was, that he was
against anything that could widen the breach, and put
it out of Fox's power to return, and drive him into desperate opposition. I, although I have often seen him
benumbed and *paralyzed*, never saw him, or any one
else, so completely so before.*—All was one dead silence
on his part; he seemed in a trance, and nothing could
be so painful as these two hours, for our conversation
lasted as long as that, reckoning intervals of ten and
fifteen minutes' silence.

Monday, December 17.

DINED at Burlington House with Lord Stormont and
Bishop of Oxford—nothing remarkable. Went with
Duchess of Portland to the play.—I talked to her in the
same style, we had talked the preceding evening to the
Duke—she felt it very much—I found from her Fox had
seen the Duke on Sunday, and that Hare had been with
her, and that both had been wrought upon by these
visits.

Tuesday, December 18.

LORD LOUGHBOROUGH called on me; he was greatly
hurt at the Duke of Portland's inaction, and Fox's violence. He adverted to our conference on the evening of
the 12th—said it was one of wrangle—that Lord Derby
was there to report to Brookes's all that passed—that it
was unfair in the Duke of Portland not to have spoken

---

* Except once, on his asking whether it became him, even if he felt or
thought as we did, to go with an offer of support ; and on my replying, Certainly not, but that we might all go in a body to the levee, and he, after it
was over, should go into the Closet, and there lay our assurances of support
and loyalty at His Majesty's feet ; and to this he said with warmth, that he
would not go like Lord Rockingham, in the year 1780, to be laughed at, and
that he never would enter the Closet unless the King sent for him to make
him his minister.—(*Original Note.*)

more out, since he had seen the King's Speech several days before, had approved it, and had been made acquainted with the Proclamation when it was yet a secret to everybody. He urged the necessity of *his* talking to the Duke, and also that of forcing him by taking the sense of the party, and going to him in a body to compel him to declare himself either decidedly for, or decidedly against Fox.—We all agreed it was absolutely necessary for the Duke of Portland to declare *his* sentiments and ours in the House of Lords. Measures were taken to recommend it to him as a necessary step—I was to go to him first, and afterwads Wyndham. This we did, and he engaged to say the next day, Wednesday, when Lord Grenville was to bring on a Bill relative to the power of the Crown over aliens, that he was disposed to support it, and in general as long as the circumstances or the crisis lasted to support the Government of the country.—Lord Fitzwilliam left London this day, from difficulty how to act, and distress of mind relative to Fox.—Wyndham, of Norfolk, also came to me; his opinions entirely coincide with ours; he was for an amicable separation, not a rupture with Fox.—I dined with the Duke of York, and staid till half-past one.—Wyndham, Lord Rawdon,* and General Bude† dined—Duke of York steady, and right in his principles to a degree.

WEDNESDAY, DEC. 19.

CALLED on Wyndham—same conversation over again about Fox—yet nothing done. I waited for the Duke of Portland to carry me to the House, which I had fixed on, in order to decide him in making his speech—he never came till the House was up—from thence to Duke of Portland—nothing material passed—he said he had been detained by people till near five, but that he would

---

* Afterwards Marquis of Hastings.

† General Bude had been preceptor to the Duke of York, and was an intimate favourite of George III.

say on Friday what he had intended to say to-day—he lamented Fox's conduct, but still reprobated the idea of breaking with him, considering it as likely to produce much real harm to the country.

Thursday, Dec. 20.

At the drawing-room—At Lord Loughborough's particular request, Sir Gilbert Elliot went to Duke of Portland to know what was his opinion as to Lord Loughborough's taking the Seals.—The Duke was decidedly against it, and said he would never consent to it.— Duke of Leeds called on me—he also thinks precisely as we do.

Friday, Dec. 21.

At the levee—King but moderately gracious—clearly supposes the Duke of Portland and his friends influenced by Fox.

The House of Lords on second reading of Alien Bill —much mischief from Lord Lansdowne—Duke of Portland spoke as he promised, but he only said that he would give his support to this specific measure, because he thought it necessary, from the situation of the country—that this motive alone influenced him—he arraigned Ministry for neglect— said he could never forget *how* they came into office, and attributed to that and their subsequent conduct, a great deal of the existing mischief —he did not, as he had intended, express his intention of supporting Government, and his speech certainly (though it was not his meaning) conveyed to the House much more the sentiments of a man intending to oppose, than one inclined to support the measures of Government. This, which we could not help considering as a breach of promise, hurt and vexed us exceedingly, and it was agreed to meet the next day and concert measures.—I

dined late at the Duke of Leeds's with Lord Bulkeley—
nothing worth notice passed.

SATURDAY, DECEMBER 22.

At three o'clock, Lords Loughborough and Porchester, Burke, Wyndham, Sir. G. Elliot, Anstruther, Dr.
Lawrence, and Elliot of Wells, met at my house.—Lord
Loughborough said he had been with the Duke of Portland; that he had had a very long and very explicit
interview with him; that the Duke had entered fairly
into the subject; that he had declared himself as averse
as he himself was to Fox's principles and motions, but
that he was of opinion that it was not yet a time to
break with him, and that it would be better to try for
every possible means of reconciliation.—He was convinced that Fox had lost himself by what Baldwin had
told him, and that he himself was a partaker of his unpopularity, yet that still he wished to keep on terms
with him. —Lord Loughborough then stated to us how
such a conduct, inasmuch as we were considered as belonging to the Portland Party, involved us in all the
unpopularity and disgrace attending Fox's principles;
that therefore it was become necessary to decide what
was to be done, and how the Duke of Portland could be
obliged to declare his sentiments to be contrary to those
of Fox.

Burke, with his usual eloquence, talked for an hour.
He said the Duke of Portland was riding in a ship, with
two anchors, one cast in the Palais Royal, the other in
Berkeley Square—that he was the instrument of Fox's
schemes, or rather the schemes of Fox's abettors; that
these had seduced Fox's principles, had made him believe that a Government like ours was not a proper one
for great talents to display themselves in, that by working on his ambition, which, carried to excess, becomes
wickedness, they had made him from these reasons approve and praise the French Revolution—that these

principles were now become inherent in him—that if he was to renounce them, it was because he must become a convert or a hypocrite—that he saw little of the first, that he dreaded we should be the dupes of the latter; and Wyndham did not think matters gone so far as to make an irreparable breach with Fox necessary. He confessed he feared he had lost himself irrevocably in the country, yet that even that might be recovered, and events rise which would bring him back to his friends; that therefore, if possible, *he* wished the separation to extend only to the present measures. This Sir G. Elliot, Anstruther, and Lawrence combated. We sat till it was time to go to the House, without coming to any other conclusion than that we would meet again in greater numbers, and the next day was fixed for that purpose.

At the House of Lords I saw Lord Carlisle; he was for Lord Loughborough's accepting the Seals, as a pledge for the good intentions of the Party. He agreed with us on all other points, and on this I was not averse to agree with him. Fox carried me home; he expressed great horror at the "décret" of the 15th December, 1792, issued* by the National Convention.—He thought war likely—The Dutch he considered as adverse to it. He was in very good humour, and talked with great liberality on the difference of opinion between him and some of his friends.

SUNDAY, DECEMBER 23.

WENT with Sir G. Elliot to Lord Loughborough; in-formed him of what had passed between Sir G. and Duke of Portland—that the Duke had declared, that from embarrassment in speaking in public, he had omit-ted to declare his general intentions to support Govern-

---

* On the 11th December, Louis XVI. was brought before the Convention. On the 15th they issued a decree, forbidding his wife and sister to have access to him.

ment under all the circumstances of the present crisis—
that he intended to do it on Friday, but found no opportunity, and certainly would avail himself of the first
which offered.   We therefore advised with Lord Loughborough, whether, these being the intentions of the
Duke, it was not rather unkind to press upon him in
the way we had agreed on the day before, and whether
some gentler mode of conveying our wishes to his knowledge might not be suggested.   To this Lord Loughborough agreed, at the same time insisting on the necessity of doing this *immediately*, as every day would diminish the number of his (the Duke's) friends.   This
led us to look over the Red Book, and we reckoned that
about 107 Members of the House of Commons, and 40
Peers were (according to our notions of their way of
thinking) disposed to think like us, and concur with us
in a sort of representation to be made to the Duke.
Lord Porchester came in, and acquiesced in what we
said, and such it was determined should be the groundwork of the plan to be proposed to the meeting to be
held at my house at three.   I went from Lord Loughborough's to Lord Beauchamp's and Lord Bute's to ask
them to attend the meeting—I also called on the Duke
of Portland—told him I was glad to hear what had
passed between him and Sir Gilbert the night before—
that it was my wish always to enrol myself under his
standard—that I was afraid his friends were falling
from him—that Fox had lost himself—that I was ready
to give him credit for no bad intentions, but that *others*,
and the great majority of the nation, did not.   The
Duke recommended patience, and said impressions of
any kind did not last long; that those Fox gave might
be done away by time, and he wished people would be
patient.   I said it was impossible to make them so;
that many of his best friends were alarmed, were uneasy
for him, whom they considered as *their* leader, and
wished most sincerely to preserve him as their leader,
and the leader of the Whig party; but their minds were
afloat, and that he must expect soon to hear more on
the subject.

At three, Lords Carlisle, Bute, Porchester, Loughborough, Beauchamp, and Anstruther, Burke, Sir G. Elliot, and Elliot of Wells, met at my house. The conversation was, in general, the same as the day before, but carried on more regularly; and it was agreed, in consideration of what the Duke of Portland had said, that instead of going in a body to Burlington House, myself, Sir G. Elliot, and Wyndham, should go, to say that several of the Duke's best friends had met; and, being all most anxious to have, and preserve, him for their leader, they wished him, *after* he had declared in the House what he had promised to say, to call a general meeting (conformable to the list we had made at Lord Loughborough's), and to take their sense what was to be done for keeping the Party;* that the *Party was*, in fact, divided by Fox's acting with a few in direct opposition to the declared principles of the Party from the time of the first Proclamation; neither the Duke of Portland, nor those known to be his friends, can act subserviently to Mr. Fox, and the Party which he has adopted; that it is necessary, on the first occasion, to disclaim his (Mr. Fox) assuming the appearance of their leader, which they will not submit to; that this must be done either individually or collectively; that it is advisable to arrange the Party on its old principles under the proper leader, the Duke of Portland, recognising him in his natural situation.

We intended to have gone to the Duke at eleven in the evening, but Wyndham came to my house; and, after discussing the matter between him, Sir G. Elliot, and myself, we agreed it would be cruel, and bear an unkind appearance, to go to the Duke abruptly; therefore, it was determined that Wyndham should go to him *alone*, prepare him for what we had to say, and that we should wait on him the next morning.

* These are Lord Loughborough's words, and were written down as a kind of instruction for us.—*Original Note.*

DECEMBER 24.

WYNDHAM came to breakfast—at eleven, he, Sir Gilbert, and myself went to Burlington House. Sir Gilbert opened the business, stated it as *now* not coming from ourselves, but from a body of the party who had had several meetings at my house; that the specific points to which the Duke's assent was desired were, that Mr. Fox, and some gentlemen formerly acting with our party, having taking a line, and expressed sentiments, in Parliament contrary to the majority of our party, and on subjects which we think too important to the interests and safety of the country to make it possible we should acquiesce in it—a division had thereby taken place in the Party. That Mr. Fox having been reputed the leader of our party in the House of Commons, we cannot otherwise avoid being involved ourselves in his opinions, or prevent their being ascribed generally to us, than by declaring explicitly that we no longer consider Mr. Fox as speaking our sentiments; that although by their own acts Mr. Fox and his present friends stand divided from the Party, yet the Party itself remains connected on its ancient principles, and under its natural leader, the Duke of Portland; that knowing him to agree with us in our own sentiments, and in our dissent from those of Mr. Fox, it is important that some declaration to that effect should be made, as an act of the Party, sanctioned by him as its leader; that he should take the proper steps for assembling those members of our party who agree with him and us, and for placing our Parliamentary proceedings on the footing of a connexion and concert, and for preventing a dispersion of his party, which was become inevitable, if some steps of that nature should not be taken. To give weight to what we said, we employed every argument which suggested itself to us—we dwelt on the very little regard or attention Fox shewed his friends; that he had followed his own opinions without consulting or communicating with them; that from the first proclamation of the twenty-first of May, 1792, he had withheld every real confidence from them, and given it, if not openly, at least to all useful effects, to Grey and the Reformers; that he did not feel what was considered as the *sole* motive of the two last steps taken by the Duke, viz., his attendance at the Whig Club, and his influencing the votes of his brother, Lord Edward Bentinck, and others in the House, the day of the opening Parliament; that these motives were, by the Duke's own avowal, to keep up *still* to the public an appearance of accord between the Duke of Portland and Fox; and they ought the more to call forth the gratitude of Fox, as in both cases the Duke acted in direct opposition to his own judgment, which he allowed on these occasions to have given way to his personal affection for Fox; that Fox, instead of prizing this as he ought, availed himself, or suffered his friends to avail themselves of it (which comes to the same), to impose on the minds of the public, by saying he and the Duke of Portland acted in union, and by making him and us, his followers, partake of all the odium and disgrace Fox had brought upon himself by his conduct. Besides these reasons for adopting the plan we had suggested, we also represented to him the very strong one of *public duty*, that called upon us for it; that in times like these it was a dereliction of that duty to allow private feelings to get the better of what ought to be our public conduct; that we owed it to him (Duke of Portland) our leader, to ourselves, and to our country, to come forward and manifest clearly and unequivocally what the Party was, by whom it was headed, of whom composed, and the principles on which it acted. The result of this conference was, that the Duke admitted the truth of these propositions—the necessity for acquiescing in the points recommended to him. He stated very strongly, and, indeed, more strongly manifested the great violence that this determination did to his private affection and attachment to Mr. Fox. He confessed it was a weakness,

arising from predilection and tenderness to Fox; and to
this cause must be ascribed the backwardness which he
had hitherto shewn to take these explicit and decisive
steps, rather than to any doubt in the reason and necessity of the thing, or on the nature of his public duty.
But that his mind was in some degree reconciled to
these strong measures from an opinion that, however
disagreeable they might appear to Mr. Fox in the meanwhile, yet they might ultimately tend even to his benefit
and comfort, because it seemed more desirable for the
interest of Mr. Fox that the Party should be held together under its old connexion, and in a form therefore
that rendered a re-union of all its parts possible, if
change of circumstances should seem to render his public principles and ours compatible with that re-union,
than that a total dissolution of the Party should happen,
which in a very short time would render its re-assem-
bling entirely impossible; that he was much flattered
and affected by the continuance of our confidence, and
that he accepted the offer we made him of acting in
Party under him both with great pride and satisfaction.
With regard to assembling us at present, he stated some
objection, which related only to the present moment,
such as the uncertainty he was in concerning the sentiments of several of his friends, the absence of others,
&c.; but he would take the earliest opportunity, and
the best means that occurred to him, of complying with
this part of our request.

With regard to a manifestation of his own sentiments, and those of his party, he would *immediately*
complete the declaration of his opinion on the present
state of public affairs, and the necessity of giving a fair
and honourable support to Government in the manner
which the interests of the country required. That
Lord Titchfield would declare the same opinions in the
House of Commons on the earliest opportunity. That
any friend of his, in declaring these sentiments which
we profess, and which have been explained in our present
communication with him, may state himself to speak his
sentiments and be authorized to say so.

This determination I reported the same evening to Lords Carlisle, Porchester, and Loughborough, at the house of the last, and they all were much pleased and satisfied with it.

December 25.

I CALLED on Lord Bute and Lord Beauchamp, and told them what the Duke of Portland had agreed to do, and they were also perfectly satisfied. I called at Burlington House: the Prince was with the Duke of Portland. I dined and supped with the Duke of York.

Wednesday, December 26.

AT Burlington House, the Duchess, whom I saw before I went in to the Duke, highly pleased with what had passed, and agreed with us entirely in opinion, reprobated Fox, admitted the impossibility of his ever regaining the confidence of the people, wished the Duke of Portland and Lord Titchfield to speak, and was on all points quite right.

The Duke of Portland carried me to the House, and went into it determined (as I thought) to speak. The Alien Bill passed; opposed by Lord Guildford and Lords Lansdowne and Lauderdale. These two made very violent and mischievous speeches.—Lord Loughborough answered them in one of the finest speeches possible; but the Duke of Portland, to the great concern and grief of his friends, *did not say a word*. I urged him repeatedly to get up, but he said he really could not, he felt it impossible: that Lord Loughborough had said all that could be said, and that it was impossible to speak after so fine a speech. I pressed him to say those very words, and nothing more, but without effect.—I dined with him afterwards *tête-a-tête*.

I had not the heart or courage to talk to him on the subject.—I perceived how greatly he felt embarrassed, and I could not bring myself to distress him more by telling him how unfairly he had disappointed his friends, and how much he had committed me by authorizing me to say he certainly would speak.—He was so very uncomfortable that it would have been cruel to have plagued him; and although he saw, by my silence and manner, how much hurt and afflicted I was at his having done nothing, yet I saved him the humiliation of making him confess his own weakness. Fox came in about half-past ten: the Duke kept him waiting as long as I staid, which he rather seemed to wish to prolong, and went to him on my going, about eleven.

Thursday, December 27.

I received a letter very early from Lord Loughborough, lamenting and complaining of the Duke of Portland's silence; lamenting it from public reasons; complaining of it from the injury it did his numerous body of friends, who wish to hold high the honour of his name.

LETTER FROM LORD LOUGHBOROUGH TO LORD MALMESBURY.

My dear Lord,—Though I am sensible that I spoke with some effect to-night, I am not young enough to feel on that account any satisfaction that can make up for the Duke of Portland's silence. The few words in which he expressed to me his approbation, pronounced upon his legs, would have had more effect on the House and on the public than ten speeches. The House had waited for his declaration; the course of the debate called for it, particularly in the latter part between Lord Lansdowne and me, and still he left it in doubt which of us spoke his sentiments; knowing too that Lord Lansdowne's party make no scruple to use his name against his intentions, and will not fail to quote his silence against my speech; and this at a moment when the connexion with Lord Lansdowne was so plainly marked. The Duke of Portland hesitates whether he shall withdraw his countenance from a party formed of Lord Lansdowne, Fox, and Grey, under the auspices of Chauvelin. What a position that is for his character, and those numerous friends who, not only from personal attachment, but as a great public point for the country, wish to hold high the honour of his name!

I do not think I shall compose myself to-morrow into a fit temper to go to Burlington House and present my remonstrance to him; but I dare to say Lord Lauderdale* will not fail to be there. I wish Sir Gilbert Elliot and you would consider what is to be done, for I cannot devise any measure to retrieve the mischief of this day to the Duke of Portland. The House of Commons will not make up for it. The only thing that could be effectual would be a positive declaration to the party that has left him, that he holds them as entirely detached, and not less in opposition to him than to Government. But that I despair of.

I could not help writing this to you, tired as I am; but yet more vexed than tired.

I ever am, my dear Lord,
Yours most sincerely,

Wednesday night.　　　　　　　　LOUGHBOROUGH.

I was prevented answering this letter from Mr. Robinson's† being in imminent danger of dying, and from being obliged to be with him and my sister. I, how-

---

* One of the Ultra-Whig party, and the most staunch friend of Mr. Grey and the Apologists of the French Revolution. He died forty years afterwards in opposition to Lord Grey's Reform Government.

† Mr. Robinson, Lord Grantham's brother, married Lord Malmesbury's sister.

ever, called first at Burlington House, where, finding
Wyndham, I did not interrupt the Duke; and afterwards, at three o'clock, on Lord Loughborough, in Bed-
ford-square. I felt as he did; and as a voucher of the
truth of what I reported from the conversation which
passed between the Duke of Portland and Wyndham,
Elliot and myself, when we were deputed by the meeting at my house on the 23rd of December, I produced
the written account of it, which had been minuted down
the moment it was over, which had been admitted as
truth by Wyndham and Elliot, and had been read
by me and Elliot to the Duke himself, the day the conversation had taken place (the 24th). Lord Loughborough had lying on his table when I came in, (he
returned at the same moment from a ride,) a letter
from the Duke of Portland. He read it, and, on giving
it me to read, said, " *This is worse and worse!*"

The letter was to explain the motives of his silence.
It stated, that after having missed the opportunity of
speaking immediately after Lord Guildford, and particularly after Lord Carlisle having so explicitly declared
that he did not wish to see any change of Administration, it was impossible for him to speak, because he
found he should be obliged to make distinctions, which,
from his want of habit in speaking in public, he felt he
could not do in a manner or in words satisfactory to
himself. That, had he spoken without any reference to
these distinctions, it would be a *renunciation and a de-
nunciation of Fox*, and to this he could not bring his
mind; and, so far from giving it as his opinion that
there should be no change of the present Administration,
he entered his solemn protest against any such doctrine.
That what had passed in the House of Lords that day
confirmed him they ought to be changed, since, without
the able and honourable support they had received from
him (Lord Loughborough), they would have been
brought to shame and disgrace; "and thus," said the
Duke in his letter, " I have accounted for my silence."

It is probable this letter was in consequence of Fox's

conversation; as I said once before, I left him at Burlington House the preceding evening.

Lord Loughborough was violent; he said he was betrayed; and it was with some difficulty I prevented his going immediately to Burlington House. We agreed, however, to meet at Burke's in the evening; but poor Robinson's illness increasing, and his death, which took place at six on the morning of the 28th, prevented my attending it. The post of this day (the 27th) brought the account of the manner in which the King's Speech on the opening of Parliament had been received at Paris, and the memorial read to the National Convention by Le Brun (the Minister for Foreign Affairs) in consequence of it. It appeared so precisely the same as the language held by Lords Lansdowne, Lauderdale, and Fox, that it is impossible not to suppose it concerted here, or to avoid suspecting that they are connected with Chauvelin.

It was agreed this evening that Sir G. Elliot should speak the next day in the House. That he should avail himself of the authority the Duke of Portland had given him in my presence, and that of Wyndham, to declare his sentiments and those of his party.

FRIDAY, DECEMBER 28.

I WAS the whole day with my sister. I heard from Elliot of Wells in the morning, that Wyndham still thought the Duke of Portland meant to separate with Fox, and that we only misconceived each other's words. Lord Beauchamp came to me in the evening, to give me an account of what had passed in the House. How much Fox was angered by Sir Gilbert's speech, how peevishly he had answered it, and how well Sir Gilbert had spoke. Lord Beauchamp's real view appeared to be a wish to know how the matter was likely to end. About one, Sir Gilbert and Wyndham came from Burlington House, where they went immediately after the debate: Fox came there soon after them. They discussed in the Duke of Portland's presence what they supposed to be his opinion, and each contended that he had pledged himself to him. He avowed Sir Gilbert as far as he had in his speech spoken of him as intending to support Government under the present crisis, but did not admit he had authority to say he would separate from Fox. This Fox contended was conveyed in Sir Gilbert's speech. Sir Gilbert said it must be from misconception, either real or wilful: that he had stated distinctly the difference of his opinions from those of Fox, as coming from himself *alone ;* and that he pledged the Duke of Portland and the Party for a general intention to support Government under the present crisis, in order to save the country and protect the Constitution; and he referred to the Duke of Portland to say whether he had not his authority for so doing. The Duke, in presence of Fox and Wyndham, said *he certainly had.*

Fox at this conference was angry, and rude in his manners; the Duke of Portland, embarrassed and perplexed beyond measure; for each side insisted that he had pledged himself to them. And on Sir Gilbert and Wyndham referring to what the Duke had said as to his intentions to support the Government, Fox with vehemence declared that nine days before (Sunday 16) the Duke had agreed with him, in the most unequivocal manner, that he saw no reason why opposition should not be carried on against the present Government on the same principles and from the same reasons as ever.

From this same conference Elliot and Wyndham came to my house, related what had passed, and seemed dissatisfied with the general appearance of the Duke of Portland, and convinced that Fox had an invariable ascendancy over him. I found a note from Lord Loughborough, wishing to see me; I went to him very early on Saturday the 29th December. He wanted to consult

me about what answer should be made to the letter he
received from the Duke of Portland on the 27th instant,
which he had left till now unnoticed, wishing to wait
the event of Sir Gilbert's speech in the House. I then
related to him all that had passed after the debate at
Burlington House; and after a great deal of conversation, in which we agreed entirely as to the necessity of
not suffering ourselves to be disavowed, I expressed my
wish to wait still a little, to postpone to the very last
moment the coming to that explanation, which must
necessarily not only make an irreparable breach between
us and the Duke of Portland, but also completely disgrace him in the public esteem. That my personal
regard for the Duke, as well as what seemed to me to
be the most judicious policy for ourselves, inclined me
to wish to temporize, and that, as Parliament was
drawing towards its prorogation, to let everything hang
over till after the recess; and then, the evening previous
to the meeting of Parliament, (if nothing could be
done during the recess to reconcile the Duke of Portland's conduct with the assurances he had given us,) to
have a general meeting of the whole party, and in that
meeting to come to a free discussion and open declaration of opinions and sentiments, and that every man
should take his own line, and follow his own principles.
That, as we knew the Party to be absolutely dissolved
in point of fact, it was dangerous to allow the public to
consider it still as holding together; since it would give
weight to pernicious measures suggested by some of the
Party, by leaving room to the public to suppose that
these measures were approved by the whole of it.
That it was unfair also to ourselves; since, thinking and
acting as we did, it was subjecting us to obloquy and
abuse, and taking away the effect of our opinions, as
long as it was a matter of doubt whether our connexion
with Fox and his followers existed or not.

Lord Loughborough acquiesced in what I said; he
afterwards met Burke and Wyndham at my house. I
could not be present at this meeting, but it was nearly

to the effect I have just mentioned. Lord Lough-borough was sent for by the Prince.

SUNDAY, DECEMBER 30, AND MONDAY, 31.

VARIOUS conversations concerning what Sir Gilbert Elliot should say in the House. Absolutely necessary he should say more, as at present it was a trick of Fox to say he misunderstood him, and that he at present stood charged with the imputation of quoting the Duke of Portland without his authority. Frederick North and Douglas were with me on Sunday evening. Frederick North strenuously on our side lamented his brother's (Lord Guildford's) motion in the House on Wednesday, and offered to speak in behalf of Sir Gilbert if called upon. Wyndham and Elliot went from my house to the Duke of Portland's. They returned late. Sir Gilbert told the Duke (in presence of Lord Fitzwilliam), that he intended to speak the next day, and what he meant to say. The Duke approved it. Lord Fitzwilliam came up in consequence of a letter from Burke; he had left town a few days after the opening of Parliament, and evidently from a wish to be absent, and from a dilemma in his mind similar to that in the Duke of Portland's.

MONDAY, DECEMBER 31.

WYNDHAM came to breakfast; he had prepared, at the Duke of Portland's request, some words Lord Titchfield was to say. They went to acquiesce in all Sir Gilbert had said, and was to say; and to express an intention to support Government, though he did not think favourably of the individuals who composed the Ministry. These Wyndham carried to the Duke of Portland, and they were approved. Sir Gilbert spoke, and distin-

guished between what he had said the preceding Saturday as his own sentiments (viz. his wide difference from
Fox), and that part of his speech in which he mentioned,
as from the Duke of Portland, his intention to support
Government.

Lord Titchfield said nearly what Wyndham had put
down, but ended his speech by so violent an abuse of
Ministry that it did away the whole effect. It was
evident Fox had come to Burlington House later than
Wyndham, and added these last sentences. Sir Gilbert
exceedingly hurt. Anstruther came and related it to
me directly, at my sister's. Burke afterwards to my
house, in a rage: he said, speaking of the Duke of
Portland, *We had killed Patroclus, and were now
fighting for the dead body.* Much conversation on what
was to be done.

JANUARY 1, 1793 (Tuesday).

LORD LOUGHBOROUGH with me early; he eager for a
further " éclaircissement " with the Duke, and for laying
the whole before the public: I still for waiting, if possible, till the end of the recess. I urged the entire ruin
it must be to the Duke of Portland, and the extreme
harm the Party must suffer at the same time; and,
under all circumstances, the bringing transactions of
this sort to light, let them be ever so clear and right,
always were misconstrued, and had an invidious object
ascribed to them.

Lord Loughborough from me went to see the Prince
of Wales in the evening. Lord Loughborough sent me
a note from Lord Carlisle, in which Lord Carlisle says
that, in a conversation with Lord Fitzwilliam, *Lord
Fitzwilliam seemed to think Sir Gilbert had not the
Duke of Portland's authority to say what he did in
the place, and in the manner he said it.* Lord Loughborough in his note said it was impossible to suffer this,
and that it would be a ridiculous delicacy to suffer our

character and honour to be sullied by having such a suspicion on them.

WEDNESDAY, JANUARY 2.

EARLY at Lord Loughborough's with Sir Gilbert Elliot.—I wished to know the *precise words* Lord Fitzwilliam used to Lord Carlisle.—Much depended on it. Staid three hours; debated what measures should be taken; my opinion invariable to spare the Duke of Portland as long as possible.—His own good character and sense might bring him round; as might also Fox's violence, and reckoning *too much* on him. — Lord Loughborough read us a very long letter, or rather manifesto, in which he recapitulated all which had passed since June. It was incomparably well done. It left not a doubt of the consistency of our conduct and principles, and of the variability of those of the Duke of Portland.—Lord Loughborough said he meant it as an answer to the Duke's letter of the 24th.—I said it was so true a statement of my sentiments, and agreed so perfectly with what I knew, that, instead of its being sent as an answer to that letter, it should be kept *till the last moment;* and if we found the Duke, when we met after the recess, persisted in his opiniative weakness for Fox, and had no consideration for our characters, then to send it, or read it to him, as the joint sentiments of us all, as accounting most perfectly for what we had done, and expressing very precisely the line we intended to follow. That *then*, if it was combated or denied, it might be made public; but that, as I could not help considering the making such a series of facts known would create great confusion and do real harm, it was my opinion that it should be avoided to the last moment. I repeated that I concurred entirely with Lord Loughborough as to the principle on which he ought to act, and we only differed as to the time. We walked towards Lord

Carlisle's. Lord Loughborough mentioned in the way the ministerial Note given in to Lord Grenville by Chauvelin* a few days ago; he said it was nearly the same as Le Brun's Memorial to the Convention; that *he believed* it would be laid before Parliament, which would be kept sitting a few days longer for that purpose.

Lord Carlisle not at home; Sir Gilbert saw him in the House of Commons. He said Lord Fitzwilliam understood the Duke of Portland did not expect Sir Gilbert would have mentioned his opinions *in the House of Commons,* and that it was as to the *place* not as to the *sentiments* delivered, that Lord Fitzwilliam questioned Sir Gilbert being authorised. This an unfair statement. Wyndham had told the Duke of Portland, the day Sir Gilbert spoke, that he did mean to speak, and what he intended to say, and the Duke stated no objection.

The Alien Bill† recommitted this day in the House of Commons, and no debate.

Thursday, January 3.

Meeting at ten in the evening at my house. Lords Carlisle, Loughborough, Bute, and Beauchamp, Wyndham, Anstruther, and Sir G. Elliot. Long discussion, which was little more than a repetition of what had passed between us and the Duke of Portland, and after

---

* Chauvelin had been accredited from the King of France, and now addressed this note to Lord Grenville as agent of the Executive Council of the French Republic. In it he deprecates any wish on the part of the Republic to interfere with any people who have not already by conquest obtained their " liberty ;" and consequently to excite sedition in England. He demands (as Lord Gower has been recalled from Paris) whether Great Britain is to be looked upon as a Belligerent or a Neutral power. Lord Grenville, in his answer, condescended to explain the policy of the Government, although he refused to acknowledge his rank, or his right to address him officially.

† The host of Royalist Emigrés and Republican agents which poured into the country rendered this measure necessary. It was supported by the Duke of Portland, Lords Loughborough, Carlisle, Spencer, and other Whigs, and opposed by Lord Lansdowne, Fox, &c.

a long conversation we decided that nothing could be done now, before Parliament adjourned, and that during the recess some measures should be taken. Wyndham and Lord Bute both agreed to go to the Duke of Portland, and urge him to take a more decided part.

FRIDAY, JANUARY 4.

DEBATE in the Commons on the passing of the Alien Bill. Wyndham metaphysical and too refined in his speech, as he had been in his language at my house the preceding night. The Bill carried without a division. Nothing passed this night week. Parliament adjourned on Wednesday, the 9th. I saw the Duke of Portland frequently, but without any effect as to his opinions relative to Fox; Lord Bute had spoken to him in the same style, but without making any impression. Lord Loughborough sent him on Saturday, the 12th January, the letter spoken of before; he had made some few alterations in it. Thursday, the 10th. Lord Loughborough, at Lady Payne's, shewed me a letter from Dundas, pressing him to decide as to taking the Great Seal, saying that he and Pitt had abstained renewing the subject for some time past, under the idea that there were still hopes of having the Duke of Portland; that this was now considered to be at an end.

Lord Loughborough answered, that he still had some hopes that a letter he intended to write would produce some effect; and, as it was of such importance to be joined by so respectable a character as the Duke of Portland, he still wished to wait.

MONDAY, JANUARY 14.

I WENT to Brookwood* and returned on the 16th.

* Lord Malmesbury's place in Hampshire.

While at Brookwood I wrote a letter to Duke of Portland, explicit of my opinions and intentions, and sent it the 16th.

Brookwood, January 16, 1793.

MY DEAR LORD,—I did not give up all hopes of coming this week to Bulstrode, till I found that it was absolutely necessary for me to pass the greatest part of it here.

In addition to the many reasons which always make me come there with pleasure, I should have been particularly glad, at this moment, to have had an uninterrupted and leisure discourse with your Grace on the state of public affairs.

Although I have never concealed from you my opinions, and I have every reason to hope they do not materially differ from your own, yet it is most essential for the comfort of *all* my feelings, that I should be perfectly clear and explicit; because, as these are feelings of the most respectful and affectionate attachment for your Grace, they would be hurt in the extreme, if it were possible that, in the event, any part of my public conduct was to appear as if I had acted with neglect or want of confidence towards you.

From this motive (a very important one indeed to me) you will, I am sure, forgive my repeating what you have often heard me say, that it is my opinion that the Government of this country ought to be cordially and strenuously supported under all the circumstances, and in all the measures arising from the present crisis; and as this crisis is one which cannot pass away suddenly, but must be depending as long as any attempts are made to maintain elsewhere, or introduce here, the French doctrines, I conceive this support cannot be confined to any fixed term, but must be unlimited as to its duration, and given without a drawback.

This sentiment I know to be so near your own, that (even with a less liberal mind than yours) I should run no risk in stating it roundly to be mine, and saying it

is one on which I intend to act. I am heartily sorry
that it is not also the sentiment of Fox. I have such a
deference for his judgment, respect for his abilities, and
so strong a personal regard for him, that it gives me
great pain to differ from him on a point of such magnitude, and in its nature so conclusive, that I do not see
a possibility of our living long enough for us ever to
meet again in our public opinions; for Fox must
either be sincere or insincere in what he has done, and
is doing. If he is sincere he is dangerous, *acting upon
principle*; if insincere he is dangerous, *acting without
principle*. The distinction only reaches his private
character (of which I need not say how well I think);
but the danger, and the determination of his mind is
precisely the same under both positions; and the consequence of his acting on such a principle, and systematically, extends so far, when supported by powers like
his, that it cannot be too much guarded against, and,
in my mind, impels a duty before which every private
consideration whatever must give way.

It grieves me to separate from him; it grieves me
still more to see how completely he has set the whole
country against him, and how far he has driven himself
from a probability of holding a high office in it! How
entirely he has broke up the Party, and how much he
has made his best friends, and those towards whom he
had obligations of the deepest nature, partakers of the
consequences of his ill-judged conduct! I know full
well your Grace's feelings on this subject; it is impossible not to honour you for them. You have heard so
much of it, that I have lately declined speaking to you
on it, from a wish not to give you pain, and I should
have avoided it even now, if I had not been apprehensive that a longer silence would have left a doubt as to
the course I mean to take when Parliament meets; and,
to do away the possibility of any such doubt existing,
is, as I before said, the object of my writing this
letter.

Were I to suffer my intentions to remain concealed

and unexplained to you, I should most deservedly for-
feit your esteem and good opinion; but I am certain of
preserving both, as long as I act sincerely and openly,
and from the conviction that I am doing right. I
do not, therefore, apologize for having written thus
freely.   I am, &c.   MALMESBURY.

His Grace the Duke of Portland.

I dined the day of my return at Batt's; Lord Loughborough there.—Nothing new from Bulstrode.—No answer from the Duke.—He had seen Dundas, and stated
to him fairly that the consequences of his taking the
Great Seal would be, that forty or fifty members *only*
would join Government.—That as many more, now with
Government, would probably return to Opposition; that
it was for Ministers to consider whether it was for their
interest to take him on these conditions.

FRIDAY, JANUARY 18.

I SAW Lord Bute in the morning; he a little warped.
Strongly against Lord Loughborough taking the Seals;
said it would make all who followed him unpopular to
a certain degree.—I dined with Lord Loughborough,
with only Anstruther.—He declared his determination
of taking the Seals; only doubted as to the time.—I advised him to see Duke of Portland first, though I was
sure he would be against it; and, above all, to fix
Wyndham to engage him to approve it on his legs in
the House of Commons.

SATURDAY, JANUARY 19.

LORD BUTE called on me. He was out of sorts and
hurt, and talked of going to Luton.

SUNDAY, JANUARY 20.

CALLED on Lord Loughborough; he returned with me, and went from my house to meet Pitt by appointment. He stayed with him about an hour and a half, and then came back to me.—He told me war was a *decided measure;* that Pitt saw it was inevitable, and that the sooner it was begun the better. That we might possess ourselves of the French islands; that the nation now was disposed for war, which might not be the case six weeks hence. That we were in much greater forwardness than the French. They had only six ships of the line in the Mediterranean—we upwards of twenty; that he had two millions ready, and that he trusted the surplus of the permanent revenue would be 600,000*l.* a-year. That the Dutch were quite right, and in earnest; that Russia was willing to go all lengths; that Spain was ready to join, and that all the little Powers only waited our giving the signal. He mentioned with concern that the King of Prussia intended to take *Great Poland,* and had declared his intentions, which we most strongly reprobated; considering it not only as unjust in principle, but as a measure which was ill-timed to a degree. After this communication, Lord Loughborough told me in Pitt's name, and from him, that Pitt wished everything that had passed between him and me at the time of the Regency to be forgotten; and that he wished to have my support, and that I would consider myself as much connected with him as ever. He likewise offered office through me to Sir Gilbert Elliot.—To all this I returned a very civil answer, but nothing more. In the evening at Nagel's; he very *coming.*

Monday, January 21.

Breakfasted with Batt; told him what I had heard from Pitt; agreed it was proper to write him a letter which Batt should carry. Called on Duke of York, and went with him to the office. News of the sentence* of death being pronounced on the King of France. Called at Burlington House twice. Duke of Portland not at home.

Tuesday, January 22.

Wrote a letter to Pitt, through Batt, at Lord Loughborough's.—Dined with Pitt and Dundas at Wimbledon. I was two hours with Duke of Portland.—He apologized for not answering my letter, and thanked me for it. He said there was very little chance of our differing in our sentiments. That perhaps we did not *quite* agree as to the extent of the support to be given. He lamented Fox's conduct, and particularly blamed it, if it were true (which he did not think), that he had given Sheridan authority to speak for him at the meeting held at the Crown and Anchor on the Liberty of the Press. In short, the Duke of Portland this day was exactly what we left him that day that Sir Gilbert, Wyndham and myself were sent to him. He clearly had not seen Fox, nor received any bad impressions whilst at Bulstrode. He talked a great deal about Ireland. Shewed me a letter in which Mr. Ponsonby stated, that he and Conolly took the idea of reforming the Parliamentary representation into their own hands, in order to prevent its getting into much worse. That from the laxity and want of confidence in the Irish Government, the measure was forced upon them, and not to be avoided.—The Duke of Portland very uneasy about this.—Dined at the Duke of York's.—He steady to a degree.

* Decreed by the Convention, Jan. 17th, having passed by a majority of eleven in seven hundred and twenty-one.

WEDNESDAY, JANUARY 23.

BATT carried my letter to Pitt.—Lord Loughborough called upon me on his return from Westminster Hall. He said, Pitt had again repeated to him what he had said before about me. I repeated to him what had passed at Burlington House. We concluded it was a favourable moment for him to see the Duke: he therefore read me a letter, stating his intention of taking the Seals, and his reasons, which he rested on the duty of every man now doing his utmost to serve his country, and the cause in which it was going to engage. This letter he asked me to carry; but on reflection it was determined that it had better go through Baldwin, of whose understanding the Duke of Portland had a high opinion, and who he thought was attached to him; Baldwin, therefore, was to go to Burlington House in the evening.

LORD MALMESBURY TO MR. PITT.

Spring Gardens, January, 23rd, 1793.

DEAR SIR,—I have felt myself exceedingly obliged by the communication which I have received from you through Lord Loughborough.* The interruption of our intercourse, I have no scruple to say, has been a subject of much regret to my mind; and the manner in which you express yourself relative to me, calls for my sincere acknowledgments. The part I have for some time past taken with respect to public affairs has been dictated by strong persuasion of the necessity of the measures which His Majesty's Ministers have taken in the present very difficult crisis. Every day furnishes additional reasons to confirm the *propriety* of that support which I am dis-

---

* On the 26th of January, 1793, Lord Loughborough succeeded Lord Thurlow as Chancellor.

posed to afford Government, and which I feel must be cordial and unequivocal, in order to be effective.

I am, dear Sir, with great truth, &c.,

MALMESBURY.

The Right Hon. Mr. Pitt.

[After this there is a hiatus in the Diary until July.]

LETTER FROM SIR GILBERT ELLIOT TO LORD MALMESBURY.

Minto, Sunday, 27th Jan. 1793.

MY DEAR LORD MALMESBURY,—I perceive by Elliot's letter, which I received this morning, as well as by your own, which I received the day before yesterday on my return from Edinburgh, that you will be very angry to see the date of this letter; and still more when I add that, as I have arranged matters here, I cannot depend on setting out before next Saturday, the 2nd of February, nor of arriving in London before Tuesday, the 5th of that month. It is *county* business which detains me, and which *cannot* be done without me. It would give great offence here, (as well as occasion the loss of a year in a considerable benefit to the country,) if I should leave it; more especially as it is the *second* time already that it has been appointed by me.

I feel very strongly the urgency of my return to London; but unfortunately the notice given by Pitt of his intention to adjourn again has involved me in the business I mention, and there is no remedy.

You will feel the difficulty, or rather the impossibility, of my forming a decisive judgment on the question you put to me,* until I have an opportunity of knowing all circumstances down to the latest date, and of communicating and comparing my own thoughts in a full and satisfactory way with you and other friends. If I were

---

* Alluding to an offer of Office that Lord Malmesbury was authorized by Pitt to make to Sir Gilbert Elliot.—Vide Diary, January 20th.

called on for a decision *now*, and where I am now writing, I should say, *No ;* and I confess my inclination runs so strongly against the coupling a separation from former friends (and perhaps from party altogether) with the acceptance of office, that I can hardly give the question a fair consideration, nor describe the circumstances in which I should think it necessary or advisable to do so. Such circumstances, however, may exist; and I should for that reason wish for the means of knowing the state of things, as well as of full consultation with friends before I should decide.

A return to Fox, or of Fox to us, appears, as you say, highly improbable; and every step he and those with whom he has exclusively connected himself seem to take, renders our separation wider, and anything like co-operation more irreconcileable with our principles. By a newspaper report of the last Whig Club, I observe that Fox is made to conclude the day by drinking very emphatically the *Majesty of the People*. I have often heard the expression; but the equivocation of the term *Majesty* appears to me to be a strong and unequivocal declaration, in the present times, of Fox's intentions, and to require more than ever the disavowal of those who are friends to the interests and liberties of the people, but decided enemies to its majesty. The last proceedings of the friends to the Liberty of the Press, who are Fox's immediate adherents, place him and us in direct opposition; and, so far from seeing any prospect of our approaching to each other, I cannot doubt that he has chosen his side in the troubles which threaten the world, and that it must be our post to oppose and combat him in Parliament and elsewhere. The Duke of Portland — I fear this part of the subject will afford but little comfort or remedy for the other evil. The existence of our party depends on his *firmness, decision, vigour, activity, consistency, uniformity of conduct*, and *honourable support* of his friends, as head of that party. And unfortunately the party is like *Snip*, and would look much better without its head. It is like the sign of the Good Woman.

I fear the Duke has proved himself *entirely* unfit for his station, both in character and talents, and that we are hopeless there. What remains ? To quit party; to do what the public good requires out of party, since we cannot do it otherwise; and to do this, as many others have done, on independent ground. The necessity for so much as this, I fear, cannot be denied; but I own that a connexion with Ministry, the acceptance of Office, with all the suspicions belonging to such a step, does not appear to me equally enjoined by public duty; and, in our circumstances, it is certainly strongly opposed by private feeling. When I parted with the Duke of Portland, he had no reason to think that I then thought such a step advisable; nor that any important change would take place in my relation with him, unless it should be grounded on some future proceedings; and I cannot be reconciled to the idea of giving him the first notice of our rupture by a step so strongly connected with private and personal interests. With regard to Lord Loughborough, I think the question stands on different ground. His acceptance of the Seals I believe sincerely to be eminently necessary for the public service. His conduct has been highly honourable, and everything like personal claim, or even party claim, on him by the Duke of Portland is certainly at least cancelled, if not converted into a direct *provocation*, by what has passed since the commencement of this session. But the public good, in my opinion, *requires* his services; and for that reason they are *due* from him. I shall certainly not only approve, but applaud, his acceptance of the Seals. It is for every man to consider whether the public has the same claim on him. I cannot feel that my services *in office* are of the smallest moment to the country; but the circumstances of the country may become such as to require all our aid in every way in which it is called for. A war in the present temper of the world concerning the cause of that war, and, in addition to this danger, any serious efforts of faction to obstruct our success by internal division and discontent, may possibly impose on us all the duty of lending a hand and setting our shoulders to the work, and of firing any gun we are placed at.

I cannot at present write more. What I have written is for you and Elliot only; and I have been literally only thinking, and, as it were, feeling my way on paper.

I am most extremely concerned at the delay in my return, more especially as you are so kind as to say, that your own judgment may be in any degree influenced by mine. The confidential and truly cordial footing on which we have lived together of late is matter of the highest satisfaction and comfort to me. I trust it will ever continue, and on my side it has a firm foundation to rest on,— I mean that of *gratitude,*—in addition to all other grounds of affection and esteem.

Ever your affectionate

G. ELLIOT.

FRIDAY, JULY 6.

AT Ranelagh with Prince of Wales—Dined at Carlton House on Sunday, 8th.—Saw Prince, Wednesday, 11th.

August 16th.—With Duke of Portland at dinner.

19th.—Bulstrode.

20th. — Lord Loughborough. — Dinner at Sir R. Payne's.

22nd.—Duke of Leeds from Pitt.—Dinner.—Fox at Burlington House.

23rd, 24th, 25th, 26th, and 27th.—Brigh t .

28th.—Returned to Brookwood.

FRIDAY, NOVEMBER 8.

WENT with Lord Darnley to Welbeck; Duke of Portland silent on Home politics, right on Foreign ones; determined to support the war—Lord Titchfield the same.

On Monday morning, early, November 11th, I received an express despatched through Mr. Batt, at the desire of the Lord Chancellor, who wrote me a letter, saying that " he had received a note from Lord Grenville,* and that both Lord Grenville and Pitt entreated me to accept a Mission on the Continent of great consequence."

I immediately gave orders to set out; but first communicated this letter to Duke of Portland, (to whom I had said, in the course of the two preceding days, that nothing had occurred relative to myself at all material for him to know since we parted in July at Oxford; and that, if there had, I certainly should have written to him, and that he should know it whenever it did happen). The Duke, however, after he had read this letter, became perfectly silent, as silent as I have seen him on several other occasions; and took no notice whatever, either by way of acknowledging the confidential communication I had made him, or by any means by animadverting on it. Strange and disagreeable as this was, I knew him well enough to know that it meant to convey his disapprobation of the step I was going to take; a disapprobation the more unreasonable, as six months before I had told him my principles on the present times, and my resolution to offer my services whenever they could be useful, and which resolution he decidedly applauded. I, however, took no notice of his silence, but appeared to take it for granted he *did approve* what I was going to do.† The few words which passed between us afterwards were on common subjects. At 11 I left Welbeck, as also did Darnley.

On the Thursday following I wrote to the Duke of Portland, to say that the Mission for which I was called up was Berlin; that it was to prevent the King of

---

* Secretary of State for Foreign Affairs.

† The Duke himself took office under Pitt on the 11th of July following, as did also Lord Fitzwilliam, Lord Spencer, and Mr. Wyndham. This broke up the old Whig party.

Prussia from withdrawing from the general alliance and plan of co-operation; that I was to pass through Holland and Brussels; and that I had not hesitated a moment to accept it, because I felt it a duty to refuse no exertion in a cause on which depended everything that was good for us, and dear to us.

On Tuesday morning I arrived in London. Saw the Chancellor about 4 P. M. He told me *what* the mission I was to be requested to undertake was, but referred me to Lord Grenville for the particulars attending it.

I saw Lord Grenville the same evening, at his house in St. James's Square. He entered very fully and minutely into the late conduct and present behaviour of His Prussian Majesty, and, after repeating nearly what he afterwards put into the form of instructions (and to which, therefore, I refer,) he said it was His Majesty's express wish that I should be requested to go to Berlin, for the end of preventing, if possible, His Prussian Majesty from departing from the general plan of co-operation.* I replied, that I was ready to undertake any service which, in the present moment, and in the support of the present cause, was thought useful. Lord Grenville said *he* was much obliged to me, and he was sure it would give the King pleasure; that he was afraid it was a difficult mission; that, however, it was of such importance that nothing should be left untried; and he was pleased to add, that if I went and did not succeed, they (Ministers) should feel they had done all in their power, and would have nothing to reproach themselves with.

* Many of His Prussian Majesty's Ministers were, from principle or corruption, favourable to the French Revolutionists, and the King himself, treacherous as well as betrayed, shewed strong symptoms of evading engagements with England, which he had contracted by his Treaty of 1788.

END OF THE SECOND VOLUME.